JESUS AND MARY REIMAGINED IN EARLY CHRISTIAN LITERATURE

Society of Biblical Literature

Writings from the Greco-Roman World Supplement Series

Ronald F. Hock, Editor

Number 6

JESUS AND MARY REIMAGINED IN EARLY CHRISTIAN LITERATURE

Edited by
Vernon K. Robbins and Jonathan M. Potter

SBL Press
Atlanta

Library of Congress Cataloging-in-Publication Data

Jesus and Mary reimagined in early Christian literature / Edited by Vernon K. Robbins and Jonathan M. Potter.

p. cm. — (Society of Biblical Literature. Writings from the Greco-Roman world Supplement series ; Volume 6)

Includes bibliographical references and indexes.

ISBN 978-1-62837-063-8 (paper binding : alk. paper) — ISBN 978-1-62837-064-5 (electronic format) — ISBN 978-1-62837-065-2 (hardcover binding : alk. paper)

1. Bible. New Testament—Criticism, interpretation, etc. 2. Jesus Christ—Biblical teaching. 3. Mary, Blessed Virgin, Saint—Biblical teaching. I. Robbins, Vernon K. (Vernon Kay), 1939– editor. II. Potter, Jonathan M.

BS2361.3.J48 2015

225.6—dc23 2015005717

Printed on acid-free, recycled paper conforming to ANSI/NISO Z39.48-1992 (R1997) and ISO 9706:1994 standards for paper permanence.

Contents

Abbreviations vii

Introduction 1
Vernon K. Robbins and Jonathan M. Potter

Part 1: Luke-Acts

Priestly Discourse in Luke and Acts
Vernon K. Robbins 13

Bodies and Politics in Luke 1–2 and Sirach 44–50: Men, Women, and Boys
Vernon K. Robbins 41

Part 2: Protevangelium of James

Who Am I To Be Blessed? Mary as Blessed Mother in the Protevangelium of James
Christopher T. Holmes 67

Temple Virgin and Virgin Temple: Mary's Body as Sacred Space in the Protevangelium of James
Meredith Elliott Hollman 103

From Prophetic Hymns to Death at the Altar: Luke 1–2 and Protevangelium of James
Michael K. W. Suh and Vernon K. Robbins 129

Part 3: Acts of John

Naked Divinity: The Transfiguration Transformed in the Acts of John
Jonathan M. Potter 181

Christ as Cosmic Priest: A Sociorhetorical Examination of the Crucifixion Scenes in the Gospel of John and Acts of John
Thomas Jared Farmer....................223

Part 4: Response Essays

Response: Luke and the Protevangelium of James
Ronald F. Hock 253

Response: The Gospel of John and the Acts of John
Susan E. Hylen....................279

Rhetorical Discourses in Gospel of John and Acts of John: A Response
L. Gregory Bloomquist....................291

Bibliography....................313

Contributors....................323

Ancient Sources Index....................325
Personal Names Index 348

Abbreviations

Primary Sources

1QS	Rule of the Community
Acts Pet.	Acts of Peter
AJohn	Acts of John
Ant.	Josephus, *Jewish Antiquities*
Apoc. El.	Apocalypse of Elijah
Apoc. Pet.	Apocalypse of Peter
Arch.	Vitruvius, *On Architecture*
b.	Babylonian Talmud
CD	Damascus Document
Cher.	Philo, *On the Cherubim*
Def. med.	Pseudo-Galen, *Medical Definitions*
Det.	Philo, *Quod deterius potiori insidari soleat* (*That the Worse Attacks the Better*)
Deus	Philo, *Quod Deus sit immutabilis* (*That God Is Unchangeable*)
El.	Euripides, *Electra*
Ep.	*Epistle(s)*
Fab.	Aesop, *Fables*
Frag.	*Fragment(s)*
Frg. Tg.	Fragmentary Targum
Fug.	Philo, *De fuga et inventione* (*On Flight and Finding*)
Geogr.	Strabo, *Geography*
Giṭ.	Giṭṭin
GJohn	Gospel of John
Gos. Mary	Gospel of Mary
Gos. Thom.	Gospel of Thomas
Haer.	Irenaeus, *Adversus haereses* (*Against Heresies*)
Her.	Philo, *Quis rerum divinarum heres sit* (*Who Is the Heir?*)

Hist. eccl.	Eusebius, *Ecclesiastical History*
Jdt	Judith
J.W.	Josephus, *Jewish War*
Leg.	Philo, *Legum allegoriae* (*Allegorical Interpretation*)
m.	Mishnah
Mem.	Xenophon, *Memorabilia*
Migr.	Philo, *On the Migration of Abraham*
Morb.	Hippocrates, *De morbis* (*On Diseases*)
Mos.	Philo, *On the Life of Moses*
Od.	Homer, *Odyssey*
Opif.	Philo, *De opificio mundi* (*On the Creation of the World*)
P.Oxy	Oxyrhynchus papyri
Parm.	Plato, *Parmenides*
Phileb.	Plato, *Philebus*
PJ	Protevangelium of James
Probl.	Pseudo-Aristotle, *Problems*
Prov.	Philo, *On Providence*
QE	Philo, *Questions and Answers on Exodus*
QG	Philo, *Questions and Answers on Genesis*
Sanh.	Sanhedrin
Stoic. rep.	Plutarch, *De Stoicorum repugnantiis*
Subl.	(Pseudo-)Longinus, *On the Sublime*
t.	Tosefta
Ta'an.	Ta'anit
Tg. Neof.	Targum Neofiti
Theaet.	Plato, *Theaetetus*
Theog.	Hesiod, *Theogony*
T. 12 Patr.	Testament of the Twelve Patriarchs
T. Benj.	Testament of Benjamin
T. Jos.	Testament of Joseph
T. Levi	Testament of Levi
T. Reu.	Testament of Reuben
T. Sim.	Testament of Simeon
y.	Jerusalem Talmud

Secondary Sources

AB	Anchor Bible
ANRW	Temporini, Hildegard, and Wolfgang Haase, eds. *Auf-*

	stieg und Niedergang der römischen Welt: Geschichte und Kultur Roms im Spiegel der neueren Forschung. Part 2, *Principat*. Berlin: de Gruyter, 1972–
ANTC	Abingdon New Testament Commentaries
BBR	*Bulletin for Biblical Research*
BDAG	Danker, Frederick W., Walter Bauer, William F. Arndt, and F. Wilbur Gingrich. *Greek-English Lexicon of the New Testament and Other Early Christian Literature*. 3rd ed. Chicago: University of Chicago Press, 2000
BIS	Biblical Interpretation Series
BTS	Biblical Tools and Studies
BJS	Brown Judaic Studies
BTB	*Biblical Theology Bulletin*
BZNW	Beihefte zur Zeitschrift für die neutestamentliche Wissenschaft
CBQ	*Catholic Biblical Quarterly*
CCSA	Corpus Christianorum: Series Apocryphorum
E-P	Ehrman, Bart D., and Zlatko Pleše. *The Apocryphal Gospels: Texts and Translations*. New York: Oxford University Press, 2011
ESEC	Emory Studies in Early Christianity
GRBS	*Greek, Roman, and Byzantine Studies*
HUCA	*Hebrew Union College Annual*
ICC	International Critical Commentary
IPM	Instrumenta Patristica et Mediavalia
JBL	*Journal of Biblical Literature*
JSNT	*Journal for the Study of the New Testament*
JSNTSup	Journal for the Study of the New Testament Supplement Series
JSOTSup	Journal for the Study of the Old Testament Supplement Series
LSJ	Liddell, Henry George, Robert Scott, Henry Stuart Jones. *A Greek-English Lexicon*. 9th ed. with revised supplement. Oxford: Clarendon, 1996
NA^{28}	*Novum Testamentum Graece*, Nestle-Aland, 28th ed.
NETS	*A New English Translation of the Septuagint*. Edited by Albert Pietersma and Benjamin G. Wright. New York: Oxford University Press, 2007
NICNT	New International Commentary on the New Testament

NPNF1	*Nicene and Post-Nicene Fathers*, Series 1
NPNF2	*Nicene and Post-Nicene Fathers*, Series 2
NRSV	New Revised Standard Version
NTL	New Testament Library
NTS	*New Testament Studies*
PG	Patrologia graeca
PL	Patrologia latina
PMS	Publications in Medieval Studies
R&T	*Religion and Theology*
RCT	*Revista catalana de teologia*
RRA	Rhetoric of Religious Antiquity
SAAA	Studies on the Apocryphal Acts of the Apostles
ScholBib	The Scholars Bible
SP	Sacra Pagina
SRR	Studies in Rhetoric and Religion
TDNT	*Theological Dictionary of the New Testament*. Edited by Gerhard Kittel and Gerhard Friedrich. Translated by Geoffrey W. Bromiley. 10 vols. Grand Rapids: Eerdmans, 1964–1976
TLG	*Thesaurus linguae graecae*
TUGAL	Texte und Untersuchungen zur Geschichte der altchristlichen Literatur
TynBul	*Tyndale Bulletin*
WBC	Word Biblical Commentary
WGRW	Writings from the Greco-Roman World
WUNT	Wissenschaftliche Untersuchungen zum Neuen Testament

Introduction

Vernon K. Robbins and Jonathan M. Potter

A majority of the essays in this volume developed from a PhD seminar titled "Luke, John, and Emerging Gospels" at Emory University during spring 2013. After some intensive sessions on the Gospels of Luke and John, everyone began to work through the Infancy Gospel of Thomas and the Protevangelium of James (PJ). Some of the highly detailed work the students were posting electronically each week on PJ caught the instructor's eye, and he started to envision the possibility of a collection of essays that might emerge from the seminar. He also noticed a keen interest among some of the students in the Gospel of John (GJohn) and its legacy, so he decided to focus for a series of weeks on the Acts of John (AJ) with them, rather than spending extended time on the Gospel of Thomas, the Gospel of Mary, and the Gospel of Judas, as had originally been planned for the seminar.

As the seminar moved along, the participants experienced a major challenge to move beyond traditional literary-historical criticism into comparative sociorhetorical exegesis of canonical and extracanonical gospels and gospel-like writings in emerging Christianity. The seminar was a remarkable exhibition of the evolving face of the study of the New Testament during the early decades of the twenty-first century. The students in the seminar were well advanced in their ability to produce literary-historical exegesis. The question for many of them was why they should engage in anything beyond good literary-historical exegesis of the extracanonical writings in relation to the New Testament gospels.

The students began to see how dramatically, in relation to canonical biblical literature, the extracanonical writings relocated biblical verses and/or reconfigured entire biblical scenes. And usually this meant a significant shift from the discursive mode in which one or more biblical writings presented the stories. In this context, the instructor emphasized how important it is to become explicitly aware of what "rhetorolect" a writer is foregrounding and the resultant "blend" of rhetorolects that results from the particular "shift" of discourse.[1] To uncover such discursive shifts and to recognize the fascinating and sometimes surprising reconfiguration of resources, the students were deeply engaged in "textural" analysis. In particular they used the heuristic tools of identifying repetitive texture and opening-middle-closing texture, procedures that proved highly productive (some of this work remains in the essays).[2]

As the final seminar papers took shape, the instructor consulted with the rest of the students to see if it might be possible to generate a volume of essays that exhibited significant coherence. An essay the instructor had published on Luke and Sirach in 2005,[3] plus an unpublished essay on priestly discourse in Luke and Acts completed in 2008, emerged as important for the papers the students were writing in the seminar. Thus the volume gradually took shape, with two essays of the instructor at the beginning, followed by essays written by the participants in the seminar.

The result is a volume that begins with two essays by Vernon Robbins on priestly rhetorolect in Luke and Acts. The first essay is a programmatic discussion of priestly statements and emphases through both Luke and Acts. Observing that Irenaeus called Luke the "priestly" gospel, Robbins proposes that there were six major rhetorical dialects, which he calls "rhetorolects," within early Christian discourse: wisdom, prophetic, apocalyptic, precreation, miracle, and priestly. This sets the stage for his

1. Vernon K. Robbins, "Conceptual Blending and Early Christian Imagination," in *Explaining Christian Origins and Early Judaism: Contributions from Cognitive and Social Science*, ed. Petri Luomanen, Ilkka Pyysiäinen, and Risto Uro, BIS 89 (Leiden: Brill, 2007), 161–95; Robbins, "Rhetography: A New Way of Seeing the Familiar Text," in *Words Well Spoken: George Kennedy's Rhetoric of the New Testament*, ed. C. Clifton Black and Duane F. Watson, SRR 8 (Waco, TX: Baylor University Press, 2008), 81–106; Robbins, *The Invention of Christian Discourse*, vol. 1, RRA 1 (Blandford Forum, UK: Deo, 2009); Robbins, "Socio-Rhetorical Interpretation," in *The Blackwell Companion to the New Testament*, ed. David E. Aune (Oxford: Blackwell, 2010), 192–219; Robert H. von Thaden Jr., *Sex, Christ, and Embodied Cognition: Paul's Wisdom for Corinth*, ESEC 16 (Blandford Forum, UK: Deo, 2012).

2. The analysis of inner texture, including repetitive texture and opening-middle-closing texture, is outlined in Vernon K. Robbins, *Exploring the Texture of Texts: A Guide to Socio-Rhetorical Interpretation* (Valley Forge, PA: Trinity Press International, 1996), 7–39.

3. Vernon K. Robbins, "Bodies and Politics in Luke 1–2 and Sirach 44–50: Men, Women, and Boys," *Scriptura* 90 (2005): 724–838. The editors of this volume are grateful for the permission granted to reprint this article here in slightly updated form.

observation that there is substantive blending of priestly rhetorolect into a dominant prophetic storyline in the Gospel of Luke. A key to the presence of priestly rhetorolect in Robbins's approach is attention to the "rhetography" of the text, namely, rhetoric in the text that prompts graphic images and pictures in the mind.[4] For priestly rhetorolect, imagery of places like altars and temples, people like priests, and activities like offering sacrifices and praying are central.[5] This means that the opening chapter of Luke, with its emphasis on the priestly lineage of both Zechariah and Elizabeth, and its portrayal of Zechariah offering incense in the temple while people outside are praying, starts Luke with special priestly emphases. Then the Jerusalem temple as a special place of blessing on the infant Jesus, followed by Jesus's return to the temple at twelve years of age, continues a focus on priestly places and activities in the context of the prophetic emphases in the opening chapters of Luke. After this, in a context of observing that Jesus's ministry is punctuated by regular times of prayer, Robbins observes how often Jesus forgives people's sins, tells others to forgive, and prays even for those who have hung him on the cross in Luke. Then before ascending into heaven, Jesus blesses his disciples and tells them to return to the Jerusalem temple, where they are continually blessing God as the Gospel ends. The priestly emphases in Luke continue in Acts, where there is special emphasis on prayer and forgiveness of sins, plus the law of Moses and the Jerusalem temple. This is especially interesting, since throughout Luke and Acts there is no assertion that Christ's death is a sacrifice for sins or that Jesus's death was a ransom for many.

After this opening essay, another essay by Robbins focuses on bodies and ritual actions in Luke, using Sirach 44–50 as an intertext that portrays vivid priestly imagery in the Jerusalem temple. Robbins observes especially how ritual actions and pronouncements of blessing, which are especially appropriate in a temple context, occur in Luke also in family households. In this context, Robbins explores how Luke produces distinctly different guidelines for "inclusion" and "exclusion" in households that are new "holy locations" for God's activity in the world.

After these two essays, the volume turns to the Protevangelium of James, which begins with circumstances around the birth of Mary, the future mother of Jesus, and ends with the martyrdom of John the Baptist's

4. Robbins, "Rhetography," 81.

5. Robbins, *Invention*, xxvi, 190–207, 499–504; von Thaden, *Sex, Christ, and Embodied Cognition*, 138–47, 233–92.

father Zechariah. A remarkable feature of PJ is its focus on the Jerusalem temple during both the first half of the story and the concluding events. Mary's parents, Joachim and Anna, have a priestly heritage, and after a miraculous pregnancy despite their childlessness, they dedicate Mary to the Jerusalem temple. Even before they take Mary to the temple, however, they keep Mary pure by making her bedroom a holy sanctuary, only allowing young, pure Hebrew girls to play with Mary, and never allowing Mary to walk on the ground. After Mary is taken to the Jerusalem temple at age three, she is watched over and fed by angels until age twelve. When priests decide she must be taken out of the temple, a time of bewilderment and challenge begins for Mary through a hastily arranged process by which Joseph is chosen by lot and a special sign to take her into his home and become her guardian. Mary miraculously becomes pregnant while Joseph is away on a building project, and this creates a time of testing for Mary as she is accused first by Joseph and then by the temple priests of inappropriate behavior. After she successfully defends herself, her pregnancy comes full term while she is traveling with Joseph for the enrollment at Bethlehem. When Joseph finds a cave as a place for Mary to give birth, Jesus comes forth from her body in the form of light and gradually becomes a suckling baby. After two midwives see that Mary's virginity remains even after her child is born, circumstances around King Herod's concern about news of the birth of a savior of Israel lead to the flight of both Mary, with the child Jesus, and Elizabeth, with the child John. The unsuccessful search for John leads to Herod's emissaries' coming to the Jerusalem temple and murdering John's father, Zechariah, who at the time is high priest of the Jerusalem temple. After Jerusalem priests find blood, but not the body, of Zechariah by the altar in the inner holy of holies, they appoint Simeon as Zechariah's successor as high priest in the Jerusalem temple.

Focusing on Mary's visit to Elizabeth after she has miraculously become pregnant in Luke and PJ, Christopher Holmes's essay discusses the different function of the topos of blessing in the prophetic discourse of the opening chapters of Luke compared to the priestly discourse in PJ. Observing that the prehistory in Luke focuses on a promised political kingdom, he perceives that the prehistory in PJ focuses on the activation of divine benefits in a priestly context around the sacred space of the temple and its personnel. This reconfiguration of discourse in PJ results in the repetitive texture of blessing in PJ 1–12 being focused on Mary with no reference to Elizabeth or her conception in the exchange between Mary and the angel of the Lord who visits her. Instead of any reference to Elizabeth's being filled with Holy Spirit, there is focus on both Elizabeth and her unborn child blessing Mary, without mention of Mary's own unborn child. At this point Mary forgets what the angel of the Lord had previously said to her and wonders why all the women on earth will bless her, rather than bursting into praise to the Lord with the Magnificat, as she does in Luke. Holmes concludes that this almost exclusive focus of blessing on Mary emphasizes not only her status as pure virgin but also her role as blessed mother of Jesus. This leads to a second observation, namely, that praise in PJ is not focused almost entirely on God, as it is in Luke, but on Mary as the means or instrument of praise to the God of Israel. In addition, the temple priests ask that God give Mary an illustrious name, everlasting in all generations, which Holmes perceives to be a reconfiguration of the Abramic blessing of Genesis 12 that applies it to Mary. This leads to the conclusion that the great name of Mary comes from her function as mother of Jesus, rather than her function solely as virgin of the Lord.

Mandy Hollman's essay, building on insights in Holmes's essay, argues that Mary is the central character in PJ in contrast to Jesus, who is the central character in the canonical gospels. Mary's chief characteristic is her absolute virginity, and this establishes the context for the rest of her functions in the story. Focusing on the opening-middle-closing texture of the movement of Mary into the temple (7.1–8.1), Hollman compares the story of Mary in PJ with the story of Samuel in 1 Sam 1:21–2:11. Comparing and contrasting these two "toddlers in the temple," she concludes that the story of Samuel functions as a resource text for PJ that is reconfigured to focus on Mary as the holy vessel of Jesus rather than a prophet-priest who anoints the ancestor of the Messiah, king of Israel. In this context, she observes the passiveness of Mary, which transcends the Hellenistic moralist's ideal for women, to point to her role as "God-bearer" (*theotokos*). This role signals her function as a new "moving temple," like the tabernacle or ark of the covenant. At this point Hollman introduces the opening-middle-closing texture of the moving of the ark of the covenant from the house of Obed-Edom to a tent in Jerusalem and Solomon's movement of the ark from the tent into the Jerusalem temple. Hollman sees similarities between the movement of the ark to Jerusalem and to the temple and the movement of Mary from the temple to Joseph's house and to the cave where she gives birth to Jesus. The dark cloud that descends on the cave and then disappears as Jesus is born as light that becomes flesh in a suckling baby leads her to conclude that in PJ Mary becomes a "moving tabernacle," a holy vessel of Jesus who comes into the world as the true light who becomes flesh to dwell among humankind. In this way, the virgin body of Mary mediates a new mode of divine presence on earth.

An essay that was inaugurated by Michael Suh comes next in the volume. In the seminar itself, he worked in detail on the prophetic nature of the four well-known hymns in the first two chapters of Luke—the Magnificat, Benedictus, Gloria, and Nunc Dimittis—with the knowledge that none of these four hymns is present in the Protevangelium of James. The question was why PJ does not contain them when they seem to be such an appealing part of the Lukan presentation of the birth of John and Jesus. As Suh developed his detailed interpretation of the prophetic dimension of these Lukan hymns, he became convinced that the foregrounding of priestly rhetorolect had led to their omission in PJ. In the process, however, the presence of one fragment of the Magnificat intrigued him. Protevangelium of James contains a noticeable reconfiguration of Mary's statement in Luke, "My soul magnifies the name of the Lord," into a magnification of Mary herself in PJ: "Mary, the Lord God has magnified your name" (7.7; 12.2). Suh began to wonder if perhaps fragments of the other three hymns might also exist in PJ. As he searched, he became convinced that fragments of the other three hymns existed in the very final scenes of PJ, which focus on the death of Zechariah, and these observations formed the conclusion of his seminar paper.

When the instructor read Suh's final paper, he considered the identification of the fragments of three of the hymns in the final events of the story to be an amazing discovery. Near the beginning of the seminar, the instructor had admitted to the students that he was puzzled with the focus on the death of Zechariah, father of John the Baptist, at the end of the story. He wondered what the significance of this conclusion might be. Since the presence of fragments of the Lukan hymns is very suggestive for new ways we might think about the ending of PJ, the instructor agreed to join Suh in a substantive revision of the second half of the paper to show, in the best way we know how at present, some of the things Suh's discovery might imply for PJ. This led to the coauthored essay in the volume.

It is important to know that the three essays on PJ in this volume were written without knowledge of Lily C. Vuong's *Gender and Purity in the Protevangelium of James*, which appeared in 2013.[6] When this excellent

6. Lily C. Vuong, *Gender and Purity in the Protevangelium of James*, WUNT 2/358 (Tübingen: Mohr Siebeck, 2013).

work became known during the editorial process, a few revisions along with some footnotes were added to the essays. However, it would have been ideal if we had all had access to Vuong's book from the outset, since it supports many insights in the essays but also pursues issues that could have produced dialogue and added some welcome nuances to certain emphases and discussions. One interesting proposal is Vuong's view that PJ 8.4 is a "narrative pivot in the text."[7] For Vuong this means that 1.1–8.3 presents Mary as ritually pure in relation to the temple and sacrifices,[8] while after 8.4 there is an emphasis on sexual purity where Mary is "first identified as a virgin and designated the title 'virgin of the Lord.' "[9] In addition, Vuong's emphases that Mary's purity follows her wherever she goes and that she functions as "Jesus' prenatal sanctuary," "symbolic temple," and "sacred temple suitable for the Son of God"[10] have an important relation to Hollman's view of Mary as a moving tabernacle. Beyond this, Vuong's argument for a Western Syrian provenance for PJ on the basis of its emphases on ascetic practices, menstrual purity laws, virginity, and both antidocetic and anti-Marcionite rhetoric has an important relation to the queries about the implications of the focus on Zechariah's martyrdom at the altar of the temple in the conclusion of the Suh and Robbins essay.

The third part of the volume contains two essays on the Acts of John, which presents Jesus as a precreation being whose death on the cross exhibits the suffering and death of the Logos, which "is suffering and death but really is not suffering and death." In AJohn, the "real" Jesus is divine light with a voice, but this Jesus appears to humans in multiple earthly forms. To some the earth-form of Jesus looks at times like a child, to others at times like a handsome young man, and still to others at times like an old man with white hair. Also, sometimes the earth-form of Jesus may have a solid, dense body, and at other times it may be soft and immaterial. Thus, while the earth-form of Jesus is dying on the cross, the divine Logos voice of the suffering and dying one speaks to John while he is in a cave on the Mount of Olives. Acts of John, therefore, elaborates and reconfigures meanings of the "glorification-death" of Jesus in GJohn with an expanded precreation conceptuality that includes substantive aspects of Middle Platonism.

7. Ibid., 146.
8. Ibid.
9. Ibid., 147.
10. Ibid., 187–91.

Beginning with an overview of AJohn, Jonathan Potter uses the designation of "the Testimonies" to refer to AJohn 87–105 and discusses multiple metamorphoses that occur in a series of twelve testimonies in 88–93. The transfiguration of Jesus on the mountain, which occurs in the three testimonies in the very middle of the unit, is just one instance among many, then, where people experience the changing appearance of the Lord. Through specific comparison of the transfiguration events in AJohn with the Lukan account, with all the Synoptic versions in the background, Potter interprets the special emphasis on the "nakedness" of the Lord, by which the "true" identity of Jesus as wholly divine is revealed. In particular, he traces the way the singular transfiguration scene in the Synoptic Gospels is reconfigured in AJohn's Johannine discourse such that in the conceptuality of AJohn, the earthly Jesus is always being "transfigured."

The final essay, by Jared Farmer, explores the function of the Lord as cosmic priestly mediator in AJohn. Farmer begins with an overview of AJohn that leads to a special focus on its opening-middle-closing presentation of the crucifixion. The remarkable thing is that instead of focusing on the earthly form of the Lord dying on the earthly cross, AJohn presents the divine Logos appearing to John in a cave as a divine voice with no shape, above a cross of light that is surrounded by a multitude having no one form. The divine Logos voice explains that the nature of the cross of light in human terms alternates among topoi the reader recognizes as major topoi in GJohn: Word, Jesus, Christ, Door, Way, Bread, Seed, Resurrection, Son, Father, Spirit, Life, Truth, Faith, or Grace. Farmer observes that AJohn adds a topos that is not in John but is prominent in Middle Platonism, namely Mind. This leads to an examination of the principle of separation in Platonism that generates the concept of "one among many," which explains the one form and one likeness of the cross of light in the context of the multiple topoi. It also explains the marking off of all things as well as the harmony amid multiple transient things on the right and the left. This leads to the middle of the explanation by the divine Logos voice of the cross of light: the cross has united all things by the Word, marked off all things transient and inferior, and compacted all into one. This explains why all earthly things have multiple forms, rather than only one united form. The important thing for John, then, is that he ignore the many and listen only to the voice of the divine Logos so that he be united with it and be as the Logos is, namely, wholly with the Father and with the Logos. The conclusion of the scene in AJohn then presents the Logos voice explaining to John that the slaying, piercing, bloodying, wounding, hanging, suffering, nailing, and death of the Logos are things John hears that the Logos suffered but did not suffer. From an earthly perspective, all of these things happened to the Logos, but from a divine perspective, none of these things really happened to the Logos. This is a mystery, the Logos voice says, that is being told only to John, and if he understands it he will truly understand the nature of the Logos in relation to all earthly things. Farmer interprets this discussion to mean that the Lord is priest and Logos who sustains the cosmos, "standing as mediator between humanity and divinity, making possible the return to unity with God through the sacrifice of the cross." In other words, the cosmos is restored through the suffering of the Logos, which is the priestly moment of sacrifice that is actually beyond human comprehension.

The fourth part of the volume contains three response essays. The response by Ronald Hock reviews and critiques the first two essays, on priestly rhetorolect, by Vernon Robbins and the essays by Christopher Holmes, Mandy Hollman, and Michael Suh and Vernon Robbins on the Protevangelium of James. Since Hock has worked so thoroughly with PJ, it is gratifying to see his response page by page to the two essays that set up the focus on priestly rhetorolect and the foregrounding of priestly rhetorolect in PJ that causes such substantive configuration of biblical stories related to it. In addition, it is a pleasure for the authors of the essays to have Hock's invitation to submit the volume for publication in the series he edited at the time, Writings from the Greco-Roman World Supplement series. The response by Susan Hylen reviews and critiques the essays by Jonathan Potter and Jared Farmer on the Acts of John both from the perspective of its relation to GJohn and the nature of the content within it. Her intimate knowledge of GJohn yields well-informed responses to the different world that AJohn creates for Jesus when John tells the Ephesians the story of his time with Jesus. The response by Gregory Bloomquist comes from intimate knowledge of the use of topoi and rhetorolects in sociorhetorical interpretation as it is applied by members of the Rhetoric of Religious Antiquity research group. Bloomquist emphasizes major differences in discourse between AJohn and GJohn, with the proposal that AJohn interacts more with literature written after GJohn than the Gospel itself.

Taken together, these essays explore the diverse character of emerging Christian narratives. From priestly beginnings at the temple in Luke to the enigmatic figure of the cross of light in Acts of John, early Christians found a variety of ways to interpret and express the storylines of Jesus,

Mary, and other important figures. By reconfiguring and relocating existing resources of texts and topoi, each of the works examined here creates new images and stories within the discursive framework of unique blends of emerging Christian rhetorolects. This volume thus offers readings that attempt to account for this richly creative and complicated process.

Part 1
Luke-Acts

Priestly Discourse in Luke and Acts

Vernon K. Robbins

This essay focuses on priestly discourse in Luke and Acts. This may seem to be a strange focus, since everyone knows that the Gospel of Luke emphasizes distribution of goods to the poor and loving one's enemies more than priestly matters. It would seem more promising to look at the Gospel of Matthew, which has a focus on "perfection" and the establishment of Peter as "the rock" on which the church is built. Luke does, however, begin with a priest named Zechariah making an incense offering in the Jerusalem temple. It is informative that Irenaeus asserts that the Gospel of Luke takes up Jesus's priestly character, "beginning with Zechariah the priest offering sacrifice to God. For now was made ready the fatted calf, about to be immolated for the finding again of the younger son" (*Haer.* 3.11.8). In contrast, he describes Matthew as the Gospel of Jesus's humanity, emphasizing Jesus as a humble and meek man! Perhaps pursuing priestly discourse in the Gospel of Luke can be an important endeavor, and when one starts with Luke, it is necessary to continue through the Acts of the Apostles.[1]

When viewed alongside the other gospels in the New Testament, it is remarkable indeed that the story of Jesus's life begins in Luke with a priestly sacrifice. The Gospel of Mark begins with a blending of Isaiah, Exodus, and Malachi; the Gospel of Matthew begins with a genealogy from Abraham through Joseph that emphasizes Davidic messiahship; and

1. This essay was first completed in January 2006 and circulated for the Rhetoric of Religious Antiquity research group but never published. When updating it in Summer 2013 for publication, my research assistant Jonathan Potter discovered Rick Strelan's book *Luke the Priest: The Authority of the Author of the Third Gospel* (Burlington, VT: Ashgate, 2008). The coincidence of our working on this subject during the same period of time is fascinating. In contrast to his work, it never occurred to me to argue that the author of Luke-Acts might be a priest. I have now read his book with interest and added references to it in various places in this essay.

the Gospel of John begins with a reconfiguration of the creation of the world. Instead, the Gospel of Luke begins with an angel appearing to a priest named Zechariah while he is making an incense offering to God in the Jerusalem temple. No scene like this appears in any of the other New Testament gospels! Does this priestly beginning have any real "priestly" significance for the presentation of Jesus and the early Christian movement in Luke and Acts? Or is this simply an interesting priestly beginning that has no significant priestly result for one's understanding of early Christian discourse?

1. Analyzing and Interpreting Priestly Rhetorolect in Luke and Acts

The initial question is how an interpreter should approach the "priestly" beginning of the Gospel of Luke. It would be possible simply to focus on priestly vocabulary, which a search reveals to be an important phenomenon in Luke and Acts. Another approach could be to use priestly aspects of Luke and Acts to support, perhaps covertly, a priestly agenda in modern Christianity.[2] Still another approach might be to interpret the priestly aspects of Luke and Acts in a manner that presents an "antipriestly" Christianity. Instead of choosing one of these angles of interpretation, the approach in this essay is self-consciously sociorhetorical, proceeding out of guidelines that have been emerging in sociorhetorical interpretation since the 1990s.[3]

The issue in this essay is the relation of the focus on priestly activities at the beginning of Luke to the wide range of interests exhibited by early Christian discourse. The approach in this essay is guided by sociorhetorical analysis and interpretation that suggests Christians blended six major

2. One should now add that another approach could be to pursue the possibility that the author of Luke-Acts was a priest; see ibid.

3. Vernon K. Robbins, *The Tapestry of Early Christian Discourse: Rhetoric, Society and Ideology* (London: Routledge, 1996); Robbins, *Exploring the Texture of Texts: A Guide to Socio-Rhetorical Interpretation* (Valley Forge, PA: Trinity Press International, 1996); Robbins, *The Invention of Christian Discourse*, vol. 1, RRA 1 (Blandford Forum, UK: Deo, 2009); Robbins, "Socio-Rhetorical Interpretation," in *The Blackwell Companion to the New Testament*, ed. David E. Aune (Oxford: Blackwell, 2010), 192–219; and David B. Gowler, L. Gregory Bloomquist, and Duane F. Watson, eds., *Fabrics of Discourse: Essays in Honor of Vernon K. Robbins* (Harrisburg, PA: Trinity Press International, 2003).

"rhetorical dialects" together during the first two centuries CE as they created early Christian discourse: wisdom, prophetic, apocalyptic, precreation, miracle, and priestly.[4] In 1996, the term "rhetorolect" was introduced to refer to these rhetorical dialects. A rhetorolect is "a form of language variety or discourse identifiable on the basis of a distinctive configuration of themes, topics, reasonings, and argumentations."[5] On the one hand, these "distinctive configurations" are a result of recitation, recontextualization, and reconfiguration[6] of biblical storylines. On the other hand, the "themes, topics, reasonings, and argumentations" have substantive relationships to belief-argumentation both in early Judaism and in broader Mediterranean culture, religion, and philosophy. Christianity emerged as a new form of Judaism through a process of selecting, reconfiguring, and blending biblical storylines with belief-argumentation in the Hellenistic-Roman world during the beginning centuries of the Common Era.

Through the presence of six major rhetorolects in early Christian discourse, the overall Christian belief-story that emerged during the first two centuries was supported by a "six storyline" Christian belief world. Each storyline worked with selective "resource zones" from the Hebrew Bible for beginning and succeeding events that flowed into the ongoing story of Jesus and his followers. Early Christian wisdom rhetorolect features God's creation of the world through light, water, spirit/wind, and earth, making Gen 1–3 one of its major resource zones. In addition, it features God's giving of torah wisdom to Moses in Deuteronomy and God's giving of

4. Vernon K. Robbins, "The Dialectical Nature of Early Christian Discourse," *Scriptura* 59 (1996): 353–62. The names wisdom, miracle, and apocalyptic have remained consistent since 1996. In contrast, precreation was first called cosmic, prophetic was first called opposition, and priestly was first called death-resurrection. These six rhetorolects provide the environment and many of the resources for the emergence of additional rhetorolects, like creedal rhetorolect, during later centuries. For blending in rhetorolects, see Vernon K. Robbins, "Conceptual Blending and Early Christian Imagination," in *Explaining Christian Origins and Early Judaism: Contributions from Cognitive and Social Science*, ed. Petri Luomanen, Ilkka Pyysiäinen, and Risto Uro, BIS 89 (Leiden: Brill, 2007), 161–95. For creedal rhetorolect, see Vernon K. Robbins, "Precreation Discourse and the Nicene Creed: Christianity Finds Its Voice in the Roman Empire," *R&T* 18 (2012): 1–17.

5. Robbins, "Dialectical Nature," 356.

6. See "intertexture" analysis and interpretation in Robbins, *Tapestry*, 96–143; and Robbins, *Exploring*, 40–70.

wisdom to Solomon in Proverbs.[7] Early Christian precreation rhetorolect features characteristics, attributes, and personages present with God prior to and during creation, making Prov 8 one of its major resource zones, and making Sir 24 and major portions of Wisdom of Solomon major continuations of precreation storytelling and belief-argumentation in the Apocrypha.[8] Early Christian prophetic rhetorolect features the emergence of God's kingdom through God's calling of people like Moses, Isaiah, and Jeremiah, who confronted the people and their leaders with God's will, making Exodus and the Major and Minor Prophets major resource zones.[9] Early Christian miracle rhetorolect features God's power unexpectedly transforming human bodies to restore them, making the Elijah and Elisha stories in 1–2 Kings major resource zones.[10] Early Christian apocalyptic rhetorolect features an overwhelming invasion of sin and death into God's world, making Gen 3–8 a major resource zone, and a decision by God to bring purifying wrath on evils that pervade both the created world and human lives, making portions of the prophetic books and the book of Daniel major resource zones.[11] Underlying each rhetorolect, then, is a "background" story that early Christians formulated by creatively selecting and retelling certain scenes and content from traditional storylines in the Hebrew Bible. This background story leads dynamically into the ongoing story of Jesus and his followers. The "ongoing" nature of the storyline in each rhetorolect is one of the key ingredients in Christian discourse. For Christians, the "overall" story never stops. One of the major questions is the twists and turns of a particular "rhetorolect" as Christians take it into new cultural, religious, and political environments. In these alternative contexts, Christians blend the rhetorolects in different ways with beliefs, dispositions, arguments, rituals, and actions in public life. During certain centuries, one or more of the rhetorolects may move into the foreground of the Christian belief-story. During other centuries, these rhetorolects may be driven into the background. This process was already at work during the first two centuries CE, and it continues into the present.

---

7. Robbins, *Invention*, 121–218.

8. Robbins, "Precreation Discourse and the Nicene Creed."

9. Robbins, *Invention*, 219–328.

10. Vernon K. Robbins, "Sociorhetorical Interpretation of Miracle Discourse in the Synoptic Gospels," in *Miracle Discourse in the New Testament*, ed. Duane F. Watson (Atlanta: Society of Biblical Literature, 2012), 17–84.

11. Robbins, *Invention*, 329–482.

In this essay, both the evocation of events from "background" storylines and the presentation of "foreground" storylines[12] in a rhetorolect are called its "rhetography."[13] Rhetography is "graphic pictorial narration." Underlying each rhetorolect is selective pictorial narration from the story world of the Hebrew Bible. As Christian discourse unfolds, it regularly blends "biblical" pictorial narration into its own ongoing pictorial narration. For example, rhetography from the story of Elijah and Elisha in the Bible at certain points blends into the rhetography in the story of Jesus. Dynamically related to the rhetography in each rhetorolect is its "rhetology." Rhetology in this essay refers to the rhetorical presentation of belief-argument. Each rhetorolect has a range of belief-arguments that function implicitly or explicitly in the context of its rhetography.

For example, a number of belief-arguments build progressively to Jesus's raising of the son of the widow of Nain in Luke 7:11–17. In Luke 5:17 the narrator asserts that "the power of the Lord was with Jesus to heal." Then the narrator asserts in Luke 6:19 that many people were trying to touch Jesus, "because power came out from him and healed all of them." This blends into the rhetology in Luke 7:16 that "God looked with favor on his people by bringing forth a great prophet among them," which is dynamically embedded in the rhetography (pictorial narration) of Jesus's raising of the son of the widow of Nain to life by touching the bier on which he was being carried and telling him to rise (Luke 7:14–15). At this point in the narration, Lukan prophetic miracle rhetology evokes the belief that power of the Lord in Jesus flowed through the bier into the body of the young man.

The rhetography and rhetology work together to present Jesus as a blended "new Elijah" (cf. 1 Kgs 17:1–24) and "new Elisha" (cf. 2 Kgs 6:32–37). The rhetorical blending creates a "new Christian story" with a dynamic intertextural relation to both the rhetography and rhetology in the stories of Elijah and Elisha in the Hebrew Bible. Recounted in this way, this Christian miracle rhetorolect also possesses a wide-reaching cultural

---

12. I am indebted to Todd Oakley for the distinction between background and foreground in discourse.

13. Vernon K. Robbins, "Rhetography: A New Way of Seeing the Familiar Text," in *Words Well Spoken: George Kennedy's Rhetoric of the New Testament*, ed. C. Clifton Black and Duane F. Watson (Waco, TX: Baylor University Press, 2008), 81–106. Compare the use of the analogous term "theography" in Jack Miles, *God: A Biography* (New York: Knopf, 1995), 11.

intertexture with stories recounting miraculous processes that brought people from death to life in many different kinds of circumstances in the Mediterranean world.[14]

Much of the success of the early Christian storylines and belief-argumentations lies in the manner in which conceptual blending occurs both within each rhetorolect and among the rhetorolects. Priestly rhetorolect focuses on altars, temples, priests, worship assemblies, and temple cities in a manner displayed in the table below.[15]

Religious Blending	**Priestly**
Social, cultural, and physical realia (first space)	Altars, temples, priests, worship assemblies, and temple city
Visualization, conceptualization, and imagination of God's world (second space)	God as holy and pure God on priestly throne in heavenly temple Selected humans as priests People as God's holy and pure priestly community (assembly, city, kingdom) Jesus as Priest-Messiah
Ongoing bodily effects and enactments: blending in religious life (third space)	Human body as giver of sacrificial offerings and receiver of beneficial exchange of holiness and purity between God and humans

2. Altars, Temples, Priests, Worship Assemblies, and Temple Cities as Spaces and Places for Priestly Rhetorolect

Sensory-aesthetic experiences of the body in various social places in the world—such as household, village, city, synagogue, kingdom, temple, and empire—are the "first-space" contexts in which people develop and perpetuate special pictures and memories in their minds. People activate cog-

14. For a recent exploration of miracle rhetorolect in emerging Christianity, see Watson, *Miracle Discourse*.

15. Cf. David A. deSilva, "The Invention and Argumentative Function of Priestly Discourse in the Epistle to the Hebrews," *BBR* 16 (2006): 295–323.

nitive and conceptual abilities to interpret these social places and actions as "second-space" cultural, religious, and ideological places. In the context of these activities, people negotiate their daily lives in ongoing contexts of sensory-aesthetic experiences, which are "third-space" "spaces of blending." In priestly rhetorolect, the experiential first spaces are altars, temples, priests, worship assemblies, and temple cities. In turn, the conceptualized second spaces are God as holy and pure, God on a priestly throne in God's heavenly temple, certain humans as priests, people as God's holy and priestly community, and Jesus as God's priestly Messiah. The third-space spaces of blending for priestly rhetorolect are the human body as giver of sacrificial offerings and receiver of beneficial exchanges of holiness and purity between God and humans.

The "reasoning" (rhetology) in priestly rhetorolect is based on a belief that "specific ritual activities" in special places produce beneficial exchange between humans and God. These ritual activities involve both physical and mental manipulation of material, verbal, emotive, and cognitive "objects." Underlying these manipulations is a belief that special "ritual" activities produce benefits both for God and for humans. The "pictorial narration" (rhetography) is based on experiences people have before altars, in temples, in worship assemblies, in temple cities, or in any place that somehow acquires special significance through activities and processes like prayer, fasting, being cleansed, being forgiven, and so on.

Early Christian priestly rhetorolect blends human experiences of temples, altars, priests, worship assemblies, and temple cities (first space) with God's cosmos (second space), and presupposes that specific actions in these "priestly" places (both first and second space) benefit both God and humans. In the space of blending (third space), people make sacrifices by giving to God things that regularly give them well being. Things like food, possessions, and money but also things like comfort and honor may be given to God. Some of these things may be given to God by giving them to other people on earth, or by allowing other people to take things like honor or fame away without protest. The greatest sacrifice people can offer to God, of course, is their entire life. Usually a person gives up only certain highly valued things in life. Sometimes, however, a person may perceive it necessary to give up one's entire life.

In sum, priestly rhetorolect features beneficial exchange between God and humans. The goal of the conceptual blending is to create people who are willing to give up things they highly value in exchange for special divine benefits that come to them, because these sacrifices are perceived to benefit God as well as humans. In other words, sacrificial actions by humans create an environment in which God acts redemptively among humans in the world.

As Luke and Acts use priestly rhetorolect in their presentation of the Christian story and the belief-arguments embedded in the story, the Christian story has a profound relationship to "priestly beginnings" when God appointed Aaron and his family as priests through Moses (Exod 28; Lev 8) and as God gave Moses commands and instructions about priestly things.[16] The Christian story also has a profound relationship to the story of the priestly prophet Samuel,[17] who anointed the first kings of Israel. When Luke and Acts extend the priestly belief-story into the story of Jesus and his followers, they and John the Baptizer all acquire certain kinds of priestly attributes and perform certain kinds of priestly functions.

3. The Christian Priestly "Background Story" in Luke and Acts

Priestly rhetorolect in Luke and Acts evokes a priestly background story as it tells its foreground story. The background story begins with Aaron and his family, continues through the tent of testimony from the time of Moses to David, includes the story of the priestly prophet Samuel, and features Solomon's building of the Jerusalem temple before the time of Zechariah's offering of the incense offering in Luke 1:8–21. This priestly background story becomes available to the hearer, reader, or interpreter through various episodes that occur in the foreground story in Luke and Acts.

3.1. Aaron and His Family

The background priestly story in Luke and Acts begins with Aaron and his family, whom God appointed as priests through Moses (Exod 28; Lev 8).

16. Since early Christians developed priestly rhetorolect with great detail, for particular writers the "beginnings" include the offerings of Cain and Abel in Gen 4, Abraham's offering of tithes to Melchizedek in Gen 14, the killing of lambs as a Passover ritual to protect the children of Israel from death, and Moses's blood covenant at Mount Sinai. In other words, different early Christian speakers and writers could use different episodes in "the biblical story" as special points of relationship to the "Christian belief-story" they were presenting.

17. E.g., the relation of the Magnificat (Luke 1:46–55) to Hannah's song (1 Sam 2:1–10); Acts 3:24; 13:20.

Aaron functions as the "founding father" of priesthood through reference to him and his successors in the presentation of Zechariah and Elizabeth. Aaron is the ancestor of Elizabeth, mother of John the Baptizer. The Gospel of Luke describes Elizabeth as "of the daughters of Aaron" (Luke 1:5). Abijah, a grandson of Aaron, received responsibility by lot for the eighth course of service in the Jerusalem temple (1 Chr 24:10, 19). Zechariah, father of John the Baptizer, is a priest "of the division of Abijah" (Luke 1:5).

3.2. Moses, Aaron, the Tent of Testimony, and the Tent of Moloch

Moses not only appointed Aaron and his family to be priests but also oversaw the building of a tent of testimony, which the people of Israel took along with them in the wilderness. Moses had it built according to the pattern God commanded to him. The people of Israel brought it along with them as they drove out the nations who possessed the land into which they were going. The people of Israel kept this tent of testimony until the time of David, who asked God for a dwelling place for the house of Jacob (Acts 7:44–46).

As the Christian priestly background story in Luke and Acts unfolds, it emphasizes that Aaron had difficulty with God's people when they were being led through the wilderness. Disobeying Aaron (Acts 7:39), the people made a golden calf, "offered a sacrifice" [ἀνήγαγον θυσίαν] to the idol, and reveled in the works of their hands" (Acts 7:41). They took along the tent of Moloch rather than the tent of testimony God commanded Moses to build. As a result, they did not offer the Lord "slain victims [σφάγια] and sacrifices [θυσίας]" during their forty years in the wilderness (Acts 7:42), but worshiped "the star of the god Rephan," which were the images they made to worship (Acts 7:43). For this reason, the Lord exiled the people of Israel to Babylon (Acts 7:43).[18]

3.3. Priestly Rituals according to the Torah of the Lord through Moses

The Christian priestly background story moves beyond its beginnings in Aaron's priestly family and its continuation through the tent of testimony

18. To understand the rhetorical nature of this account of the biblical events in Acts, see the detailed discussion in Todd C. Penner, *In Praise of Christian Origins: Stephen and the Hellenists in Lukan Apologetic Historiography*, ESEC 10 (New York: T&T Clark, 2004), 315–23.

and the tent of Moloch into Moses's presentation of priestly commandments that are important for God's people to follow. One of these commandments requires the circumcision of all males. According to Acts, Abraham received the covenant of circumcision (Acts 7:8). Circumcision became a "custom," however, through Moses (Acts 15:1), and by this means it became a requirement of the law of Moses (Acts 15:5; 16:3; 21:21), which is intimately related to the Jerusalem temple. In addition, the law of Moses requires a ritual of purification after the birth of a child, with a command that the mother offer two turtledoves or two pigeons as a sacrifice in the temple, if she cannot afford a sheep (Luke 2:22, 24; cf. Lev 12:1–8). In addition, the law of the Lord requires that "every firstborn male shall be designated as holy to the Lord" (Luke 2:23: cf. Exod 13:2, 12, 15). There is also a ritual sacrifice of purification whereby one is cleansed from leprosy (Luke 5:14; 17:14; cf. Lev 13–14). Also, it is good to take a vow for a period of time and end it with a ritual of purification in the temple, which includes shaving of the head (Acts 18:18; 21:20–26; cf. Num 6:1–21).

According to Acts, there is a list of minimum requirements from Moses that gentile believers must follow: abstaining from things polluted by idols, from fornication, from whatever has been strangled, and from blood (Acts 15:20–21, 29; 21:25; cf. Lev 3:17; 17:3–18:30; 19:26; Exod 34:15–16; Deut 12:16, 26–27). One line of interpretation considers these requirements to represent the covenant of Noah, since God gives a command to Noah that humans must not eat blood or flesh with blood in it (Gen 9:4). Acts, however, never mentions Noah in relation to these requirements.[19] Most scholars today understand these rules as having their basis in the laws for resident aliens dwelling among the Israelites (Lev 17–18).[20]

3.4. Samuel, Saul, and David

After the time of Moses and the judges, the priestly prophet Samuel anointed both Saul and David as kings of Israel. The Gospel of Luke never

19. In the Gospel of Luke, 3:36 mentions Noah in the genealogy of Jesus back to Adam, and 17:26–27 refers to the time of Noah, but there is no reference to a special covenant or a command not to eat blood in either context.

20. For a careful evaluation of the options, see C. K. Barrett, *A Critical and Exegetical Commentary on the Acts of the Apostles*, 2 vols., ICC (Edinburgh: T&T Clark, 1998), 2:730–36; and see also the excursus "Apostolic Decree" by Richard I. Pervo, *Acts: A Commentary*, Hermeneia (Minneapolis: Fortress, 2009), 376–78.

refers to Samuel by name, but Luke's account of the birth of John the Baptizer exhibits dynamic intertexture with patterns and content in the Samuel story. When Acts 3:24 refers to Samuel, it includes him among the prophets who "foretold these days." Acts 13:20 also refers to Samuel as a prophet in a context that recounts how God gave both Saul and David to the people of Israel as kings.

3.5. Solomon Built a House for God, but God Does Not Dwell in a House Made with Hands

Solomon, David's son, built a temple for God in Jerusalem (Acts 7:47). There is, however, a prophetic assertion that the Most High does not dwell in a house made with human hands (Acts 7:48). Rather, heaven is the throne of God, and the earth is the footstool for God's feet (Isa 66:1–2; Acts 7:49–50). What, then, is the future role of the Jerusalem temple that Solomon built? The answer to this unfolds in the foreground story in Luke and Acts.

4. The Christian Priestly Jesus Story in the Gospel of Luke[21]

The priestly story of Jesus begins with priestly aspects of the account of John the Baptizer's birth that create a priestly environment for the birth of Jesus and his subsequent activities in the Gospel of Luke.

4.1. The Priestly Story of John the Baptizer

John the Baptizer had both a mother and a father who had priestly lineage. As noted above, Elizabeth was "of the daughters of Aaron" and Zechariah was a descendant of Aaron's grandson Abijah (Luke 1:5). One of the results of the priestly context for John the Baptizer's birth is a Nazirite vow that continues over his entire life in the form of never drinking wine or strong drink (Luke 1:15). The Holy Spirit with which John is filled "even before his birth" (Luke 1:15) appears to have priestly connotations of holiness as a result of the "blameless" (ἄμεμπτοι), righteous lives of his priestly parents (Luke 1:6). When Zechariah speaks prophetically after John has been circumcised and named (Luke 1:59–66), his first act is to "bless [εὐλογῶν]

21. Cf. Rick Strelan, "Luke the Priest," in *Luke the Priest*, 117–44.

God" (1:64, 68). In the context he speaks of the people's ability to serve God without fear, "in holiness and righteousness before him all our days" (Luke 1:75). One of the specific roles of John will be to give knowledge of salvation to God's people "in the forgiveness of their sins" (Luke 1:77: ἐν ἀφέσει ἁμαρτιῶν), which is an action specifically assigned to priests in the Torah (Lev 4:20, 31, 35; 5:6, 16, 18).[22]

It is well known that the Gospel of Luke inaugurates the adult activity of John the Baptizer by naming the emperor, the governor of Judea, the tetrarchs of three nearby regions, and the high priests at the time he appeared in public (Luke 3:1–2). An interpreter attentive to priestly rhetorolect in Luke will observe that the list of names moves to a final emphatic focus on "the high priesthood of Annas and Caiaphas" before it introduces "John the son of Zechariah," who preaches a baptism of repentance for the purpose of "the forgiveness of sins" (Luke 3:2–3). The priestly heritage and nurturing of John the Baptizer produces a "priestly" prophet. John is not simply a prophet who announces to God's people that they must "bear fruits worthy of repentance" (Luke 3:8). Rather, the goal of the baptism he offers is forgiveness of sins, which is the special domain of priests in the story of Israel.

Embedded in the priestly story of John the Baptizer is a beginning point that includes prayer. When Zechariah was offering the incense on the altar inside the Jerusalem temple, the whole assembly of people outside were praying (1:10). When the angel Gabriel speaks to Zechariah inside the temple, he asserts that Zechariah's "prayer has been heard" (1:13). An attribute of the priestly father of John the Baptizer, then, was prayer in the context of the righteousness "before the Lord" of both Zechariah and Elizabeth (1:6). In addition, part of the priestly ritual of the incense offering in the temple was an assembly of people at the time to offer prayers. Prayers offered to God, then, are an important aspect of priestly rhetorolect in the Christian story in Luke.

4.2. The Priestly Story of the Infant Jesus

After the Gospel of Luke introduces the promise of the birth of John to his priestly parents (1:5–25), it introduces the promise of the birth of Jesus

22. See, e.g., Lev 4:20 LXX: καὶ ἐξιλάσεται περὶ αὐτῶν ὁ ἱερεύς, καὶ ἀφεθήσεται αὐτοῖς ἡ ἁμαρτία.

(1:26–38). The initial emphasis on Jesus is that "he will be great, and will be called the Son of the Most High, and the Lord God will give to him the throne of his ancestor David" (1:32). Therefore, Davidic messiahship comes into the foreground when Lukan narration introduces Jesus to the Gospel story. In this context, however, there is also an emphasis that "the Holy Spirit will come upon" Mary, and this will make the child born to her "holy" (1:35). As the angel Gabriel continues to speak, he reveals that Mary is "a relative" of Elizabeth (1:36: συγγενίς). Mary, then, not only has a relationship to "the house of David" (1:27); she has a kinship relationship to a woman who is one "of the daughters of Aaron" (1:5). Once this "priestly" relationship of Mary is announced in the story, special priestly things begin to happen in relation to Jesus.

When Mary enters "the house of Zechariah" to visit her relative Elizabeth, she is entering a priestly household. When Elizabeth hears Mary's greeting, the child John leaps in her womb (1:41). When Elizabeth is filled with Holy Spirit, she cries out two "blessings." The activity of "blessing" is a special activity of priests (cf. Sir 50:20–21). Elizabeth, a daughter of Aaron, speaks to Mary like a priest during a time when her priestly husband is unable to speak! First, Elizabeth blesses Mary herself "among women" everywhere; second, she blesses Jesus as "the fruit" of Mary's womb (1:42). Through Holy Spirit that has filled Elizabeth through the presence of Mary, who is pregnant with Jesus, Mary has received blessings in a priestly household from a priestly wife.

The priestly nature of Elizabeth's speech becomes especially evident when it is compared with speech by priests to Mary in the Protevangelium of James (PJ). On Mary's first birthday, her father "Joachim presented her to the priests, and they blessed [ηὐλόγησαν] her: 'God of our fathers, bless [εὐλόγησον] this child and give her a name which will be on the lips of future generations forever'" (PJ 6.7).[23] The reference to "all generations" (πάσαις ταῖς γενεαῖς) is obviously an adaptation of Mary's own speech in Luke 1:48.[24] After this, the high priests bless Mary with the "ultimate blessing" (PJ 6.9: ἐσχάτην εὐλογίαν), which includes a request that God "look

23. The Greek and English are based on Ronald F. Hock, *The Infancy Gospels of James and Thomas*, ScholBib 3 (Santa Rosa, CA: Polebridge, 1995).

24. This accepts, of course, that the Magnificat is Mary's speech rather than Elizabeth's, as it is in some ancient manuscripts: see Joseph A. Fitzmyer, *The Gospel according to Luke (I–IX): Introduction, Translation, and Notes*, AB 28 (New York: Doubleday, 1981), 365–66.

upon" (ἐπίβλεψον) this child (cf. Luke 1:48a). When Joachim and Anna commit Mary to live in the temple at three years of age, the priest blesses (εὐλόγησεν) her by saying: "The Lord has exalted your name among all generations. In you the Lord will disclose his redemption to the people of Israel during the last days" (PJ 7.7). After Mary spins purple and scarlet thread for the high priest, he blessed (εὐλόγησεν) her and said: "Mary, the Lord God has magnified your name [cf. Luke 1:46] and so you will be blessed [ἔσῃ εὐλογημένη] by all the generations of the earth" (PJ 12.2; cf. Luke 1:48). Instead of priests blessing Mary in the Gospel of Luke, the priestly wife Elizabeth, Mary's relative, blesses her. Priestly kinship, priestly holiness, and priestly blessings establish an environment in which priestly heritage, attributes, and effects blend with the portrayal of Mary and Jesus in the Gospel of Luke.

After Jesus is born, only in Luke is he circumcised in the context in which he is named Jesus (2:21). Circumcision is understood in Acts to be one of the customs of Moses, which is, in turn, closely associated with holiness and the temple (cf. Acts 6:13–14).

After the circumcision and naming of Jesus, his parents take him to the Jerusalem temple and offer a priestly sacrifice for purification (Luke 2:22). When they offer two turtle doves or two pigeons for the purification offering (2:24), they follow the priestly guidelines of Lev 12:8 in a manner that indicates they could not afford to offer a sheep. In this context, Luke asserts that "it is written in the law of the Lord, 'Every male that opens the womb shall be called holy to the Lord'" (2:23: ἅγιον τῷ κυρίῳ). This is a recitation that blends words from Exod 13:2, 12, 15, and Luke 1:35 to create an abbreviated commandment of Moses in the form of an oral proverb.[25] Lukan narration blends the ritual sacrifice in the temple for purification and the consecration of all firstborn males to God. The wording that they brought him up (ἀνήγαγον αὐτόν) to Jerusalem "to present him to the Lord" (παραστῆσαι τῷ κυρίῳ) "imitates the presentation of Samuel by his mother, Hannah, in 1 Sam 1:22–24."[26] The closest wording is actu-

25. The recitation abbreviates, rearranges, blends, and revises Exod 13:2, 12, 15, in relation to Luke 1:35 (πᾶν and διανοῖγον μήτραν are present in Exod 13:2, 12, 15; τὰ ἀρσενικά [rather than ἄρσεν] in Exod 13:12, 15; τῷ κυρίῳ in Exod 13:12, 15; and ἅγιον κληθήσεται is present in Luke 1:35). The end result is a commandment from the torah in an oral, proverbial form; see Robbins, *Exploring*, 41–42; cf. Robbins, *Tapestry*, 103–6.

26. Fitzmyer, *Luke I–IX*, 425.

ally 1 Sam 1:25 LXX, where Hannah and Samuel "go up before the Lord" (προσήγαγον ἐνώπιον κυρίου). According to Num 18:15–16 (cf. 3:47–48), his parents should have paid five shekels to a member of the family of Aaron when Jesus was one month old. In contrast, the consecration of Jesus as a firstborn son is simply part of the presentation of him in the temple.[27] For the Gospel of Luke, the presentation of Jesus in the temple is part of an overall environment of doing things according to the law of Moses at the time of Jesus's birth (2:23, 24, 27, 39). This establishes an early stage in Jesus's life where his parents lived "according to the law of Moses" and did nothing "against" the Jerusalem temple (cf. Acts 21:28).

In the context of the presentation of Jesus to the Lord in the Jerusalem temple, various people engage in a ritual of blessing. Simeon's words while he is holding Jesus in his arms are considered to be an action of "blessing [εὐλόγησεν] God" (2:28). After his words of blessing about Jesus, he blesses (εὐλόγησεν) Jesus's parents (2:34). While Simeon blesses Jesus and his parents like a priest, the prophet Anna functions like those who assemble during priestly activities. She "worships" (λατρεύουσα) night and day in the temple, "fasting and praying" (2:37). The activities of prayer and blessing that are part of the story of the birth of John the Baptizer, then, extend into the context of the presentation of Jesus to the Lord in the Jerusalem temple.

4.3. A Turning Point in Jesus's Relation to the Jerusalem Temple

When Jesus returns to the temple at twelve years of age, he comes as a young man who sits "among the teachers [τῶν διδασκάλων]," and all of the people who hear him are "amazed at his understanding and his answers" (2:46–47). This is the beginning of a program in which Jesus turns the temple into a place of teaching and prayer, rather than a place of sacrificial ritual. When Jesus returns to the Jerusalem temple at the height of his adult career, he drives out those who were selling things to support the sacrificial rituals and announces that the temple is to be "a house of prayer" (19:46).

After Jesus drives the sellers out of the temple, he turns the temple into a place of teaching from Luke 20:1 to 21:38. In the context of his temple

27. According to ibid., 425, there is no evidence of a temple ritual with the firstborn son "either in the OT or in the Mishnah."

teaching, the only "ritual" he observes is rich people putting their gifts into the treasury and a poor widow putting in two small copper coins (21:1–2). This, along with his response to a question about paying taxes to the emperor (20:22–26), turns part of the teaching toward issues concerning the rich and the poor that are present at various points from Jesus's announcement of his "good news for the poor" in Luke 4:18 through his encounter with the chief tax collector Zacchaeus, who was very rich (19:1–10), and through the parable of the wealthy and powerful nobleman in Luke 19:11–27.

The question, then, becomes: What is Jesus's authority to reconfigure the Jerusalem temple from a place of priestly sacrifice to a place of teaching and prayer? This appears to be what is at stake in the question of the chief priests and scribes: "Tell us, by what authority are you doing these things? Who is it who gave you this authority?" (20:2). One of the questions for the hearer of the Lukan story can be: Does Jesus have any "priestly" credentials that would allow him to "authoritatively" change the function of the Jerusalem temple?

This essay now turns to a set of activities by Jesus in Luke that a hearer may consider to be priestly activities. These activities might be considered, then, to qualify Jesus to confront the chief priests and scribes on priestly matters and to insist on a reconfiguration of the function of God's temple.

4.4. The Priestly Story of the Adult Jesus

4.4.1. Jesus Commands a Healed Leper to Offer Temple Sacrifices

Like the account of the cleansing of the leper in Mark 1:40–45 // Matt 8:1–4, the Lukan account also features Jesus telling the healed leper, "Go and show yourself to the priest, and, as Moses commanded, make an offering for your cleansing, for a testimony to them" (5:14). When Jesus cleanses ten lepers in Luke 17:11–19, however, there is no similar command. Instead, the emphasis is on one who was a Samaritan, who "turned back, praising God with a loud voice; and he fell on his face at Jesus's feet, giving him thanks" (17:15–16).

A command by Jesus to the Samaritan to make priestly offerings in the Jerusalem temple according to the law of Moses would have been interesting indeed in Lukan discourse! It may be appropriate to notice, however, that neither Luke nor Acts exhibits clear knowledge that Samaritans do not worship in the Jerusalem temple. Only the Gospel of John in the writings of the New Testament exhibits this knowledge (4:20–21). In fact, only Luke, John, and Acts refer to Samaritans. Luke 10:29–35 alongside Luke 17:11–19 could give the impression that Samaritans were "foreigners" (cf. 17:18: ὁ ἀλλογενής) who, like the Ethiopian eunuch in Acts 8:27, go up to Jerusalem to worship. This is especially possible, since Acts puts the mission to the Samaritans (Acts 8:4–25) directly before the account of the baptism of the Ethiopian eunuch (Acts 8:26–40). We may observe, then, that in only one instance, an instance where most interpreters would suggest that Luke simply is following Mark, does Jesus give a command that someone should offer a sacrifice in the Jerusalem temple according to the priestly commandments of Moses.

4.4.2. The Continuous Prayer Life of Jesus in Luke

If a priest is supposed to offer prayers regularly, Jesus admirably fulfills this requirement. In the spirit of Heb 5:7: "In the days of his flesh, Jesus offered up prayers and supplications, with cries and tears, to the one who was able to save him from death." The hearer sees Jesus praying for the first time after he is baptized by John. While he is praying, the heaven opens, the spirit descends like a dove on him, and he hears a voice from heaven: "You are my Son, the Beloved; with you I am well pleased" (3:21). After this, Jesus "often" withdraws "to lonely places" and prays (5:16). Once he went out to a mountainside and prayed the entire night (6:12). One time when he was praying in private with his disciples, he asked his disciples: "Who do the crowds say I am?" (9:18). On one occasion when Jesus took Peter, John, and James with him onto a mountain to pray, while he was praying "the appearance of his face changed, and his clothes became dazzling white," Moses and Elijah came and talked with him, and a voice from the cloud that overshadowed the disciples said: "This is my Son, my Chosen, listen to him" (9:29–35). At still a later time when Jesus was praying at a certain place, one of his disciples asked Jesus to teach them how to pray, and he did so (11:1–4). In the context of Jesus's last supper with the apostles, he told Simon that he had prayed for him that his faith may not fail (22:32). After the supper, Jesus went out to the Mount of Olives and told them to "pray that you may not come into the time of trial" (22:40). Then he himself went a short distance away, knelt down, and prayed: "Father, if you are willing, remove this cup from me; yet not my will but yours be done" (22:41–42). In some manuscript traditions, an angel from heaven appears and gives Jesus strength as he prays in anguish and "great drops of blood fall down on the ground" (22:44).[28] When Jesus finishes praying, he discovers that the disciples are sleeping "from grief," and again he tells them that they must get up and pray that they may not come into the time of trial (22:45–46).

4.4.3. Jesus Describes Persistent and Appropriate Prayer

Alongside Jesus's regular ritual of prayer in Luke stand occasions in which he discusses with his followers how they should pray, and in some of these contexts he criticizes how certain other people pray. In two instances, Jesus instructed people about prayer with parables. First, he told the disciples (17:22) a parable "about their need to pray always and not to lose heart" (18:1). The parable describes a judge "who neither feared God nor had respect for people" (18:2). When he is persistently approached by a widow, requesting that he grant her justice against her opponent, he finally does so (18:3–8). In this instance, the judge acts in a manner befitting a priest who pronounces a blessing of justice on an unfortunate widow who petitions in a manner that is like persistent prayer. Second, he tells "some who trusted in themselves that they were righteous and regarded others with contempt" about a Pharisee and a tax collector who went up to the temple to pray (18:9–10). The Pharisee, addressing God, focuses entirely on himself in contrast to others, describing others as "thieves, rogues, adulterers, or even like this tax collector" and himself as one who fasts twice a week and gives a tenth of all his income (18:11–12). This man does not receive justification before God (18:14). Alternatively, the tax collector stands far off, beating his breast and not looking up to heaven, saying, "God, be merciful to me a sinner!" (8:13). Jesus describes the tax collector as the one who "went down to his home justified," because he humbled himself (18:14). In this context, the tax collector engages in prayer in the Jerusalem temple in a manner that produces a result similar to the blessing of a priest. In these instances, then, persistent and appropriate prayer brings blessings from God on those who engage in it.

Later, when Jesus is in the Jerusalem temple, he pronounces "condemnation" (κρίμα) on scribes who "for the sake of appearance say long

28. See Joseph A. Fitzmyer, *The Gospel according to Luke (X–XXIV): Introduction, Translation, and Notes*, AB 28A (New York: Doubleday, 1985), 1443–44, for an extensive discussion of the addition and omission of Luke 22:43–44 among manuscripts and versions.

prayers" at the same time that they "devour widows' houses" (20:47). In contrast, Jesus explains that people should "be alert at all times, praying that you may have the strength to escape all these things that will take place, and to stand before the Son of Man" (21:36). Jesus's prayer life, which is like the life of a righteous priest, should be a model for people to follow through all the tests and trials of life. In the manner of a priest, Jesus not only lives in the discipline of a life of prayer but also explains to people the difference between appropriate and inappropriate prayer.[29]

4.4.4. Jesus Forgives People's Sins, Tells Others to Forgive, and Blesses People

In two instances, Jesus forgives sins of people. The first occurs when some men bring a paralyzed man to him. Jesus heals the man by pronouncing that his sins are forgiven (5:20). When scribes and Pharisees argue that no one can forgive sins but God alone, Jesus responds that "the Son of Man has authority on earth to forgive sins" (5:24). This action by Jesus would appear to portray Jesus enacting the role of a priest in a context where he also is a healer. The second occurs when a sinful "woman of the city" (7:37) comes into a Pharisee's house and performs a ritual of weeping, bathing Jesus's feet with tears, drying Jesus's feet with her hair, kissing Jesus's feet, and anointing them with expensive ointment (7:38). Jesus responds to her ritual by saying, "Your sins are forgiven" and telling her to "go in peace" because her faith has saved her (7:48–50). In contexts where other people engage in persistent ritual actions of petition and devotion, then, Jesus may respond like a priest who pronounces the forgiveness of a person's sins.

In addition to forgiving people their sins, Jesus explains in Luke 6:37 that if people forgive, they will be forgiven. Later, when the sinful woman bathes, anoints, and dries Jesus's feet with her hair, Jesus uses a story about a creditor and two debtors to argue that a person who shows great love receives forgiveness for their sins (7:47). In some instances, then, Jesus's wisdom includes knowledge about priestly effects. According to Luke 7:47,

---

29. Jesus defends his disciples' not praying and fasting in only one instance. When Jesus is with the disciples, they "eat and drink with tax collectors and sinners" (5:30), in contrast to John's disciples and the disciples of the Pharisees who "frequently fast and pray," because Jesus himself has come "to call not the righteous but sinners to repentance" (5:32).

"showing great love" functions as a priestly ritual that brings the effect of "receiving forgiveness of sins." In addition, Jesus teaches the disciples to pray, "Forgive us our sins, for we also forgive everyone who sins against us" (11:4), and if a brother sins but then repents, forgive him even "seven times in a day" (17:4).

Jesus engages in an especially defining priestly act when he uses prayer to intercede with God for those who are crucifying him, saying: "Father, forgive them, for they do not know what they are doing" (23:34). Here Jesus enacts a principle he taught his disciples: "bless [εὐλογεῖτε] those who curse you, pray for those who mistreat you" (6:28). Jesus uses the prayer to petition God to forgive them for the death they are inflicting on him.

At the end of the story of Jesus in the Gospel of Luke, Jesus looks forward to the time when his followers will perform a priestly function by proclaiming "repentance and forgiveness of sins" in his name "to all nations, beginning from Jerusalem" (24:47). The final act of Jesus, just before he ascends into heaven, reconfigures the priestly beginnings of the Gospel of Luke. "Lifting up his hands," Jesus "blessed" (εὐλόγησεν) his followers, and while he is blessing (ἐν τῷ εὐλογεῖν) them, he ascends into heaven (24:50–51). Some manuscripts add that Jesus's followers bow down in worship (προσκυνήσαντες) while Jesus ascends into heaven.[30] Then his followers return to Jerusalem and are continually "in the temple blessing [εὐλογοῦντες] God" (24:53). In this scene, Jesus acts like a priest in relation to his followers, and his followers go to the Jerusalem temple and engage in proper worship that includes "blessing" God.

It is noticeable that both Jesus and his followers perform actions of "blessing" (εὐλογεῖν), rather than simply actions of "praising." Persistently throughout Luke many people engage in glorifying (δοξάζειν) or praising (αἰνεῖν) God.[31] "Blessing" God and other people, however, is associated specifically with priestly activities in Luke. It is informative that there is a concentration of language of blessing in the two opening chapters of the Gospel of Luke and in its final verses. While the story of Luke begins with priestly offerings in the temple that brings blessings on the family of John the Baptizer and the family of Jesus, the story ends with Jesus blessing his followers in a priestly manner and sending them to the Jerusalem temple,

30. See Fitzmyer, *Luke X–XXIV*, 1590.

31. Luke 2:13–14, 20; 4:15; 5:25–26; 7:16; 13:13; 17:15; 18:43; 19:37–38; 23:47; Acts 2:47; 3:8, 9, 13; 4:21; 11:18; 12:23; 13:48; 21:20.

where they engage in "continually [διὰ παντός] blessing [εὐλογοῦντες] God" (24:53). Not only do priestly activities extend from the beginnings of the Lukan story into priestly activities by Jesus throughout his life. At the end of the Lukan story, Jesus's priestly activity of blessing sends his followers to the Jerusalem temple, where they "bless God" in a manner that creates an environment where they themselves will begin to function in a priestly manner "to all nations" (24:47).

4.5. "Almost" Sacrificial Language about Jesus's Death in Luke

In the midst of the "priestly" attributes exhibited by Jesus in Luke, there is no direct statement that Jesus died a sacrificial death to save humans from their sins. Neither Luke nor Acts contains a statement like Mark 10:45 // Matt 20:28: "For/Just as the Son of Man came not to be served but to serve, and to give his life a ransom for many" (cf. Luke 22:27).[32] Alongside 1–2 Corinthians and Romans, in particular, which assert so directly that Christ died for the sins of many (or "for us"), it is remarkable that there is not one statement like this in the preaching of Jesus's followers in Acts.[33] Instead, Jesus's followers repeatedly preach a "baptism in the name of Jesus Christ" that brings forgiveness of sins and the gift of the Holy Spirit. Peter's argument in Acts 2 is that God's resurrection of Jesus to the right hand of God, which makes him both Lord and Messiah, puts him in an authoritative position whereby "baptism into his name" brings forgiveness of sins, much like a priest would pronounce a "blessing" that a person's sins are forgiven at the end of an appropriate sacrificial ritual in the temple.

There is one verse in Luke to which interpreters point to suggest that this gospel actually does contain language about Jesus's sacrificial death for others. Luke 22:20, toward the end of the account of the Last Supper, features Jesus saying: "This cup which is poured out for you [ὑπὲρ ὑμῶν] is the new covenant in my blood." This verse does not mention "ransom" or "sin," but the phrase "for you" moves beyond the new covenant of Jer 31:31 toward the domain of the blood covenant in Exod 24:8.[34] The presence of this verse in Luke makes it all the more remarkable that there is not sacrificial language in the preaching in Acts, as we will see below.

---

32. The only statements in Luke and Acts that use a word with a λυτρ- base are in Luke 1:68; 2:38; 24:21; Acts 7:35.

33. 1 Cor 15:3; 2 Cor 5:14–15; cf. Rom 8:32; 1 Pet 3:18; Heb 9:12.

34. See Fitzmyer, *Luke X–XXIV*, 1402.

5. The Christian Priestly "Followers Story" in the Acts of the Apostles

The Acts of the Apostles begins with a strong focus on prophetic rhetorolect blended with apocalyptic rhetorolect. This discourse emphasizes the restoration of the kingdom to Israel (1:6–7), "the last days" (2:17–21), and the "certainty that God has made Jesus both Lord and Messiah" (2:36).

5.1. Prayer, Casting Lots, Baptism, and Forgiveness of Sins at the Beginning of Acts

Priestly rhetorolect blends with prophetic and apocalyptic rhetorolect already in Acts 1:12–14, which portrays the eleven apostles returning to Jerusalem. After listing the eleven apostles by name, the narrator asserts that all of them "constantly devoted themselves to prayer, together with certain women, including Mary the mother of Jesus as well as his brothers" (1:13–14). Thus, in a manner parallel to Jesus's beginning of his adult life with prayer after his baptism (Luke 3:21), an assembly of Jesus's followers sets the context for the events that occur in the opening chapters of Acts through their worship together in an upper room in Jerusalem (1:13).

Prayer continues to establish the context for their activities as they choose the replacement for Judas. Praying, "Lord, you know everyone's heart. Show us which one of these two [Justus or Matthias] you have chosen to take the place in this ministry and apostleship from which Judas turned aside to go to his own place" (1:25), they establish a priestly environment for God's choice as the lot falls on Matthias (1:26).[35]

Priestly precedent for the use of lots to determine the Lord's choice lies in Lev 16:8–9, where Aaron casts lots to determine which goat the Lord had chosen for the sin offering, and in 1 Chr 24–25, where the specific duties of the descendants of Aaron and the workers in the temple are determined through the casting of lots. Once again there is a precedent at the beginning of Luke, where the narrator asserts that Zechariah had been "chosen by lot" to "enter the sanctuary of the Lord and offer incense" (1:9).

---

35. For a discussion of the casting of lots in Acts 1:26, see Arie W. Zwiep, *Judas and the Choice of Matthias: A Study on Context and Concern of Acts 1:15–26*, WUNT 2/187 (Tübingen: Mohr Siebeck, 2004), esp. 168–72. Zwiep calls the procedure in Acts 1:26 "the 'perfect' biblical scenario" (171).

Priestly rhetorolect continues in Acts in the context of Pentecost, immediately after Peter's interpretation of the death and resurrection of Jesus to the people assembled in Jerusalem. After concluding that God "with certainty" had made Jesus both Lord and Messiah (2:36), Peter instructs all the people to "repent, and be baptized every one of you in the name of Jesus Christ so that your sins may be forgiven; and you will receive the gift of the Holy Spirit" (2:38). With this assertion, Peter continues the reconfiguration of priestly activity by John the Baptizer and Jesus with a ritual of baptism "in the name of Jesus Christ" that brings "forgiveness of sins" and "the gift of the Holy Spirit." This discourse at the beginning of Acts now builds on all the priestly precedents of baptism of repentance, forgiveness of sins, and presence of the Holy Spirit in the events at the "beginning" of the John the Baptist and Jesus story, as well as major activities by Jesus during his adult life. After being baptized, the people devote themselves not only to the apostles' teaching, to fellowship, and to the breaking of bread (2:42), but also, the narrator asserts in the final emphatic position in the sentence, "in prayers" (2:42). Again, an entire configuration of "priestly" activities both at the beginning of the story of Jesus and throughout Jesus's adult life pervades the beginning of the story in Acts about the formation of a "worshiping community" of people who will engage in "priestly" activities as they become Jesus's "witnesses … to the ends of the earth" (1:8).

5.2. Prayer throughout Acts

Much as prayer pervades the story of Jesus in Luke, so prayer is present virtually everywhere with Jesus's followers in Acts. With this activity, Jesus's followers become a "priestly" community of people as they spread their activities from Jerusalem all the way to Rome. As the story progresses, the continual "priestly" activity of prayer blends with miracle rhetorolect as well as wisdom, prophetic, and apocalyptic rhetorolect. When Peter and John are going up to the temple to pray, people bring a man who was lame from birth to the temple to ask for alms, and Peter and John heal him of his lameness (3:1–10). When Peter and John are released from the Jerusalem council, which includes the high priest and the high priestly family (4:5), they return to their associates and immediately raise their voices to God in prayer (4:23–26). After they had prayed, "the place in which they were gathered together was shaken; and they were all filled with the Holy Spirit and spoke the word of God with boldness" (4:31). Once again the story relates to the beginning of the story of Jesus, where, when Jesus is praying, the heavens are opened, the Holy Spirit descends on Jesus, and a voice from heaven establishes Jesus as God's Son, the Beloved One (Luke 3:21–22). For Jesus's followers, boldness comes for their task when God sends the Holy Spirit to them in the context of special prayers they offer when they gather together.

The episode with Stephen begins and ends with prayer as an important phenomenon (Acts 6:4, 6; 7:59). The appointment of seven men to distribute daily to the widows was motivated by a desire of the twelve apostles to have time to devote themselves "to prayer and to serving the word" (6:4). The Twelve naturally set the context for their appointment of the seven men with prayer (6:6). In addition, they lay their hands on them, a ritual perhaps most closely related to Moses's appointment of Joshua as his successor in the presence of Eleazar the priest and the whole congregation (Num 27:22–23; Deut 34:9; cf. Num 8:10–11). Laying on of hands occurs frequently after this in Acts (8:17, 19; 9:12, 17; 13:3; 19:6; 28:8, 10), and usually prayer accompanies it (8:15, 22, 24; 9:11; 13:3 [also fasting; cf. 14:23]; 28:8). When Stephen dies, he prays, "Lord Jesus, receive my spirit," before kneeling down and crying out with a loud voice, "Lord, do not hold this sin against them" (Acts 7:59–60: cf. Luke 23:34, 46). For the first time in the story, a follower of Jesus prays to Jesus, rather than solely to God. Seeds for Jesus as a priestly intercessor that were planted when Jesus asked God to forgive those who were killing him (Luke 23:34),[36] then, are exhibited in the narration in Acts to bear fruit in Stephen's prayers to Jesus.

On various occasions in Acts, kneeling accompanies prayer (7:60; 9:40; 20:36; 21:25). In one instance, there is singing of hymns to God (16:25) alongside prayer. In the context of the acceptance and baptism of Cornelius and his family into the community of Jesus's followers, there is extensive prayer. There is an emphasis that Cornelius and his family, as devout and God-fearing people, pray to God regularly, as well as giving generously to the poor and needy (10:2, 30, 31). In turn, a voice confronts Peter with the acceptance of Cornelius in a context where he had gone up on the roof to pray and had become hungry (10:9–10; 11:5). When Peter is in prison, there is an emphasis that the church gathered and prayed ear-

36. Luke 23:34 is lacking in some major ancient manuscripts like $\mathfrak{P}^{75}$, B, and D*. If it was not originally in Luke, scribal transmission shows an interest in the role of Jesus as a priestly intercessor during the first centuries of Christianity.

nestly for him (12:5, 12). When Paul comes into the story, he seeks a place of prayer on the Sabbath (16:13, 16), prays at the Jerusalem temple (22:17), and prays for safety when traveling on the sea (27:29).

5.3. Forgiveness of Sins

From the beginning to the end of the story, there is emphasis on forgiveness of sins through belief in Jesus. Peter and the apostles tell the high priest that God exalted Jesus at his right hand so that "he might give repentance to Israel and forgiveness of sins" (5:31). Peter tells those in the house of Cornelius that all the prophets testify that all who believe in Jesus "receive forgiveness of sins through his name" (10:43). Paul tells the Israelites gathered in Pisidian Antioch that through Jesus, whom God raised up, "forgiveness of sins is proclaimed to you" (13:38). Then later Paul tells King Agrippa that the Lord Jesus appeared to him and sent him out so that people "may receive forgiveness of sins and a place among those who are sanctified" (26:18). In this overall context, there is a specific assertion in Acts 13:39 that through Jesus "everyone who believes is set free from all those sins from which they could not be freed by the law of Moses." The discussion of forgiveness of sins, therefore, leads to a discussion of the law of Moses and the temple.

5.4. The Law of Moses and the Jerusalem Temple

Throughout Acts Paul frequently observes the priestly laws of Moses (16:3; 18:18; 20:16; 21:20–26). Nevertheless, Jews from Asia charge that he teaches against the people of Israel, their law, and their temple (21:28). Indeed, they charge specifically that he brought Greeks into the temple and defiled it (21:28–29). The law or "customs" of Moses are associated intimately with the Jerusalem temple. In Acts 6:13–14, people from the synagogue of the Freedman along with Cyrenians, Alexandrians, Cilicia, and Asia (6:9) blend together an assertion against Stephen that "this man never ceases to speak words against this holy place [the Jerusalem temple] and the law; for we have heard him say that this Jesus of Nazareth will destroy this place, and will change the customs Moses delivered to us" (6:13–14). Later, Jews from Asia accuse Paul of teaching against the people of Israel, against the law, and against the temple, in addition to actually defiling the temple by bringing Greeks into it (21:27–28). The discourse in Acts argues, in contrast, that Jesus's followers offer forgiveness of sins through Jesus without actually defiling the temple or forsaking all the laws of Moses.

As indicated above, in Acts 13:39 Paul argues that "by this Jesus everyone who believes is set free from all those sins from which you could not be freed by the law of Moses." Gradually there is opposition from "people from Judea" (15:1) and from Pharisees (15:5) that people cannot be saved unless they are circumcised according to the custom of Moses and ordered to keep the law of Moses. When James, the apostles, and elders agree not to require circumcision for gentile believers but to require that they abstain from things polluted by idols, from fornication, and from whatever has been strangled and from blood (15:20, 29; 21:25), the discourse in Acts implies that this is a matter of following major laws of Moses (15:21; 21:20–21). Jesus's followers like Jesus, then, follow some of the laws of Moses but do it in such a way that they reconfigure the function of the Jerusalem temple. Presumably, the rationale is that "God does not dwell in a temple made with hands" (Acts 7:48).[37] Rather, "Heaven is my throne," says "the prophet" (7:49), and for Jesus's followers, Jesus has been made Lord and Christ in heaven by being given a seat at the right hand of God (2:34–35). On the basis of Christ's status in heaven, repentance and baptism "in the name of Jesus Christ" brings forgiveness of sins and the gift of the Holy Spirit (2:38).

In addition to following the particular laws agreed on at the council in Jerusalem (15:20; 21:25), Paul is willing to perform a special rite of purification in the Jerusalem temple, presumably according to a Nazirite vow for a specific period of time (21:23, 26). Jesus's followers, including Paul, follow some of the laws of Moses, worship and pray in the Jerusalem temple when they have an opportunity, and sometimes may even take a special vow of purification in the context of the temple. They do not understand these activities, however, as bringing forgiveness of sins and the gift of the Holy Spirit, which are the means by which a person receives redemption from God.

5.5. "Almost" Sacrificial Language about Jesus's Death in Acts

There is one verse in Acts that gains attention of interpreters as potential sacrificial language about Jesus's death. In the account of the Ethiopian

37. See Penner, *In Praise of Christian Origins*, 316–17.

eunuch, the narrator in Acts 8:32 recites Isa 53:7–8 in a manner that compares Jesus's death to the slaughter of a lamb. The entire recitation is as follows: "Like a sheep he was led to the slaughter, and like a lamb silent before its shearer, so he does not open his mouth. In his humiliation justice was denied him. Who can describe his generation? For his life is taken away from the earth" (Acts 8:32; Isa 53:7–8). This Scripture passage, which created the context for Philip's "proclamation of the good news about Jesus" (Acts 8:35), makes no assertion about Christ's death as a sacrifice or ransom for people's sins. Nor does the recitation include "By his wounds you have been healed" (cf. 1 Pet 2:24). Rather, the point is that the death of Jesus created a context where Jesus was taken away from the earth by God to a place where he is "both Lord and Messiah" (Acts 2:36). Everyone who repents and is baptized "in the name of Jesus Christ" will have their sins forgiven and will receive the gift of the Holy Spirit (Acts 2:38). For this reason, Philip baptized the Ethiopian eunuch (8:39). For the followers of Jesus, the ritual of baptism becomes the "priestly" ritual through which people receive forgiveness of their sins from God.

6. Conclusion

Alongside other New Testament writings, it is remarkable that the priestly rhetorolect in Luke and Acts does not contain a straightforward assertion that Jesus died as a sacrifice to remove the sins of believers. Rather, the story of Jesus in Luke has priestly beginnings in the Jerusalem temple that set the stage for a priestly John the Baptizer who announces the forgiveness of sins to people on the basis of repentance and a praying Jesus who pronounces people's sins to be forgiven and announces that "repentance and forgiveness of sins is to be proclaimed in his name to all nations, beginning from Jerusalem" (Luke 24:47). In a related manner, the Acts of the Apostles presents the story of a praying and worshiping community equipped with a message that those who are baptized in the name of Jesus receive forgiveness of sins and the gift of the Holy Spirit. The basis for forgiveness of sins in Luke and Acts appears to be the "priestly" ritual of a devout life, rather than a priestly "blood sacrifice" through which God removes the sins of individual people and the community.

There is no direct assertion in Luke or Acts that Christ offered a sacrifice for sins (cf. Heb 10:12). The term "sacrifice" (θυσία) occurs four times in Luke and Acts. First, Jesus's parents offer a sacrifice (τοῦ δοῦναι θυσίαν) "according to the law of the Lord, 'a pair of turtledoves or two young pigeons'" as a rite of purification after Jesus is born (Luke 2:24). Second, Pilate mingled the blood (τὸ αἷμα) of the Galileans with their sacrifices (τῶν θυσιῶν αὐτῶν) in Luke 13:1. Third and fourth, Stephen asserts that the "ancestors" (Acts 7:39: οἱ πατέρες ἡμῶν) of Jesus's followers "offered a sacrifice" (ἀνήγαγον θυσίαν) to the calf they had made with their own hands as an idol (7:41), rather than offering "slain victims and sacrifices" (σφάγια καὶ θυσίας) forty years in the wilderness (7:42).

There is also no assertion that Jesus gave his life as a ransom for many, that he laid down his life for others, or that he died for the sins of many. We may, however, have found reasons why Irenaeus viewed the focus of the Gospel of Luke to be on the priestly character of Jesus (*Haer.* 3.11.8). Circumcised on the eighth day, purified and consecrated through temple ritual, guided daily by a life of prayer, and empowered by the Holy Spirit, Jesus forgave sins and announced that repentance and forgiveness of sins "in his name" would be proclaimed to all nations. This portrayal of Jesus and his priestly function for the world is distinctive to Luke and Acts. Using a sociorhetorical approach, however, it is possible to describe in detail how a Christian priestly rhetorolect in Luke and Acts has multiple dimensions of relationships, in the context of its differences, to a Christian priestly rhetorolect in other writings both in the New Testament and in noncanonical early Christian literature.

Bodies and Politics in Luke 1–2 and Sirach 44–50: Men, Women, and Boys*

Vernon K. Robbins

1. Body in the World and World in the Body

The special topic of this paper is the manner in which the body is present in language and in interpretation of language, and how "politics" develops in, through, and around language about bodies. The topic emerges in an environment where some literary interpreters are talking about a transition from a "linguistic turn" during the twentieth century to a "corporeal turn" at the beginning of the twenty-first century.[1] A major issue is how humans fill words with meaning. Horst Ruthrof argues that "the body is always already part of language as discourse."[2] Gleaning insights from Peirce, Husserl, Heidegger, Wittgenstein, and Derrida, and drawing on recent research in cognitive science, cognitive linguistics, and cognitive rhetoric, he develops a position he calls "corporeal semantics." From this perspective, "When a meaning event occurs, the body enters language in the form of quasi-perceptual readings of the world."[3] The point is that speakers and interpreters are always negotiating language by means of "the

---

* An earlier version of this essay was published as "Bodies and Politics in Luke 1–2 and Sirach 44–50: Men, Women, and Boys," *Scriptura* 90 (2005): 724–838. The editors of this volume are grateful for the permission granted to reprint this article here in updated form.

1. Mark Johnson, *The Body in the Mind: The Bodily Basis of Meaning, Imagination, and Reason* (Chicago: University of Chicago Press, 1987); George Lakoff and Mark Johnson, *Philosophy in the Flesh: The Embodied Mind and Its Challenge to Western Thought* (New York: Basic Books, 1999); Horst Ruthrof, *The Body in Language* (London: Cassell, 2000), 6–21.

2. Ruthrof, *The Body in Language*, vii.

3. Ibid., 1.

body" in the form of nonverbal signs. "The body is present in discourse in the form of nonlinguistic signs: as olfactory, tactile, gustatory, aural, visual, and many other subtle, nonverbal readings of the world."[4]

This paper will not address the relation of corporeal semantics to cognitive semantics,[5] nor will it address the fundamental function of nonverbal signs in the production of meaning in language.[6] Rather, it will start with an observation made during the eighteenth century by Giambattista Vico that humans give meaning to the world outside of them by using terms related to their bodies. The result is the presence of "body language" in the world.

> Thus, head for top or beginning; the brow and shoulders of a hill; the eyes of needles and of potatoes; mouth for any opening; the lip of a cup or pitcher; the teeth of a rake, a saw, a comb; the beard of wheat; the tongue of a shoe; the gorge of a river; a neck of land; an arm of the sea; the hands of a clock; heart for centre (the Latin uses *umbilicus*, navel, in this sense); the belly of a sail; foot for end or bottom; the flesh of fruits; a vein of rock or mineral; the blood of grapes for wine; the bowels of the earth. Heaven or the sea smiles; the wind whistles; the waves murmur; a boat groans under a great weight. The farmers of Latium used to say the fields were thirsty, bore fruit, were swollen with grain; and our rustics speak of plants making love, vines going mad, resinous trees weeping.[7]

A very important part of meaningful language is a matter of placing "body" in the world. And in the midst of this, we know not to try to thread the eye of a needle with the hands of a clock, or to lick the lip of a cup with the tongue of a shoe! In other words, we place our body in the world in ways that we understand and can negotiate without significant difficulties.

In the context of human activity in which we place "body" in the world, it is remarkable how pervasively early Christian discourse places "world" in the body. All of us are familiar with the exhortation in 1 Pet 2:5 that, "like living stones," followers of Christ should let themselves "be built into a spiritual house." We also know that "the eye is the lamp of the body" (Matt 6:22; cf. Luke 11:34) and that Jesus is "the vine" and those who

---

4. Ibid., vii.

5. Ibid., 166–68.

6. Ibid., 22–139.

7. Giambattista Vico, *The New Science of Giambattista Vico* (Ithaca, NY: Cornell University Press, 1968), [405], 129. Quoted in Ruthrof, *The Body in Language*, 38.

"abide in him" are "the branches" (John 15:5). And we seem to know what is meant when it says that bodies should be full of light (Luke 11:34–36).

With these things in mind, the beginning place for interpretation in this paper is a commitment to a theory of semantic corporeality.[8] The analysis is grounded in a sociorhetorical presupposition that bodies are essential participants in the creation of meaning in a text. In other words, the interpreter is committed to an approach that places body in mind and mind in body, intentionally moving away from a post-Kantian body-mind dualism.[9] In addition, the interpreter is committed to an analysis of "culture" in body and mind.[10] Building on Vico's insight that humans place their bodies in the world to create a meaningful world, this paper moves into the ways in which humans create different kinds of "bodies" by placing different social and cultural spaces into them. The issue, then, is society and culture in body and mind. One of the questions is: How do you place a house, a kingdom, or parts of the created world into a human body? If we can begin to answer this question, another question is: Why? Why would anyone want to place a house, a kingdom, or parts of the created world into a human body? The answer is political: a matter of creating a political space, a polis, where there is order. "Significant others" mediate society and culture to a new member of the world, selecting "aspects of it in accordance with their own location in the social structure, and also by virtue of their individual, biographically rooted idiosyncrasies."[11] Those who make the selections and mediate them are "brokers," mediators who move power and benefits of power around in the world.[12] Movement of "order" is therefore movement of power.

---

8. Ruthrof, *The Body in Language*, 7. Johnson, *The Body in the Mind*.

9. Johannes N. Vorster, "Construction of Culture through the Construction of Person: The *Acts of Thecla* as an Example," in *The Rhetorical Analysis of Scripture: Essays from the 1995 London Conference*, ed. Stanley E. Porter and Thomas H. Olbricht, JSNTSup 146 (Sheffield: Sheffield Academic, 1997), 447–57; Vernon K. Robbins, *The Tapestry of Early Christian Discourse: Rhetoric, Society and Ideology* (London: Routledge, 1996), 6–10, 26–30.

10. Bradd Shore, *Culture in Mind: Cognition, Culture, and the Problem of Meaning* (New York: Oxford University Press, 1996); Vernon K. Robbins, "Making Christian Culture in the Epistle of James," *Scriptura* 59 (1996): 341–51; cf. Johnson, *The Body in the Mind*; Lakoff and Johnson, *Philosophy in the Flesh*.

11. Peter L. Berger and Thomas Luckmann, *The Social Construction of Reality: A Treatise in the Sociology of Knowledge* (Garden City, NY: Doubleday, 1967), 131.

12. Bruce J. Malina, *The New Testament World: Insights from Cultural Anthropology*, rev. ed. (Louisville: Westminster John Knox, 1993), 102.

The author of this paper presupposes that early Christian discourse blended six different types of "Christian body" together through the medium of six different rhetorolects: wisdom, miracle, prophetic, priestly, precreation, and apocalyptic. "A rhetorolect is a form of language variety or discourse identifiable on the basis of a distinctive configuration of themes, topics, reasonings, and argumentations."[13] Each rhetorolect blends "locations" in the world with the human body in distinctive ways. In addition, it blends the human body with "locations" in the world. This reciprocal activity between the human body and "locations" creates a dynamic system of Christian discourse that simultaneously reconfigures images of the human body and images of locations in the world.

This paper engages in the beginning steps of an investigation that exhibits the manner in which the Jerusalem temple and households in Luke interact reciprocally with human bodies to create prophetic, priestly bodies who move the story forward into households, where prophetic speech creates new configurations of "holy community," and finally back into the Jerusalem temple, where a new community of men and women "live daily" until special promises occur.[14] These beginning steps focus on the first two chapters of the Gospel of Luke to analyze the ways in which divine powers in the temple move out into households through the bodies of Zechariah, Elizabeth, and Mary, and subsequently into John the Baptist and Jesus. The analysis and interpretation begins directly with Luke 1:5, where events occur that lead to the birth and infancy of John the Baptist and Jesus.

2. Zechariah and Elizabeth Take Center Stage in Luke 1:5–7

Lukan narration[15] in 1:5 begins in a manner that evokes seven mental spaces[16] for human bodies or body-like personages: King Herod of Judea;

13. Vernon K. Robbins, "The Dialectical Nature of Early Christian Discourse," *Scriptura* 59 (1996): 356.

14. For an alternative approach, which nevertheless makes many similar observations about the priestly data in Luke, see Rick Strelan, *Luke the Priest: The Authority of the Author of the Third Gospel* (Burlington, VT: Ashgate, 2008).

15. From the perspective of this essay, Luke 1:1–4 is paranarration, namely, narration about the narrative itself (see Todd V. Oakley, "Conceptual Blending, Narrative Discourse, and Rhetoric," *Cognitive Linguistics* 9 [1998]: 331).

16. Gilles Fauconnier, *Mental Spaces: Aspects of Meaning Construction in Natural Language* (Cambridge: Cambridge University Press, 1994).

a priest named Zechariah; a priest named Abijah, of whom Zechariah is a descendant; a priestly wife named Elizabeth; a priest named Aaron, who is the "founding father" of Elizabeth's family; a child who has not been born to Zechariah and Elizabeth; and God.

Herod, king of Judea, is mentioned only once in Luke (1:5). His body serves only as "background," evoking a temporal-spatial location for the events that bring forth the births of John and Jesus.[17] Lukan narration uses eight Greek words to name Herod and refers to the location of the story in "Judea" during "the days of King Herod." Political boundaries within time and geophysical space establish the location for the opening part of the Lukan story: a time and place in which a man named Herod reigned as king.

The Gospel of Luke never mentions King Herod of Judea again, although members of the Herodian family appear in five later chapters as the story progresses.[18] Thus King Herod exists in the background, functioning as the "founding father" of political government. The Gospel of Matthew, in contrast to Luke, brings King Herod prominently into the story of Jesus's birth and childhood. Referring to Herod nine times by name,[19] Matthew's account creates a dynamic relation between the "religious politics" surrounding the birth and childhood of Jesus and the religious politics of Israel's journey from the land of Canaan to Egypt and then back out of Egypt into the land of Canaan. The Gospel of Luke, in contrast to Matthew, uses the political presence of King Herod only as background for a story that begins in the Jerusalem temple.

Lukan narration refers to Abijah when it introduces Zechariah and to Aaron when it introduces Elizabeth. Aaron, the brother of Moses, was the "founding father" of priestly families in Israel (Exod 28:1–43). Abijah was a grandson of Aaron, receiving responsibility by lot for the eighth course of service in the Jerusalem temple (1 Chr 24:10, 19). A man with a family heritage going back to Abijah would probably travel from his household to Jerusalem twice a year to perform a week of daily duties in the temple.[20]

---

17. Ruthrof, *The Body in Language*, 48: "Together, spatial and temporal deixis govern the technical aspects of the point of view from which a text is spoken."

18. Luke 3 (vv. 1, 19); 8 (v. 3); 9 (vv. 7, 9); 13 (v. 31); 23 (vv. 7, 8, 11, 12, 15).

19. Matt 2:1, 3, 7, 12, 13, 15, 16, 19, 22. After this, there are only three references to a member of the Herodian family in the Matthean account: 14:1, 3, 6.

20. Joseph A. Fitzmyer, *The Gospel according to Luke (I–IX): Introduction, Translation, and Notes*, AB 28 (New York: Doubleday, 1981), 322.

Lukan narration embodies both Elizabeth and Zechariah with priestly heritage that reaches back to Aaron, the brother of Moses, whom God gave responsibility for all priestly things in Israel. Aaron functions as the "founding father" of priesthood in the Lukan story, then, much like Herod functions as the founding father of political government.

There is only one reference in Luke to Abijah and one to Aaron (Luke 1:5), like there is only one reference to Herod, king of Judea. A major difference emerges, however, when Lukan narration uses fifty-four Greek words in 1:5–7 to bring the priestly attributes of Zechariah and Elizabeth into the foreground of the story. After Luke 1:5 introduces the names and ancestors of Zechariah and Elizabeth, 1:6 presents them as interrelated "priestly" bodies of action. In the spirit of Gen 2:24, this priestly male and female function as "one flesh." Together, they were "righteous before God, living blamelessly according to all the commandments and regulations of the Lord" (1:6). Their bodies functioned in unity as they enacted the most honorable deeds of priestly heritage possible to humans on earth. By all accounts, their actions should be at the center of Israel's functioning as "a priestly kingdom and a holy nation" (Exod 19:6).

There is, however, a problem. The "priestly flesh" of Zechariah and Elizabeth has produced no offspring. Is this deficiency in blessing the result of a problematic relation between political and priestly domains in the kingdom of Judea? In other words, do people with special holiness in Herod's kingdom not receive abundant blessings from God as a result of "evil" in the political realm? Or is there somehow a problem in the temple itself that causes the righteous people of Israel not to receive God's blessings? Is this a story where miraculous powers in God's temple will bring forth children who rise up against the political powers in the region, or will they somehow reform the temple? Or will these children rise up against both the political powers and the Jerusalem temple?

No narrational commentary tells the hearer or reader why Zechariah and Elizabeth are childless, but first-century "cultural knowledge" probably created an expectation that Zechariah and Elizabeth would "miraculously" have a child during their advanced years. There would also be an expectation that this child would somehow play a role in religious-political renewal. This new story, then, is really an old story. The newness of the story will emerge from the particular way in which Zechariah and Elizabeth hear the news that they will have a child and the particular circumstances that surround the birth and infancy of the child.

As Lukan narration unfolds, it creates a mental space for an unborn child in the context of Herod, king of Judea; a priest named Zechariah; a priestly order of Abijah; a priestly wife named Elizabeth; and a priestly family descended from Aaron. But a divine being also has emerged, with alternative names of "God" and "the Lord" (1:6). This being named God and the Lord has a greater presence in relation to the bodies of Zechariah and Elizabeth than Herod, Abijah, or Aaron. The righteousness of Zechariah and Elizabeth is righteousness "before God" (1:6: ἐναντίον τοῦ θεοῦ). The narration evokes an image of God "opposite" Zechariah and Elizabeth, as though God were continually on the other side of an envisioned space that includes God, Zechariah, and Elizabeth. The importance of God's presence is underscored by the "commandments and regulations of the Lord," which guide Zechariah and Elizabeth as they "blamelessly" enact righteousness with their bodies (1:6). In other words, Zechariah and Elizabeth give priority in their lives to the personage and decrees of God, rather than the personage and regulations of Herod, the king of Judea. This is, again, an old story in the story of Israel. But every old story has the potential to be a new story. What will be new about this old story?

3. Zechariah Enters the Temple in Luke 1:8–10

The next fifty-four Greek words in Lukan narration (1:8–10) introduce decisively new personages engaged in new actions. When the narration brings Zechariah onto center stage, performing his duties in the temple (1:8–9), it also brings into focus "a whole multitude of people praying outside at the time of the incense offering" (1:10). Lukan foregrounding of the "blameless" bodily enactment of priestly heritage by Zechariah and Elizabeth moves fully onto center stage in 1:8–9 when Zechariah enters "the sanctuary of the Lord" to serve "as priest before God." When Lukan narration repeats the phrases "before God" (1:8) and "of the Lord" (1:9), the hearer or reader conceptually blends the space that contained Zechariah, Elizabeth, and God (1:6) with the Jerusalem temple, which contains Zechariah and God (1:8–9). And now a very important question emerges: Is the initial space containing Zechariah, Elizabeth, and God implicitly the "household" of Zechariah and Elizabeth, or is it a space that could be located anywhere "in God's cosmos"? My conclusion is that the hearer or reader creates an implicit image of the bodies of Zechariah and Elizabeth in a household. The reason lies in the presupposition in the narration that they should have a child. Lukan narration makes a transition from the household of Zechariah and Elizabeth, where God is present at all times to both Zechariah and Elizabeth—and a child also should be present—to the household of God, into which only Zechariah can enter to serve as a priest before God.

And now we must make another decision. Is Zechariah's body separate from Elizabeth's body as he enters the temple, or is it still an interrelated unity with Elizabeth's body? Lukan narration indicates that Zechariah's body is still thoroughly unified with Elizabeth's body, but here we enter into a very important step in "body politics." In the context where Zechariah's body enters the temple, the hearer or reader sees that his "priestly" body has a special relation not only to a "blamelessly righteous" wife (1:6) but also to a "whole multitude of praying people" (1:10). The "double-focus" in this new space introduces another religious politics. Zechariah's male body is invested "politically" with authority to move "closer" to the presence of God than either his priestly wife or the "whole" multitude of people who stay on the outside and pray. At this point, then, Lukan narration leaves whatever politics may exist between King Herod and the temple in the background and places the "body politics" of a priest in the Jerusalem temple in the foreground.

In other words, Lukan narration elaborates priestly rather than political rhetorolect as it moves from background information, which includes political reference, into a story about Zechariah and Elizabeth. The priestly focus of the narration brings forth one of the most vivid pictures of priestly activity in New Testament discourse. The initial focus is on purposeful action by Zechariah's body, which accords fully with the focus on Zechariah's and Elizabeth's purposeful enactment of "blameless" righteousness in 1:6. As Zechariah's feet carry him into the sanctuary of the Lord, where he will use his hands to offer the burning offering of incense, the hearer or reader is transported into the Jerusalem temple. When Zechariah comes to the special incense altar, he is standing just outside the curtain that shields the holy of holies from view.[21]

21. See the description of the high priest's entry into the holy of holies on the Day of Atonement in m. Yoma 5:1: "The outer curtain was looped up on the south side and the inner one on the north side. He went along between them until he reached the north side; when he reached the north he turned round to the south and went on with the curtain on his left hand until he reached the Ark. When he reached the Ark he put the fire pan between the bars. He heaped up the incense on the coals and the whole place became filled with smoke. He came out by the way he went in, and in the outer space he prayed a short prayer. But he did not prolong his prayer lest he

4. Wisdom Enters the Temple in Sirach 44–50

At this point, a recent study by Claudia V. Camp can help our analysis and interpretation of Luke 1–2. She focuses on Sir 44–50 to exhibit how the text of Sirach "tells" a temple.[22] In Sirach's "person story" of Israel, Aaron receives the longest description of all the "famous men" of Israel except for the high priest Simon, son of Onias, who forms the conclusion.[23] Of particular interest for our investigation of Luke 1–2 is the depiction of the high priest Simon in Sir 50:1–21.

First, Sir 50:1–4 describes the high priest Simon on the basis of his purposive action concerning the temple and the city in which the temple was located. He "repaired the house," "fortified the sanctuary," "laid the foundation for the high double walls," "dug a water cistern," "considered how to keep his people from ruin," and "strengthened the city against siege."

Second, Sir 50:5–8 describes the high priest Simon's body in relation to God's created cosmos to depict "how glorious he was, surrounded by the people, as he came out of the house of the curtain" (50:5). This description is a matter of blending God's good and bounteous creation, which is the primary image undergirding wisdom rhetorolect,[24] with the body of the high priest Simon. At the moment Simon comes out of the house of the curtain, he is like the morning star among the clouds, the full moon at the festal season, the sun shining on the temple of the Most High, the rainbow gleaming in splendid clouds, roses in the days of first-fruits, lilies by a spring of water, a green shoot on Lebanon on a summer day (50:6–8), an olive tree laden with fruit, and a cypress towering in the clouds (50:10).

In the midst of the blending of the high priest with God's bounteous cosmos, he is also blended with the special materials of the house of God. The high priest Simon is like fire and incense in the censer, and

---

put Israel in terror" (trans. Danby; quoted in M. Eugene Boring, Klaus Berger, and Carsten Colpe, eds., *Hellenistic Commentary to the New Testament* [Nashville: Abingdon, 1995], 184–85).

22. Claudia V. Camp, "Storied Space, or, Ben Sira 'Tells' a Temple," in *"Imagining" Biblical Worlds: Studies in Spatial, Social and Historical Constructs in Honor of James W. Flanagan*, ed. David M. Gunn and Paula M. McNutt, JSOTSup 359 (London: Sheffield Academic, 2002), 64–80.

23. Sir 45:6–22; 50:1–21; Camp, "Storied Space," 75.

24. Sir 24:13–22 describes the manner in which wisdom becomes good and bounteous creation.

he is like a vessel of hammered gold studded with all kinds of precious stones (50:9).

The description of the high priest Simon in Sir 50 can help us understand how the Gospel of Luke is reconfiguring the space of the Jerusalem temple in the mind of the hearer or reader. Sirach 50 focuses on the high priest, rather than on a priest who performs daily duties in the temple. This sets the stage for a very different picture of the relation of the priest to the assembly of people related to him. In Sir 50, the high priest gives the congregation direct access to blessings as they are able to see things inside the temple. Sirach 50:5 describes the high priest in glorious array, "surrounded by the people, as he came out of the house of the curtain." The people quite obviously see the high priest, just as the hearer or reader sees him, as he performs his priestly activities in the temple. As he goes up to the holy altar, the high priest makes "the court of the sanctuary glorious" (50:11). At this point there is an amazingly vivid sequence of activity by the high priest, "all the sons of Aaron," "all the people," and the singers:

1. The high priest "received the portions from the hands of the priests, as he stood by the hearth of the altar with a garland of brothers around him." At this point the high priest is "like a young cedar on Lebanon, surrounded by the trunks of palm trees" (50:12).
2. In this context "all the sons of Aaron in their splendor held the Lord's offering in their hands, before the whole congregation of Israel" (50:13).
3. When the high priest finished his rituals and the offering at the altars (50:14) "he held out his hand for the cup and poured a drink offering of the blood of the grape; he poured it out at the foot of the altar, a pleasing odor to the Most High, the king of all" (50:15).
4. At this point "the sons of Aaron shouted; they blew their trumpets of hammered metal; they sounded a mighty fanfare as a reminder before the Most High" (50:16).
5. "Then all the people together quickly fell to the ground on their faces to worship their Lord, the Almighty, God Most High" (50:17).
6. "Then the singers praised him with their voices in sweet and full-toned melody" (50:18).

7. "And the people of the Lord Most High offered their prayers before the Merciful One, until the order of worship of the Lord was ended, and they completed his ritual" (50:19).
8. "Then Simon came down and raised his hands over the whole congregation of Israelites, to pronounce the blessing of the Lord with his lips, and to glory in his name" (50:20).
9. "And they bowed down in worship a second time, to receive the blessing from the Most High" (50:21).

This remarkable picture of the high priest, "all the sons of Aaron," the "whole congregation of Israel," and the singers is the result of a blend of biblical wisdom tradition with biblical priestly tradition. Instead of seeing the magnificent pilasters, entrance, sidewalls, inner room, side chambers, passageway from story to story, stairway, raised platform, chambers of the court, and so on of the temple (Ezek 41:1–42:12), which is characteristic of priestly tradition, the hearer or reader sees "people," which is characteristic of wisdom tradition. The temple is in the background, while people are in the foreground. In Sirach, the Jerusalem temple has become a "house of God" filled with glorious people who have attributes of God's bounteous, fruitful creation!

5. Receiving Blessings in the Temple in Luke 1:11–25

In the Gospel of Luke, Zechariah is not a high priest. He is an "ordinary" priest who performs "daily duties" in the temple during two weekly time periods each year.[25] This ordinary priest brings powers of God out of the temple by means of his body and takes these powers into his household. This is the beginning of a story in which God's miraculous powers move from the Jerusalem temple into two households in such a manner that these households, rather than the temple as "the house of God," become God's "power base" for the renewal of Israel.

As the story unfolds in Luke, a picture of the Jerusalem temple and the people of Israel that is very different from Sirach emerges in the mind of the hearer or reader. First, the "whole" multitude of people are restricted to an area "outside" the sanctuary (Luke 1:10). This means they are not able to see what Zechariah does nor participate in an overall ceremony

25. Cf. Strelan, *Luke the Priest*, 119–23, 125–30.

of song, praise, and bowing down in worship (cf. Sir 50:17–21). Second, an unexpected and astonishing event occurs during the incense offering that transmits a special kind of blessing into the bodies of two interrelated priestly people. This focusing of God's blessings creates a dramatically different function for the Jerusalem temple. Instead of being an open location filled with glorious people who participate in God's bounteous blessings, it is a closed location filled with an ordinary priest who carries a special blessing in his body out to a particular household. Third, when Zechariah comes out of the temple, he is not able to perform one of the most customary priestly functions: "to pronounce the blessing of the Lord with his lips, and to glory in his name" (Sir 50:20). The absence of this ability has an important relation to the miracle in his body. But why this absence in the midst of this blessing?

The scene in Luke features remarkable reciprocity between the bodies of Zechariah and Elizabeth. When the messenger by the altar begins to speak, his statements build on the unified relation between the body of Zechariah and the body of Elizabeth asserted in 1:5–7. Zechariah should remove fear from his body, because Elizabeth will have a son in her body. At this point the hearer or reader becomes aware of three preceding events the narration has not recounted: (a) Zechariah has prayed to God; (b) God has heard his prayer; and (c) God has sent the messenger with a special word for Zechariah. This creates a picture of Zechariah speaking with his mouth in a manner that successfully reached the hearing of God. When the messenger speaks, he tells him to remove the fear that has overwhelmed his body (1:12–13). At this point, a sequence of events in the book of Daniel between a messenger from God and Daniel may be instructive. When the messenger comes, he tells Daniel not to fear (μὴ φοβοῦ), because his words have been heard (εἰσηκούσθη: Dan 10:12). Nevertheless, Daniel turns his face toward the ground and becomes speechless (ἐσιώπησα: Dan 10:15). Daniel is able to open his mouth and speak only after the angel touches his lips (Dan 10:16). It would be possible to think that the fear which overwhelmed Zechariah would move him into a state of speechlessness. If it did, the remarkable news that he would soon have a son whom he could name John (1:13–14) removed his speechlessness. When the messenger completes his speech of good news, Zechariah boldly speaks with language that may sound like a challenge of false prophecy. Discussing the problem of false prophecy, Deut 18:21–22 asserts:

> You may say to yourself, "How shall I know [πῶς γνωσόμεθα] the word [τὸ ῥῆμα] that the LORD has not spoken?" If a prophet speaks in the name of the LORD but the thing does not take place [μὴ γένηται] or prove true, it is a word that the LORD has not spoken. The prophet has spoken it presumptuously; do not be frightened by it.

Zechariah speaks to the messenger Gabriel with language that reverberates with reasoning about false prophecy: "How will I know this [κατὰ τί γνώσομαι τοῦτο]?" (Luke 1:18). In the Lukan sequence, Gabriel takes great offense at Zechariah's inquiry. He does not answer Zechariah's question by focusing on God's power to do remarkable things or by reminding Zechariah of Abraham and Sarah, or some other barren couple who had a child late in their lives. He interprets the inquiry as a personal assault on his reliability. Therefore, he presents his identity and credentials as though he had been confronted by an investigating officer: "I am Gabriel. I stand in the presence of God, and I have been sent to speak to you and to bring you this good news" (1:19). The response essentially means: "How could you dare question my identity and status by implying that I could be presenting a false prophecy to you?" The context evidently is very important for the perceived offense. Could a false prophet suddenly appear on the right sight of the altar of incense, just outside the holy of holies, in the Jerusalem temple? Gabriel identifies himself through his close relation to God. Gabriel's persona is a full representation of the "presence of God" (1:19: ἐνώπιον τοῦ θεοῦ) as he stands before Zechariah. Zechariah's speech has implied that false prophecy has come forth from a representative of the presence of God! The punishment of Zechariah is not as severe as death, which came upon Uzzah when he reached out and touched the ark of God (2 Sam 6:6–7). Rather, it is the removal of his ability to function as a priest (Deut 21:5). Without speech he can neither bless God nor pronounce a blessing on the multitude of people gathered in prayer outside the temple. In contrast to Aaron, the "founding father" of priesthood who had a special task of speaking for his brother Moses (Exod 4:14–16, 30; 7:1; 16:9–10), Zechariah leaves the temple with no ability to communicate words from God to the people.

The end result of this sequence is an ailment in the body of Zechariah until the day "these things occur" (γένηται ταῦτα: Luke 1:20). The special gift of a priest to bless has been removed. Nevertheless, a special gift of life resides in his body as he goes out of the temple. The multitude waiting outside would have expected Zechariah to pronounce a blessing to God and a blessing on them when he came out of the temple. In addition, the hearer or reader may have expected that Zechariah would receive a command from the angel to announce a prophetic message to the people, like Isaiah did after his vision of God in the temple (Isa 6:1–13). In Luke, however, the angel does not touch the lips of Zechariah (cf. Isa 6:7; Dan 10:16) so he can speak. In contrast to Aaron, who spoke for Moses, or Isaiah the prophet, Zechariah becomes barren of speech. Zechariah's body now has even a more substantive barrenness in relation to his wife Elizabeth's body as he exits the temple. Both lack an attribute fundamental to their honor in the realm of their social status.

According to the Lukan story, the people waiting outside interpret Zechariah's inability to speak in precisely the manner one expects from Daniel's speechlessness when God's messenger comes to him: they perceive that Zechariah is not able to speak, because he has seen a vision in the sanctuary (1:22). But this means that Zechariah is not able either to pronounce a priestly blessing on the people or to prophesy about the birth of John. It is necessary for a miracle to remove this ailment from Zechariah's body. And how will this occur? By means of purposive action by his body that takes him to his home (1:23) and joins him with Elizabeth in the conception of a son (1:24).

The reciprocal relation of the bodies of Zechariah and Elizabeth comes dramatically in view at the end of the scene when Elizabeth speaks. In a context of Zechariah's inability to bless God with his lips, Elizabeth speaks out in prophetic praise in a manner one might have expected Zechariah to speak when he came out of the temple: "This is what the Lord has done for me when he looked favorably on me and took away the disgrace I have endured among my people" (1:25). This praise of God could just as naturally be on the lips of Zechariah as on the lips of Elizabeth! But Zechariah is unable to speak at this point in the story. An additional miracle must occur before God gives the attribute of speech back to him. This miracle occurs on the eighth day of the life of their son, when he is circumcised and named (1:64).

6. Blessing in Sirach 50:22–24 and Zechariah's Blessing in Luke 1:68–79

At the end of the description of the high priest Simon in Sirach, the final act of the high priest is "to pronounce the blessing [εὐλογίαν] of the Lord with his lips, and to glory in his name" (50:20). At this point, the whole congregation of Israelites bows down a second time "to receive the blessing [εὐλογίαν] from the Most High" (50:21). Then Ben Sira adds his own benediction:

> And now bless [εὐλογήσατε] the God of all,
> who everywhere works great wonders [τὸν μεγάλα ποιοῦντα],
> who fosters our growth [τὸν ὑψοῦντα] from birth,
> and deals with us according to his mercy [κατὰ τὸ ἔλεος αὐτοῦ].
> May he give us gladness of heart [εὐφροσύνην καρδίας],
> and may there be peace [εἰρήνην] in our days
> in Israel, as in the days of old.
> May he entrust to us [ἐμπιστεῦσαι μεθ' ἡμῶν] his mercy [τὸ ἔλεος αὐτοῦ],
> and may he redeem [λυτρωσάσθω] us in our days.

In the context of the circumcision of John at eight days of age, Zechariah "immediately has his mouth opened and his tongue freed, and he begins to speak" (Luke 1:64). Naturally, the speech from Zechariah's lips is priestly when he speaks in the midst of the neighbors who have gathered for the occasion. Zechariah begins by blessing (εὐλογῶν) God (1:64), like the blessing in Sir 50:22–24 (cf. 45:15), rather than glorifying (δοξάζων) God like nonpriestly people do in Luke.[26] Filled with God's Holy Spirit, when Zechariah prophesies (1:67), his speech is filled with priestly blessing (cf. Exod 7:2). He opens with: "Blessed [εὐλογητός] be the Lord God of Israel, who has looked with favor and redeemed [ἐποίησεν λύτρωσιν] his people" (1:68). This has a close relation to the opening and closing of the priestly benediction in Sir 50:22, 24. As Zechariah continues, he speaks of God doing mercy (ἔλεος) (1:72), much like Sir 50:22. In addition, he refers to the people's ability "to serve in holiness and righteousness before him" (1:74–75) all their days, in a manner related to the liturgy of worship in Sir 50. When Zechariah speaks directly about the attributes of John, he speaks again about God's mercy (1:78) and about peace (1:79), like Sir 50:22–24. When Zechariah states that "the dawn from on high [ἐξ ὕψους] will break upon us" by the tender mercy of God (1:78), one is reminded of the high priest in Sir 50 standing "like the morning star among the clouds" (50:6) and "the sun shining on the temple of the Most

26. Luke 2:20; 4:15; 5:25, 26; 7:16; 13:13; 17:15; 18:43; 23:47.

High (ὑψίστου)" (50:7). Zechariah has taken temple worship and blessing as envisioned in Sirach out of the temple into the hill country where he and Elizabeth live. The body of the child born to Zechariah and Elizabeth creates the context for God's blessings to be present outside the temple in the midst of God's people.

7. The House of Mary and the Priestly House of Blessing in Luke 1:26–56

Zechariah is not the only one responsible for the presence of God's blessings outside the Jerusalem temple. The angel Gabriel, who "stands in the presence [ἐνώπιον] of God" (1:19), was sent by God not only to Zechariah but also to Mary (1:26). The repetition of the "sending" links Gabriel's visit to Zechariah (1:19) with his visit to Mary (1:26).[27] When Mary is introduced to the hearer or reader, Lukan discourse adds "kinship" information like it did with Zechariah and Elizabeth. There is no priestly lineage for Mary nor for the house in which she lives. In contrast, the reader or hearer sees in the background "a man named Joseph of the house of David" (1:27), to whom she is "engaged." David, of course, is the "founding father" of "kingship" in Israel. As a result, the episode featuring Gabriel and Mary shifts decisively away from priestly topics to language about kingship. There are, however, important relationships between the discourse in the Mary episode and the scene with the high priest Simon in the temple in Sir 50. When Gabriel speaks to Zechariah, he refers to "the Lord" (1:15, 17), "God" (1:19), and the "Lord God" (1:16). When Gabriel speaks to Mary, he not only refers to "the Lord" (1:28), "God" (1:30, 35, 37), and "Lord God" (1:32) but also to the "Most High" (1:32, 35). In the midst of language about "the Lord" (Sir 50:17, 19, 20),[28] Sirach shifts decisively to "Most High" as the title for God (Sir 50:7, 14, 15, 16, 17, 19, 21). This language about God is further intensified by reference to God as "the Almighty" (παντοκράτωρ) in Sir 50:14, 17. In Sirach, the Jerusalem temple is not only a place for God's "holy" power but also a place for God's "mighty" power. This emphasis is present in the high priest Simon's "fortifying" of the temple (50:1, 4) and in the emphasis on

27. Lukan discourse says that the angel Gabriel was sent "from God to [εἰς] a city … to [πρός] a virgin … and the virgin's name was Mary" (1:26–27).

28. In Ben Sira's benediction, there is a reference to "the God of all" (Sir 50:22).

"peace" in the benediction (50:23). In Luke 1:26–38, Gabriel moves this language outside the Jerusalem temple into the house of Mary.[29]

When Gabriel brings God's mighty power into the Davidic house of Mary, he concludes his speech with reference to the pregnancy of her kinswoman Elizabeth (1:36). As a result, as soon as the angel departs from her, Mary "makes haste to a Judean town in the hill country" (1:39) to visit her. When Mary "enters the house of Zechariah" (1:40), much like Zechariah "entered the sanctuary of the Lord" (1:9), Elizabeth is filled with Holy Spirit in the presence of Mary's pregnant body (1:41), much like Zechariah later is filled with Holy Spirit in the presence of his eight-day-old son (1:67).[30] Gabriel told Zechariah that John would be filled with Holy Spirit before his birth (1:15). The coming of the Holy Spirit upon Mary in her own household (1:35) makes her a bearer of Holy Spirit outside her household to Elizabeth, much like Zechariah brought God's miraculous powers of birth from the Jerusalem temple to Elizabeth. Elizabeth's house becomes a "house of blessing" when Mary enters it. Elizabeth's body, "filled with Holy Spirit" (1:41), functions in a manner that makes her home an inner sanctum of blessing both for Mary and for Jesus. When Elizabeth speaks to Mary, she speaks in the manner of a priest. Elizabeth begins by blessing Mary among women (1:43a). Adopting a priestly role, Elizabeth's blessing evokes the presence of "all women" as she "ritualizes" Mary's status as a person "favored by God" (1:28, 30). The house of Zechariah and Elizabeth has become a special "house of God" that not only includes two women but also invokes the presence of all women through its priestly activity! After the blessing on Mary, Elizabeth blesses the fruit of Mary's womb (1:42b). Elizabeth's house becomes the location for the priestly wife Elizabeth to be the first human to bless the son who will be named Jesus (1:31). But her speech also participates in another dynamic in the discourse. Gabriel assured Mary that her son would be "holy" (ἅγιον: 1:35) as a result of the role of God's Holy Spirit in her pregnancy. Through Elizabeth's speech, the activity of God's

29. Along with an emphasis on God "Most High" in Sir 50 is an emphasis on God's "mercy." Both Ben Sira's benediction and Zechariah's priestly prophecy refer to God's mercy (Sir 50:22, 24; Luke 1:72, 78). In a context of reference to God "Most High," Sir 50:19 refers to the people's prayers "before the Merciful One" (κατέναντι ἐλεήμονος).

30. The anarthrous references to Holy Spirit refer to God's spirit and power in a manner that is not Trinitarian, though they helped to prepare the way for Trinitarian doctrine (Fitzmyer, *Luke I–IX*, 350–51).

Holy Spirit returns to Mary in the form of a holy, priestly blessing on Mary's son Jesus. Elizabeth has become a mediator of the blessings of God's Holy Spirit back to Mary. Elizabeth concludes her priestly activity with the pronouncement of a beatitude. This shifts the second person address of all of her previous speech to a third person announcement of the blessedness of Mary: "Blessed is she who believed that there would be a fulfillment of what was spoken to her by the Lord" (1:45). To whom is this beatitude addressed? It is as though all the hearers or readers have become a congregation of people participating in worship at Elizabeth's house. The beatitude Elizabeth speaks is a response to the "joy" (1:44: ἀγαλλίασις) of the child in her body. The mode of Elizabeth's speech is related to the shouting, the trumpeting, and the singing in the midst of the blessings in the Jerusalem temple in Sir 50:16–21. In this final act, Elizabeth functions not only as priest but also as a son of Aaron, a trumpeter, and a singer! The blessedness of Mary, which causes the child in Elizabeth's womb to leap for joy, brings forth a beatitude from Elizabeth that tells the story of a woman who believed what was spoken to her by the Lord. After Elizabeth's beatitude, Mary fulfills the role of the joyous congregation by responding with a song of joy and gratitude for all of God's mighty and merciful works (1:46–55).

As noted above, the priest Zechariah is absent from the scene with Mary and Elizabeth. During this time, we must remember, Zechariah is not able to speak. As a mute priest, he has no place in the scene. Only women blessed with child are present in this priestly house and its activity of worship. The presence of these pregnant women creates the context for God's Holy Spirit to be active both in the women and in the children in their bodies. But more than this happens as Elizabeth functions as the priest who gives blessings in "Zechariah's house" (1:40). If Sirach has "told" a Jerusalem temple where Woman Wisdom has been taken into, or excluded from, a "male inner sanctum" which functions as a "womb of holiness,"[31] the house of Zechariah and Elizabeth puts significant pressure on this tradition. Fecundity of holiness is present in the house of Elizabeth, and priestly blessing flows from the mouth of a priestly wife onto a pregnant woman who brought God's Holy Spirit into her house. When the child in Elizabeth's womb leaps for joy, she participates in the joy of her child by pronouncing a beatitude of blessing. Zechariah's priestly wife

31. Cf. Camp, "Storied Space," 78–80; Nancy B. Jay, *Throughout Your Generations Forever: Sacrifice, Religion, and Paternity* (Chicago: University of Chicago Press, 1992), 40.

functions as a priest in the absence of the male priest who usually could pronounce the blessings. In "their own house of holiness" in a Judean town in the hill country, the balance has tipped from priestly activity by a man to priestly activity by a woman. Women are centrally present in this "holy place." As the powers of God have moved outside the Jerusalem temple, women have become the priestly mediators of God's blessings to two very important men in the story of God's renewal of Israel.

8. Blessing the Infant Jesus and His Return to the Temple in Luke 2:21–52

After a simple reference to the circumcision of Jesus on the eighth day and the naming of him according to the name given by the angel (2:21), the Gospel of Luke presents a scene of "cleansing" in the Jerusalem temple according to the law of Moses (2:22).[32] At this point, the torah discourse that began in 1:6 with the description of Zechariah and Elizabeth continues in narration about Jesus. The beginning (2:22–24), middle (2:27), and end (2:39) of the narration contains five references to "the law." This establishes a context of righteous performance of torah throughout the scene that rivals the introduction of Zechariah and Elizabeth to the hearer or reader at the beginning of the story. The repetitive texture of the narration is remarkable as it refers to "according to the law of Moses" (2:22), "as it is written in the law of the Lord" (2:23), "according to what is stated in the law of the Lord" (2:24), "according to what was customary under the law" (2:27), and "everything according to the law of the Lord" (2:39). The overall scene creates a sequence of faithful ritual performance in the temple, followed by prophetic speech and blessing, that is related to the scene with Zechariah in the temple and the scene with Elizabeth and Mary after it. The body of the infant Jesus, which the angel assured Mary would be born "holy" (1:35), is taken into the Jerusalem temple and "presented to the Lord" through a ritual sacrifice of "a pair of turtle doves or two young pigeons" (2:22–24). The effect of this ritual is to enact the name of Jesus as "holy" not only in Mary's "house of David" but also in the Jerusalem temple. Fifty Greek words describe the detail of this activity with an even greater specificity of detail than the narration that described Zechariah's offering of the incense in 1:8–10. Much as the incense offering created a

32. Either "their" cleansing or "his" (Jesus's) cleansing.

picture of bodily devotion in the temple that brings forth God's miraculous powers in the form of a child "filled with the Holy Spirit" (1:15, 41), so the "cleansing" creates a picture of bodily devotion in the temple that secures the "holiness" of the firstborn child (2:23), which the Holy Spirit brought into being in the body of Mary (1:35). Performance of torah in the Jerusalem temple is a means by which "priestly" holiness transfers from the context of the temple to the bodies of both John the Baptist and Jesus.

Instead of the sudden appearance of a messenger of the Lord in the context of the cleansing offering, a righteous and devout man named Simeon and a fasting and praying prophet named Anna come forward and perform actions of blessing and prophecy. These two "temple-bodies" create a picture of a space of blessing in the Jerusalem temple that is open to both men and women. In other words, instead of the cleansing offering being on the inside in the sanctuary (ναός: 1:9, 21–22) while the parents and the child are praying outside (cf. 1:8–23), the Jerusalem temple is a space of blessing (ἱερόν: 2:27, 37) open to both women and men.[33] The infant Jesus and his parents (2:27, 33) enter the temple, and a special man and woman come forward and bless not only the child but also the parents (2:34). The narration endows Simeon with Holy Spirit three times (2:25, 26, 27) as it describes his "righteous and devout expectation" (2:25), the promise that he "would not see death before he had seen the Lord's Messiah" (2:26), and his entrance into the temple (2:27). Then it pictures him taking the child into his arms, "blessing God," and speaking (2:28). Simeon is clearly an embodiment of the Holy Spirit in the location of the Jerusalem temple! When Simeon speaks, his references to peace (2:29), salvation "before the face of all people" (2:30–31), and "glory to your people Israel" (2:32) creates the picture of the Jerusalem temple as a special place of "revelation to nations."

When Simeon finishes speaking, he blesses (εὐλόγησεν) Jesus's father and mother (2:34), again in the manner of a priest.[34] When he speaks to Jesus's mother Mary about the destiny of her child, he refers to the falling (πτῶσις) of many in Israel (2:34) with language that relates in a special way to the description of the activities of the high priest Simon in Sir 50. At the end of the description of all the good things Simon did for the temple and the city of Jerusalem, the narration states that "he considered how to save

33. Ἱερόν obviously refers to an open court of the Jerusalem temple rather than the ναός, the "closed" sanctuary (see Fitzmyer, *Luke I–IX*, 427).

34. See, e.g., 1 Sam 2:20; Num 6:23–27; Gen 14:18–19.

his people from ruin [πτῶσις], and fortified the city against siege" (50:4). While the image of rising and falling has a close relation to Isa 8:14–15,[35] the Greek word πτῶσις has a special place in the LXX of Isa 51:17:

> Rouse yourself, rouse yourself! Stand up [ἀνάστηθι], O Jerusalem,
> you who have drunk at the hand of the Lord the cup of his wrath,
> For the cup of ruin [πτῶσις], the bowl of wrath, you have drunk and you have emptied.[36]

The "ruin" to which Isaiah refers is the same kind of "falling" that concerned the high priest Simon in Sir 50:4. This "falling" is also on the lips of Simeon as he stands before Jesus and his parents, and it appears to have a special relation to the destruction of Jerusalem to which Jesus refers in Luke 21:24: "And Jerusalem will be trampled on by the nations, until the times of the nations are fulfilled."

"Finishing everything" according to the torah of the Lord while Jesus is an infant (Luke 2:39) results in the child Jesus growing, becoming strong, and becoming "filled with wisdom" (2:40). In this way the "favor" (χάρις) of God was upon him. In other words, the blessing in the priestly house of Zechariah and Elizabeth, and the "cleansing" of Jesus in the Jerusalem temple, result in "wisdom" in Jesus. This is a reversal of the movement of God's powers in Sirach, where God's wisdom moves into the holiness of the temple.

When Jesus is twelve years old, he returns dramatically to the temple. He does not return in a priestly mode, but in the mode of a person filled with wisdom. When Jesus enters the temple, the hearer or reader begins to view the temple as a place of teaching! Instead of being primarily a closed sanctuary or primarily a court of blessing, it begins to become a place where people gather to receive special wisdom from God. As the narrative progresses, Jesus will return to the temple as a prophetic teacher who reconfigures the temple into a household where his followers can gather to

35. Cf. Luke 20:17–18; 1:51–53.

36. Another passage is Jer 6:13–15 LXX: "For from the least of them to the greatest, everyone carries out lawlessness, from priest even unto false prophet all act falsely. They have healed the affliction of my people with spitefulness, and they say, 'Peace, peace,' where is peace?… Therefore they will fall in their ruin [πτώσει]; at the time of their visitation [ἐπισκοπῆς] they will be destroyed, says the Lord."

receive the Holy Spirit for their work in the world (24:44–53). The stage is set for this in Luke 2:41–52.

When Jesus's parents find Jesus in the temple after the festival of Passover, he is "sitting among the teachers [διδασκάλων], listening to them and asking them questions" (2:46). All who heard him were "amazed at his understanding [συνέσει] and his answers [ἀποκρίσεσιν]" (2:47). The twelve-year-old Jesus does not go to the temple to pray, to give or receive a blessing, to offer forgiveness, or to give praise to God. This young man, who received blessing from the priestly house of Zechariah and Elizabeth, and from the Jerusalem temple, already embodies these blessings in the form of a person filled with remarkable wisdom. After Jesus establishes contact with John the Baptist (Luke 3:21–23) and spends time in the wilderness (4:1–13), his wisdom becomes prophetic wisdom (4:18–19) rather than priestly wisdom. This new story recounts the transmission of God's powers from the Jerusalem temple through priestly procedures into a prophetic teaching Messiah who preaches good news to the poor; heals the blind, lame, and maimed; and raises people from the dead! As the story comes to an end in the Gospel of Luke, the Jerusalem temple has become a space where men and women can gather much as they did in Sir 50. Instead of receiving blessings from the rituals of a glorious high priest, however, these people receive God's Holy Spirit while hearing the preaching of prophetic wisdom (Acts 2). The Jerusalem temple remains a place of God's power, but a new story of "important persons" begins to "tell" the temple in ways that present decisively new challenges for the story of Israel.

9. Conclusion

The Gospel of Luke features an amazing amount of "blessing" in its opening chapters. Elizabeth blesses Mary "among women," and she blesses the child in Mary's womb (1:42). Zechariah blesses God when his mouth is opened and his tongue is freed (1:64), and he blesses God again when he begins to speak about the child John (1:68). Simeon blesses God when he sees Jesus in the temple as an infant (2:28). Then Simeon blesses Jesus's parents and communicates a special message to Mary (2:34). In addition, the Gospel of Luke contains an amazing focus on priestly people and priestly rituals. The story begins with a priestly offering of incense by Zechariah, and it emphasizes that both Zechariah and Elizabeth are members of priestly families. Then a priestly offering is made by Jesus's parents, and the narration emphasizes that these activities fulfilled the torah of the Lord in the temple.

The priestly activity at the beginning of the story bears fruit in a "prophet in the wilderness" named John, whom tax collectors called "Teacher" (3:12), and in a "prophet who preaches good news to the poor" named Jesus (4:18). God's powers have moved out of the Jerusalem temple into the bodies of two people who reform society, households, and the temple through their prophetic teaching. Jesus returns to the Jerusalem temple as an adult to reform it with his teaching (Luke 20:1–38). The priestly powers that went out of the temple now come back into the temple as prophetic wisdom in the body of Jesus. This prophetic wisdom reconfigures the temple into a "household" where Jesus's followers themselves perform the priestly activity of blessing God daily (24:53: εὐλογοῦντες). In Luke, then, the "telling" of the temple at the beginning of the story has a dynamic relation to the "telling" of the temple at the end of the story. At the beginning, God's miraculous powers move through an angel and a priest out from the Jerusalem temple into households. At the end, people move from their households into the Jerusalem temple, where they become the new "bodies" who will take God's power out into cities, towns, and households throughout the Mediterranean world.

Part 2
Protevangelium of James

Who Am I To Be Blessed? Mary as Blessed Mother in the Protevangelium of James

Christopher T. Holmes

Scholarship has explored the relationship between the Protevangelium of James (PJ) and the canonical gospels, especially the Gospel of Luke.[1] Protevangelium of James demonstrates a close relationship to Luke, in terms of concepts and themes as well as verbal and syntactical agreement. It is relatively apparent that the author of PJ has made use of Luke as a source text and reconfigured it in places.[2]

This essay considers one such reconfiguration in PJ: Mary's visit to Elizabeth as found in PJ 12.2–3 and Luke 1:39–56. After a comparative exegesis of the two passages, I will explore the topos of "blessing" as it

1. See, e.g., Mary F. Foskett, *A Virgin Conceived: Mary and Classical Representations of Virginity* (Bloomington: Indiana University Press, 2002); Vernon K. Robbins, *Who Do People Say I Am? Rewriting Gospel in Emerging Christianity* (Grand Rapids: Eerdmans, 2013), 157–73; Pieter A. van Stempvoort, "The Protevangelium Jacobi: The Sources of Its Theme and Style and Their Bearing on Its Date," in *Studia Evangelica III*, ed. F. L. Cross, TUGAL 88 (Berlin: Akademie, 1964), 410–26. Willem S. Vorster, "The Protevangelium of James and Intertextuality," in *Text and Testimony: Essays on New Testament and Apocryphal Literature in Honour of A. F. J. Klijn*, ed. T. Baarda et al. (Kampen: Kok, 1988), 262–75, provides particular attention to the dynamic between "pretexts" and subsequent texts. For general introduction, see Bart D. Ehrman and Zlatko Pleše, *The Apocryphal Gospels: Texts and Translations* (New York: Oxford University Press, 2011), 31–38; J. K. Elliott, "The Protevangelium of James," in *The Apocryphal New Testament: A Collection of Apocryphal Christian Literature in an English Translation*, ed. J. K. Elliott (Oxford: Clarendon, 2005), 48–67; and Paul Foster, "The Protevangelium of James," in *The Non-Canonical Gospels*, ed. Paul Foster (London: T&T Clark, 2008), 110–25.

2. "The main inspiration and sources behind PJ have been the birth stories in Matthew and Luke and the Old Testament. Like Luke 1–2 the language of PJ is heavenly influenced by the LXX" (Elliott, "Protevangelium of James," 51).

appears in both of these passages and in the whole of each composition. My analysis will highlight the different role that blessing plays in the environment of prophetic discourse in Luke 1–2 compared to the role it plays in the environment of priestly discourse in PJ. Finally, I will seek to amplify particular use of the topos in PJ. Since Mary is almost the exclusive recipient of blessing, I will attempt to answer Mary's question in PJ 12.2, "Who am I, Lord, that all the women of the earth will bless me?"[3] Ultimately, I hope to show that the author of PJ draws attention to Mary's function as mother, in addition to her identity as pure virgin, which distinguishes her as blessed.

1. Comparative Exegesis of Luke 1:39–56 and Protevangelium of James 12.2–3

1.1. Considering the Context

Before analyzing the two passages themselves, it will be helpful to place each within its respective narrative context. Mary's visit to Elizabeth in Luke 1:39–56 falls within Luke's treatment of the "prehistory" of Jesus's life and ministry (1:5–4:13). In Luke 1–2, Luke presents the birth of John the Baptist and the birth of Jesus in parallel to one another. I will highlight just a few details of Luke's parallel presentation: an angel foretells the birth of each in advance (John in 1:5–25; Jesus in 1:26–38); the birth of each child is described (John in 1:57–66; Jesus in 2:1–20); both infants are named and circumcised (John in 1:59–63; Jesus in 2:21); and, the development of both infants is mentioned (John in 1:80; Jesus in 2:40). Luke situates Mary's visit to Elizabeth in the midst of divine promises being fulfilled through the twin births of John and Jesus.

Luke's description of the births of John and Jesus is filled with poetic and hymnic language. In addition to Mary's hymn of praise in Luke 1:46–55, the narrative contains Elizabeth's blessing of Mary and her child (1:42–45), Zechariah's prophetic blessing of John in 1:67–79, Simeon's praise in 2:29–32, and Anna's praise in 2:38. These hymnic portions in particular demonstrate Luke's attempt to portray the birth of Jesus, the Messiah, and

---

3. Unless otherwise noted, translations and Greek text of PJ are from Ehrman and Pleše, *The Apocryphal Gospels* (hereafter designated E-P). English translations generally follow the NRSV, although modifications have been made in places, especially to highlight similarities between Luke and PJ.

the birth of John, the Messiah's forerunner, as fulfillment of God's promises to Israel.

Based on Vernon K. Robbins's work on "rhetorolects" in early Christianity, this section of Luke clearly demonstrates what he calls "prophetic discourse."[4] Beyond obvious motifs of prophecy such as the future orientation of divine messages delivered through angels (Luke 1:20) and the connections between John the Baptist and Israel's prophets of old (Luke 1:16–17), the logic of the narrative itself aligns with the pattern of thought characteristic of prophetic discourse. Robbins explains: "The goal of prophetic rhetorolect is to create a governed realm on earth where God's righteousness is enacted among all of God's people in the realm with the aid of God's specially transmitted word in the form of prophetic action and speech."[5] A few examples confirm the primacy of prophetic rhetorolect in Luke 1–2. Throughout, Jesus is depicted as the royal Messiah of God. He is promised the throne of David and is said to reign over the house of Jacob (1:32–33); he is described as the "Lord" in Mary's interaction with Elizabeth (1:43, see more below); he is Israel's "mighty savior" (1:69) who will save God's people from the power of their enemies (1:69, 74); the angels tell the shepherds of the birth of the Messiah Lord (2:11). God too is depicted in ways that align with the conceptual world of prophetic discourse: God is the "Mighty One" (1:49) characterized by the "strength of his arm" and his remembrance of his promises to Israel (1:54–55).

There are elements that resemble priestly discourse in Luke 1–2, such as Jesus's visit to the temple and the role of Simeon and Anna, but these are largely subsumed within prophetic discourse. Simeon, who is not explicitly identified as a priest in Luke (as in PJ),[6] blesses Mary and her child, but the motivation for his doing so appears in the form of prophetic discourse rather than priestly. He blesses Jesus because he sees God's salvation in Jesus (2:29); just a few verses earlier in Luke, Simeon is said to be waiting for "the consolation of Israel" (2:25), which comes to fruition

---

4. For an overview of Robbins's work on rhetorolects, see Vernon K. Robbins, "Conceptual Blending and Early Christian Imagination," in *Explaining Christian Origins and Early Judaism: Contributions from Cognitive and Social Science*, ed. Petri Luomanen, Ilkka Pyysiäinen, and Risto Uro, BIS 89 (Leiden: Brill, 2007), 161–95; and Robbins, *The Invention of Christian Discourse*, vol. 1, RRA 1 (Blandford Forum, UK: Deo, 2009).

5. Robbins, "Conceptual Blending," 166.

6. Elliott says flatly, "Simeon was not a high priest" ("Protevangelium of James," 51).

when he sees Jesus. The "blessedness" of both Mary and Jesus is cast in prophetic overtones: for both, blessing concerns the fulfillment of God's promises to Israel related especially to a political kingdom. Even when the narrative takes place in or near the temple, the temple is not characterized by the activation of divine benefits. Rather, it is the platform for prophetic speech.[7] The dominance of prophetic discourse, even when the "first space"[8] of priestly discourse (the temple) is employed, can be seen more clearly when compared to the dominant mode of discourse in PJ.

Much of PJ, like Luke 1–4, concerns the prehistory of Jesus, but it extends the prehistory of Jesus back even further than the Gospel of Luke does. Rather than starting the narrative with the story of John's birth, PJ describes the conception, birth, childhood, and betrothal of Mary, the mother of Jesus. The Protevangelium of James opens with Joachim and Anna who, though childless for many years, become the parents of Mary (PJ 1–4). The next major section of the composition concerns Mary: her birth (PJ 5), her childhood (PJ 6–7), her "betrothal"[9] to Joseph (PJ 8–10), her conception of Jesus (PJ 11–16), and the events surrounding his birth (PJ 17–21). The text ends with Herod's slaughtering of the innocent children, Mary's hiding Jesus in a manger, and Elizabeth's flight to the hills (PJ 22); the death of Zechariah (PJ 23–24); and an epilogue by the author, "James" (PJ 25). In light of this broad outline, PJ 12.2–3 occurs in the middle of the middle section concerning Mary. Though not a perfect division, the middle section of PJ is essentially split in half by Mary's conception of Jesus (PJ 11–12). As will become clear in what follows, Mary's visit to Elizabeth itself functions as a hinge connecting the first and second parts of this major section concerning Mary.

Much of PJ acts as a reconfiguration of Luke 1:5–2:40. The author of PJ has expanded Luke's narrative, though, by including the details of Mary's parents, Joachim and Anna.[10] This addition not only expands the narrative

---

7. See Luke 1:5–24. Even though Zechariah is attending to his priestly duties, the emphasis of the pericope is on the appearance of the angel and his prophetic message. Likewise, in Luke 2:25–36 the temple is the site of Simeon's prophetic praise of God.

8. For a discussion of "first space" in rhetorolects, see Robbins, "Conceptual Blending," 164–66.

9. Compared to the Synoptic Gospels, PJ presents the relationship between Mary and Joseph in more ambiguous terms.

10. For example, Joachim's religiosity in PJ 1.1 compared to that of Zechariah and Elizabeth in Luke 1; Anna likening herself to Sarah and Abraham (PJ 1.3; 2.4) compared to the old age of Zechariah and Elizabeth in Luke 1:5–7; and the hearing of

but also results in the removal of many of Luke's details about Zechariah, Elizabeth, and John.[11] As pointed out above, Luke presents the birth of John and Jesus in parallel to one another; as a result, John can properly be understood as Jesus's forerunner in Luke. In contrast, it is Mary, not John, who acts as the forerunner for Jesus in PJ. It is Mary's parents, not the parents of John, who receive a visit from a heavenly messenger (PJ 4; cf. Luke 1:8–20). It is Mary's birth, not John's, that precedes the birth of Jesus (PJ 5; cf. Luke 1:57–66).[12] The "prehistory" of Jesus found in PJ concerns not the birth of two prophets as it does in Luke, but the birth of two figures who are distinguished because of their blessedness and the blessings they bestow on others.

The reconfiguration of Luke's narrative by the author of PJ results in a major shift in the dominant rhetorolect employed: from prophetic discourse to priestly discourse. Robbins highlights the temple as the "first space" in priestly discourse, which "presupposes that ritual actions benefit God in a manner that activates divine benefits for humans on earth."[13] Priestly discourse is characterized by "thanksgiving, praise, prayer, and blessing."[14] The goal of priestly discourse is undergirded by the assumption

---

Anna and Joachim's prayers (PJ 4.1–2) compared to the hearing of Zechariah's prayer in Luke 1:13.

11. As a result of this reconfiguration, all three play a more muted role in PJ than they do in Luke. Zechariah appears first in the narrative in PJ 8.3 to determine which widower will become Mary's guardian. After mention of Zechariah's silence in PJ 10.2, Zechariah does not appear again until his death is described in PJ 23–24. Likewise, Elizabeth is not mentioned at all until the pericope under investigation (PJ 12.2–3) and is not mentioned again until PJ 22.3, which concerns Herod's pursuit of John. The narrative reveals later that Herod is pursuing John, and is angry with Zechariah, because Herod thinks that John will rule Israel (PJ 23.2). Most significantly, John is first mentioned in PJ 22.3, and it is only here that we learn of Elizabeth's bearing a child; it is not until 23.1 that Zechariah is identified as John's father.

12. Many details in PJ suggest that birth and life of Mary foreshadow the birth and life of Jesus in the canonical gospels: both grow stronger every day (PJ 6.1; cf. Luke 1:80; 2:52); both are presented in the temple (PJ 7.1–2; cf. Luke 2:22); both receive angelic care (PJ 8:1; cf. Mark 1:13); both have significant experiences at the temple at the age of twelve (PJ 8.2; cf. Luke 2:41–51); both are tried by Jewish religious leaders (PJ 14–15; cf. Luke 22:66–71); and both are seated on a donkey on their climactic journeys (PJ 17.2; cf. Luke 13:15).

13. Robbins, "Conceptual Blending," 170.

14. Ibid.

that "sacrificial actions by humans create an environment in which God acts redemptively among humans in the world."[15]

One of the major results of PJ's reconfiguration of Luke is that Jesus's "prehistory" is told in PJ not in terms of a promised political kingdom, but in terms of the activation of divine benefits. Much of PJ revolves around the sacred space of the temple: the narrative begins with offerings in the temple and ends with the installation of a new high priest in the temple. Likewise, PJ demonstrates a great concern for the temple's sacred personnel—priests and the high priest appear in nearly every part of the composition. Finally, the holiness of Mary, her entertainers, and her dwelling is also emphasized throughout the composition.[16]

The shape of priestly discourse in PJ, however, demonstrates its own focus in two important ways. First, PJ subtly calls into question the effectiveness or power of the temple and its priesthood to activate divine benefits. As I will point out below, Mary is depicted as a "moving temple" in PJ, which is distinct from the Jerusalem temple.[17] As such, her presence activates divine benefits for other characters in the story. Second, the author of PJ focuses the activation of divine benefits around the blessings of childbearing.

The opening chapters demonstrate the way in which childbearing activates divine benefits. Joachim is portrayed as an ideal character in the mode of priestly discourse: he not only makes offerings at the temple but also has the habit of offering double what is prescribed. As he explains, "The part of [the offering that is] my excess will be for all people and the part [of the offering that is] for forgiveness will be for the Lord God for my atonement" (PJ 1.1). His religious devotion is threatened, however, by an impediment in his life. This impediment is not cultic or even moral in nature; it is biological. Joachim does not have a child. As a result, Reuben

15. Ibid.

16. For an excellent analysis of the role of purity and its various forms (ritual, menstrual, and sexual) in PJ, see Lily C. Vuong, *Gender and Purity in the Protevangelium of James*, WUNT 2/358 (Tübingen: Mohr Siebeck, 2013), esp. 25–26. Many thanks to the reviewer who drew my attention to Vuong's monograph as well as to the monograph of Jennifer A. Glancy and the earlier article of Shaye J. D. Cohen (see note 64 below).

17. Many thanks to Vernon Robbins for the image of Mary as a "moving temple." Vuong also discerns PJ's depiction of Mary as an instantiation of the temple, but suggests this only happens *after* she has been dismissed from the temple (see Vuong, *Gender and Purity*, 133–36).

says, "It is not permitted for you to offer your gifts in the first place [πρώτῳ], because you have not produced an offspring in Israel" (PJ 1.2). Joachim's failure to produce an heir threatens his ability to experience divine benefit, which in this case is forgiveness. One of the major consequences of Mary's birth is that she becomes the instrument by which Joachim and Anna receive divine benefits.[18]

When one considers the larger narrative of PJ, it becomes evident how the author has added an additional parallel between Mary and Jesus. Just as Mary is Jesus's forerunner in terms of his birth, she is also his forerunner in terms of the ability to activate divine benefits. In parallel to Mary, the birth of Jesus causes the midwife to recognize Mary's child, Jesus, as the instrument by which divine benefits are restored to Israel (PJ 19.2). With this shift from prophetic to priestly discourse clearly in mind, we may proceed with a closer comparative exegetical analysis of the two accounts of Mary's visit to Elizabeth.

1.2. Exegetical Analysis

1.2.1. Opening[19]

PJ 12.2–3	Luke 1:39–56
2 Full of joy, Mary went off to her relative [συγγενίδα] Elizabeth.	39 In those days Mary set out and went with haste to a Judean town in the hill country,

The first thing to note is that determining where to start the opening of the pericope in PJ is more difficult than it is in the Gospel of Luke.[20] There

18. Though she rightly calls attention to concerns for purity and the central place of the temple in this early section of PJ, Vuong underplays the inability of Joachim and Anna to receive divine benefits *prior to* the conception of Mary. She suggests instead that characters in PJ simply "misread" and "misunderstand" the state of Joachim and Anna vis-à-vis the temple (see Vuong, *Gender and Purity*, 70–88). On my read, Joachim and Anna's childlessness proves a significant impediment to the activation of divine benefits, which is only resolved through the conception of Mary.

19. Font guide: Greek in bold font = identical word agreement in the Greek; Greek with underline = similar word agreement in the Greek; English in bold font = repetitive word or theme in passage.

20. For a description of the analysis of "opening-middle-closing" (OMC) texture,

are several important reasons to think that PJ 12.1 should be read together with 12.2–3.[21] In 12.1, Mary brings her scarlet and purple thread and is blessed by the priest Samuel. The priest's blessing, "you will be blessed among all the generations of the earth," may be better understood as part of the opening of PJ's version of Mary's visit to Elizabeth. Modern editions have chosen to break chapter 12 and chapter 11 in such a way that suggests that 12.1 should be read with 12.2–3. Further, the threefold repetition of εὐλογέω in 12.1–3—priest, Elizabeth, Elizabeth's unborn child—suggests a persistent repetitive texture.[22] Finally, the mention of Elizabeth's scarlet in 12.2 connects to Mary's in 12.1.

For the purposes of this essay, I have decided to read Mary's visit to Elizabeth in 12.2–3 as separate from, but related to, the priest's blessing in 12.1. Since chapter and verse divisions are not original to the text, but have been suggested by modern editors, they should not entirely restrict exegetical analysis. In addition, there is a clear geographical shift between 12.1 and 12.2–3. Finally, opening with 12.2 rather than 12.1 highlights a close syntactical resemblance between the two "openings." Both accounts open with a participle followed by a finite verb; the main verb in PJ is in the imperfect tense, while the verb in Luke is in the aorist.[23]

The question of repetitive texture is more difficult. One can make an argument for the persistence of the repetitive texture of εὐλογέω in much of PJ 1–12. As I read PJ, the priest's blessing in 12.1 can be understood as the final blessing in a cycle of "priestly blessings" that stretch from PJ 6.2 until 12.1. The blessings in 12.2–3 suggest slight, but significant, differences from the blessings elsewhere in the composition. The blessing in 12.2–3 comes from the lips of Elizabeth—the first woman and nonpriest to bless Mary—and from "that which is inside of her." Also, the blessing more explicitly pertains to Mary's role as mother (PJ 12.2; cf. Luke 1:43). Finally, the priest's final blessing introduces irony into the narrative of PJ

see Vernon K. Robbins, *Exploring the Texture of Texts: A Guide to Socio-Rhetorical Interpretation* (Valley Forge, PA: Trinity Press International, 1996), 19–21.

21. In the seminar, this was a topic of much debate. With Vernon K. Robbins's constructive questions in mind, I have retained the break at 12.2 for reasons that will be explained more fully below. It is my hope, though, that my larger analysis will prove cogent and helpful regardless of where one places 12.1.

22. For the notion of repetitive texture, see Robbins, *Exploring*, 8–9.

23. Luke 1:39: Ἀναστᾶσα δὲ Μαριάμ … ἐπορεύθη….
PJ 12.2: χαρὰν δὲ λαβοῦσα Μαριὰμ ἀπῄει….

because the same priest will become Mary's accuser in PJ 15. Though these differences are important, the proximity of the blessings in 12.2–3 to those in 12.1 demands that they not be understood independently of the preceding blessings.

On the whole, I have set out to compare a single event that occurs in the two compositions: Mary's visit to Elizabeth. This event, though, is highly contextualized in both compositions. A good case could be made for reading Gabriel's annunciation (Luke 1:26–38) as the "opening" for Mary's visit to Elizabeth in Luke; it is also equally possible, however, to treat the annunciation and Mary's visit as two distinct events with their own distinct "openings." In the narrative of both Luke and PJ, the "opening" of one section often functions as the "closing" of another. With the case of the priest's blessing in 12.1, the relationship between the "closing" of one part and the "opening" of another appear to overlap substantially.

With these caveats in mind, the opening of PJ appears to be shorter and omits several details found in Luke.[24] It is worth noting the addition of συγγενίς in PJ 12.2. In Luke's annunciation (Luke 1:26–38), the same lexeme is found in the angel's message to Mary; there, it indicates that her "relative" Elizabeth has also conceived a child (Luke 1:36). The angel's annunciation in PJ 11 contains no reference to Elizabeth or her conception.

1.2.2. Middle

PJ 12.2–3	Luke 1:39–55
O: 2 She knocked on the door; and when Elizabeth heard she cast aside the scarlet and ran to the door.	40 where she entered the house of Zechariah and greeted Elizabeth. 41 When Elizabeth heard Mary's greeting, the child leaped [ἐσκίρτησεν] in her womb.
M: When she opened it	And Elizabeth was filled with the Holy Spirit 42 and exclaimed with a loud cry,

24. E.g., the chronological setting of her journey (ἐν ταῖς ἡμέραις ταύταις); the manner in which she went (μετὰ σπουδῆς), and the destination of her journey (εἰς πόλιν Ἰούδα).

she **blessed** [εὐλόγησεν] Mary	“**blessed** [εὐλογημένη] are you among women, and **blessed** [εὐλογημένος] is the fruit of your womb.
and said, “How is it [**Πόθεν μοι τοῦτο**] that the mother of my Lord should come to me [ἵνα ἡ μήτηρ τοῦ κυρίου μου ἔλθη πρὸς ἐμέ]?	43 And how is it [**πόθεν μοι τοῦτο**] that the mother of my Lord comes to me [ἵνα ἔλθη ἡ μήτηρ τοῦ κυρίου μου πρὸς ἐμέ]?
For see [**ἰδοὺ γάρ**], the child in me [τὸ ἐν ἐμοί] leapt up [**ἐσκίρτησεν**]	44 For see [**ἰδοὺ γάρ**] as soon as I heard the sound of your greeting, the child in my womb [τὸ βρέφος ἐν τῇ κοιλίᾳ μου] leapt up [**ἐσκίρτησεν**] for joy.
and **blessed** [εὐλόγησέν] you.”	45 And **blessed** [μακαρία] is she who believed that there would be a fulfillment of what was spoken to her by the Lord.”
C: But Mary forgot the mysteries that the archangel Gabriel had spoken to her, and gazed at the sky	
and said,	46 And Mary said,
“Who am I, Lord, that all the women of earth [πᾶσαι αἱ γυναῖκες τῆς γῆς] **will bless me** [**μακαριοῦσίν με**]?”	“My soul magnifies the Lord, 47 and my spirit rejoices in God my Savior, 48 for he has looked with favor on the lowliness of his servant. Surely, from now on all generations [πᾶσαι αἱ γενεαί] **will bless me** [**μακαριοῦσίν με**]; 49 for the Mighty One has done great things for me, and holy is his name. 50 His mercy is for those who fear him from genera-

tion to generation. 51 He has shown strength with his arm; he has scattered the proud in the thoughts of their hearts. 52 He has brought down the powerful from their thrones, and lifted up the lowly; 53 he has filled the hungry with good things, and sent the rich away empty. 54 He has helped his servant Israel, in remembrance of his mercy, 55 according to the promise he made to our ancestors, to Abraham and to his descendants forever."

(1) Opening of the Middle: The narrative in both compositions describes the initial interaction between Mary and Elizabeth. Here, PJ adds details that relate to the response of Elizabeth. In Luke, there is no reference to Elizabeth's actions before blessing Mary in Luke 1:42. In comparison, PJ adds that Elizabeth heard, dropped her scarlet thread, ran to the door, and opened it. In addition to this, PJ makes no mention of the οἶκος Ζαχαρίου as in Luke 1:40. Here, and elsewhere in PJ, Elizabeth and Zechariah are depicted separately from one another. Finally, PJ does not include a reference to the response of Elizabeth's βρέφος to Mary's greeting as found in Luke 1:41.

(2) Middle of the Middle: This section contains Elizabeth's blessing of Mary and the description of her unborn child's response to Mary. The two accounts display strong verbal similarity in reference to Elizabeth's question, "And why has this happened to me that the mother of my Lord has come to me?" The only differences between the two accounts are the omission of καὶ in PJ and the variant location of the verb ἔλθῃ. At the end of this section the reference to Mary's being "blessed" (μακαρία) because she believed completely does not appear in PJ. Though a small detail, this omission reflects the change in rhetorolect describe above. Emphasis on complete belief is more appropriate for prophetic discourse than for priestly discourse. In addition to these general observations, several important elements in the two accounts deserve further comment.

Elizabeth's blessing: One of the first notable differences in PJ is that it contains no reference to Elizabeth's being filled with the Holy Spirit. This omission also aligns with the switch from prophetic to priestly rhetorolect in PJ. Likewise, PJ does not attribute direct speech to Elizabeth in her blessing of Mary as in Luke. While Luke 1:42 has Elizabeth exclaim "with a loud cry, 'Blessed are you among women,'" PJ has "she [Elizabeth] blessed Mary." In addition, Elizabeth's blessing in PJ applies only to Mary, and does not include the "fruit" of her womb as in Luke.

The unborn child's response: There is some verbal similarity in how the two accounts report the response of Elizabeth's unborn child, such as the identical verbal form ἐσκίρτησεν; but the two differ in important ways. First, the subject of ἐσκίρτησεν is more ambiguous in PJ than it is in Luke. In Luke, the subject can fairly be described as an embryo or fetus—it is τὸ βρέφος ἐν τῇ κοιλίᾳ μου that leaps. In PJ, however, the subject of the verb is less clear: τὸ ἐν ἐμοί. In addition, there is no reference to Mary's greeting being connected to or the cause of the unborn child's response. Luke 1:44 has Elizabeth say, "For see as soon as I heard the sound of your greeting"; in contrast, Elizabeth only mentions the "leaping" of the unborn child in PJ 12.2. Finally, and most importantly, the unborn child is said to join with its mother in blessing Mary. As noted above, the blessing of a nonpriestly woman and her unborn child distinguish this blessing from the previous blessings in the composition.

The significance of blessing: PJ adds εὐλόγησέν σε for Luke's ἐν ἀγαλλιάσει ("in gladness"). The verb εὐλογέω occurs sixteen times in PJ (compared to thirteen times in Luke) and will be discussed more fully below. In PJ, Mary and her mother are almost always the objects of blessing. The only use of εὐλογέω that does not apply to Mary or her mother applies to the offspring of Joseph (PJ 15.4). In this case, the priest implies that Joseph's offspring will not be blessed because of Mary's apparently illicit conception.

(3) Closing of the Middle: Here we read of Mary's response. The two accounts differ greatly in terms of length and in terms of the tone of her response. Protevangelium of James 12.2 states that Mary forgets what has been spoken to her by Gabriel, which is referred to as τῶν μυστηρίων.[25]

25. The lexeme μυστήριον occurs two times in PJ (12.2, 3). The frequency with which μυστήριον occurs in PJ is significant in comparison to the singular occurrence in each of the Synoptic Gospels and the twenty-eight total occurrences in the NT. "Mysteries" refer exclusively to Mary's virgin birth in PJ. This use of "mystery" does

Mary's forgetfulness in PJ stands in contrast to her exalted response in Luke 1:46–54. Mary speaks of her soul and spirit magnifying God (μεγαλύνει), for looking "with favor" on Mary, God's humble servant (Luke 1:46–48).[26] In addition, the Lukan version contains an emphatic claim to Mary's blessedness: "Surely, from now on all generations [πᾶσαι αἱ γενεαί] will call me blessed [μακαριοῦσίν με]" (Luke 1:48). PJ contains no such laudatory response, and instead of an emphatic statement about Mary's blessedness, PJ reconfigures the Lukan version as a question—"Who am I, Lord, that all the women of earth [πᾶσαι αἱ γυναῖκες τῆς γῆς] will bless me [μακαριοῦσίν με]?" (PJ 12.2).[27] The rest of Mary's famous "Magnificat" (Luke 1:49–54) is omitted entirely in the account found in PJ.[28]

Overall, the middle section closes with a very different feel in each. In Luke, Mary's response is confident and full of praise. In PJ, the middle ends with a question. The author's reconfiguration of the closing—especially Mary's forgetfulness and the significance of her question—is puzzling for many reasons. It seems to me that Mary's question represents the "turn" in the narrative that results from the angel's annunciation in chapter 11.[29] Her question ultimately relates to the question of this essay: Why, indeed, is Mary to be blessed by all the women of the earth?

---

not align with the use of the term in the shared saying of Jesus concerning the "mystery/mysteries" of the kingdom (Matt 13:11 // Mark 4:11 // Luke 8:10). Rather, the usage sounds more Pauline (see esp. 1 Cor 2:1; Eph 1:9; Col 1:26; 1 Tim 3:16), but the emphasis is slightly different. In the Pauline writings, "mystery" applies more to the Christ-event than it does to Jesus's miraculous conception and birth (but cf. 1 Tim 3:16).

26. In PJ, the fact that God looks on Mary with favor has already been underscored in PJ 7, when Mary dances on the steps of the altar in the temple, and in PJ 11 in the voice's greeting of Mary.

27. It is worth noting that PJ 12.1 retains the laudatory response of "all generations," but there it comes on the lips of the priest and employs the verb εὐλογέω, not μακαρίζω. This is the singular usage of μακαρίζω in both PJ and Luke (cf. μακάριος, which occurs fifteen times in Luke and never in PJ).

28. Foskett notes the significance of this speech for the characterization of Mary in Luke-Acts: "As the first speech in Luke-Acts and the only such form ascribed to Mary, its importance for understanding the Lucan portrayal of Mary cannot be overestimated" (Foskett, *A Virgin Conceived*, 14). The omission of this speech not surprisingly alters the characterization of Mary in PJ.

29. Mary's ambivalence at this point in the narrative could reflect her (even overwhelmed) response to the task God has given her. Mary has already learned that she will conceive and give birth to the "son of the Most High" (PJ 11.2). The exact same

1.2.3. Closing

PJ 12.3	Luke 1:56
O: 3 She stayed with Elizabeth for three months [τρεῖς μῆνας].	56 And Mary remained with her about three months [μῆνας τρεῖς]
M: Day by day her own belly grew.	
C: Mary then returned home [ἐν τῷ οἴκῳ αὐτῆς] in fear, and hid herself from the sons of Israel.	and then returned to her home [εἰς τὸν οἶκον αὐτῆς].
She was sixteen when these mysteries happened to her.	

The two accounts close in similar ways. They both mention that Mary stayed with Elizabeth for three months and then returned home. The account in PJ is significantly longer, however, because it adds details not found in the Lukan account: reference to Mary's growing stomach, her fear,[30] and her hiding herself from the sons of Israel. The reference to Mary's belly growing is consistent with attempts elsewhere in PJ (cf. 13.1) to add details to her pregnancy; in Luke, in contrast, the annunciation (Luke 1:26–38) leads to the birth of Jesus (2:1–7) without any further reference to her pregnancy. The account of PJ adds an epilogue to the account that provides Mary's age at the time of these events.

2. Interpretation

On the whole, the account of Mary's visit to Elizabeth in PJ is shorter than its counterpart in the Gospel of Luke. The general outline, though,

verbal phrase (τίς εἰμι) in Mary's question occurs also in LXX Exod 3:11, where Moses questions his ability to carry out the tasks of speaking to Pharaoh and leading the people of Israel to freedom. The same phrase occurs also in 2 Sam 7:18 (= 1 Chr 17:16); 9:8; 1 Chr 29:14; Jdt 12:14; 1 Macc 10:72). The exact verbal phrase does not appear in the NT.

30. "Fear" and "hiding" are connected with the sons of Israel also in PJ 14.1. The "sons of Israel" appear elsewhere as the cause of consternation for the protagonists in PJ: of Anna (PJ 3.1; 6.3); of Joseph (9.2; 15.2, 4); and of Mary (12.3; 14.1).

is very similar in both: Mary travels to see Elizabeth, receives a blessing from her, stays with her for three months, and then returns home. Despite this similarity, PJ has thoroughly reconfigured the account. In Luke, the mood is one of joyful doxology throughout, on the part of both Mary and Elizabeth. Although PJ begins with a reference to Mary's joy (PJ 12.2), it ends with Mary's doubtful question about her worthiness (12.2) and her hiding herself in fear (12.3). In addition to filling out the stages of her physical pregnancy (i.e., her belly growing day by day and reference to the sixth month), PJ adds intensity to the suspense and fear brought about by Mary's supernatural conception and role as mother.[31]

For the purposes of this essay, however, the preceding comparison of PJ 12.2–3 and Luke 1:39–56 calls attention to the nature of Mary's blessedness. The state of Mary's blessedness,[32] which has been emphasized in the narrative of PJ to this point, begins for the first time to be doubted or disputed. Mary's question—"Who am I?"—gives voice to a reconsideration of the cause or significance of her blessedness that began in PJ 7. Earlier in the narrative, her proximity to and service in the temple appear to be the cause of her blessedness (see PJ 6.2; 7.2; 12.1). In PJ 12.2 and earlier in PJ 11.1–2, Mary's blessedness is connected with her identity as mother. In an attempt to highlight and understand this shift, it is necessary to analyze the topos of "blessing" in each composition more fully.

2.1. Praise and Blessing in Luke and Protevangelium of James

The attempt to analyze the topos of blessing in Luke and PJ requires one to think beyond individual words to related words and concepts. The table below presents several of the more important "synonyms" that may help outline the topos of blessing in the compositions.

Lexeme	Number in PJ	Number in Luke	Number in NT*
αἰνέω	1	3	8
αἶνος	0	1	2
δόξα	1	13	166

31. Vernon K. Robbins, *Who Do People Say I Am*, 163.

32. On Mary's blessedness, see Foster, "Protevangelium of James," 122; and E-P 34–35.

δοξάζω	5	9	61
ἐπιβλέπω	1	2	3
εὐλογέω	15	11	41
εὐλογία	2	0	16
μακαρίζω	1	1	2
μακάριος	0	15	50
μεγαλύνω	4	2	8

* This table is based roughly on Louw and Nida's lexicon based on semantic analysis. See "Praise" (33.354–33.364) in Johannes P. Louw and Eugene A. Nida, eds., Greek-English Lexicon of the New Testament: Based on Semantic Domains, 2nd ed. Accordance electronic edition, version 4.0 (New York: United Bible Societies, 1989).

References for praise and blessing language in PJ: αἰνέω: 8.1; δόξα: 25.2; δοξάζω: 6.3; 14.2; 16.3; 24.1; 25.1; ἐπιβλέπω: 6.2; εὐλογέω: 2.4 (bis); 3.3; 4.4; 6.2 (3×); 7.2; 11.1; 12.1 (bis); 12.2; 15.4; εὐλογία: 6.2; 24.1; μεγαλύνω: 5.2; 7.2; 12.1; 19.2.

References for praise and blessing language in Luke: αἰνέω: 2:13, 20; 19:37; αἶνος: 18:43; δόξα: 2:9, 14, 32; 4:6; 9:26, 31, 32; 12:27; 14:10; 17:18; 19:38; 21:27; 24:26; δοξάζω: 2:10; 4:15; 5:25, 26; 7:16; 13:13; 17:15; 18:43; 23:47; ἐπιβλέπω: 1:48; 9:38; εὐλογέω: 1:42, 64; 2:28, 34; 6:28; 9:16; 13:35; 19:38; 24:30, 50, 51, 53; μακαρίζω: 1:48; μακάριος: 1:45; 6:20, 21, 22; 7:23; 10:23; 11:27, 28; 12:37, 38, 43; 14:14, 15; μεγαλύνω: 1:46, 58.

A few general comments about the table are in order. First, words related to praise and blessing occur thirty times in PJ and fifty-seven times in the Gospel of Luke. Second, the two compositions share a group of frequently occurring words: δοξάζω, εὐλογέω, and μεγαλύνω. Third, each composition employs words with more frequency than the other. For example, αἰνέω/αἶνος is more prominent in Luke; εὐλογία occurs only in PJ; and μακάριος does not occur in PJ at all (though μακαρίζω occurs once in both compositions).

The concentration of the words is also revealing. Although εὐλογέω and μεγαλύνω occur nearly the same number of times in the two compositions, PJ employs both more frequently since PJ is only one-fourth the length of Luke.[33] In addition, the number of occurrences of μεγαλύνω in PJ would account for half of the total occurrences in the New Testament, and the number of occurrences of εὐλογέω would account for more than one-third of the total New Testament occurrences. This prevalence of lau-

33. According to Accordance software, Luke has 19,495 words and PJ has 5,175 words; PJ is thus 26.5 percent as long as Luke.

datory language in PJ arises from the mode of priestly discourse in the composition. Although the two compositions demonstrate some similarities in their use of language related to praise and blessing, PJ presents its own "lexicon" of praise and blessing.

One aspect of this divergence is the use of μεγαλύνω. In Luke, the verb is always related to God—it either describes a response to God (Luke 1:46) or an act of God (Luke 1:58). In PJ 5.2 and 19.2, μεγαλύνω is used with reference to God, specifically as an act of praise to God (similar to δοξάζω or αἰνέω). Nevertheless, it also attains a "special" sense in reference to making the name of Mary great. Although μεγαλύνω does not attain this sense in the New Testament, there are important instances in the LXX in which the name of a biblical character is made great (e.g., Gen. 12:2); these will be discussed in the section concerning Mary's blessedness in PJ below.

With these general comments in mind, I will analyze more fully the topos of praise (αἰνέω/αἶνος and δοξάζω) and the topos of blessing (εὐλογέω/εὐλογία and μακαρίζω/μακάριος) in order to ascertain more clearly the similarities and differences between the two compositions.

2.2. The Topos of Praise in Luke and Protevangelium of James

As the word frequency table above suggests, the Gospel of Luke contains a higher frequency of language related to praise. In Luke, glory (δόξα) and praise (αἶνος), and their related verbal forms are nearly synonymous.[34] For example, the crowd is said to give praise to God (ἔδωκεν αἶνον τῷ θεῷ) in Luke 18:43; similarly, the healed person in Luke 17:18 gives God glory (δοῦναι δόξαν τῷ θεῷ). The overlap of verbal forms appears clearly in Luke 2:20: "And the shepherds returned, giving glory [δοξάζοντες] to and praising [αἰνοῦντες] God for all the things that they heard and saw just as it was spoken to them." With only one exception, the object of both praise and glory is always God (θέος);[35] in Luke 4:15, the singular exception, it is Jesus who is glorified (δοξάζω) by "everyone" who hears his teaching in the synagogues. In Luke, the praise of God frequently comes from those who have been healed by Jesus (5:25; 13:13; 17:15, 18; 18:43) or those who wit-

---

34. Δόξα frequently denotes "glory" in the sense of "fame" or "reputation" (see BDAG, s.v. δόξα). The "fame" of various individuals and entities in mentioned in Luke: Israel (2:32), the nations (4:6), Israel's leaders (9:31; 12:27), the Son of Man (9:26; 21:27), and the Messiah (24:26). These fall outside of the semantic range of "praise."

35. Luke 2:13, 14, 20, 28; 5:25, 26; 7:16; 13:13; 17:15, 18; 18:43; 19:37; 23:47; 24:53.

nessed the healing (5:26; 7:16; 18:43); in addition, angels (2:13), shepherds (2:20), and a centurion (23:47) praise God.

This brief survey suggests a few observations about the nature of praise language in Luke. First, praise is almost entirely *theocentric*: God is the object of praise and glory in nearly every occasion. Second, Jesus is the *instrument* that brings about God's praise: the act of praise is prompted by the advent or activity of Jesus. Jesus's miraculous birth, healing power, and innocent death all lead characters in Luke to praise God.

Turning to consider the use and nature of praise language in PJ, one notices an intriguing reconfiguration: while the object of praise is the same in PJ, the means or instrument is often Mary, not Jesus. In PJ 6.3, the religious leaders give the God of Israel glory (ἐδόξασαν τὸν θεὸν Ἰσραήλ) after they leave the feast at Joachim's house. Given the context of their blessing Mary in 6.2, it's very likely that their giving God glory is caused by Mary. Mary as the instrument of God's praise can be seen more clearly when her parents entrust her to the temple. After leaving her at the temple, Mary's parents return "praising" (ἐπαινοῦντες[36]) and "glorifying" (δοξάζοντες) God because she did not turn back (PJ 8.1). Likewise, in 14.2, Joseph is said to glorify the God of Israel (ἐδόξασεν τὸν θεὸν τοῦ Ἰσραήλ) because of the favor (χάρις) given to him; the immediate context suggests that this "favor" is Mary's betrothal to him. In each case, Mary is the cause of God's praise. The author of PJ has reconfigured the notion of praise as found in the Gospel of Luke. In Luke, praise is *theocentric* and is caused by *Jesus*; in PJ, praise is also *theocentric*, but it is caused by *Mary*.

The final two occurrences of δοξάζω differ from those above. The epilogue to the composition ends with the author "James" saying that he returned to Jerusalem safely and there glorified God (δοξάζων τὸν Δεσπότην θεόν) after Herod's slaughter of the children (PJ 25.1). This adds little to our analysis. The final occurrence, however, is more helpful. In 24.1, the narrative describes the priests who are awaiting Zechariah's blessing. Unbeknownst to them, Zechariah has been murdered and they will receive no blessing. Contingent upon Zechariah's blessing, the priests hope to glorify God (δοξάσαι τόν … θεόν). As the narrative moves forward, however, it becomes clear that this hope will not be fulfilled. They receive

36. Some manuscripts have αἰνοῦντες rather than ἐπαινοῦντες. Compared to αἰνέω, the lexeme ἐπαινέω occurs less frequently in the NT (6× total) as well as in Luke (1×). In Luke 16:8, Jesus's parable speaks of the master's "commending" (NRSV) the shrewdness of his manager.

no blessing and do not glorify God. Instead, they become afraid (24.2), eventually enter into the sanctuary to find Zechariah murdered (24.3), and then leave in fear (24.3). In other words, the narrative of PJ ends with the priests lacking the power to activate divine benefits and thus unable to respond appropriately to God. Though subtle, this confirms the shifting role of the temple elsewhere in PJ: the activation of divine benefits occurs in proximity to Mary, not the temple or its personnel.

2.3. The Topos of Blessing in Luke

The Gospel of Luke employs two word groups to denote blessing: μακαρίζω/μακάριος and εὐλογέω/εὐλογία. The verb μακαρίζω is quite rare in the New Testament. It occurs only in Luke 1:48 and in Jas 5:11. The occurrence in Luke appears in Mary's Magnificat. Mary exclaims, "For behold, from now on, all generations will bless me [μακαριοῦσιν με πᾶσαι αἱ γενεαί]." James 5:11 says, "Behold, we bless [μακαρίζομεν] those who endured."[37] Both Luke 1:48 and Jas 5:11, then, employ μακαρίζω to denote one person or group of people regarding another person or group as blessed or fortunate.[38]

The word μακάριος itself is used most often in biblical tradition to describe fortunate people, locations, and events. The term occurs fifteen times in Luke, and four of these occur in the Sermon on the Plain.[39] In general, the use of μακάριος in Luke aligns with the use of μακαρίζω described above: the term is employed to describe those whom the audience should

37. N.B., the NRSV glosses the verbal form in each with "to call blessed."

38. Because it occurs somewhat rarely in the NT, a brief survey of the use of μακαρίζω in the LXX is in order. Μακαρίζω occurs twenty-four times in the LXX: Gen 30:13; Num 24:17; 4 Macc 1:10; 16:9; 18:13; Pss 40:3; 71:17; 143:15; Song 6:9; Job 29:10; Wis 2:16; 18:1; Sir 11:28; 25:7, 23; 31:9; 37:24; 45:7; Mal 3:12, 15; Isa 3:12; 9:16. The verb also carries the sense of human regard or judgment on another. Gen 30:13 employs language that is very close to that of Luke 1:48. At news of her conception, Leah says, "Fortunate am I [μακαρία ἐγώ] because the women will bless [μακαρίζουσιν] me." See further Ps 143:15 and Mal 3:12. This human perception of μακάριος, though, can be distorted. For example, Isa 3:12 says, "My people, those who bless you [οἱ μακαρίζοντες], mislead you." The only time that God is the subject of μακαρίζω (i.e., the one who perceives or bestows μακάριος on another) is in Sir 45:7.

39. Cf. Matthew's use of μακάριος. It occurs thirteen times, nine of which appear in the Sermon on the Mount.

regard as fortunate.[40] In the Sermon on the Plain, those whom Jesus deems fortunate contrasts with those whom others might think fortunate: he calls fortunate the poor (6:20), the hungry (6:21), those who weep (6:21), and those who are hated (6:22).[41] Elsewhere, the fortunate denote those who properly recognize Jesus (7:23; 10:23) as well as those who hear and obey God's word (11:28).[42]

Mary is called μακαρία twice in the Gospel of Luke. In the first instance, Elizabeth says of Mary, "And fortunate [μακαρία] is the one who believed that the things that have been spoken to her by the Lord will come to fruition" (Luke 1:45). In the second, a woman interrupts Jesus's teaching by saying, "Fortunate [μακαρία] is the womb [κοιλία] that bore you and the breasts [μαστοί] that nursed you!" (Luke 11:27). Something about Jesus—most likely his teaching, but possibly his reputation—leads the woman in the crowd to regard Mary as fortunate to have Jesus as a son. Jesus redirects her perception of who is fortunate: "On the contrary, fortunate [μακάριοι] are those who hear the word of God and obey it" (11:28).

Luke also narrates the performance of blessings on other people and objects. These blessings in Luke are frequently denoted by the verb εὐλογέω, which occurs thirteen times.[43] The character who most frequently bestows blessings in Luke is Jesus—he blesses bread in the miraculous feeding (9:16) and in his meal after the resurrection (24:30), and he blesses the disciples (24:50–51). Jesus is also the beneficiary of pronounced blessings—first by Elizabeth (1:42) and then by Simeon (2:34). The blessing of Jesus is often tied to the blessing of Mary (by Elizabeth in 1:42) and the blessing of both his parents (by Simeon in 2:34). Finally, Simeon (2:28), Zechariah (1:64), and the disciples are all said to bestow

---

40. Μακάριος occurs sixty-eight times in the LXX. Like the use of the term in Luke, μακάριος in the LXX plays a descriptive function, especially in the wisdom literature.

41. Jesus's parables confirm and expand on the description of those described as fortunate elsewhere in Luke. See, e.g., Luke 12:37–38, 43; 14:14. In the context of Luke's rendering of the "Synoptic Apocalypse," the distress caused by the geopolitical turmoil has the power to reverse typical notions of blessedness: barren women, who would normally not be regarded as "fortunate," are deemed μακάριαι because of the swiftness with which they are able to avert the coming disaster.

42. Cf. Luke 14:15: "After hearing these things, one of the fellow diners said to him, 'Blessed [μακάριος] is whoever eats bread in the kingdom of God.'"

43. Three of these occurrences resemble the use of μακάριος discussed above: Luke 6:28; 13:15; 19:38. It is possible to understand εὐλογέω here as indicating a divine favor in contrast to a human interpretation of another person as μακάριος.

"blessing" on God. This use of εὐλογέω denotes a response to God, which is caused by actions or events in the narrative context.

Before turning to PJ, it will be helpful to note the way in which the topos of blessing functions within the prophetic rhetorolect of Luke 1–2. First, the blessings often take place in the first space of priestly rhetorolect and are spoken by people of priestly descent.[44] As I mentioned above, even the apparently priestly language in Luke is blended, if not subsumed, within the more dominant mode of prophetic discourse. Elizabeth's blessing of Mary in Luke 1:39–45 highlights this: Mary is blessed because she *believes* in God's *future* promises declared by God's appointed *messenger*. All of these features align more with prophetic discourse than with priestly discourse.[45]

2.4. The Topos of Blessing in Protevangelium of James

As mentioned above, the topos of blessing in PJ differs from that of the Gospel of Luke, at least lexically, in two clear ways. First, PJ employs εὐλογέω/εὐλογία exclusively to denote blessing; μακάριος does not occur in PJ, and μακαρίζω appears only once in Mary's question in PJ 12.2–3. Second, there are more occurrences of both verbal and nominal forms of the εὐλογ- root in PJ than in the Gospel of Luke. As the following analysis of each instance of εὐλογέω/εὐλογία will demonstrate, the author of PJ has significantly reconfigured the topos of blessing, not only by extracting it from prophetic discourse and embedding it in priestly discourse, but also in the particular way he employs the topos in relationship to Mary.

2.4.1. The Blessing of Anna: Barrenness Turned to Bounty

The first occurrences of εὐλογέω in PJ allude to the first blessings in the LXX: "And God blessed [ηὐλόγησεν] them, saying 'Increase and multiply…'" (Gen 1:22, 28). The first instance of the bestowal of divine favor in the LXX is indicated by the ability to "increase and multiply." In PJ 2–4, εὐλογέω occurs four times, and the topos of blessing is tied closely with

---

44. For Elizabeth's priestly descent, see Luke 1:5. As mentioned above, Simeon is not explicitly described as a priest in Luke's Gospel.

45. See further Vernon K. Robbins, "Bodies and Politics in Luke 1–2 and Sirach 44–50: Men, Women, and Boys," *Scriptura* 90 (2005): 824–38, reprinted in updated form in this volume, pages 41–63.

producing offspring. As discussed above, the fact that Joachim does not have a child seems to prohibit his full participation in the first space of priestly discourse. Likewise, in PJ 2.4, Anna prays, "God of my fathers, bless [εὐλόγησον] me and attend to my prayer, just like when you blessed [εὐλόγησας] the womb [μήτραν] of Sarah and gave her a son, Isaac." While mourning her barrenness, she contrasts herself and her infertility with both the earth and the fish, who bless (εὐλογεῖ) God by producing offspring and fruit (PJ 3.3). Finally, in PJ 4.4, the author relates the praise of Anna at the fulfillment of her prayer in PJ 2.4: "Now I know that the Lord God blessed [εὐλόγησεν] me greatly. For behold, the widow is no longer a widow, and see, the childless [ἄτεκνος] has conceived [ἐν γαστρὶ εἴληφα[46]]." In PJ 2–4, the topos of blessing concerns reproduction: Anna's conception of a child demonstrates her blessedness and results in the activation of divine benefits for her and Joachim.

2.4.2. The Blessed Mary in Protevangelium of James 6–12

The topos of blessing plays a significant role also in PJ 6–12. Here, Mary is the sole recipient or object of blessing. These blessings of Mary occur in key places in the narrative of PJ: in the feast celebrating Mary's first birthday (PJ 6), in the presentation of the three-year-old Mary to the temple (PJ 7), in the annunciation of Mary's conception (PJ 11), in Mary's presentation of her purple and scarlet fabric (PJ 12.1), and in the blessing of Elizabeth and "that which is inside" of her (PJ 12.2). The characters who utter the blessings on Mary are mostly of priestly status: priests in PJ 6.2, 7.2, and 12.1, and the high priest in 6.2. In contrast, there is no hint that the blessings of a "voice" in PJ 11 and of Elizabeth and her unborn child in 12.2 are of a priestly nature. We will discuss each of these in turn.

2.4.2.1. Mary Blessed at One: A Name and the Ultimate Blessing

Mary is blessed twice in PJ 6. The first comes on the lips of a group of priests; the second is spoken by the high priest. The context provides important clues to the meaning of εὐλογέω in this chapter. In 6.1, the author describes the first year of Mary's life, including her ability to stand and walk at six months of age. Mary's precociousness prompts Anna to build a sanctuary

46. In place of the perfect form of λαμβάνω, some manuscripts read the future, λήψομαι.

(ἐποίησεν ἁγίασμα)[47] in the infant girl's bedroom (κοιτών) until she is of an appropriate age to be taken to the temple (ναός). Mary's ritual purity is emphasized, as is the purity of her "entertainers," the "undefiled daughters of the Hebrews."

Anna's actions represent the relocation of God's ἁγίασμα, or "holy precinct."[48] In the LXX, the phrase ποιέω ἁγίασμα occurs in Exod 25:8 and 1 Chr 22:19. In Exod 25:8, this holy precinct is the locus of God's revelation—God says, "and I shall appear [ὀφθήσομαι] among you." In 1 Chr. 22:19, the holy precinct is the place where the ark of the covenant and the holy vessels are to be kept. In 1 Chr. 28:10, Solomon is selected to build a house (οἶκος) for a holy precinct (εἰς ἁγίασμα). In other places, such as 1 Maccabees, the ἁγίασμα is functionally equivalent to the temple (ναός). By saying that Anna has built a "holy precinct" in which Mary dwells, the author of PJ likens Mary to an object or vessel of the temple, although not the temple located in Jerusalem.[49]

---

47. There is ambiguity in how to properly understand the reference to the ἁγίασμα in PJ 6.1 (καὶ ἐποίησεν ἁγίασμα ἐν τῷ κοιτῶνι αὐτῆς) and 6.3 (ἐν τῷ ἁγιάσματι τοῦ κοιτῶνος). It is not clear if Anna's effort results in the construction of a sanctuary *in* Mary's bedroom or if it transforms Mary's bedroom *into* a sanctuary entirely. Ehrman and Pleše render both instances as if the sanctuary is *in* her bedroom (E-P, 47). Hock translates both as though Mary's bedroom has been converted *into* a sanctuary: "And so she turned her bedroom into a sanctuary," and "Her mother then took her up to the sanctuary—the bedroom" (PJ 6.4, 10; Ronald F. Hock, *The Infancy Gospels of James and Thomas: With Introduction, Notes, and Original Text Featuring the New Scholars Version Translation*, ScholBib 3 [Santa Rosa, CA: Polebridge, 1995], 43). Neither version supplies a note supporting the translation. Smid notes a variant reading in 6.3 that "indicates a very close agreement between the sleeping apartment and the sanctuary." He concludes, "In any case it is the author's aim to stress that Mary spends the first years of her life in holy seclusion" (Harm Reinder Smid, *Protevangelium Jacobi: A Commentary* [Assen: Van Gorcum, 1965], 50).

48. The NETS renders ἁγίασμα as "holy precinct" forty-three of the sixty-five times it occurs.

49. Cf. Foskett, *A Virgin Conceived*, 164: "By retaining her virginity *ante partum*, *in partum*, and *post partum*, Mary is transformed from being a *parthenos* in the cult to being a cult object." This in particular emphasizes Mary's passivity: "From the day that she is born, Mary functions less as an active subject and more as an object of exchange and offering" (ibid., 160). Vuong suggests that the depiction of Mary in her early years is analogous to that of a sacred gift prepared for the temple (see Vuong, *Gender and Purity*, 88–106).

Turning now to the blessings themselves, there are several important things to note. First, the blessings are uttered by a group of priests and then by the high priest. In this way, the blessings in chapter 6 differ from how the topos of blessing appears in the Anna cycle discussed above. The relocation of the temple and these "priestly blessings" that are applied to Mary intensify the priestly rhetorolect of PJ. Second, the blessings of the priests and high priest are intended to bestow divine benefit upon Mary:

> God of our fathers, bless [εὐλόγησον] this child and give [δός] to her an illustrious [ὀνομαστός] name forever, in all generations.
> God of the heights, look upon [ἐπίβλεψον] this child and bless [εὐλόγησον] her with an ultimate blessing, which is unsurpassable.[50]

Though the priests or high priest utter the blessing, God is ultimately responsible for fulfilling it. Third, and finally, the imperatives (εὐλόγησον [bis], δός, and ἐπίβλεψον) emphasize the performative nature of these blessings (cf. the perfect form [εὐλογημένη] in Luke 1:42).

Two questions remain to be answered concerning the priests' blessing in PJ 6.2: What is the motivation or cause of the priests' and high priest's blessings of Mary, and what is the nature or intention of their blessings? The answer to the first question—the motivation or cause of the priests' blessing—is not entirely clear from the immediate context, which gives us little reason to think that the priests know of Mary's premature walking or Anna's construction of the ἁγίασμα in Mary's bedroom.

The blessing here may be related to the portrait of Mary earlier in the composition. With Anna's construction of the ἁγίασμα, the author of PJ has depicted Mary as a sacred vessel or even a sacred space. She is surrounded by holy, pure people, even though she is not physically at the temple in Jerusalem. In similar fashion, the blessings of the priests can be understood as the passing-on of their priestly function to Mary. The LXX contains many examples in which a father blesses his son just before he dies,[51] which may be applied to the priestly blessings of Mary here. As a father's final blessing on his son bestows an inheritance in the form of continuing the father's legacy, so also the blessing of the priests represents Mary's inheritance of the legacy of the priests. As a priestly personage,

50. For this translation of ἥτις διαδοχὴν οὐκ ἔχει, see BDAG, s.v. διαδοχή.
51. H. Beyer, "εὐλογέω, εὐλογητός, εὐλογία, ἐνευλογέω," *TDNT* 2:754–65, esp. 756.

Mary has already been the instrument that activates divine benefit in her parents' lives, and the angel's message later in the narrative suggests that she will be used to bring about the benefit of the forgiveness of sins for others (see PJ 11.3). In these important details, PJ has displaced the Jerusalem temple as first space of priestly discourse and has centered it on Mary.

The nature of blessings bestowed on Mary is clearer. The priests ask that God give Mary an "illustrious name, everlasting in all generations," and the high priests ask God to bless Mary with an ultimate and unsurpassable blessing.

An illustrious, everlasting name. The adjective "illustrious" (ὀνομαστός) does not occur in the New Testament, but it appears twenty-one times in the LXX.[52] There are three related uses of the adjective in the LXX: it denotes (1) fame based on action, especially related to political or martial superiority;[53] (2) fame based on one's identity, especially the identity indicated by Israel's special relationship with God; and (3) the fame of one's name.[54]

One example of a "famous name" from the LXX may help clarify the nature of the priests' blessing here. In Gen 12:2, Abraham's name is directly tied to God's blessing. God says to Abraham, "I will make you into a great nation and I will bless [εὐλογήσω] you and I will exalt your name [μεγαλυνῶ τὸ ὄνομα σου], and you will be blessed [ἔσῃ εὐλογητός]." Genesis 12:2 offers a compelling parallel to the blessing of Mary here for two reasons. First, God's blessing of Abram includes the promise of progeny—God promises to make him into a "great nation" that consists of innumerable offspring. This connects with the notion of blessing as procreation in PJ 2–4. Second, and more importantly, God promises to make Abram's name great. In PJ 7.2 and 12.1, the same phrase (μεγαλύνω τὸ ὄνομα σου) is applied to Mary in a priestly blessing. Likewise, in PJ 12.1, the priest

52. The usage in the LXX does not appear to diverge significantly from the use in classical Greek; cf. LSJ. s.v. ὀνομαστός.

53. For fame, see, e.g., Ezek 22:5: "Your fame [ἡ ὀνομαστή] is unclean and great in lawless acts" (NETS); cf. Ezek 23:3. For men of renown (οἱ ἄνθρωποι οἱ ὀνομαστοί), see, e.g., Gen 6:4; cf. ἄνδρες ὀνομαστοί in, e.g., Num 16:2. Judith is said to be famous beyond the whole earth (παρὰ πᾶσαν τὴν γῆν) because of her beauty and wisdom (cf. Jdt 11:21) and presence in Nebuchadnezzar's court (Jdt 11:23).

54. In Isa 56:5, "fame" is connected with one's "name." God speaks of righteous eunuchs: "I will give to them, in my house and within my wall, an esteemed place [τόπον ὀνομαστόν], better than sons and daughters; I will give them an everlasting name [ὄνομα αἰώνιον], and it shall not fail" (NETS).

declares, "You will be blessed [ἔσῃ εὐλογημένη]," which bears strong verbal similarity to God's promise to Abram in Gen 12:2 (ἔσῃ εὐλογητός). On the whole, the priestly blessing in PJ 6.2, in light of the blessings in 7.2 and 12.1, suggests the possibility that the author of PJ has reconfigured the Abramic blessing of Gen 12 and applied it to Mary.[55] Just as Abram activates divine benefit for "all the nations" of the earth (cf. Gen 22:18) as father, Mary similarly activates divine benefit as mother.

An ultimate, unsurpassable blessing. The blessing of the high priest not only repeats aspects of the blessing of the priests earlier in the narrative but also intensifies it in two ways. First, it intensifies the status of the one who utters the blessing: it is said by the high priest, not a group of priests. Second, the nature of the blessing itself is intensified by calling for an "ultimate, unsurpassable" blessing.

The language of the high priest's blessing is rare. The precise meaning of ἔσχατος here is not entirely clear, but it seems to differ from the dominant sense of ἔσχατος in the New Testament, which pertains to the "last" or "end" of something in sequence. The exact phrase ἐσχάτη εὐλογία does not occur in the New Testament or the LXX. For the purposes of this essay, I accept the suggestion that ἔσχατος here means "to furthest extremity in rank, value, or situation."[56] This leads to the translation "ultimate" in the sense that Mary's blessing is "to the furthest extremity" of any possible blessing.

In addition to imploring God for Mary's "ultimate" blessing, the high priest asks for a blessing that is literally "without successor." The feminine noun διαδοχή does not occur in either the New Testament or the LXX; the masculine noun διάδοχος occurs one time in the New Testament (Acts 24:27) and seven times[57] in the LXX. In both the New Testament and the LXX, it refers to a political or religious successor. That Mary's blessing "does not have a successor" suggests that the two modifiers should be understood together to emphasize the utter singularity of the blessing spoken upon Mary. It is the highest "rank" of those blessings that precede it, and there will be no equivalent blessing in the future.

55. Exegetically, this is not far from Paul's reading of Gen 12 in Gal 3. Just as Paul restricts the meaning of Abraham's seed to Jesus (Gal 3:15–16), the reconfiguration of the Abramic blessing to Mary makes her unique offspring the source of blessing to all nations.

56. BDAG, s.v. ἔσχατος.

57. 1 Chr 18:17; 2 Chr 26:11; 28:7; 2 Macc 4:29; 14:26; Sir 46:1; 48:8.

2.4.2.2. Mary Blessed at Three: The Revelation of God's Redemption

The third scene in which Mary is blessed occurs in PJ 7.2. In this chapter, Mary's parents fulfill the promise they had made to dedicate Mary to the temple. Though they originally intend to do so when she is two years old, they decide to wait until she is three lest she "be homesick for her father and mother" and leave the temple (7.1). At three, Anna and Joachim deploy the "undefiled daughters of the Hebrews" with lit torches to prevent the heart of the three-year-old Mary from being enticed (αἰχμαλωτισθήσεται)[58] away from the temple (7.2). It is important to remember that Mary has already been "housed" in God's "holy precinct." Although the location of Mary's dwelling place changes and does so in a significant way, Mary's role as a sacred vessel or sacred space has already been established in PJ 6 by Anna's construction of the ἁγίασμα and by the blessing of the priests.

After Mary's reception into the temple, the narrative recounts the blessing of Mary:

> And the priest received her [ἐδέξατο] her and, after kissing her, he blessed her and said, "The Lord God has begun to make your name great [ἐμεγάλυνεν][59] in all generations. By you [ἐπὶ σοί][60] at the end of days, the Lord will reveal [φανερώσει] his redemption [τὸ λύτρον αὐτοῦ] to the sons of Israel." (PJ 7.2)

The blessing here demonstrates both points of convergence and divergence from the blessings in PJ 6. Most obviously, this blessing, like those in chapter 6, is uttered by a priestly personage. Like the blessing of the priest in PJ 6, the blessing in PJ 7 also concerns the "name" of Mary and its importance "in all generations." The priest's speech contains both a recognition of Mary's blessedness in the present as well as a degree of future orientation, conveyed by the future tense of φανερόω.

The blessing in chapter 7 also contains unique details. This is the only blessing of Mary that includes the priest "kissing" (φιλέω) Mary. Likewise, the location of the blessing has changed—it takes place not in Joachim

58. For this translation of αἰχμαλωτισθῇ ἡ καρδία αὐτῆς ἐκ ναοῦ κυρίου, see BDAG, s.v. αἰχμαλωτίζω.

59. N.B., the form of ἐμεγάλυνεν used here can be translated as either an aorist or an imperfect. An inceptive imperfect ("to begin to…") may be the most appropriate translation given the repetitive nature of εὐλογέω and μεγαλύνω in PJ.

60. For an "instrumental" sense of ἐπί + dative, see Matt 4:4; Mark 10:24; Luke 1:29.

and Anna's house, but in the temple in Jerusalem. The speech itself builds on the blessing of the priest in chapter 6. The tense of μεγαλύνω suggests that the priest's blessing in chapter 6 has been "fulfilled" at least in part—Mary has been given a "famous" name, which is indicated by the fact that the priest here recognizes that it has begun to be "made great." Finally, the priest's blessing indicates that Mary is the instrument by which God's redemption (λύτρον) will be revealed at the end of days.

On the whole, this scene shows that the author of PJ has reconfigured a number of topoi from the New Testament. First, the priest's "reception" of Mary appears to be a reconfiguration of Simeon's "reception" of Jesus in Luke 2:28:

> Luke 2:28: αὐτὸς **ἐδέξατο** αὐτὸ εἰς τὰς ἀγκάλας καὶ **εὐλόγησεν** τὸν θεὸν **καὶ εἶπεν**.
> PJ 7.2: καὶ **ἐδέξατο** αὐτὴν ὁ ἱερεύς, καὶ φιλήσας **εὐλόγησεν** αὐτὴν **καὶ εἶπεν**.

Whereas Simeon has seen God's salvation (εἶδον … τὸ σωτήριον σου) in the infant Jesus, the priest in PJ recognizes the blessing of "redemption" that will be seen through Mary. Here again the author of PJ creates a parallel between the "prehistory" of Jesus—as it emerges in Luke—and that of Mary. Finally, the author of PJ reconfigures the "audience" of this revelation. In Luke, it is directed toward both the gentiles and God's people Israel (Luke 2:32). In PJ, the revelation is exclusively for the sons of Israel.

Next, the priest declares that redemption (λύτρον) will be revealed through Mary. This suggests the reconfiguration of tradition in the New Testament as well. The noun λύτρον occurs only two times in the New Testament and twenty times in the LXX. In the LXX, λύτρον appears most frequently in the legal material: seventeen of the twenty occurrences appear in Exodus, Leviticus, or Numbers. The two occurrences in the New Testament derive from a shared saying in Matt 20:28 and Mark 10:45. In the saying, Jesus states, "The son of Man did not come to be served, but to serve and to give himself [τὴν ψυχὴν αὐτοῦ] as a ransom [λύτρον] for many." Though the precise meaning of λύτρον here may be debated, it likely pertains to the salvific power of Jesus's offering himself for others.[61] Given the likely reconfiguration of Luke 2:28 noted above, it is plau-

61. See discussion in M. Eugene Boring, *Mark: A Commentary*, NTL (Louisville: Westminster John Knox, 2006), 302–4; and W. D. Davies and Dale C. Allison, *A Criti-*

sible to read λύτρον in PJ with the same sense, almost as a replacement for σωτήρια in Simeon's speech.[62] The priest declares that God's saving redemption is revealed "by Mary." His prediction is confirmed later in the narrative when the midwife declares in PJ 19.2, "My soul has been magnified today, because my eyes have seen a paradox, because salvation has been born [ἐγεννήθη] to Israel." In other words, Mary is portrayed as the instrument by which divine benefit is activated for Israel.

Finally, the revelation of God's saving redemption through Mary takes place "at the end of days" (ἐπ᾽ ἐσχάτου τῶν ἡμερῶν). Though this may denote the "end of days" as the time when God's salvation is revealed as in prophetic-apocalyptic discourse,[63] it is also possible to take it as a decisive point in history (e.g., Heb 1:2). In either case, the larger narrative of PJ suggests that the salvation that will be revealed through Mary does not take place at some time in the eschaton, but rather takes place at the end of her pregnancy. Thus the midwife witnesses God's salvation as a present reality (PJ 19.2); the priest's prediction in PJ 7.2, then, comes to fruition and is "seen" by the midwife.

2.4.2.3. Mary's Blessing as a Young Woman: Recognizing Mary's Name

The scene in PJ 7 ends with God casting his grace (χάρις) upon Mary and her dancing on the steps of the altar. The author adds that "all of the house of Israel loved her" (7.3). This in many ways is the high point of Mary's childhood as the object of blessing by priestly personages. The set-apart and multiply blessed "vessel" of God has been relocated from the "holy precinct" of her parent's house to her "proper" place at the steps of the altar in the Lord's house. The fortune of Mary, however, begins to change in PJ 8.2. With the onset of puberty and the inevitable impurity that follows, the priestly personages must find another "house" for Mary.[64] Mary's "guard-

---

cal and Exegetical Commentary on the Gospel according to Saint Matthew, 3 vols., ICC (Edinburgh: T&T Clark, 1988–1997), 3:94–100.

62. See similarly, Foskett, *A Virgin Conceived*, 146: "Just as Luke's Simeon proclaimed the dawning of God's salvation when he beheld Jesus in the temple (Lk 2.30), so does PJ's priest immediately recognize that in Mary the deity will reveal redemption to Israel."

63. E.g., Jer 23:20; Dan 10:14.

64. For a discussion of the purity issues associated with the onset of puberty, specifically associated with menstruation, see Vuong, *Gender and Purity*, 119–47. Her conclusion about the literary significance of the onset of Mary's menstruation aligns with the overall force of my argument: "Most notably, as we shall see, Mary's departure

ian" is selected by miraculous sign, and she is given to Joseph (8.3–9.3). Abandoned (καταλείπω) in Joseph's house, she is nonetheless under the special protection of God: Joseph rightly says to her, "The Lord will guard [διαφυλάξει] you" (9.3). Mary's physical distance from the temple in Jerusalem solidifies her function as the "roving temple" that stands in distinction to the Jerusalem temple.

The next section of PJ (10.1–12.1) concerns the spinning of a curtain for the temple. This section extends the change in Mary's fortune intimated above. Up to this point in the narrative, Mary has been singled out by the priests. In this section, however, her individuality in the eyes of the priests is diminished. Mary, who was blessed with an "ultimate" and "unsurpassable" blessing, fades to near anonymity with the other "undefiled virgins" of Davidic heritage (10.1). The holy vessel of the temple is demoted to one of its many servants. She is selected to spin the purple, not because of her special identity or exceptional blessedness, but rather by the decision of casting lots (10.2).[65]

---

from the Temple allows her to take on her new role as a potential mother" (129). While Vuong derives evidence for her suggestion mostly from biblical and Jewish sources, Jennifer A. Glancy (*Corporal Knowledge: Early Christian Bodies* [Oxford; New York: Oxford University Press, 2010]) doubts the plausibility of exclusively Jewish interests in this incident. Rather, she calls attention to the broader concerns over menstruation in the ancient Mediterranean world, especially the virulent view of menses: "Mary's body is clean and dry in the *Protevangelium of James* because the effluvia associated with pregnancy and childbirth were thought to converge" (Glancy, *Corporal Knowledge*, 112). Protevangelium of James's overall portrait of Mary relates to her sacred role: "The text implies that Mary's body is a sacred space. Mary's womb is Jesus' prenatal sanctuary. It should not be sullied by the usual sordid byproducts of femininity" (109). Given this cultural script, Glancy insists that Mary in PJ never experiences menstruation, but conceives Jesus shortly after leaving the temple. Glancy's position stands in contrast to the earlier position of Shaye J. D. Cohen, "Menstruants and the Sacred in Judaism and Christianity," in *Women's History and Ancient History*, ed. Sarah Pomeroy (Chapel Hill: University of North Carolina Press, 1991), 273–99. He insists, rather, that it "was not paganism but Judaism (and/or Leviticus) that taught early Christianity to regard the menstruant as impure" (287). He adds that excluding menstrauting women from sacred space occurs in early Christianity long before it does in rabbinic Judaism (ibid.). See also Foskett, *A Virgin Conceived*, 149.

65. That Mary's task is actually determined by lot stands in contrast to Joseph's selection as her guardian. The "lot" to determine her guardian was ultimately unsuccessful. It was only after this initial failure that Joseph was selected by a miraculous sign.

It is important to note, then, the way that Mary's identity has changed, especially as it relates to her virginity and purity. Even in Matthew and Luke, Mary is portrayed as a singular virgin—even *the singular* virgin of Isa 7:14. Here, however, she is one among many virgins, one in the company of other undefiled young women. The child who stood at the center of the undefiled daughters of the Hebrews and who was illuminated by their torches in PJ 7 has been subsumed into their midst, barely distinguishable. This has important ramifications for understanding the nature of Mary as a sacred vessel or sacred space. As a virgin, Mary is just one among many before conception.

In the midst of this apparent diminishing in the importance of Mary, a voice reaffirms Mary's blessedness and unique identity. Mary's hearing of the voice and the angel's visit in PJ 11 reconfigures the annunciation found in Luke 1:26–38, and to a degree, the baptism of Jesus as found in Matthew.

First, Mary's hearing of a voice that declares her true identity resembles the baptism of Jesus in the Synoptic tradition, especially in Matthew. In PJ 11, a voice speaks (ἰδοὺ φωνὴ λέγουσα) to Mary and reveals her identity as the one who will conceive by the power of God (11.1, 3). Likewise, in Matthew, a voice speaks (ἰδοὺ φωνή … λέγουσα) of Jesus's true identity as God's Son (Matt 3:17). Though not as immediate in PJ, the declaration in each composition leads the protagonist into the wilderness for testing. In Matt 4:1–11, Jesus faces an adversary in the wilderness whose tests confirm the manner in which he is God's Son (i.e., the refrain, "If you are God's son …"). Similarly, the drink test in PJ 16, which drives Mary into the wilderness, confirms the manner in which she has conceived (i.e., she is declared innocent of any illegal sexual activity).

In addition, the scene in PJ 11 represents the reconfiguration of the Lukan annunciation scene. The beginning of the voice's greeting in PJ 11.1 is identical to Gabriel's greeting in Luke 1:28: "Greetings, favored one. The Lord is with you."[66] Then, the angel adds, "You have been blessed [εὐλογημένη] among women." The perfect form of εὐλογέω reminds Mary (and the reader) of the numerous blessings that have been bestowed on her up to this point in the narrative. It may be significant to note as well that the angel declares that she is blessed "among women" not "among virgins."

66. Unlike Luke, the author has already indicated that Mary is the object of God's favor (χάρις) and protective presence in PJ 7.

Unlike the version in Luke, Mary does not ponder the meaning of the greeting (Luke 1:29). Instead, she returns to her house in fear and takes up her spinning project again (11.2). Shortly after, an angel appears to her inside of her house.

The narrative of PJ at this point more closely aligns with that of Luke 1:30–38, albeit it with important reconfigurations. Many of these reconfigurations move beyond the scope of this essay, but the reconfiguration of Mary's question is of utmost importance. In Luke 1:34, after news of that she will conceive, Mary asks, "How will this be, since I have not known [i.e., had sexual relations with] a man?" Mary's question in Luke relates to her virginity. In PJ 11.2 , she asks, "Will I conceive from the living Lord God, and will I give birth to a child [γεννήσω] as every woman bears children [ὡς πᾶσα γυνὴ γεννᾷ]?" Mary does not ask about the state of her virginity but about the manner of her conception and delivery.[67] In other words, Mary's question concerns the manner in which she will be a mother.[68] In like fashion, the angel's answer conveys how she will become the mother of the "son of the Most High." The angel answers, "Not really, Mary. For the power of the Lord will overshadow you. For this reason, indeed, that set-apart thing [ἅγιον] which is born from you will be called the son of the Most High" (PJ 11.3)[69]

At this point, the author of PJ relocates the angel's saying found in Matt 1:21, which is addressed to Joseph, and applies it to Mary's role as mother: "And you will call his name Jesus; for he will save his people from their sins." The author's relocation of tradition concerning Jesus's birth and purpose aligns with Mary's blessed "instrumentality" elsewhere in PJ, especially in the priest's prediction in 7.2. The priest's prediction, which anticipates the midwife's declaration in 19.2, is here validated by God's heavenly messenger. Mary is blessed with the "ultimate" blessing as mother because she will bear the "ultimate" son, the son of the Most High who is the saving redemption of God's people. With this, the narrative

67. Cf. Edouard Cothenet, "Le Protévangile de Jacques: origine, genre et signification d'un premier midrash chrétien sur la Nativité de Marie," *ANRW* 25.6:4265: "Il no sera question du voeu de virginité de Marie qu'à partir du IVe s., ici la question semble porter sur le mode de l'enfantement et prépare le récit relatif â la *virginitas in partu*."

68. In her otherwise excellent attention to the character development of Mary in PJ, Foskett undervalues the way in which Mary's question in PJ differs from her question in Luke (see Foskett, *A Virgin Conceived*, 151–53).

69. Once again, the account in PJ bears a strong verbal relationship to Luke 1:35.

again resembles Luke's text, in which Mary accepts the angel's message and declares, "Behold, the slave of the Lord who is before him. Let it be to me according to your word" (PJ 11.3; cf. Luke 1:38).[70]

On the heels of Mary's acceptance of the angel's message comes the final "priestly blessing" in both the cycle concerning Mary's blessedness in PJ 6–12 and in the composition as a whole. This final blessing functions as an inclusio around the "priestly blessings" of Mary: PJ 6.2 contains the first blessing of Mary uttered by a priest; PJ 12.1 contains the last. The text reads,

> And she made the purple and the scarlet, and brought[71] [them] up to the priest. And, having received [them], the priest blessed [εὐλόγησεν] her and said, "Mary, the Lord God has begun to make your name great [ἐμεγάλυνεν … τὸ ὄνομά σου], and you will be blessed [ἔσῃ εὐλογημένη] by all the generations of the earth."

In dramatic irony, the astute reader knows that Mary's "great name" pertains not to the material created by her hands for the temple; her great name is not the result of her "work" as one of the undefiled virgins. Rather, her great name pertains to that creation which results from God's power growing inside of her; her great name is due to her "work" as a mother. The language of the second half of the blessing (ἔσῃ εὐλογημένη) bears strong verbal similarity to God's promise to Abram in Gen 12:2 (ἔσῃ εὐλογητός), confirming the suggestion above that the author of PJ has reconfigured God's blessing of Abraham and applied it to Mary.

3. Conclusion

In this essay I have given sustained attention to the meaning of the topos of blessing in PJ. By comparing the depiction of Mary's visit to Elizabeth in PJ with the similar depiction in Luke, I have made several suggestions about the nature of Mary's blessing.

---

70. PJ adds the word κατενώπιον to the Lukan text.

71. Though it lies beyond the scope of this essay, it is interesting to note that in the Synoptics, the verb ἀνάγω is used in reference to Jesus's being brought up before the Jewish religious elite and up to his crucifixion (see Matt 27:2, 31; Mark 14:44, 53; 15:16; Luke 22:66; 23:26. Cf. Luke 21:12, where the verb is used to describe the followers of Jesus being brought up before a variety of accusers.

First, I have emphasized the importance of priestly discourse for understanding not only Mary's visit to Elizabeth, but the whole topos of blessing in PJ. Though at first glance the topoi of praise and blessing appear to be similar in Luke and PJ, the dominant mode of discourse in each creates a unique trajectory for each. In Luke 1–2, praise and blessing come as a result to the fulfillment of God's promises to the nation of Israel in the birth of two prophets, John the Baptist and Jesus. In PJ, praise and blessing result in the activation of divine benefit in the birth of two blessed personages, Mary and Jesus.

Second, I have highlighted the changing nature of Mary's character, especially in the eyes of the priests. In the cycle of "priestly blessings" that begins in 6.2 and extends to 12.1, Mary is depicted as an instrument that leads the priests to praise and glorify God (6.3). With the onset of puberty (8.2), however, the priests' regard for Mary begins to change. She is physically separated from the temple in Jerusalem and is entrusted to another caregiver. Though the priest blesses her in 12.1, he does so not for her singularity, but for her role as one of the many holy virgins of Israel. By PJ 15–16, the priests' regard for Mary has changed completely: she is no longer worthy of blessing, but fit for a curse because of her apparent illicit pregnancy. Though she is absolved of any wrongdoing, she nevertheless falls completely from the attention of the priests.

Third, I have hinted at the ways in which the author of PJ refocuses priestly discourse on Mary. With Anna's construction of the ἁγίασμα for her, Mary inhabits a sacred space and to some degree displaces the Jerusalem temple as a result. Likewise, as a priestly instrument, she supplants the function of the Jerusalem priesthood. She, not the priests, activates divine benefits for other characters in the story. It is not surprising, then, that the narrative ends with priests awaiting the activation of divine benefit, which they do not ultimately receive. They do not receive divine benefit, because they refuse to accept the manner in which Mary is a priestly instrument after she leaves the temple.

Finally, I have suggested that Mary's function as an instrument of God's presence is tied in particular to her role as mother. My argument rests on the particular way in which the topos of blessing has been reconfigured in PJ around conception and childbearing. Anna and Joachim are "blessed"—that is, divine benefits are activated for them—through the conception and birth of Mary. Likewise, Mary is blessed with an ultimate and unsurpassable blessing through conceiving and giving birth to Jesus. I have made the suggestion that the magnification of Mary's name represents a reconfiguration of the Abramic blessing of Gen 12. Just as Abraham's function as father results in the blessing of all people, so Mary's function as mother results in the blessing of all people. In sum, Mary is the ultimate priestly instrument by which God's "saving redemption" is extended to Israel.[72]

The emphasis on Mary's role as mother is related to her role as virgin. As previous scholars have pointed out, one function of PJ as a whole may have been motivated by apologetic concerns about Jesus's identity as the Son of God.[73] I am not denying that Mary's purity and virginity are major emphases in PJ. By calling attention to Mary's role as mother, however, I am suggesting an additional purpose: PJ casts Mary's role as mother in a positive light. By tying Mary's blessedness to her role as mother, PJ suggests that her sanctity does not extract her from "traditional" social norms of childbearing;[74] rather, she is embedded within them, even as she remains a virgin. In this sense, the midwife's response to the virgin birth highlights the significance of Mary's blessing. The midwife has indeed seen a "paradox" (παράδοξος): she has witnessed a virgin be blessed by becoming a mother (PJ 19.2).[75] Her declaration that "salvation has been born to Israel" (PJ 19.2) solidifies the reconfiguration of priestly material from Luke. This statement, spoken by Simeon in the temple, is relocated to the desert, and it comes from the lips of a Hebrew midwife. Mary is a priestly vessel—she is the one who will be blessed by all women—insofar as she is the vessel of God's saving presence, Jesus.

---

72. Elliott comments that Mary "is seen in PJ as an instrument of divine salvation in her own right" (Elliott, "Protevangelium of James," 51).

73. See the pithy summary of the apologetic motives in E-P, 34–45. See further Foskett, *A Virgin Conceived*, 141–64.

74. See, e.g., Peter Brown, *The Body and Society: Men, Women, and Sexual Renunciation in Early Christianity* (New York: Columbia University Press, 1988), 5–9, 53–64. From the perspective of Brown, the emphasis in PJ on childbearing as a source of blessing, in contrast with radical sexual renunciation, may align with the outlook of the Pauline school: "It is striking how many of these [later writers in Pauline tradition] wished to present Paul, an apostle notably fired by the ideal of an 'undistracted' life in Christ, as a man concerned to validate the structures of the married household" (57).

75. "L'insistance du Ps-Jacques à affirmer la virginité dans l'enfantement luiméme est particulièrement déconcertante" (Cothenet, "Le Protévangile de Jacques," 4265). Cothenet suggests the "disconcerting" element may resemble a nascent form of doceticism (cf. Irenaeus, *Haer.* 1.7.2).

Temple Virgin and Virgin Temple: Mary's Body as Sacred Space in the Protevangelium of James

Meredith Elliott Hollman

1. Telling Mary's Story

It is easy to see why early Christians would have been curious about Mary. Despite her essential role in the story of redemption, the New Testament reveals little about her. In the infancy narratives of Matthew and Luke, she takes the stage with no introduction and then fades into the background. The audience is left to wonder who Mary was and why she, of all the young women in Israel, was chosen to bear the Son of God. The Protevangelium of James (PJ) takes up these tantalizing questions, filling in the gaps of the canonical accounts to give Mary a biography and an identity.[1]

In PJ, Mary is *the* central character. An examination of its opening-middle-closing (OMC) texture[2] demonstrates her essential place in the narrative.

Opening (1.1–8.1): Mary's Early Life
- O (1.1–5.2): Miraculous birth, to Anna and Joachim
- M (6.1–3): Infancy
- C (7.1–8.1): Dedication at the temple

1. References to PJ are based on the chapter and verse divisions in Bart D. Ehrman and Zlatko Pleše, *The Apocryphal Gospels: Texts and Translations* (New York: Oxford University Press, 2011), which is also the translation used.

2. For OMC texture as a mode of analysis, see Vernon K. Robbins, *Exploring the Texture of Texts: A Guide to Socio-Rhetorical Interpretation* (Valley Forge, PA: Trinity Press International, 1996), 19–21. O, M, and C in the OMC outlines designate the opening, middle, and closing subsections of the larger opening, middle, and closing sections. Thus, e.g., the O under Middle means the Opening of the Middle.

Middle (8.2–16.3): Mary's Trials as "the Virgin of the Lord"
- O (8.2–10.2): Relocation to Joseph's house
- M (11.1–12.3): The Virgin conceives
- C (13.1–16.3): Accusation and vindication

Closing (17.1–24.4): Mary as Virgin Mother
- O (17.1–18.1): Preparation for birth
- M (18.2–20.4): The virgin birth
- C (21.1–24.4): Herod's wrath

[Epilogue (25.1–4): The Testimony of James]

The canonical gospels tell the story of Jesus, but PJ tells Mary's story.[3]

Mary's chief characteristic in PJ is her absolute virginity. While the Gospel of Luke only calls Mary παρθένος three times (1:27 [2x]; 1:34), in PJ "virgin" becomes her typical designation (9.1; 10.1; 13.1 [2x]; 15.2 [2x]; 16.1; 19.3 [2x]). Protevangelium of James also pushes the topos of virginity further. In Luke, Mary's virginity simply refers to her sexual status; she has not "known a man" (1:34). The miracle of the "virgin birth" is the manner of conception. In PJ, virginity is connected to purity in a broader sense. From birth, Mary is set apart as holy to God—her body guarded against anything "unclean," her movements confined to sanctified places,[4] and her affections directed solely toward "the temple of the Lord." Her condition as *virgo intacta* is the physical sign that Mary's body remains sacred and undefiled. In PJ, the climactic miracle is not the virginal conception, but that giving birth does not violate the Virgin's physical "condition" (φύσις).[5]

As "the Virgin of the Lord," Mary makes an unusual protagonist. On the one hand, she is the main character, whom others bless and praise.

---

3. "In contrast to Luke-Acts, where Mary is at best a secondary character, PJ's extraordinary protagonist is the narrative's *raison d'etre*. Like the heroines of the [Hellenistic] novels, she is a figure of socio-economic, familial, and cultic status that not only is rendered in direct and indirect detail, but explicitly recognized by all the characters with whom she interacts. From the very opening of the narrative, the reader is prepared to construct a Mary who will stand in sharp relief against the unknown virgin of Luke's account" (Mary F. Foskett, *A Virgin Conceived: Mary and Classical Representations of Virginity* [Bloomington: Indiana University Press, 2002], 145–46).

4. Joseph's house, though not a sanctuary, is given special status as Mary's divinely appointed refuge.

5. See PJ 19.3–20.1.

Protevangelium of James may even be described as an encomium of Mary.[6] On the other hand, she is hardly a "character" at all. While Mary is passive and silent, others decide the course of her life, guard her from defilement, and assess her virtue. This is not as surprising as it may seem, since the virtues for which Mary is honored—virginity, purity, innocence—primarily denote a *lack* of something, namely, no sexual experience, no pollution, no blame. Her utter purity seems to leave little room for human personality. She functions like a sacred vessel, receiving and imparting divine blessing, ultimately in her role as *theotokos* (God-bearer).[7] As will be demonstrated later, Mary's body may also be considered a sort of "moving temple," or tabernacle, by which "the Word became flesh and tabernacled among us" (GJohn 1:14).

This paper will focus on PJ 7.1–8.1 (Mary's dedication at the temple) as a window into Mary's role in PJ. In the above OMC schema, this pericope constitutes the closing of the opening in the overall narrative. It is a turning point, marking Mary's transition from the domestic setting of her parents' home to the public (though still enclosed) setting of the temple. This is the culmination of the Anna and Joachim story, as they present their promised "gift" at the altar of God. The opening has begun at the temple, with Joachim presenting offerings but grieved by his lack of children and estranged from his wife. It now closes at the temple, as both Joachim and Anna joyfully present their child as a perfect, living offering. Mary's arrival at the temple also sets the stage for the main story, that of her own career. Her extraordinary upbringing has made her uniquely qualified to serve as "the Virgin of the Lord" (9.1).

---

6. See Foskett, *A Virgin Conceived*, 145–46; and Ronald F. Hock, *The Infancy Gospels of James and Thomas: With Introduction, Notes, and Original Text Featuring the New Scholars Version Translation*, ScholBib 3 (Santa Rosa, CA: Polebridge, 1995), 17. "Hock notes significant correspondence between topoi that occur in the early chapters of *PJ* and the rhetorical conventions of the *egkomion*.... By speaking of Mary's lineage in terms of race (*genos*), providing details about her parents (*pateres*) and ancestry (*progonoi*), and including illustrations of her upbringing (*anatrophe*), the narrative highlights those aspects of Mary's character that the ancients considered most worthy of commendation" (Foskett, *A Virgin Conceived*, 145).

7. Though this precise title was not attributed to Mary until later, the concept is germane to PJ; see Vasiliki Limberis, *Divine Heiress: The Virgin Mary and the Creation of Christian Constantinople* (New York: Routledge, 1994).

2. Mary Moves to the Temple (PJ 7.1–8.1)

OMC Analysis (all caps indicates repetitive texture):

Opening

O: [1] Months passed for the child.

M: When she became two, Joachim said, "Now we should take her up to THE TEMPLE OF THE LORD, to fulfill the promise we made; otherwise the Master may send some harm our way and our gift be deemed unacceptable." Anna replied, "Let's wait until she is three; otherwise she may be homesick for her father and mother."

C: Joachim agreed, "Let us wait."

Middle

O: [2] When the child turned three, Joachim said, "We should call the undefiled daughters of the Hebrews and have them each take a torch and set them up, blazing, that the child not turn back and her heart be taken captive away from THE TEMPLE OF THE LORD." They did this, until they had gone up to THE LORD'S TEMPLE.

M: And the priest of the Lord received her and gave her a kiss, blessing her and saying, "The Lord has made your name great among all generations. Through you will the Lord reveal his redemption to the sons of Israel at the end of time."

C: [3] He set her on the third step of the altar, and the Lord cast his grace down upon her. She danced on her feet, and the entire house of Israel loved her.

Closing

O: [1] Her parents went away

M: marveling, praising and glorifying God, the Master, that the child did not turn back.

C: Mary was in THE TEMPLE OF THE LORD, cared for like a dove, receiving her food from the hand of an angel.

The basic structure of this pericope follows Mary's movement from one place to another. In the opening, she is at her parents' home. The middle describes her transport from home to the temple in Jerusalem. At the closing, Mary is left in the temple, and her parents depart. Although Mary is the centerpiece, she cannot be described as the main character of this pericope. "The child" does very little and has no part in the dialogue. Instead, Anna and Joachim are the main actors. The unit opens with dialogue between them and closes with their reaction to the events. They make the decisions about Mary and move her to the temple. Their faithfulness in bringing their "gift" emerges as a major focus. The repetitive texture ("the Lord's temple," 4x) highlights the temple setting, with its accompanying priestly rhetorolect.[8]

This plot structure recalls familiar scenes from the Old Testament, blending topoi and their clustered associations. One set of associations surrounds the topos of an exceptional child dedicated to God from birth, recalling the story of Hannah and Samuel (1 Sam 1:21–2:11). The cultic setting and priestly rhetorolect also suggest another, more subtle topos: moving the ark of the covenant—or, more broadly, the ritual relocation of divine presence. These streams merge, as Mary's parents dedicate a child so exceptionally set apart that she becomes the locus of God's presence on earth.

3. Toddlers in the Temple: Mary and Samuel (PJ 7.1–8.1; 1 Sam 1:21–2:11)

Let us first reread this pericope through the topos of "a child dedicated to God." Several Old Testament precedents come to mind—Isaac, Samson, Jephthah's daughter—but the most similar story is that of Hannah and Samuel (1 Sam 1:21–2:11). Both tales feature a miraculously conceived child whose mother has promised to offer it for service at the house of God. In each case, the parents rear the child until it is old enough to leave home, then fulfill their promise by "going up" to the temple/sanctuary and delivering the child to the priest. While this tale in PJ is infused with topoi from 1 Samuel, it recasts them to create a different focus. Though the texts are similar, they have few, if any, verbal parallels. Anyone familiar with the story of Hannah and Samuel cannot help but recall it when reading the pericope in PJ, but the resemblance is on the level of plot and topoi rather than particular lexemes.

8. On rhetorolects, see Vernon K. Robbins, *The Invention of Christian Discourse*, vol. 1, RRA 1 (Blandford Forum, UK: Deo, 2009).

Each story's opening (PJ 7.1; 1 Sam 1:21–23) centers on a dialogue between the parents in which the mother suggests keeping the infant home until it can endure separation from its parents. Hannah wishes to wean her son first, and Anna is concerned that if they give Mary up before she is three she will be homesick. Both husbands agree, but they also give mild warnings against failing to deliver the children when the time comes. The structure of the dialogue in the opening of each story, however, is different: in PJ the man speaks first, suggesting that they take the child immediately, while in 1 Samuel the woman begins the conversation, proposing to keep the child home for a couple of years. Unlike in 1 Samuel, in PJ 7.1 the spouses initially disagree, though Joachim quickly concedes to Anna. In both stories, the opening scenes show the women demonstrating more initiative and authority than one might expect in their sociohistorical contexts. This positive portrayal of women's agency and piety is borne out in PJ as a whole, while in 1 Samuel it is less so.[9] By describing a dialogue by both parents rather than a decision by one (accepted by the other), the PJ account gives the impression that both Joachim and Anna are closely caring for Mary, while in 1 Samuel 1 the child is mainly Hannah's concern. Eli allows Hannah to do as she pleases, but Joachim actively participates in Anna's plan for Mary (contrast 1 Sam 1:23, "may the Lord establish the word of *your* mouth" with PJ 7.1, "to fulfill the promise *we* made," though in 4.1 the promise was Anna's alone). Their shared commitment to delivering Mary as an "acceptable gift" reflects their piety. It also reveals Mary's unusual status as a child set apart. Her parents do not regard her as their own (they refer to her as "the child"), but as a holy person temporarily in their care. The obsessive measures Anna has taken to preserve Mary's purity go far beyond anything in the Old Testament stories of dedicated children. Mary is truly exceptional. Unlike Samuel, who receives yearly visits from his mother (1 Sam 2:19–20), Mary apparently has no further contact with her parents. Anna and Joachim disappear after PJ 8.1, leaving her with no family. Mary belongs to the Lord alone.

The middle sections of the two accounts (PJ 7.2–3; 1 Sam 1:24–2:10) both describe the parents' bringing their children up to the sanctuaries and presenting them to the priests. They differ, however, at two significant points. First, while both stories include someone's uttering a benediction

9. For example, the young women serving at Shiloh are a cause of sin, since Eli's wicked sons sleep with them (1 Sam 2:22).

(PJ 7.2; 1 Sam 2:1–10), in 1 Samuel it is Hannah's praising God, while in PJ it is the high priest's blessing Mary. Second, PJ concludes the middle section with details of Mary's happy reception in her new home: the Lord bestows grace on her, she dances "on her feet" (presumably the first time she has been "on her feet" since her seven steps at age six months; 6.1),[10] and "the entire house of Israel" loves her (7.3). In 1 Samuel the middle section ends with Hannah's praise to God. These two differences in PJ create a greater emphasis on the exceptional nature of the child being dedicated (Mary). In 1 Samuel 1–2 the focus is on God's grace to Hannah, and nothing is said at this point about Samuel's character.

The closings (PJ 8.1–2; 1 Sam 2:11) also exhibit similar structures. The parents depart, and the children begin temple service. Two distinctive elements in PJ, however, emphasize Mary's perfection. In the middle of the closing, Mary's parents are amazed and praise God because "the child did not turn back" (8.1). First Samuel contains no such detail. Considering the extreme circumstances of the parting in PJ (Mary is only three, has never known anyone but her parents and the "undefiled daughters of the Hebrews," and is being left with strangers for the rest of her life), the child's not turning back borders on the miraculous. It certainly demonstrates her single-minded (pure) devotion (cf. 7.2, "that the child *not turn back* and her heart be taken captive away from the Temple of the Lord"). Mary's parents also exhibit their absolute devotion to God (cf. Hannah's song in 1 Sam 2:1–10), by being pleased when their child does not even watch them leave. A second distinction also portrays Mary's unparalleled purity. While 1 Samuel simply reports, "The lad was ministering to the face of the Lord" (2:11), PJ adds that while Mary was in the temple, she was "cared for like a dove, receiving her food from the hand of an angel" (8.1).

Overall, the structural similarity between the two pericopes suggests that the Old Testament story of Hannah and Samuel serves as a resource text for PJ 7.1–8.1, though not a "source text" in the sense of direct literary

10. "When she was six months old, her mother set her on the ground, to see if she could stand. She walked seven steps and came to her mother's bosom. Her mother lifted her up and said, 'As the Lord my God lives, you will not walk at all on this ground until I have taken you up to the Temple of the Lord' " (PJ 6.1). The Greek syntax (ἕως σε ἀπάξω ἐν τῷ ναῷ Κυρίου) does not specify whether Mary will be allowed to walk when the family sets out for the temple ("until I *take* you up to the temple") or only once they have arrived ("until I *have taken* you up to the Temple," as in Ehrman's translation). I find the latter more likely, based on narrative details to be discussed below.

dependence.[11] In addition, the placement of the account of Joachim and Anna taking Mary to the temple gives the PJ story a special focus. First Samuel 1:21–2:11 centers on Hannah's faith and God's grace to her. Protevangelium of James 7.1–8.1 is partly about the faith of Mary's parents, but in light of the internal narrative structure and the pericope's place in PJ as a whole, the main focus is on the perfection of the child Mary. There is a detail about Mary's pure and acceptable state before God at the center of the opening, the middle, and the closing of the PJ account. At the center of the opening is Joachim's concern to fulfill their promise about Mary so that she will be acceptable as a gift to God. At the center of the middle (and thus at the emphatic center of the entire pericope), the high priest pronounces his blessing on the little girl: her parents have fulfilled their trust, and Mary is pleasing to God. At the center of the closing section the child does not turn back as her parents leave her at the temple. This is the final sign to the parents that Mary is absolutely pure in her affections.

4. Mary as "Acceptable Gift" and Sacred Vessel

Like Samuel, Mary is dedicated "to minister" before the Lord (λειτουργῶν, 4.1; the same word is used of Samuel in LXX 1 Kgdms 2:11, 18). Her ministry, however, takes a very different shape. Samuel immediately begins assisting Eli with priestly duties, and a few years later he begins receiving "the word of the Lord." He becomes a leader in Israel, active and vocal. Mary, however, is remarkably passive and silent. The difference is already present at the end of these parallel accounts. After Samuel's parents leave, "the boy remain[s] to minister to the Lord" (1 Sam 2:11); after Anna and Joachim leave, "Mary was in the Temple of the Lord, cared for like a dove, receiving her food from the hand of an angel" (PJ 8.1). Mary is not "ministering" in the temple; she is just present there. Furthermore, she herself *is being ministered to*, "cared for" and fed by an angel.

In contrast to the account of Samuel, therefore, Mary arrives at the temple strictly as a "gift" prepared by others, and once she is in the temple the careful bodily care continues. Mary functions like a sacred *object*, pure but passive. In PJ 6.1–8.1, Mary's parents show complete control over her. She is their "gift" to God, apart from any decision on her own part, and they take it upon themselves to guard her against any hint of impurity. Anna

11. On resource texts, see examples in Robbins, *Invention*, 405–6, 504–5.

has controlled every detail of Mary's young life. She will not nurse the baby until after her own ritual purification, makes an extra vow that she will not let Mary "walk at all on this ground" until she goes to the temple, confines Mary to her bedroom sanctuary, meticulously monitors her kosher diet, and recruits "the *undefiled* daughters of the Hebrews" to entertain the child. The parents' extreme care continues when Joachim calls the "undefiled daughters of the Hebrews" to escort Mary on the journey to the temple. They carry torches (presumably at night) to prevent the three-year-old from seeing anything beyond the circle of her entourage, lest she "turn back and her heart be taken captive away from the Temple of the Lord." Mary's purity is thus the result of her parents' fulfilling of their "promise"; she herself has been passive. She arrives at the temple as a human present, and the priest "receive[s] her." He blesses her, not for anything she has done, but because of what God will do in and through her: "The Lord has made your name great.... Through you will the Lord reveal his redemption" (7.2). He sets her on the altar steps, symbolically giving her to God, and God responds by "cast[ing] his grace down upon her" (7.3).

To this point, Mary has been passive, exercising no control over her own body. After she is at the altar, however, she "dance[s] on her feet" (7.3). This moment in the story stands out as an apex in Mary's life. She exercises agency over her own body and dances before the Lord, as though accepting her place as "the Lord's Virgin" in the temple. Her contentment with her new home is further demonstrated when her parents leave and she does not "turn back," as a normal toddler would do. She is loved by "the entire house of Israel" and seems to be a favorite of the priests. The account ends with Mary's being "cared for like a dove" (a symbol of purity, but also a helpless pet). She does not even feed herself or eat common food; she is fed "from the hand of an angel" (8.1).

This pattern of passivity is consistent with Mary's character in the rest of PJ. When she turns twelve, others decide what to do with her, and she is handed over to Joseph for safekeeping. Joseph does not want her in his house, so he leaves her alone there for four years while he travels for work. We are not told anything about Mary's reaction. When the angel announces her coming pregnancy, she submits to God's will, but her primary emotions are fear and confusion. There is no Magnificat. Instead, Mary inexplicably *forgets* the angel's words! When confronted first by Joseph and then by the high priest, she can give no explanation for her pregnancy; she can only weep and insist that she is a virgin. Even when she becomes a mother, she does not "give birth" in the usual sense. The baby simply *appears*, as light. Even after her time as a gift in the temple, then, her passive life continues as she is assigned to Joseph, pronounced into pregnancy, and manifested into motherhood.

In the context of Mary's passivity, the small amount of her speech exhibits well her lack of agency. Mary does not speak at all in chapters 6–10. All of her speech occurs in chapters 11–17, even though she continues to be present in the narrative into chapter 22. All in all, Mary speaks a total of eight times, and each time she speaks only briefly. Her first statement is a question, occurring at 11.6: "If I actually conceive by the Lord, the living God, will I also give birth the way women usually do?"[12] The second time she speaks, she submits to God's will: "Here I am, the Lord's slave before him. I pray that all you've told me comes true" (11.9). After this, Mary asks a second question, at 12.6: "Who am I, Lord, that every generation on earth will congratulate me?" This question indicates Mary's puzzlement with what is happening to her, and this puzzlement continues as the story moves forward. The next three times Mary speaks, she defends herself against accusations that she has not been true to her holiness: (1) "I'm innocent. I haven't had sex with any man" (13.8). (2) "As the Lord my God lives, I don't know where it came from" (13.10). (3) "As the Lord God lives, I stand innocent before him. Believe me, I've not had sex with any man" (15.13). With no speech either in chapter 14 or 16, her last two statements occur in chapter 17. Along the road to Bethlehem, a concerned Joseph asks why Mary appears downcast at one moment and joyful the next. She responds by describing a prophetic vision: "Joseph, it's because I imagine two peoples in front of me, one weeping and mourning and the other celebrating and jumping for joy" (17.9).[13] The last time Mary speaks, she instructs Joseph to help her off the donkey because it is time for the baby to be born (10). After this, Mary does not speak, either in the context of the birth of Jesus or afterward.

---

12. The PJ text and numbering in this paragraph is based on Hock, *Infancy Gospels* (see n. 6).

13. This lone prophecy by Mary may be explained by the nearness of the birth. Immediately afterward, Mary says, "The child inside me [τὸ ἐν ἐμοί] is pressing on me to come out" (17.3 [Ehrman and Pleše]). "That which is in her" is the Word, so it is fitting that a prophetic word would "come out" of Mary at this point. The prophecy of "two peoples, one weeping and mourning and the other happy and rejoicing" (17.2 [Ehrman and Pleše]), soon finds at least partial fulfillment. The midwives rejoice at the birth of Jesus, while Herod's cruelty causes mourning in Bethlehem.

Why should Mary be so passive? A feminist hermeneutic might attribute it to androcentric gender stereotypes. This was my initial hypothesis. Mary's quiet submission, childlike innocence, and lack of sexual desire resemble Hellenistic moralists' ideals for women, as well as many early Christian portraits of female saints and martyrs. Qualities like these continue to be valued as "feminine" in many cultures today. For men, however, assertiveness and powerful speech were (and are) prized. While gender likely plays some role, an unbiased look at the text of PJ reveals that it cannot be the entire basis for Mary's passive characterization. Other female characters (Anna, Judith, Elizabeth, the two midwives) have more than their share of agency and speech. Anna even takes the lead in dealing with Mary, and at the beginning of this pericope she overrules Joachim (7.1). The female characters often demonstrate more understanding than the males.[14] The very nature of PJ, as an "infancy gospel" about Mary, makes it "the only narrative in earliest Christian tradition that recounts the birth of a female protagonist."[15]

The dedication of a female to serve in the temple is unusual, since the Old Testament priesthood was exclusively male. The virgin daughters of priests and Levites were allowed to share their fathers' food from the offerings, but there is no positive mention of their sharing in cultic responsibilities. In the Second Temple period, women were not permitted into the temple proper, but were allowed only in the "Court of the Women."[16] There are, however, a few biblical examples of women serving in or around the temple/tabernacle. Exodus 38:8 mentions "the women who served at the entrance to the Tent of Meeting" (LXX: τῶν νηστευσασῶν αἳ ἐνήστευσαν παρὰ τὰς θύρας τῆς σκηνῆς τοῦ μαρτυρίου), who apparently donated their mirrors to make the bronze basin for the tabernacle. First Samuel 2:22 also mentions "the women who served at the entrance to the Tent of Meeting," with whom Eli's wicked sons sinned. In the New Testament,

14. Faced with their childlessness, Joachim goes out into the desert and sulks (1.4), while Anna, at the rebuke of her maid, cleans herself up and prays to God (2.4). The priests make no prior preparations for Mary's inevitable menarche, but must rush to find a last-minute solution (8.2). Joseph tries to refuse his role as guardian, then shirks his duty by leaving home (9.2–3). The priests and Joseph blame Mary when they discover her pregnancy (13.1–14.1; 15.1–16.2), but Elizabeth seems to have prophetic insight (12.2). The midwives respond to the birth of Christ with praise (19.2–20.3), but Herod goes on a killing spree (21.1–23.3).

15. Foskett, *A Virgin Conceived*, 141.

16. See Josephus, *J.W.* 5.2–3, 6.

there is the old widow Anna, a "prophet" who "never left the temple, but worshipped day and night, fasting and praying" (Luke 2:36–37).[17] Even these few female ministers may be viewed as liminal figures. The women at the Tent of Meeting serve "at the entrance," not inside. Though the text is not explicit, it is possible that these women had to be virgins,[18] which would explain why the sin of Eli's sons was so heinous. Anna occupies a somewhat ambiguous social status, as a woman who became a widow very early in life and separated herself from society. On the whole, women are rarely associated with the Jewish temple, much less with ministerial roles.[19] While PJ stretches historical plausibility by assuming that a young girl *could* be dedicated to the temple, the priests' consternation over what to "do with" Mary when she reaches age twelve indicates that her situation was unusual. The portrayal in PJ is motivated by the theological and literary goals of the author(s).[20] The narrative's purpose of showing Mary's exceptional holiness overrides a concern for historical realism.

In any case, Mary's role as "God-bearer" (*theotokos*)[21] problematizes her place in the gendered hierarchy of the ancient world. As the "virgin

17. The account of Anna may provide an "opening" in the Lukan resource text for the author of PJ to envision a similar temple ministry for Mary.

18. The Hebrew, נָשִׁים, is the generic term for "women," and reveals nothing about their age or sexual status. The LXX omits the second half of 1 Sam 2:22 and reads only, "Now Eli was very old and he heard of the things his sons were doing to the sons of Israel" (translation mine). The omission is understandable because the sons' crime of sleeping with these women is not mentioned earlier in 1 Sam 2:12–17, where their sin involves "treating the Lord's offering with contempt" (2:17) by taking the best portions of sacrificial meat for themselves.

19. Greek and Roman cults, however, required women as well as men for their rites. Most relevant to PJ are the Vestal virgins, who tended the sacred hearth of Vesta in the city of Rome.

20. On PJ 7.1–9.11, Foskett comments, "The narrative continues to chronicle Mary's *anatrophe* [upbringing] with a development that reveals ignorance of Jewish cultic traditions" (*A Virgin Conceived*, 146). Contrast Megan Nutzman, "Mary in the Protevangelium of James: A Jewish Woman in the Temple?" *GRBS* 53 (2013): 551–78. Nutzman argues that PJ's account of Mary in the temple does *not* demonstrate the author's ignorance of Judaism. Instead, "the author structures his narrative to evoke three groups of Jewish women with special privileges in the temple cult"—"accused adulteresses," "girls who wove the temple curtains," and "female Nazirites" (552). Though this article is well worth reading, I find its argument unconvincing.

21. This title was not formally adopted until the third ecumenical council (431 CE), where the debate centered on the two natures of Christ rather than on Mary's

of the Lord," Mary embodies uncompromised receptivity to the divine. In this receptive role, she may be considered supremely "feminine" by ancient Mediterranean standards—submissive, obedient, and passive. But her receptivity is toward the *divine*, not toward a man. Her function as the physical locus of the incarnation gives her greater proximity to God than any other human being (except Jesus). Mary's silence arises not from her gender, but from her role in salvation. She is the pure *vessel* through which the Logos becomes incarnate. "Vessel" may be an especially helpful metaphor when reading PJ. Mary is called "blessed" because of what God does in and through her, not because of her own merit or actions.[22] While PJ certainly portrays Mary as an extraordinary individual, her personal credentials are the result of her divine election, not its cause. She proves herself worthy of her calling by her composure at the well (11.1–3), her endurance before unjust accusations (13.2–3; 15.3), and her hiding of Jesus in a manger (22.2). Still, only her delivery of the spun thread to the high priest (12.1) and her journey to visit her relative Elizabeth (12.2–3) show her engaged in positive actions driven by her own motivation. All of her other actions are defensive, reactions to problematic circumstances that come upon her. Overall, she is rarely an active agent in the story. Her primary role is to be a holy, pure vessel that can carry the Logos in her body for nine months. In this light, Mary's first action at the temple is especially appropriate. She does not speak, but instead she *dances*—presenting her embodied self to God as a pure vessel of grace.

5. The Locus of Divine Presence

As a holy vessel on which the divine presence comes to rest, Mary's body becomes the locus of sacred space. She is like a new "moving temple," tabernacle, or ark of the covenant. Indeed, comparison with the temple/tabernacle/ark of God's presence in the Hebrew Bible reveals another dimension of PJ 7.1–8.1—its structural similarity with the movement of the Old

role. It is, however, attested earlier in theological works (possibly in Origen's *Commentary on Romans*, as cited in Socrates, *Ecclesial History* 7.32; confirmed use by Athanasius in 330) and liturgy (Coptic Orthodox Hymn *Sub Tuum Praesidium*, ca. 250). These too probably postdate PJ, but even if the title was not officially being used, the topos of Mary as "God-Bearer" or "Mother of God" likely existed at an earlier date.

22. See Christopher T. Holmes, "Who Am I To Be Blessed? Mary as Blessed Mother in the Protevangelium of James," in this volume, 67–101.

Testament ark, under the topos "relocation of sacred space." This topos is less obvious, but comparison with Exod 39–40, 1 Chr 15–16, and 2 Chr 5–7 gives strong evidence of its presence.

These Old Testament passages narrate the three major movements of the ark of the covenant before Nebuchadnezzar took it. In Exod 39–40, Moses finishes constructing the tabernacle and places the ark inside it. In 1 Chr 15–16 (parallel 2 Sam 6), David moves the ark from the house of Obed-Edom to a tent in Jerusalem. In 2 Chr 5–7 (parallel 1 Kings 8), Solomon brings the ark from the tent into the temple. These five texts (counting the parallels) demonstrate a remarkably similar plot structure.[23] Together, they reflect a basic narrative pattern and conventional elements for the topos "moving the ark." Here is a generalized account:

Opening

O: The ark's movement is delayed, as preparations must be made.[24]
M: The leader assembles the Israelites to "bring up" the ark.[25]
C: A select group of priests picks up the ark, and the procession starts.[26]

Middle

O: The procession advances, with rejoicing and ritual observances.[27]
M: The ark reaches its destination and is placed there.[28]
C: The glory of God descends on the ark's new home.[29]

---

23. Slightly less so for Exod 39–40, but the basic pattern holds.

24. Exod 39:32 (the Israelites make preparations); 1 Chr 15:1 (delay at the house of Obed-Edom; David's building projects; David prepares the tent); 2 Chr 5:1 (Solomon finishes building the temple and brings in the things David has dedicated).

25. Exod 39:33–43 (the Israelites bring what they have made to Moses); 1 Chr 15:3 (David assembles "all Israel," "to bring up the ark of the Lord to its place"); 2 Chr 5:2–4 (Solomon assembles "all the Israelites" "to bring up the ark of the covenant of the Lord").

26. 1 Chr 15:2, 4–15 (Levites carry the ark); 2 Chr 5:4 (Levites carry the ark); cf. Exod 40:1–15 (God instructs Moses on setting up tabernacle; no one else may enter).

27. 1 Chr 15:25–29; 2 Chr 5:5–6; Exod 40:16–33 (Moses does the work of setting up the tabernacle).

28. 1 Chr 16:1; 2 Chr 5:7–10; Exod 40:30–31.

29. Exod 40:34–35; 2 Chr 5:11–14; 7:1–4. This element is absent in 1 Chr 15–16 and its parallel in 2 Sam 6.

Closing

O: The leader blesses the congregation and leads them in praise/prayer.[30]

M: The sanctuary and/or its ministers are dedicated, with prayers, sacrifices, and rejoicing.[31]

C: The congregation goes home happy.[32]

Now let us look at PJ 7.1–8.1 (Moving Mary) again, in light of the above pattern:

Opening

O: [1] Months passed for the child.

M: When she became two, Joachim said, "Now we should take her up to the Temple of the Lord, to fulfill the promise we made; otherwise the Master may send some harm our way and our gift be deemed unacceptable." Anna replied, "Let's wait until she is three; otherwise she may be homesick for her father and mother."

C: Joachim agreed, "Let us wait."

Middle

O: [2] When the child turned three, Joachim said, "We should call the undefiled daughters of the Hebrews and have them each take a torch and set them up, blazing, that the child not turn back and her heart be taken captive away from the Temple of the Lord." They did this, until they had gone up to the Lord's Temple.

M: And the priest of the Lord received her and gave her a kiss, blessing her and saying, "The Lord has made your name great among all generations. Through you will the Lord reveal his redemption to the sons of Israel at the end of time."

C: [3] He set her on the third step of the altar, and the Lord cast his grace down upon her. She danced on her feet, and the entire house of Israel loved her.

---

30. 1 Chr 16:2–36; 2 Chr 6:1–42; cf. Exod 39:43.

31. 1 Chr 16: 4–42; 2 Chr 7:4–9; in Exodus, the dedication takes place later, but instructions for it are given in 40:9–15.

32. 1 Chr 16:43; 2 Chr 7:10; the parallel in Exodus is later, after the dedication, though this pericope ends with a reference to the Israelites' movements (40:36–38).

Closing

O: [1] Her parents went away

M: marveling, praising and glorifying God, the Master, that the child did not turn back,

C: Mary was in the Temple of the Lord, cared for like a dove, receiving her food from the hand of an angel.

In the opening, Mary's transport is anticipated but delayed (7.1; cf. O of O [i.e., "opening of opening"] in "moving the ark" above). The middle opens with the assembly of "the undefiled daughters of the Hebrews," for the purpose of "taking up" Mary to the temple (7.2); compare above the leader's assembling of "the Israelites to bring up the ark" (M of O), and "a select group picks up the ark and the procession begins" (C of O; they are also "undefiled").

In the Old Testament accounts, the ark is carried on the shoulders of Levites (1 Chr 15:15; 2 Chr 5:7–8). Protevangelium of James does not explicitly say that Mary is being carried to the temple, but the surrounding material implies it. We know from PJ 6.1 that Mary is not allowed to walk on the ground until her parents have "taken her up to the Temple of the Lord,"[33] so she probably does not walk to the temple. In 7.3, the priest "set[s] her on the third step of the altar," which suggests that after "receiving" her (from her parents' arms), he has carried her to the altar. Joachim, Anna, and the Hebrew virgins surround Mary in a little procession (7.2, O of M), as in the Old Testament the Israelites process around the ark (O of M, "moving the ark"). Their "torches" add a ritualistic and perhaps celebratory touch, though the musical instruments, songs, and wild dancing of the Old Testament processions are absent. Protevangelium of James does mention dancing later, as Mary "dances on her feet" upon the step of the altar (7.3, C of M).

Mary's arrival at the temple occurs at the very center of the pericope (7.2, M of M), just as the ark's arrival marks the center point of the three Old Testament scenes (M of M above). The priest then "blesses" Mary (7.2; M of M), as the king blesses the congregation upon the ark's arrival at its destination (O of C above). The content of this "blessing" also fills the narrative role of the praises and prayers in the Old Testament ark-moving

33. After Mary's first seven steps, "Her mother lifted her up and said, 'As the Lord my God lives, you will not walk at all on this ground until I have taken you up to the Temple of the Lord'" (6.1). At the birthday feast, they apparently carry her around.

scenes. Though there is no bright cloud in this PJ pericope (it comes later, in ch. 20), the descent of divine presence is not absent. After the priest has presented Mary by placing her on the altar, "the Lord cast[s] his grace down upon her" (7.3; C of M; cf. the descent of the cloud at C of M in 2 Chr 6). This receipt of grace foreshadows God's "overshadowing" Mary in the future (11.3; 19.2), making a connection to the Old Testament cloud of glory all the more likely.

Like the Old Testament sanctuaries with their priests and instruments, Mary is then dedicated/consecrated and installed in her office of service (7.3–8.1; C of M and C of C; compare "moving the ark," M of C). The element of communal rejoicing (M of C, "moving the ark") is also present here in PJ: "The entire house of Israel" loves Mary (7.3; C of M). As our pericope closes, Anna and Joachim go home "marveling, praising and glorifying God, the Master" (8.1; M of C), like the Israelite congregations before them (C of C, "moving the ark"; cf. 2 Chr 7:10, "He sent the people away to their homes, joyful and in good spirits because of the goodness that the Lord had shown to David and to Solomon and to his people Israel").

In addition to its opening-middle-closing texture, the repetitive texture of PJ 7.1–8.1 also links it to these Old Testament scenes about moving the ark. "The Temple of the Lord" occurs four times in this small unit and receives frequent mention in the rest of PJ as well. The "moving the ark" scenes of Exodus and 1–2 Chronicles[34] all exhibit the repetitive texture of "the ark of the Lord" and its variants ("the ark of God," "the ark of the covenant of the Lord," "the ark," etc.). They also repeat the name of the ark's destined sanctuary: in Exod 39–40, "the tabernacle" (also "the tent of meeting," "the tabernacle of the tent of meeting," etc.); in 1 Chr 15–16, the "place" prepared for it; in 2 Chr 5–7, "the temple" or "the house of God" ("house of the Lord," "the house," "the house for the name of the Lord," etc.). The priestly rhetorolect further reflects the cultic setting within which the topos "moving the sanctuary" naturally belongs.

The Mary/tabernacle correlation is reflected not only in the manner of her relocation, but also in the fact that she is relocated. In the course of the narrative, she is frequently transported from place to place. Changes of residency occur at turning points in the narrative—from her sanctuary bedroom to the temple (7.2), from the temple to Joseph's house (9.3). In addition to these major movements, there are many minor changes

34. Also true of their parallels in 2 Samuel and 1 Kings.

of location. Mary rarely "goes" anywhere; instead, someone else usually "takes" or "brings" her, as a holy object like the tabernacle would be carried about. The locations seem to have little significance in themselves, with the major exception of the Jerusalem temple. The climactic event of Mary's career, the birth of Jesus, occurs in the most insignificant of places—a cave in the "wilderness" (ἔρημος, 17.3) far from her intended destination. Protevangelium of James here diverges from Matthew and Luke, both of which locate Jesus's birth in Bethlehem.[35] By placing the birth in the middle of a journey (μέσον τῆς ὁδοῦ, 17.3), the author highlights Mary's itinerancy and links it to her role as embodied tabernacle.

A "tabernacle" is a mobile tent, not a fixed structure. Movement itself belongs to the topos "sacred space" in the Old Testament, related to the prominent topoi of "wandering," "wilderness," and election.[36] The people of God are "wanderers on the earth," who leave the security of what they know to pursue what God has promised them (Heb 11:13–16; Ps 105:8–13). God commands Abram, "Go from your country and your kindred and your father's house to the land that I will show you" (Gen 12:1; cf. Heb 11:8). Israel becomes "God's own possession" when God leads them out of Egypt, towards the promised land (Ps 114:1–2). At the exile, they are again uprooted, to become "sojourners and aliens" again. Early Christians, who saw themselves in continuity with Old Testament Israel, adopted this cluster of topoi to describe themselves as "foreigners" and "exiles" in the present sinful world (Heb 11:39–40; 1 Pet 1:1, 17; 2:18; cf. Phil 3:20; GJohn 17:14–16). Pilgrimage becomes a metaphor for the life of faith, which surrenders worldly sources of security (leaving a familiar, settled place) and places its trust in God's promise (the "inheritance" at the journey's end) (1 Pet 1:1–5). The wilderness is the in-between, in which the journey of faith takes place. In the wilderness, God encounters people in a formative way (see Exod 40:36–38; Ezek 20:35; Hos 2:14; Acts 7:38; the Hebrew name for the book of Numbers means "in the wilderness").[37]

---

35. Luke 2:4–6; Matt 2:1. Luke's statement that Mary "laid [the baby] in a manger, because there was no place for them in the inn" (2:7) provides a potential opening for this development in PJ.

36. From *lectio* ("to choose") plus *ex* ("out of"). Being "elect" thus implies a dissociation from the commonplace and familiar, like a spiritual change of address. The following discussion reads OT theology in light of its reception in the NT (especially Hebrews), under the assumption that the Christian author of PJ would have done so.

37. "Wilderness" may function similarly to the primordial chaos ("the deep" in

Unlike the "gods of the nations," the God of Israel has dominion over the whole earth and is not bound to one place. When God delivers the Israelites from bondage in Egypt, the visible sign of divine presence goes before them as a cloud of fire or smoke (Exod 13:21–22). The ark and tabernacle, upon which the cloud periodically settles, become permanent physical signs of God's presence among the people. They are carried at the head of the caravan by day and placed in the center of the camp each night (Exod 40:36–38; Num 10:33–36).[38] The ark leads the Israelites' procession into the promised land; as long as the priests carrying it stand in the Jordan, the people can cross on dry land (Josh 3:1–4:18). During the time of the Judges, the ark moves about periodically, coming to rest in various sanctuaries. First Chronicles suggests that the transition from tabernacle to temple was problematic precisely because the temple was a fixed structure (a "house," instead of a "tent").

> Now when David settled in his house, David said to the prophet Nathan, "I am living in a house of cedar, but the ark of the covenant of the Lord is under a tent." Nathan said to David, "Do all that you have in mind, for God is with you."
>
> But that same night the word of the Lord came to Nathan, saying: "Go and tell my servant David: Thus says the Lord: You shall not build me a house to live in. For I have not lived in a house since the day I brought out Israel to this very day, but I have lived in a tent and a tabernacle. Wherever I have moved about among all Israel, did I ever speak a word with any of the judges of Israel, whom I commanded to shepherd my people, saying, Why have you not built me a house of cedar?" (1 Chr 17:1–6)

David's well-intentioned plan seems to be at fault for two related reasons. First, it is *David's* plan, rather than God's ("Did I ever speak a word…?" v. 6);

Gen 1:2). Both represent potentiality yet unformed (or uninhabited, uncivilized), out of which God creates. As the material world receives form out of "the deep," the covenant community develops its character "in the wilderness." God also uses wilderness experiences to shape individuals. From an anthropological perspective, "wilderness" in the OT is related to liminality.

38. In Num 14:44, an ill-fated group "presumed to go up to the heights of the hill country" for battle, "even though the ark of the covenant of the Lord, and Moses, had not left the camp." The absence of the ark represents their attempt to seize what God has promised on their own terms and by their own strength. God is not "with them" in their purpose.

in the Old Testament cultus, correct worship is dictated by God. Second, a fixed temple might appear to anchor God to one location, as though God no longer "moved about among all Israel" (v. 6). Both of these errors represent an attempt to domesticate God, to have religion on human terms.[39] Israel's relationship to the covenant God depends on divine grace, which must always be received as a gift rather than presumed as a fixed possession. God is thus free to act unexpectedly, even paradoxically. Protevangelium of James portrays the birth of Mary's child as the paradox by which God bestows grace in a completely new way. Access to God is no longer bound to a building, a nation, or a priesthood.[40]

The presentation of Mary as virgin temple implies a critique of the previous temple and, by extension, the entire "old covenant." The Romans destroyed the Second Temple long before PJ was written, but "James" never mentions the fact. Instead, the narrative's progression implicitly characterizes the old temple as defunct, even while it stood. The Protevangelium opens at the temple, with Joachim offering sacrifices. The temple cultus appears functional, but it is already being called into question. When the high priest forbids the childless Joachim to offer his sacrifices, he presumptuously passes judgment on a person favored by God. Anna and Joachim receive God's promise when they are far from the temple. The temple authorities are not vilified, but they do not understand what God is doing through Mary. Protevangelium of James ends where it began, at the temple, which has become dysfunctional. Stones covered in priestly blood portend its coming destruction. Against this backdrop, Mary's tabernacle-like movements suggest the provisional nature of the old cultus. Hebrews reasons that the ritual institutions of the Old Testament, including ark, tabernacle, and temple, had been "shadows" of the new covenant in Christ (10:1).[41] God's promise to Abraham was only provisionally fulfilled when

---

39. A constant threat to Israel's covenant identity is the desire to be "like all the other nations," especially by adopting their forms of worship. A more serious misjudgment is recounted in 1 Sam 3–5, a generation before David. The Israelite army attempts to secure God's aid against the Philistines by irreverently carrying the ark into battle. As punishment for trying to manipulate God, the Israelites are routed, the responsible priests (Eli's sons) killed, and the ark captured.

40. Cf. GJohn 2:13–22; 4:19–26; Rev 21:22 ("I saw no temple in that city, for its temple is the Lord God the Almighty and the Lamb."). See also Eph 2:11–22.

41. The author of PJ would have understood the OT through a similar christocentric lens. Early Christian interpreters quickly adopted prophecy-fulfillment and typology as ways to reconcile the OT and the NT. Even if PJ is not directly influenced

the Israelites settled in Canaan. In a spiritual sense, the people of God continued to be "strangers and foreigners on the earth," awaiting the promised "rest" (Heb 4:8–11; 11:13, 39–40). Mary's vagrancy in PJ reminds readers that neither the Jerusalem temple nor the land of Israel—both lost to the Romans a century earlier—was ever the final destination for the wandering people of God. Through Mary, the promised eschatological salvation is "born" to Israel (PJ 6.2; 7.2; 19.2).

Through the lens of the "ark/tabernacle/temple" topos, surrounding details in PJ come into focus to create a unified portrayal of Mary's body as the new locus of divine presence. For example:

(1) The collection of staffs from the widowers (chs. 8–10) recalls another group of staffs in Num 17:1–11. As the miraculous budding of Aaron's staff signifies his election to care for the most holy things, the dove's descent onto Joseph's staff indicates his election to be Mary's guardian.

(2) When the priests enroll virgins of the tribe of David to spin thread for a temple curtain, Mary's Davidic ancestry comes to the fore (PJ 10.1). It was David who purposed to build the Jerusalem temple, and more importantly, it was he who received the divine promise of an heir—a descendant who would build the temple and establish a never-ending dynasty (2 Sam 7:14). This promise receives emphasis in Solomon's prayer at the dedication of the temple. Solomon thanks God for the fulfillment in his own reign and temple construction, and he also petitions God to continue fulfilling the promise, as though part of it remains. At this point in the prayer, Solomon muses on the impossibility of God's dwelling on earth with humankind, much less in the "house" being dedicated (2 Chr 6). In Mary and her child, the ancient promise to David comes to fruition "at the end of days" (PJ 7.2). Jesus is to be both the promised Son of David and the temple of divine presence. Mary has received "the ultimate[42] blessing" (6.2) by being the vessel for God's embodied arrival into human history.

(3) Spinning thread for the temple curtain is also an appropriate task for Mary in her capacity as "the *Virgin* of the Lord." This is probably the curtain that separated the holy place from the holy of holies, as Mary's intact virginity closes off her sanctified body from the realm of the profane. As the holy of holies housed the ark of the covenant,[43] the locus

---

by Hebrews, similar hermeneutical strategies were widespread among the second-century church.

42. "Ultimate" translates ἐσχάτην, which has an eschatological connotation.

43. Before the exile, that is. In the first-century temple, the ark was notably absent.

of divine presence in the Old Testament cult, Mary bears within her the incarnate Son of God.

(4) Mary's "Who am I?" (PJ 12.2) becomes pregnant[44] with Old Testament significance. As Christopher Holmes[45] has demonstrated, PJ alters the tone of its Lukan source text by reconfiguring Mary's response to the annunciation and Elizabeth's blessing. Luke's Mary speaks prophetically in the Magnificat, proclaiming with joyful assurance, "Surely, from now on all generations will call me blessed!" (μακαριοῦσίν με πᾶσαι αἱ γενεαί; Luke 1:48). The Mary of PJ, confused and afraid, utters no Magnificat. All that remains to her is a question: "Who am I, Lord, that all the women of earth will bless me?" (Κύριε, τίς εἰμι ἐγὼ ὅτι πᾶσαι αἱ γυναῖκες τῆς γῆς μακαριοῦσίν με; 12.2). This statement may serve a bivalent function in PJ. On the one hand, it simply shows Mary's ignorance, and perhaps humility. On the other hand, the question echoes another response to divine blessing—that of King David in 2 Sam 7:18. Through the prophet Nathan, God promises to establish David's "house":

> Moreover the Lord declares to you that the Lord will make you a house. When your days are fulfilled and you lie down with your ancestors, I will raise up your offspring after you, who shall come forth from your body, and I will establish his kingdom. He shall build a house for my name, and I will establish the throne of his kingdom forever. I will be a father to him, and he shall be a son to me. (2 Sam 7:11–14)

David prays, "Who am I, O Lord, my Lord, and what is my house, that you have brought me thus far?" (LXX: τίς εἰμι ἐγώ κύριέ μου κύριε καὶ τίς ὁ οἶκός μου ὅτι ἠγάπηκάς με ἕως τούτων; 2 Sam 7:18). Note the parallel construction of Mary's question: Κύριε, τίς εἰμι ἐγὼ ὅτι πᾶσαι αἱ γυναῖκες τῆς γῆς μακαριοῦσίν με; (PJ 12.2). The topos of "blessing" is also shared with David's prayer:[46]

> Now therefore may it please you to bless the house of your servant, so that it may continue forever before you; for you, O Lord God, have spoken, and with your blessing shall the house of your servant be blessed forever. (2 Sam 7:29)

44. Pun intended!

45. Holmes, "Who Am I to Be Blessed."

46. Though it uses εὐλογέω.

This blessing comes to David in the context of temple-building. David has planned to build the Jerusalem temple, but God commands him to leave the task to Solomon. Still, the king's heart is in the right place, so God promises to bless him with an heir who will build the temple and reign forever. As a descendant of David, Mary shares in David's blessing. She herself becomes a sort of temple, and her son becomes the ultimate fulfillment of the Davidic covenant.

6. The Glory of God Fills the Tabernacle (PJ 17–20)

The topos of Mary as temple/tabernacle reaches its clearest expression near the end of PJ, at the birth of Jesus (chs. 17–20).[47] On the road to Bethlehem, Mary is being relocated again. Joseph "seats her" on a donkey, with his son walking ahead of her and Samuel following (17.2). These three men form a humble entourage. When it is time for the birth, Joseph "takes her down" from the donkey (17.3), "finds a cave and takes her into it," and leaves his sons to guard her (18.1). Again, Mary is like an object being moved about (compare descriptions of the ark in transit: 2 Sam 6:3–6, 12–17; 1 Chr 15:25–16:1; 2 Chr 5:4–8). As discussed above, the cave's location "in the wilderness" (17.3) is reminiscent of the tabernacle.

When Joseph and the midwife approach the cave, "a bright cloud overshadow[s] it" (19.2; cf. 11.3, "The power of God will *overshadow* you"), so they must halt "at the entrance" until it dissipates. A reader immediately recalls the cloud of God's presence at the dedication of the tabernacle (Exod 40:34–35)[48] and the dedication of Solomon's temple (2 Chr 7:1–2),[49] which similarly prevents the ministers from entering the sanctuary and evokes praise from the gathered witnesses (2 Chr 7:3, "when all the people

47. Although the main focus of this essay has been PJ 7.1–8.1, an overview of the tabernacle topos in PJ's nativity story is irresistible. It also provides further evidence of the PJ topos "Mary as Tabernacle," supporting the above interpretation of 7.1–8.1.

48. "Then the cloud covered the tent of meeting, and the glory of the Lord filled the tabernacle. Moses was not able to enter the tent of meeting because the cloud settled upon it, and the glory of the Lord filled the tabernacle."

49. "When Solomon had ended his prayer, fire came down from heaven and consumed the burnt offering and the sacrifices; and the glory of the Lord filled the temple. The priests could not enter the house of the Lord, because the glory of the Lord filled the Lord's house."

saw …";[50] cf. PJ 19.2, "The midwife said, 'My soul has been magnified today, for *my eyes have seen* a miraculous sign'").

In the presence of such holiness, people must take care not to incur divine wrath. Salome's punishment recalls the incident with Uzzah, during David's first attempt to move the ark to Jerusalem:

> When they came to the threshing floor of Nakon, Uzzah reached out and took hold of the ark of God, because the oxen stumbled. The Lord's anger burned against Uzzah because of his irreverent act; therefore God struck him down, and he died there beside the ark of God. (2 Sam 6:6–7)

In PJ, Salome dares to "insert her finger in order to examine [Mary's] condition" (20.1),[51] and God's wrath breaks out against her. Her hand [χείρ] "is falling away by fire,"[52] as God's wrath had "burned" (LXX: ἐθυμώθη) against Uzzah for "stretching out his hand" (ἐξέτεινεν Οζα τὴν χεῖρα αὐτοῦ) to the ark. Salome repents of both her unbelief and her "lawlessness" (ἀνομία, 20.1), as though she has violated cultic restrictions. She benefits from the divine grace present in the Christ child, as despite her more severe offense she does not suffer Uzzah's fate (20.3–4).

Vernon Robbins has noted the presence of the Johannine topos "light" in this remarkable nativity scene.[53] The Word, who is "the true Light," becomes flesh to dwell among humankind.[54] The nativity in PJ also draws on GJohn for its body-as-tabernacle topos ("The Word became flesh and

---

50. "When all the people of Israel saw the fire come down and the glory of the Lord on the temple, they bowed down on the pavement with their faces to the ground, and worshiped and gave thanks to the Lord, saying, 'For he is good, for his steadfast love endures forever.'"

51. This is probably a euphemistic translation. The Greek could more literally be translated, "And Salome thrust [ἔβαλε] her finger into/to her *physis* [which in this context is likely a euphemism for either genitals or the hymen]" (see Foskett, *A Virgin Conceived*, 159).

52. Πυρὶ ἀποπίπτει, translation mine.

53. Vernon K. Robbins, *Who Do People Say I Am? Rewriting Gospel in Emerging Christianity* (Grand Rapids: Eerdmans, 2013), 166–69.

54. GJohn 1:1–5, 9, 14; compare PJ 11.2, "You will conceive a child from his Word" and PJ 19.1.

tabernacled [ἐσκήνωσεν][55] among us"; GJohn 1:14).[56] Protevangelium of James pushes GJohn's metaphor one step further. If Jesus is the divine presence "tabernacling" on earth, his mother's body is also a sanctuary. The Old Testament imagery allows flexibility. The "glory of God" sometimes resides in a cloud of light. When the cloud rests on the tabernacle or temple, it signifies that God is "moving in." God's presence in Israel also has a physical locus in the tablets of the covenant, which are placed in the ark, which is in turn placed in the tabernacle. All of these may be considered loci of divinity, so it is no contradiction for both Jesus and Mary to be "tabernacles" or "temples." At the same time, such physical objects of the Old Testament cultus "contain" God only in a limited sense, for God is omnipresent. Even as he dedicates the magnificent temple, Solomon prays, "But will God indeed reside with mortals on earth? Even heaven and the highest heaven cannot contain you, how much less this house that I have built!" (2 Chr 6:18). God has "set his name" on "this house," but Solomon does not suppose God literally lives there, confined to a physical form. Instead, he asks, "May your eyes be open day and night toward this house … and may you hear from heaven your dwelling place" (6:19–21). Through Mary and in her child, God becomes *physically* present on earth, in human form.[57] The midwife thus exclaims, "My eyes have seen a paradox [παράδοξα], that salvation for Israel has been *born* [ἐγεννήθη]." The miraculous birth brings the "ultimate blessing" to humankind. Mary's absolute purity is a necessary condition for her role. Thus her extraordinary virginity, even *in partu*, demonstrates the physical sanctity of the vessel fit to "give birth to God."[58]

7. Conclusion: The Virgin and the Temple

In summary, PJ's narrative of Mary's arrival at the temple (7.1–8.1) employs the topoi of "a child dedicated to God" and "relocation of sacred space" to

55. Occurs only five times in NT, once in GJohn (1:14) and four times in Revelation (7:15; 12:12; 13:6; 21:3). See BDAG, s.v. σκηνόω (σκηνή), "Live, settle, take up residence." For Rev 12:12, "Perhaps an expression of continuity with God's 'tenting' in Israel." See 1.b.α for σκηνή: "Yahweh's tabernacle ἡ σκηνὴ τοῦ μαρτυρίου the Tabernacle or Tent of Testimony (Ex 27:21; 29:4; Lev 1:1; Num 1:1 and often; …) Ac 7:44. Also simply ἡ σκηνή (LXX; Jos. Ant. 20,228; Just., D. 127,3; s. Iren. 1,18,2 …) Hb 8:5; 9:21; 13:10."

56. Cf. GJohn 2:21 and Rev 21:3.

57. That is, God the Son, the second person of the Trinity.

58. According to Mary's later title, *theotokos*.

illuminate Mary's significance. The first topos places Mary in continuity with several Old Testament figures destined for special roles in Israel's history. The second topos portrays Mary's body as a holy vessel, like the ark of the covenant, the tabernacle, or the first temple. Both of these associations depend on Mary's physical purity, which her virginity represents. As the exceptionally pure "Virgin of the Lord," Mary surpasses the Old Testament precedents within both topoi. Her consecration to God is so complete that her own body becomes the "tabernacle" on which the grace of God comes to rest. This bestowal of grace foreshadows the miraculous conception and birth by which the Virgin's body mediates a new mode of divine presence on earth.

From Prophetic Hymns to Death at the Altar: Luke 1–2 and Protevangelium of James

Michael K. W. Suh and Vernon K. Robbins

The goal of this essay is to present comparative exegetical analysis and interpretation of Luke 1–2 and the Protevangelium of James (PJ).[1] On a first reading, the four well-known prophetic hymns in Luke 1–2—the Magnificat, Benedictus, Gloria, and Nunc Dimittis—are absent from PJ. Careful analysis, however, shows that fragments of these appear in significant places in PJ. An underlying goal of this essay is to present the rhetorical skill of the author of PJ in the context of the rhetorical skill of the author of Luke. It is typical to think of PJ as simply performing a "supplementing function"[2] on opening events in the Gospel of Luke. This approach does not do justice to the rhetorical nature of PJ, since its primary modus vivendi is to use Luke's narrative as a resource within its overall agenda. PJ does not only "fill in gaps" in the Lukan account; rather, it establishes and maintains its own agenda in an overall context of the agenda of the Lukan account. The author of PJ exhibits significant literary training.[3] Therefore,

1. The translations used are the NRSV for biblical texts, and for PJ, Ronald F. Hock, *The Infancy Gospels of James and Thomas: With Introduction, Notes, and Original Text Featuring the New Scholars Version Translation* (Santa Rosa, CA: Polebridge, 1995), whose Greek text was also employed. At times there is deviation from these translations with our own translations, especially for purposes of comparison. Note that PJ references are also based on Hock, whose verse numbering differs from some other editions.

2. "Ergänzungsfunktion": Silvia Pellegrini, "Kindheitsevangelien," in *Antike christliche Apokryphen in deutscher Übersetzung*, ed. C. Markschies and J. Schröter, 2 vols. (Tübingen: Mohr Siebeck, 2012), 2:891; J. K. Elliott, *The Apocryphal New Testament: A Collection of Apocryphal Christian Literature in an English Translation* (Oxford: Clarendon, 2005), 50–51.

3. Hock, *Infancy Gospels*, 10. Cf. Aelius Theon on "paraphrase," in *Progymnas-*

it should not be surprising to discover that the four programmatic hymns in Luke 1–2 have been appropriated in unexpected ways in PJ.

The argument of this essay is twofold: (1) the four hymns in Luke 1–2 play a strong role in the prophetic discourse of the canonical gospel; (2) the new mode of discourse in PJ—that is, priestly discourse—guides the author in relocating and reconfiguring aspects of the Lukan hymns as he refashions the story of Mary to present her holiness and blessedness.[4] The essay will unfold in relation to this twofold argument. First, there will be detailed analysis of both the context and prophetic role of each of the four hymns in the Lukan account of the birth of John the Baptist (hereafter simply "John") and Jesus. Second, comparative exegesis of the hymns in Luke 1–2 and PJ will show the relocation, sometimes remarkable, of fragments of the Lukan hymns in PJ. The goal of the essay will be to show how the priestly agenda in PJ not only drives the prophetic emphasis of Luke into the background but also produces a wholesale fragmentation of the Lukan hymns. Since PJ uses Luke as one of its major resources, fragments of the Lukan hymns make surprise appearances as the story unfolds. While the initial means of identifying the fragments in their new location is lexical, the fragments contain significant topoi that have been taken from their Lukan context and placed in another context in PJ. Identification of the topoi reveals that major fragments of three of the Lukan hymns appear in the events of priestly Zechariah's martyrdom. The rhetorical effect of this, we will argue, is to push John into the background and bring his martyred father, high priest Zechariah, into the foreground as priestly forerunner of the crucified Jesus. Careful attention to the effect of the priestly discourse in PJ on the Lukan storyline may lead us into some new ways of understanding and interpreting PJ in emerging Christianity.

---

mata 110P–111P, in George A. Kennedy, *Progymnasmata: Greek Textbooks of Prose Composition and Rhetoric*, WGRW 10 (Atlanta: Society of Biblical Literature, 2003), 71–72, based on the edition and French translation of the Armenian (the Greek does not survive for this portion) by Michel Patillon and Giancarlo Bolognesi, eds., *Aelius Theon: Progymnasmata*, Budé 376 (Paris: Belles Lettres, 1997). See Kennedy, *Progymnasmata*, 64, for his rationale in utilizing the Armenian textual tradition.

4. On the definition of "rhetorolects," see Vernon K. Robbins, *The Invention of Christian Discourse*, vol. 1, RRA 1 (Blandford Forum, UK: Deo, 2009), 7–17. Recently Rick Strelan has proposed that the author of Luke was a priest, and therefore the hymns have primarily a priestly function. He does not analyze the hymns in detail so that he observes their prophetic function; Rick Strelan, *Luke the Priest: The Authority of the Author of the Third Gospel* (Burlington, VT: Ashgate, 2008), 140–44.

1. The Prophetic Hymns in Luke 1–2

The reader of Luke's Gospel encounters four hymns in rapid succession in the first two chapters: Luke 1:46–55 (Magnificat); 1:67–79 (Benedictus); 2:14 (Gloria); and 2:28–32 (Nunc Dimittis). They are frontloaded in the Lukan corpus as key statements that predict how the narrative will unfold, specifically with respect to how God has worked and will work with his people.[5] This is a clear indication that these hymns are operating within the realm of prophetic rhetorolect, which "emerges when God decides to create a kingdom of people on earth who have special responsibility to live according to *God's will*."[6] Within the birth narratives of Luke 1–2, the various angelic and prophetic disclosures point to the will of God (βουλὴ τοῦ θεοῦ) as the unifying force in the story.[7] The focus, therefore, is on inscribing the rule of God on earth, and Jesus's programmatic statements in Luke 4:16–30 confirm this prophetic rhetography of the Third Gospel.[8]

It is well known that the Greek of Luke 1–2 differs markedly from the rest of Luke-Acts.[9] W. L. Knox describes Luke 1–2 as "an orgy of Hebraic Greek," and concerning the origin of these vestiges of Semitic influence, scholars have offered various explanations.[10] The argument of this essay

5. Stephen Farris, *The Hymns of Luke's Infancy Narratives: Their Origin, Meaning and Significance*, JSNTSup 9 (Sheffield: JSOT Press, 1985), 9. Raymond E. Brown (*The Birth of the Messiah: A Commentary on the Infancy Narratives in the Gospels of Matthew and Luke*, updated ed. [New York: Doubleday, 1993], 242) calls Luke 1–2 "a true introduction to some of the main themes of the Gospel proper."

6. Robbins, *Invention*, 219 (emphasis added).

7. Robert C. Tannehill, *The Narrative Unity of Luke-Acts: A Literary Interpretation*, 2 vols. (Philadelphia: Fortress, 1986), 1:20. The phrase βουλὴ τοῦ θεοῦ is quite uncommon in the NT, found only in the Lukan *Doppelwerk* in Luke 7:30; Acts 2:23; 13:36; 20:27. In the LXX: Jdt 8:16 (τὰς βουλὰς κυρίου τοῦ θεοῦ ἡμῶν); Wis 6:4; 9:13. It occurs only sparsely outside of the Judeo-Christian context: Homer, *Od.* 16.402 (θεῶν … βουλάς); Hesiod, *Theog.* 960, 993 (βουλῇσι θεῶν); Strabo, *Geogr.* 14.1.4 (θεῶν βουλῇ).

8. Luke 4:16–30 is the well-known scene in which Jesus unrolls the prophet Isaiah (61:1–2) and perceives himself to belong to the long line of prophets in the likeness of Elijah and Elisha of the OT. See Vernon K. Robbins, "The Socio-Rhetorical Role of Old Testament Scripture in Luke 4–19," in *Z Noveho Zakona / From the New Testament: Sbornik k narozeninam Prof. ThDr. Zdenka Sazavy*, ed. Hana Tonzarova and Petr Melmuk (Prague: Vydala Cirkev ceskoslovenska husitska, 2001), 85–86.

9. François Bovon, *Luke 1: A Commentary of Luke 1:1–9:50*, trans. Christine M. Thomas (Minneapolis: Fortress, 2002), 30.

10. W. L. Knox, *The Sources of the Synoptic Gospels*, ed. Henry Chadwick, 2 vols.

does not depend on identifying a particular source—LXX or otherwise—for what is found in Luke 1–2.[11] However, the rhetorical texture of the Hebraic Greek in the opening chapters of Luke led early Christians to characterize Luke as a "priestly gospel."[12] We will argue that in Luke 1–2 the priestly language has been subsumed under the dominant prophetic rhetorolect. The priestly rhetography in Luke 1–2, however, likely contributed substantively to how the author of PJ shaped his material.

In form-critical terms, the hymns of Luke 1–2 can be understood as "declarative psalms of praise" directed toward God with characteristics of Hebrew poetry.[13] Along with this definition, there is a typical structure governing each of the hymns in Luke 1–2.[14] The three longer hymns contain the following elements: (1) introductory praise, (2) motive clause(s)

(Cambridge: Cambridge University Press, 1953), 2:40. Farris (*Hymns*, 31) lists two options that scholars have posited: (1) Luke 1–2 as translation of Semitic source(s) or (2) Luke 1–2 written in imitation of LXX style. For this line of inquiry, see, e.g., Richard J. Dillon, "The Benedictus in Micro- and Macrocontext," *CBQ* 68 (2006): 457–80; Randall Buth, "Hebrew Poetic Tenses and the Magnificat," *JSNT* 21 (1984): 67–83; Robert Simons, "The Magnificat: Cento, Psalm or Imitatio?," *TynBul* 60 (2009): 25–46.

11. See a summary of various positions in Strelan, *Luke the Priest*, 142.

12. Irenaeus, *Haer.* 3.11.8, "But that according to Luke, taking up [his] priestly character commenced with Zechariah the priest offering sacrifices to God."

13. Farris, *Hymns*, 11. It is beyond the scope of this essay to deal with the specifics of deriving the "form" of the hymns in Luke 1–2, and therefore we will assume the work of important form critics who have delved into this issue in detail. See Hermann Gunkel, *The Psalms: A Form Critical Introduction*, trans. Thomas M. Horner (Philadelphia: Fortress, 1967), 10; Claus Westermann, *The Praise of God in the Psalms* (London: Epworth, 1966), 115. Ambrose of Milan—who was himself known for his hymnography—writes, "A hymn is a song containing praise of God. If you praise God but without song you do not have hymn. If you praise anything that does not pertain to the Glory of God, even if you sing it, you do not have a hymn. Hence a hymn contains three elements: *song* and *praise* of *God*" (*De cantu et musica sacra* 1.14 [emphasis added]).

For helpful introductions to biblical poetry generally, see Robert Alter, *The Art of Biblical Poetry* (New York: Basic Books, 1985), 3–84; David Noel Freedman, "Pottery, Poetry, and Prophecy: An Essay on Biblical Poetry," *JBL* 96 (1977): 5–26; Floyd V. Filson, "How Much of the New Testament is Poetry?," *JBL* 67 (1948): 125–34. For its application to a specific hymn, see Robert C. Tannehill, "The Magnificat as Poem," *JBL* 93 (1974): 263–75.

14. The only exception here is the Gloria of Luke 2:14, which does not fit this structure; given its brevity, its content and form need to be examined in their own right below.

as the grounds for praise, (3) amplification or summary statements that conclude the hymn.[15] Additionally, the various individual stories in Luke 1–2 demonstrate a progression leading up to the hymns: (1) promise, (2) fulfillment, and (3) praise (i.e., the hymns).[16] It is quite remarkable, in our view, how the author of PJ redirected the prophetic emphasis in this strong narrative-hymnic storyline toward a priestly storyline that, nevertheless, used fragments of the hymns in newly crafted narrative environments. What we might consider to be "irresistible" rhetorical forms may, for writers in antiquity, have simply been "resources" that contained fragments for their own agendas!

Once we have emphasized the strong poetic character of the hymns in Luke 1–2, there is nevertheless one other feature to be noticed. Many interpreters have proposed that some of the hymns in Luke 1–2 have an awkward placement in the narrative. This means that, to varying degrees, if these hymns are removed from their present location, the narrative flows naturally without them. This is less of a problem for the shorter hymns, Nunc Dimittis and Gloria,[17] though for both the Magnificat and the Benedictus a case can be made that these hymns interrupt the flow of the Lukan narrative. Given his literary training, the author of PJ detected some disjunctures in the rhetorical flow of Luke 1–2 that he could then freely use to relocate parts of the hymns. The specifics of these details will be discussed in the sections dealing with the respective hymns.

1.1. The Prophetic Context and Content of the Magnificat: Luke 1:46–56

The climactic section that contains the Magnificat is part of a major progression of promise–fulfillment–praise in Luke 1–2. Prior to the Magnificat of Luke 1:46–55, the angel Gabriel foretold to Mary the birth of Jesus (1:26–38). While Mary is initially troubled (1:29), Gabriel exhorts her not to be afraid (1:30), and she is given details concerning the nature of her conception (1:31, 35a) along with details about the fate of her child (1:32–33, 35b). By the end of this encounter she appears to be convinced of the veracity of Gabriel's words—given more force with evidence that Mary's barren kinswoman Elizabeth is also going to bear a son (1:36). Though she is not told to go see Elizabeth specifically, Mary "went with haste" (1:39,

15. Farris, *Hymns*, 29.
16. Ibid., 101.
17. Ibid., 29–30.

ἐπορεύθη … μετὰ σπουδῆς) to visit her. This could be Mary's own prerogative to confirm for herself what Gabriel had told her earlier in 1:36. Whatever the case, Mary enters the home of Elizabeth's husband Zechariah and is met by Elizabeth, who proclaims words of blessing on Mary under the aegis of the Holy Spirit (1:41b–42). It is at this point that Mary responds with the Magnificat, a lengthy song of praise from 1:46 to 1:55.

The Magnificat is the culmination of the character transformation that Mary undergoes in Luke 1–2 and, in fact, stands as the last time the reader hears the voice of Mary in the entire Gospel. The change is evident when considering the context in which the Magnificat is situated. When Mary encounters the angel Gabriel and his greeting in Luke 1:28, her immediate reaction is consternation rather than joy (1:29).[18] The doubt that might have been at work here continues through her conversation with Gabriel. To the angel's words that she would conceive a preeminent son (1:31–33), Mary responds skeptically: "How will this be since I have not known a man?" (1:34). It is not until Gabriel provides three additional pieces of information that Mary finally appears to be convinced of his words: (1) her conception through the Holy Spirit (1:35); (2) the pregnancy of her formerly barren (στεῖρα) kinswoman Elizabeth (1:36); and (3) these seemingly impossible conceptions[19] described as being possible with God (1:37).[20] From Mary's first encounter with the angel Gabriel to her even-

18. Mary was both "troubled" (διαταράσσω) by and "thought" (διαλογίζομαι) about Gabriel's words. Διαταράσσω is a *hapax legomenon* in the entire biblical corpus (it occurs only once here in the LXX and NT) with the BDAG (s.v. διαταράσσω) defining it as "to confuse or to perplex (greatly)." Cf. T. Sim. 4.9; Josephus, *Ant.* 2.120; Diodorus Siculus, 18.7.7. Διαλογίζομαι occurs twenty-seven times in the LXX and NT, and BDAG (s.v. διαλογίζομαι) defines it as (1) "to think or reason carefully, esp. about the implications of something" or (2) "to discuss a matter in some detail." In Luke 1, however, the word is laden with some aspect of uncertainty as it is elsewhere in the NT (see Matt 16:7–8; 21:25; Mark 2:6, 8; Luke 3:15; 5:21–22).

19. The context is not immediately clear what was formerly understood to be impossible, i.e., (1) Mary's conception by the Holy Spirit or (2) Elizabeth's conception in barrenness. It is likely that both events are in view in Luke 1:37.

20. Luke 1:37 is an allusion to Gen 18:14 with clear verbal similarities. Both accounts activate the same topos, i.e., one in which a divine figure describes the unlikelihood of conception to a soon-to-be parent. In Luke 1, the angel Gabriel speaks to Mary about her (and Elizabeth's) conception, and in Gen 18 the Lord tells Abram that his elderly wife Sarah will soon give birth to a son. See the parallel statements below:

Luke 1:37 (Gabriel): οὐκ ἀδυνατήσει παρὰ τοῦ θεοῦ πᾶν ῥῆμα.

Gen 18:14 (The Lord): μὴ ἀδυνατεῖ παρὰ τῷ θεῷ ῥῆμα.

tual outburst of praise in the Magnificat, there is an inclination to characterize Mary positively. The once fearful young woman now assumes an air of responsibility as the upcoming mother of Jesus, the Son of the Most High, and breaks forth in worship as a demonstration of her newfound confidence and courage. The blessing of Elizabeth in 1:45 confirms that Mary has moved beyond the realm of uncertainty and/or doubt to one of resolute belief. Indeed, Mary is indirectly called by Elizabeth "the one who believed" (ἡ πιστεύσασα), and the object of that belief is the fulfillment of what was spoken from the Lord.

The implications of the study of the context of the Magnificat should now be obvious: there is the giving of "prophecy" or things that are going to take place according to the will of God; and there is the eventual "fulfillment" of these promises. In other words, the context and language leading up to the Magnificat demonstrate the operative work of prophetic rhetorolect, and it would be surprising if the Magnificat did not move within that discourse. This leads us to more specific analysis of the Magnificat.

When reading the ten verses of praise in the Magnificat, it is astonishing to see how many of the words and phrases have a relationship to the Hebrew Bible. The margins of the NA^{28} point to no less than forty different possible biblical allusions running the entire gamut from Genesis to Isaiah to Psalms.[21] This constant recall back to Israel's Scripture produces what Tannehill calls a "savoring mood,"[22] in which the importance of remembrance gains intensity as the hymn progresses. There is a repetitive texture of the contrast between the Lord's actions and human rulers. A clear antithesis can be seen between how God acts for the reverent (v. 50), humble (v. 52b), hungry (v. 53a), Israel (v. 54), and Abraham (v. 55) over against his acts against the proud (v. 51b), mighty (v. 52a), and rich (v. 53b).

The Magnificat begins with Mary's own specific situation with phrases such as "*my* soul" (v. 46a, ἡ ψυχή μου), "*my* spirit" (v. 47, τὸ πνεῦμά μου), "they will bless *me*" (v. 48b, μακαριοῦσίν με), and "great things for *me*" (v. 49a, μοι μεγάλα). As the canticle progresses, Mary slowly recedes into the background and the acts of God for Israel and Abraham move to the

21. The full list of possible allusions is impressive: Genesis; Deuteronomy; Numbers; Deuteronomy; 1–2 Samuel; Psalms; Proverbs; Job; Sirach; Micah; Habakkuk; Malachi; Isaiah; Ezekiel. See Brown, *Birth of the Messiah*, 357–65.

22. Robert C. Tannehill, *The Shape of Luke's Story: Essays on Luke-Acts* (Eugene, OR: Cascade, 2005), 33.

foreground. In a way, Mary has taken on the persona of the entire people of God, singing on their behalf "to remember" what God has done (v. 54b, μνησθῆναι), in order to look forward to what God is going to do for his people (v. 55b, τῷ σπέρματι αὐτοῦ εἰς τὸν αἰῶνα).[23]

The prophetic rhetorolect that was present in the wider context of Luke 1–2, therefore, has heavily influenced the shaping of the Magnificat. Mary's song maintains the storyline of God's people beginning with God's promise to Abraham in Genesis all the way forward to the present circumstances and beyond.[24]

One striking aspect of the Magnificat (Luke 1:46–55) is that its presence in the narrative interrupts the natural flow of the story. In Luke 1:45, Elizabeth blesses Mary, and it would make perfect sense to pick up in 1:56 with the narrator's statement that "Mary remained with her about three months and returned to her house." Stephen Farris surmises that "the intelligibility of the narrative would not suffer from the absence" of the Magnificat. The lack of an airtight connection has led scholars to posit a secondary insertion by the author or editor of the text.[25]

If we grant the current location of the Magnificat within the narrative, two other issues compound the problem of narrative flow, one external and the other internal to the text. First, in 1:46, there are versional and patristic witnesses that support reading *Elizabeth*, rather than Mary, as the speaker of the Magnificat.[26] On external evidence alone, the textual witnesses heavily favor "Mary" as the correct reading. But why would there ever have been an attribution of the Magnificat to Elizabeth? In verse 41, Elizabeth is "filled with the Holy Spirit" (ἐπλήσθη πνεύματος ἁγίου), and this topos does significant work in the Lukan corpus in characterizing figures that subsequently speak in inspired speech or song.[27] Zechariah, for example, is also filled with the Spirit (ἐπλήσθη πνεύματος ἁγίου) in 1:67 prior to his Benedictus in 1:67–79. Furthermore, in content the Magnificat

23. Bovon, *Luke 1*, 56, 62–65.

24. Robbins, *Invention*, 219–21.

25. Farris, *Hymns*, 21; Bovon, *Luke 1*, 60.

26. NA^{28} lists the following witnesses for "Elisabeth": a, b, l*; Ir^{arm}, $Or^{lat\ mss}$, Nic. These would suggest a Greek original that reads Καὶ εἶπεν Ἐλισάβετ rather than Καὶ εἶπεν Μαριάμ.

27. The phrase πίμπλημι πνεύματος ἁγίου is quite specific to Luke in the biblical corpus, as it occurs only one other time outside of Luke-Acts, in Prov 15:4 LXX. All other occurrences are found in the Lukan *Doppelwerk*: Luke 1:15, 41, 67; Acts 2:4; 4:8, 31; 9:17; 13:9.

imitates Hannah's Song in 1 Sam 2:1–10, one that contains elements that suit the circumstances surrounding Elizabeth's life better than Mary's.[28]

This is related to the second point, regarding the unfolding of the narrative itself. In Luke 1:45, Elizabeth blessed Mary, and in 1:46–55, Mary breaks forth in song. In 1:56, however, the author tells us that "*Mary* remained with *her* for about three months" (emphasis added). The flow of the narrative would make better sense if it actually read the opposite: "*she* [i.e., Mary, the one who was the subject of the Magnificat just prior] remained with *Elizabeth* for about three months." There is also one other internal detail that lends credence to Elizabeth as the speaker of the Magnificat: in Luke 1:46, if the speaker had changed from verse 45 to verse 46, one would expect to find εἶπεν δέ rather than καὶ εἶπεν. Therefore, while the external evidence overwhelmingly favors Mary, the internal evidence favors Elizabeth as the speaker of the Magnificat.[29] The ambiguity regarding the speaker of the Magnificat and the different character development of Mary may have contributed to its relocation and reconfiguration in PJ.[30] In a later section where we will engage in comparative exegesis of the hymns of Luke 1–2 and PJ, we will assume Mary as the subject of the Magnificat; despite the possible internal evidence against reading Mary as the subject, the textual tradition far outweighs any narrative conflicts that may be detected.

1.2. The Prophetic Context and Content of the Benedictus: Luke 1:67–79

Just as in the other hymns, the Benedictus (1:67–79) stands as a section of praise within the overall promise—fulfillment—song nexus of the stories found in Luke 1–2. In Luke 1:5–25, the birth of John is foretold to Zechariah as he ministers at the temple as a priest (1:8). The reader is told that he has a wife, Elizabeth, who also is of priestly descent (1:5). For whatever reason, Elizabeth is "barren" (1:7, στεῖρα), and the prospect

---

28. Bovon, *Luke 1*, 60; Dietrich Rusam, *Das Alte Testament bei Lukas*, BZNW 112 (Berlin: de Gruyter, 2003), 65–75. For a helpful overview of the history of interpretation, see Stephen Benko, "The Magnificat: A History of the Controversy," *JBL* 86 (1967): 263–75.

29. Farris, *Hymns*, 109–10.

30. See our comparative analysis of PJ 12.1–9 and Luke 1:36–56 below.

of their rearing of a child is slim because they are both advanced in age (προβεβηκότες ἐν ταῖς ἡμέραις).[31]

At some point during Zechariah's time of service as a priest, an angel of the Lord, who reveals himself to be Gabriel in 1:19, appears before him, and Zechariah becomes troubled and fearful (1:12, ἐταράχθη … καὶ φόβος ἐπέπεσεν ἐπ' αὐτόν).[32] Despite Zechariah's priestly lineage, his son is described in language that locates him in a line of prophets. John's being filled with the Spirit even from the womb resonates with prophetic calling,[33] and he is even associated closely with one of the greatest prophets of Israel's story, Elijah. However, just as he does with Mary in Luke 1:26–38, Gabriel has to convey to Zechariah positive proclamations in order to dispel any initial notions of fear or doubt. The words of the angel are quite similar to one another in form and content (see appendix 1). Following these words, Zechariah still displays some measure of doubt as he speaks to Gabriel: "How will I know this? For I am an old man and my wife is advanced in years" (1:18). What transpires at this point is a bit unusual given our knowledge of the rest of Luke 1–2.

As shown above, the speeches of Gabriel to Zechariah and Mary are parallel to one another, and both appear to be incredulous in their immediate response (1:18; 1:34).[34] At this point, Mary is given further proof about what will take place (1:35–37), while Zechariah is censured and made mute with a charge of unbelief regarding Gabriel's words (1:19–20). What was so particularly different about his question that it necessitated a punishing response? If Mary is later called "blessed" by Elizabeth for believing in the soon-to-be-fulfilled words of God (1:45), then in some sense, Zechariah is depicted as cursed—albeit only briefly—for his doubt. The narrative continues in 1:21–25 with Zechariah's ongoing status as mute, while his wife Elizabeth has indeed conceived a child as Gabriel foretold earlier.

---

31. The language here (underlined in the following) is reminiscent of the story of Abram and Sarai in Genesis. In Gen 11:30, the reader is told that Sarai was barren: καὶ ἦν Σαρα στεῖρα καὶ οὐκ ἐτεκνοποίει, and in Gen 18:11, the reader is given information regarding the age of Abram and Sarai along with the impossibility of Sarai's conceiving due to menopause: Αβρααμ δὲ καὶ Σαρρα πρεσβύτεροι προβεβηκότες ἡμερῶν, ἐξέλιπεν δὲ Σαρρα γίνεσθαι τὰ γυναικεῖα.

32. Cf. Mary's response in Luke 1:29.

33. Judg 13:5–7 LXX; Jer 1:4–5.

34. Zechariah (Luke 1:18): κατὰ τί γνώσομαι τοῦτο; ἐγὼ γάρ εἰμι πρεσβύτης καὶ ἡ γυνή μου προβεβηκυῖα ἐν ταῖς ἡμέραις αὐτῆς. Mary (Luke 1:34): πῶς ἔσται τοῦτο, ἐπεὶ ἄνδρα οὐ γινώσκω.

This event, which marks the fulfillment of what was promised to Zechariah, echoes the earlier story of Sarah and Abraham and the birth of their son Isaac. Again, the portrayal of these characters is being shaped by prophetic rhetorolect that moves the story along in Luke's Gospel. From 1:26 to 1:56, Zechariah's story is put on hiatus, to resume with the birth of John in 1:57–66. When the priest Zechariah regains his tongue with the proper naming of John, he interrupts the narrative with the Benedictus (1:67–79), a song that opens with hints of influence from prophetic rhetorolect.[35]

More detailed analysis shows yet further important aspects of the Benedictus and its setting. In many ways, Zechariah continues to parallel Mary in Luke 1–2. In content, the Benedictus has less to do with Zechariah's son than it does with how God has acted and will act on behalf of his people. The opening words of praise bless the Lord as the God of Israel because "he visited and redeemed his people" (v. 68, θεὸς τοῦ Ἰσραήλ, ὅτι ἐπεσκέψατο καὶ ἐποίησεν λύτρωσιν τῷ λαῷ αὐτοῦ). What does the birth of a son to a minor priest belonging to a small division of the priestly family have to do with God's plan of redemption?[36] John does not enter the conversation until verses 76–79, and even then his primary role is to be "the prophet of the Most High" within the overarching plan of God (v. 76).

From verses 69–75, the issue at hand is the affirmation of God's faithfulness to his promises. At various points there is the recall of what he has done: (1) God's speech through "his holy prophets from of old" (v. 70, τῶν ἁγίων ἀπ᾽ αἰῶνος προφητῶν αὐτοῦ); (2) mercies that were "promised to our fathers" (v. 72a, μετὰ τῶν πατέρων ἡμῶν); (3) covenant remembrance (v. 72, μνησθῆναι διαθήκης ἁγίας αὐτοῦ); and (4) oath sworn to Abraham (v. 73a, ὅρκον ὃν ὤμοσεν πρὸς Ἀβραάμ). All of these details situate the contemporary event (i.e., the birth of John) within the larger storyline of God's saving purposes for Israel.[37] This is a continuation of what has been revealed in Israel's Scriptures. As will be evident in the birth of Jesus in Luke 2 specifically—and even in the rest of the

35. Luke 1:67, ἐπροφήτευσεν λέγων.

36. Bovon (*Luke 1*, 33): "Despite the *Protoevangelium of James*, Zechariah is not the high priest, nor is he from the high-priestly family; he is a simple priest. Of the twenty-four classes of the priesthood, the division of Abijah is the eighth, not one of the more prestigious."

37. Again, we point the readers to the outside margins of the NA^{28}, which list around thirty cross-references to NT/LXX and T. 12 Patr. See also Brown, *Birth of the Messiah*, 386–89.

Gospel more generally—the figure of the Davidic Messiah is the ultimate fulfillment of God's prophecies, and consequently, all other characters are subservient to this program. François Bovon sums up correctly: "In the Benedictus, salvation history is not only recounted but sung."[38]

1.3. The Prophetic Context and Content of the Gloria: Luke 2:14

The occurrence of the Gloria in the next segment of the narrative adds still additional dimensions to the ongoing story. Luke 2:1–7 begins with narration that the thing foretold to Mary in Luke 1:26–38 has come to fruition with the birth of Jesus to Joseph and Mary. One of the main points of focus here is Joseph's own lineage as belonging to the line of David, and Jesus is now part of that heritage. This connection is important because at multiple points throughout Luke 1–2, the narrative has been pointing toward a Davidic Messiah, and therefore a confirmation of those predictions is necessary for rhetorical integrity.[39] It is at this point that the narrative takes a quick turn away from Jesus and moves to a new scene.[40]

Out in the field, an angel of the Lord appears to some shepherds and speaks in a manner similar to how Gabriel spoke to both Zechariah (1:13–17) and Mary (1:30–33).[41] The angelic proclamation here is brief in comparison to Gabriel's speech to Zechariah and Mary in Luke 1, but there remains striking similarity in form.[42] Immediately following the proclamation concerning the baby lying in a manger (2:12), a "multitude of the heavenly host" appears and begins to praise God (v. 13, αἰνούντων τὸν θεόν[43]) in a brief exclamation of song known as the Gloria.

38. Bovon, *Luke 1*, 77–78. He continues, "Even in the middle of time, God acts neither directly nor alone.... Human beings are called to work along with God. The people of God receive not only salvation; the participation God expects of them is also an expression of his compassion." This is precisely the mode of prophetic rhetorolect.

39. Cf. Luke 1:27, 32, 69 (and in the divine announcement to follow in 2:11).

40. Bovon aptly states (*Luke 1*, 86): "We are instructed less about person of Jesus than about his effect."

41. Although this "angel of the Lord" is not identified by himself or the narrator, he is likely the same angel Gabriel of Luke 1. Given the parallel form along with Gabriel's role throughout Luke 1, there is no reason to suspect otherwise here in Luke 2.

42. See the consistency of form of the speeches in appendix 1.

43. The verb αἰνέω—which Raymond Brown (*Birth of the Messiah*, 403) describes as a "Lucan favorite"—is uncommon in the NT (Luke 2:13, 20; 19:37; Acts 2:47; 3:8, 9; Rom 15:11; Rev 19:5) but frequently attested in the LXX, particularly in the Psalms

Structurally, the Gloria is a chiasm with "glory" (A) and "peace" (A') forming the bookends and "highest" (B) and "earth" (B') sandwiched in between.[44] In addition, "God" is juxtaposed to "men" within the rhetoric of this brief hymn. As in the other canticles, even this short proclamation by the host of angels situates what has just preceded within the wider context of God's activity in history. The unique aspect of this hymn is that whereas the other three are found on the mouths of human characters, the Gloria is recited by the heavenly hosts, angels who are supposed to dwell in the presence of God. As the chart in appendix 1 demonstrates, there is continuity in the structure of the proclamations that belies a consistency of rhetoric. If this is indeed the case, it implies that even in terms of rhetorolects, the Gloria is very much at home within the prophetic mode of discourse.

As in the first two hymns, there is a recall of the history of salvation as told within the history of Israel.[45] In fact, the context of the Gloria *begins* with that proclamation, as the angels declare, "Great joy shall be to all people" (χαρὰν μεγάλην ἥτις ἔσται παντὶ τῷ λαῷ; Luke 2:10c[46]). This "people" can be none other than Israel; therefore, this designation implies that all that is to follow pertains to this particular group of people with their own narrative of God's acts as foretold in the Jewish Scriptures.[47] More significantly, this scene provides an important insight to these shepherds concerning the identity of Jesus that has not been revealed thus far in Luke's Gospel, namely, Jesus as σωτήρ.[48] As Dietrich Rusam puts it

(52×). After Psalms, the word occurs most frequently in Sirach (16×) and 1 Chronicles (10×) while found a handful of times in other books. Given this rhetorical signal and connection to the Psalms, it is difficult to know why Farris has so quickly dismissed this material from his book dealing with hymns in Luke's infancy narratives (*Hymns*, 12). We can only guess that its brevity has eluded his attempt to interpret Luke 2:14. By situating this verse within the wider context as we have done in the appendix, one can more quickly detect the consistent rhetography of all three hymns, therefore rendering intelligible the rhetorical force of this highly abbreviated hymnic material.

44. Bovon, *Luke 1*, 90–91.

45. Rusam, *Das Alte Testament*, 75.

46. As the Gloria only spans two verses, the letters designate specific sections of the hymn as displayed in the chart in the appendix.

47. Ibid.

48. This is not a common designation for Jesus among the canonical gospels, occurring only in Luke 1:47; 2:11; GJohn 4:42 (occurs also in Acts 5:31 and 13:23).

succinctly, "This title encircles the entire future work of Jesus."[49] The use of such a title along with χριστός brings to the fore the hope of a political triumph by Israel's Messiah, a component of prophetic discourse.[50] The compact narrative of christological significance in Luke 2:10–11 functions in two ways here: (1) the readers of Luke's Gospel—"prepared" by the annunciation (1:26–39) and the Benedictus (1:67–79)—are now confronted with that which was foretold earlier in the narrative,[51] and (2) the brief summary serves to quickly move the story forward as the plot continues to unfold.

The Gloria itself activates topoi that stretch back to the OT and interweave throughout the Lukan *Doppelwerk*. The call to give "glory to God in the highest" (2:14a) finds its counterpart in Luke's version of the triumphal entry in which the people declare, "Glory in the highest" (19:38).[52] Also, the declaration of divinely given peace recalls two prophetic texts in particular. In both instances, the nexus of topoi that are described in the Gloria can be found: Isa 9:5–6 LXX describes the birth of a child who brings peace while reigning on the throne of David, and Mic 5:3–4 LXX envisions a figure who himself would act as the shepherd, bringing glory and establishing peace.[53]

---

49. "Mit diesem Titel wird das gesamte künftige Wirken Jesu umschrieben" (Rusam, *Das Alte Testament*, 76).

50. Cf. Vernon K. Robbins, "Rhetography: A New Way of Seeing the Familiar Text," in *Words Well Spoken: George Kennedy's Rhetoric of the New Testament*, ed. C. Clifton Black and Duane F. Watson, SRR 8 (Waco, TX: Baylor University Press, 2008) 88–90; Robbins, "Conceptual Blending and Early Christian Imagination," in *Explaining Christian Origins and Early Judaism: Contributions from Cognitive and Social Science*, ed. Petri Luomanen, Ilkka Pyysiäinen, and Risto Uro, BIS 89 (Leiden: Brill, 2007), 166–71.

51. Rusam (*Das Alte Testament*, 78) states that this announcement to the shepherds is "für den Leser v.a. durch die Verkündigung an Maria (Lk 1,31–33) und das Benedictus des Zacharias (Lk 1,68–79) vorbereitet."

52. There is, however, a reversal of the location of "peace." It is described in the Gloria as found "upon earth" (2:14b, ἐπὶ γῆς εἰρήνη), while in the triumphal entry it is located "in heaven" (19:38, ἐν οὐρανῷ εἰρήνη).

53. Concerning the third line of the Gloria, "among those whom he favors" (Luke 2:14c), NA[28] lists two possible allusions: Pss 50:20 and 88:18.

1.4. The Prophetic Content and Context of the Nunc Dimittis: Luke 2:28–32

Simeon's Nunc Dimittis is recited on the heels of Jesus's presentation at the temple (2:22–28). With respect to Jesus and John (the objects of the prophetic discourse of Luke 1–2) and the temple (the object of priestly ritual), there is a blending of the two types of discourse in the narrative. There are multiple mentions of "the law" and the need to uphold the proper customs for purity for the child Jesus.[54] When thinking about the similarities between Mary of PJ and Jesus of Luke 2:22–28, it is not surprising to find that priestly discourse finds significant energy with Mary and the temple in the noncanonical story.

This is not to say that prophetic rhetorolect has disappeared completely, as the narrator tells us two things about Simeon that move naturally toward the Nunc Dimittis: (1) he has been waiting for the consolation of Israel (v. 25), and (2) he was under special supervision of the Holy Spirit (v. 25–27). With regard to the first point, the phrase, παράκλησιν τοῦ Ἰσραήλ, has an "eschatological tenor,"[55] in which a human figure—who becomes the subject of a hymn—serves as the mediator (yet again) of God's saving activity not on behalf of one *individual* but for the *nation* of Israel. Also, notice the repetitive reference to "Israel" in this storyline of Simeon, when Simeon is described as waiting for the "consolation of *Israel*" (2:25), and within the Nunc Dimittis, when Simeon himself declares that salvation has arrived in the form of a child "for glory to your people *Israel*" (2:32).[56] Just as in the Magnificat, Benedictus, and the Gloria, there is an insistence that *Israel's* story is what matters. Concerning the latter point, the Holy Spirit continues to play a major role in shaping the narrative context of these hymns. Here, the influence of the Holy Spirit on Simeon confirms his place as a prophet.[57]

At this point, we would like to draw attention to the formal consistency across all four hymns in Luke 1–2 (see the table below; see also appendix 1). By doing so, it lends credence to our thesis that rhetorically speaking,

54. In Luke's Gospel, νόμος occurs nine times, with five located here in Luke 2 (vv. 22, 23, 24, 27, 39), once in 10:26, twice in 16:16–17, and once in 24:24; cf. Strelan, *Luke the Priest*, 117–25, 129–30.

55. Bovon, *Luke 1*, 100.

56. Cf. Strelan, *Luke the Priest*, 137–38.

57. Tannehill, *Narrative Unity of Luke-Acts*, 1:39. See also n. 27 above.

all four hymns are similar in how they are situated within the narrative of Luke 1–2.

	1:45–55	1:68–79	2:14	2:29–32
Words of Praise	1:46–47	1:68a	2:14a	2:29
First Motive Clause	1:48	1:68b	2:14b	2:30
Second Motive Clause	1:49a			
Amplifying Statements	1:49b–53 (amplifies motive 2)	1:69–75 1:76–77 (about John)	2:14c	2:31–32
Summary	1:54–55	1:78–79		

In terms of actual content, the Nunc Dimittis (2:29–32) is no different from the other three hymns in that prophetic rhetorolect is doing significant work here. In Luke 2:29, Simeon opens with the statement that he is now being dismissed "according to your word" (κατὰ τὸ ῥῆμά σου), and when reading the broader context of this statement, it is clear that the τὸ ῥῆμα to which Simeon refers is the promise he had earlier received through the Holy Spirit that he would not die until he laid his eyes upon the "Lord's Messiah" (2:26). It is rather striking to see the consistent activation of the same topoi over and over again throughout these four hymns. First, there is often the prior work of the Holy Spirit to move the characters along (1:41, 67). Second, the readers encounter multiple references to the "first space" of prophetic discourse, that is to say, a geopolitical kingdom (1:16–17, 32–33, 51–55 68–74; 2:11, 26, 32).[58] Related to this is the third point, that this political kingdom would mean "salvation" for God's people through a "savior." It is striking that all four hymns contain a form of the

58. See Robbins ("Conceptual Blending," 164–67) for a good description of the various "first spaces" within early Christian rhetorolects, including prophetic discourse.

σωτηρ- word group: Luke 1:47 (Magnificat); 1:69, 71, 77 (Benedictus); 2:11 (Gloria); and 2:30 (Nunc Dimittis).[59] Fourth, each of the hymns demonstrates the significance of reaching back to Israel's Scriptures.[60] Despite the spatial location of Simeon in the temple, the context of the Nunc Dimittis and the words spoken therein reveal the dominant mode of discourse at work, one of early Christian prophetic discourse.

1.5. Summary

The foregoing discussion of the context and content of the four hymns in Luke 1–2 indicates that the author of Luke's Gospel is highly motivated by prophetic interests. The words spoken by angels, priests, prophet-like figures, and others continually draw on Israel's Scriptures as a way to *describe* the present reality with implications for the geopolitical kingdom of Israel. It should be reiterated here that this conclusion does not preclude the presence of priestly (or otherwise) elements in Luke 1–2, but only to highlight the fact that if one *dominant* mode of discourse must be named, it is prophetic rhetorolect. In PJ, is it possible to detect the sleight of hand that puts a different rhetorolect in the foreground and causes the prophetic discourse of the resource text to move into the background (Luke 1–2)?

2. Relocation of Hymnic Material in the Protevangelium of James

In this section, we will engage in a comparative exegesis of the hymns of Luke 1–2 that displays and interprets the relocation of fragments of the Lukan hymns in PJ. Here at the outset, it is important to keep in mind that the dominance of prophetic rhetorolect moves the narrative energetically along in Luke 1–2. Also, we need to remember that, from a technical standpoint, PJ does not reproduce any one of Luke's four hymns. In other words, we could say that the author of PJ omits all of Luke's hymns from the story he tells about Mary. The question we must ask about PJ is, Does the author of this infancy narrative operate within the same early Christian discourse

59. In fact, these four hymns account for 75 percent of all occurrences in Luke's Gospel (the other two are found in Luke 3:6; 19:9).

60. For a description of each of the hymn's allusions to the OT, see their respective analyses above. The Nunc Dimittis recalls the story of Abraham in Gen 15 (cf. Rusam, *Das Alte Testament*, 78–81).

as Luke, that is, early Christian prophetic rhetorolect? Or has he adopted a different rhetorolect that has significantly influenced how he uses aspects of the hymns in his narrative? If the opening and closing chapters of PJ are any indication, the dominant rhetorolect appears to be priestly. However, it remains to be seen whether this is indeed the case throughout this protogospel. Before moving to the analysis of Luke 1–2 and PJ, it may be helpful to rehearse the definition of these two types of rhetorolects with general comments about the texture of this infancy gospel.[61]

Prophetic rhetorolect is the blending of speech and actions of a prophet's body in an experiential space of God's kingdom on earth with conceptual space of God's cosmos. This rhetorolect presupposes that the prophet has received a divine message about God's will. The prophet speaks and acts in contexts that envision righteous judgments and actions by kings, who should be God's leaders who establish justice on the earth. *Priestly rhetorolect* is the blending of human experiences in a temple or other place of worship with a concept of temple city and God's cosmos. This rhetorolect presupposes that ritual actions benefit God in a manner that activates divine benefits for humans on earth.[62]

2.1. General Observations

In the very first chapter of PJ, Mary's father Joachim bears gifts (PJ 1.2, προσέφερε τὰ δῶρα) to give to the Lord. Unfortunately, despite his generosity before God, Joachim is disqualified from offering his gifts because of his childlessness (1.5), and even his wife, Anna, experiences ostracism due to her barrenness (2.6–7). While both Joachim and Anna know that they are unlikely to bear a child, they also understand God's acts in the past that make impossible things possible on behalf of his people. Joachim "remembered the patriarch Abraham" and how the Lord gave him a son late in life (1.8, ἐμνήσθη τοῦ πατριάρχου Ἀβραάμ), and Anna prayed to the Lord: "bless me … just as you blessed our mother Sarah and gave her a son" (2.9, εὐλόγησόν με … καθὼς εὐλόγησας τὴν μήτραν Σάρρας καὶ ἔδωκας αὐτῇ υἱόν). Conceptually, there is a measure of blending between priestly rhetorolect and prophetic rhetorolect. The temple functions immediately in PJ 1 as a place of importance and continues to do so as the narrative

61. This is only a partial definition of prophetic and priestly rhetorolects, adapted from Robbins, "Conceptual Blending," 166–71.

62. Robbins, *Invention*, xxvi–xxvii, cf. 219–328.

continues. However, the prophetic undertones that were present in Luke 1–2 have not been completely effaced, as the readers are told that the first two main figures of the story (Joachim and Anna) both recalled some act of God in the past that would be the lens through which they understand their present situation of barrenness.

Anna laments (3.3) that she has been "mocked and banished from the temple of the Lord" (ἐξεμυκτήρισαν καὶ ἐξώρισάν με ἐκ ναοῦ κυρίου[63]). She has been barred from participation in the temple cultus,[64] and in the psyche of PJ, this is a severe punishment indeed. Anna's response to her banishment is a series of "woe is me!" (6×, οἴμοι) statements in 3.4–8 that draws from prophetic pronouncements of woes upon those who have not lived in righteousness. Fortunately for Anna, an angel of the Lord

63. The underlined portion of the verb denotes a variant here, with some texts displaying the prefix (e.g., H. R. Smid, *Protevangelium Jacobi: A Commentary* [Assen: van Gorcum, 1965], 35–36) and others omitting it (e.g., Bart D. Ehrman and Zlatko Pleše, *The Apocryphal Gospels: Texts and Translations* [New York: Oxford University Press, 2011], 42–43; Hock, *Infancy Gospels*, 36–37). Regardless of which verb is displayed, the translators seem to detect no difference in meaning by translating the word as "to mock": Smid, *Jacobi*, 36; Ehrman and Pleše, *Apocryphal Gospels*, 43; Hock, *Infancy Gospels*, 37; Elliott, *Apocryphal New Testament*, 58; Silvia Pellegrini, "Das Protevangelium des Jakobus," in *Antike christliche Apokryphen in deutscher Übersetzung*, ed. C. Markschies and J. Schröter, 2 vols. (Tübingen: Mohr Siebeck, 2012), 2:903–29 (916; verspottet).

64. Ἐκμυκτηρίζω ("to deride, sneer"; BDAG, s.v.) is not a common word, found 5× only in 1 Esd 1:49; Pss 2:4; 21:8; 34:16; Luke 16:14; 23:35. A TLG search yields LXX and NT as the only attestations of this word prior to the early church fathers. Μυκτηρίζω ("turn up the nose at, treat with contempt"; BDAG, s.v.) occurs somewhat more frequently in the biblical text (15×): 1 Kgs 18:27; 2 Kgs 19:21; 2 Chr 36:16; 1 Macc 7:34; Ps 79:7; Prov 1:30; 11:12; 12:8; 15:5, 20; 23:9; Job 22:19; Isa 37:22; Jer 20:7; Ezek 8:17. Again, biblical use of the word far outweighs what we find in other sources. Cf. Hippocrates, *Morb.* 7.1.123; Dionysius Thrax, *Frag.* 43.2; Sib. Or. 1.171. Most instructive is 1 Esd 1:47–49: "Now also the leaders of the people and of the priests [τῶν ἱερέων] committed many acts of impiety and lawlessness, more than all the unclean deeds of all the nations, and they defiled the temple of the Lord [τὸ ἱερὸν τοῦ κυρίου] that had been sanctified in Jerusalem. And the God of their fathers sent word through his messenger to call them back, because he tried to spare them and his covert. But they mocked [ἐξεμυκτήρισαν] at his messengers, and on the day the Lord spoke, they were scoffing at his prophets until in his anger against his nation, on account of their impious acts, he ordered that the kings of the Chaldeans go up against them" (NETS). Here the priests themselves are the source of pollution for the temple and are the ones ridiculing divine messengers.

announces to her that she will indeed bear a child (4.1), and her response in 4.2 is instructive for discerning the mode of Christian discourse that is dominant: "Whether I give birth to a boy or a girl, I will offer it as a gift to the Lord [δῶρον κυρίῳ].... it will serve him [ἔσται λειτουργοῦν αὐτῷ] its whole life." There is no question here that the author of PJ envisions this child (i.e., Mary) serving as a priestly figure in the environs of the temple.

When Mary is yet a toddler, Anna no longer allows her to walk on ground until the child is brought to the temple of the Lord (6.3). Even her bedroom is converted into a sanctuary (6.4, ἁγίασμα), and nothing profane or unclean is allowed to pass through it/her.[65] At age one, Mary is blessed, first by the priests during her first birthday banquet (6.7), and then by the high priests (6.9). At age three, Mary is dedicated to the temple—here she is blessed yet again (7.7)—to live there until the age of maturity (8.2). She later joins a special retinue of virgins to spin threads for a veil (καταπέτασμα[66]) for the temple (10.1–10).

In summary, two conclusions may be drawn regarding the storyline of Mary up to this point in PJ. First, it is clear that the temple is the main location that energizes the narrative; the story of the infancy gospel begins and ends here. Also, Mary has become so closely identified with the temple that anything else that lies in proximity to this topos has been

65. The Greek is not as ambiguous as the translations make it out to be: καὶ ἐποίησεν ἁγίασμα ἐν τῷ κοιτῶνι αὐτῆς, καὶ πᾶν κοινὸν καὶ ἀκάθαρτον οὐκ εἴα διέρχεσθαι δι᾽ αὐτῆς ("And she made a sanctuary in her bedroom and all profane and impure thing she did not allow to pass through her.") Furthermore, there are no variants that seem to be at play here. The personal pronoun is in singular feminine form, so it is not clear why some translators have decided to read αὐτῆς as connected to the bedroom. See, e.g., Elliot (*Apocryphal New Testament*, 59): "did not permit anything common or unclean to pass through it"; Pellegrini ("Das Protevangelium des Jakobus," 2:917): "und weder Profanes noch Unreines ließ sie zu ihm gelangen." (If Pellegrini was referring to Mary, she would have used the dative feminine, *ihr*.) If the pronoun did in fact refer to the bedroom (masc.) or the sanctuary (neut.) one would expect to find αὐτοῦ. On the other hand, Ehrman and Pleše (*Apocryphal Gospels*, 47) and Hock (*Infancy Gospels*, 43) translate αὐτῆς more freely: "to pass through her lips" and "to pass the child's lips" respectively. The phrase δι᾽ αὐτῆς occurs 8× in the LXX (Num 4:8; Josh 2:18; Mic 2:13; Joel 4:17; Zech 2:15; Jer 18:16; twice in Ezek 44:2) and 5× in the NT (Matt 7:13; GJohn 11:4; Rom 7:11; Heb 11:4; 12:11, 15), and in none of these instances is αὐτῆς used to refer to a masculine or neuter antecedent.

66. This refers to the veil of the holy of holies in the Jerusalem temple (e.g., Exod 26:31–37; Lev 4:17; 16:2; Num 3:10, 26 LXX; 2 Chr 3:14; Matt 27:51; Mark 15:38; Luke 23:45; Heb 6:19; 9:3; 10:20).

brought into its orbit, even at the cost of dislodging it from its original anchor. For example, Zechariah loses his "role" as the husband of Elizabeth and gains the role of high priest of the temple.[67] Second, ritual practices in the temple continue to find their rationale in this text. Throughout the narrative, various characters are going to the temple, bringing gifts to the temple, interacting with priests, and concerning themselves with ritual purity. Silvia Pellegrini aptly summarizes the important theological interests of PJ as "righteousness, belief, purity."[68] Given these features, it can certainly be inferred that priestly rhetorolect energizes PJ. If one can accept the role of Mary as the "feminine bodily intermediary between God and Jesus,"[69] then we can go one step further to add that as the only human figure who enjoys this special relationship with both God and Jesus, she also serves as a mediating figure between God/Jesus and other humans in the story. This type of conceptual hierarchy works within a priestly rhetorolect in which the priest(s), in this case Mary as a type of priest/temple, supervise "beneficial exchange between God and humans."[70] A comparative exegesis below will provide a careful analysis of how the prophetic hymns of Luke 1–2 have been read through the lens of priestly rhetorolect by the author of PJ.

---

67. While Luke explicitly identifies Zechariah as the husband of Elizabeth (Luke 1:5), the narrator of PJ is not so concerned with this fact. Zechariah is mentioned in the following accounts, none of which explicitly involves the figures of Elizabeth or John (with the exception of one example): (1) Zechariah is charged by an angel of the Lord to gather widowers, one of whom will take the virgin Mary to be his wife (PJ 8.3–9); (2) the narrator adds a brief note that at some point during Mary's spinning of the threads, Zechariah became mute (PJ 10.8–10) without any narrative detail concerning his doubt about the birth of his son as in Luke 1:13–20; (3) Herod was seeking John and asks Zechariah where he has hidden his son (PJ 23.1–2; this is the only exception where their parent-child relationship is implied); and (4) Zechariah is murdered with his death reported to the people (PJ 23.7–24.12). Regarding the question of Zechariah's death and the possible connection to 2 Chr 24:20–22, see Sheldon H. Blank, "The Death of Zechariah in Rabbinic Literature," *HUCA* 12–13 (1937–1938): 327–46; Charles L. Quarles, "The *Protevangelium of James* as an Alleged Parallel to Creative Historiography in the Synoptic Birth Narratives," *BBR* 8 (1998): 139–49.

68. "[D]ie Gerechtigkeit, der Glaube, die Reinheit" (Pellegrini, "Das Protevangelium des Jakobus," 2:912).

69. "[L]eiblichen Mittlerin zwischen Gott und Jesus" (Pellegrini, "Kindheitsevangelien," 2:891).

70. Robbins, "Conceptual Blending," 181.

2.2. Relocation of Topoi in the Magnificat: Protevangelium of James 12.1–3 and Luke 1:36–56

Comparison of the opening of PJ 12.1 with the Lukan scene that introduces Elizabeth's pregnancy (see the table below) shows how prophetic knowledge about Elizabeth in Luke is reconfigured into early Christian priestly discourse that places the temple and its blessings to the people of Israel in the foreground.[71]

Step 1: From Prophetic Knowledge about Elizabeth to Blessing at the Temple*

Luke 1:36, 39	PJ 12.1–3
(1) [36] And now, your **relative Elizabeth** in her old age [Ελισάβετ ἡ συγγενίς σου … ἐν γήρει αὐτῆς] has also conceived a son; and this is the sixth month for her who was said to be barren.	(1) [1] She [Mary] made the **PURPLE** and the **SCARLET** [τὴν πορφύραν καὶ τὸ κόκκινον], and brought them to the **TEMPLE**.
(2) See below Luke 1:46, "My soul **magnifies** the Lord [Μεγαλύνει ἡ ψυχή μου τὸν κύριον]" See below Luke 1:48, "**all the generations will bless** me" [μακαριοῦσίν με πᾶσαι αἱ γενεαί]	(2) [2] The **PRIEST** took them and **BLESSED** her [ὁ ἀρχιερεὺς εὐλόγησεν αὐτήν], "Mary, the Lord God has **magnified** your name [ἐμεγάλυνεν … τὸ ὄνομά σου]; **you will be BLESSED** among **all the generations** of the earth [ἔσῃ εὐλογημένη ἐν πάσαις ταῖς γεναῖς τῆς γῆς]."

71. The following tables are an adaptation of the method of analyzing opening-middle-closing texture presented in Vernon K. Robbins, *Exploring the Texture of Texts: A Guide to Socio-Rhetorical Interpretation* (Valley Forge, PA: Trinity Press International, 1996), 19–21.

(3) [39] In those days **Mary** set out and **went** [Μαριὰμ … ἐπορεύθη] with haste to a Judean town in the hill country,	(3) [3] Full of joy, **Mary went** [Μαρία ἀπῄει] to her **relative Elizabeth** [συγγενίδα … Ἐλισάβεδ].

* Note the specific stylistic markers in the OMC tables: bold = same (or similar) wording; bold caps = repetitive texture or important topoi; underlined = important data in Luke 1–2 or PJ not parallel in the other text. N.B.: For some words/phrases, multiple markers may be overlaid unto the text.

It was already noted above how important the Mary-temple relationship is for the narrative of the infancy gospel. Here, Mary has finally completed the task that was set before her in PJ 10.6–10, namely, to spin scarlet and purple threads for the veil of the holy of holies in the temple. Mary brings the fruit of her labor to the high priest and is subsequently doubly blessed by him. It is striking that the very first word of Mary in Luke 1:46, μεγαλύνει (Lat.: *magnificat*), occurs here on the lips of the high priest. This is one of the four instances in which the topos of "magnification" has been expanded into a repetitive texture that begins with the birth of Mary and reaches its highpoint when Mary is about to give birth to Jesus. The concept of "being magnified" first occurs when Anna finds out she has given birth to a girl. Anna exclaims, "My soul has been magnified this day" (PJ 5.8, Ἐμεγαλύνθη ἡ ψυχή μου ἐν τῇ ἡμέρᾳ ταύτῃ). It occurs the second time when Mary, at the age of three, is brought to the temple in order to dwell there. When Mary goes up the steps to the temple, the priest blesses her, saying, "The Lord God has magnified your name among all generations" (PJ 7.7, Ἐμεγάλυνεν κύριος τὸ ὄνομά σου ἐν πάσαις ταῖς γενεαῖς). Here it is noticeable that the priest does not magnify the name of the Lord for Mary's coming, as one might expect from Mary's Magnificat in Luke. Rather, the Lord God magnifies Mary's name. The reader expects that Mary has become the center of attention by this time in the story. But one might not expect the Lord God to "magnify the name of Mary," since remarkable events in the entire story really should magnify "the name of the Lord God." The verb of "magnification" occurs a third time in the scene discussed above when Mary, after her stay in the temple is over, completes her task of spinning purple and scarlet threads for the veil (10.1–10; 12.1). When she takes the completed work to the high priest, he accepts it and blesses Mary with an alternative version of PJ 7.7: "Mary, the Lord God has magnified [ἐμεγάλυνεν] your name and so you will be blessed by all the generations of the earth" (12.2). At this point, Mary rejoices and leaves to visit her relative Elizabeth. The fourth and final occurrence of the verb emerges on the midwife's lips when a dark cloud overshadows the cave in which the birth of Jesus will occur. The midwife exclaims, "My soul has been magnified today [ἐμεγαλύνθη ἡ ψυχή μου σήμερον], because my eyes have seen a paradoxical wonder in that salvation has come to Israel" (19.14). This creates the repetitive pattern shown in the table below.

Being Magnified in Protevangelium of James

Anna, mother of Mary, at the birth of Mary	**"My soul has been magnified** this day" (5.8).
Priest when three-year-old Mary comes to stay at the temple	**"The Lord God has magnified your name** among **all generations.** In you the Lord will disclose his redemption to the people of Israel during the last days" (7.7–8).
High priest when Mary brings the completed purple and scarlet threads to him	"Mary, **the Lord God has magnified your name** and so you will be blessed by **all** the **generations** of the earth" (12.2).
Midwife when a dark cloud overshadows the cave where Jesus will be born	**"My soul has been magnified** today, because my eyes have seen a paradoxical wonder in that salvation has come to Israel" (19.14).

The first and fourth occurrences, which are both aorist passive, "magnified" (ἐμεγαλύνθη), frame the section of the repetitive texture from the birth of Mary to the birth of Jesus. Each one reconfigures Mary's statement in the Magnificat, "My soul magnifies the Lord" (μεγαλύνει ἡ ψυχή μου τὸν κύριον) to "My soul has been magnified" (ἐμεγαλύνθη ἡ ψυχή μου). The central two occurrences present a magnification of the name of Mary. Both focus totally on Mary, repeating the assertion, "The Lord God has magnified your name" (ἐμεγάλυνεν ... τὸ ὄνομά σου), with an additional statement about "all generations." The second occurrence in the center highlights the focus on Mary's name by starting with direct address, "Mary."

Mary's immediate response to the blessing of the high priest (PJ 12.2) is to go to her relative Elizabeth. In Luke 1:39, in contrast, Mary's decision to visit Elizabeth is motivated at least in part by Gabriel's message to her that Elizabeth is pregnant in her old age. In Luke 1 Mary proceeds "with haste,"[72] and this appears to be motivated by the prophetic speech from the angel Gabriel. In PJ 12.3 Mary goes off to Elizabeth "full of joy" (lit. "taking joy"; χαρὰν δὲ λαβοῦσα) after the priest has blessed her so magnanimously. Yet Mary shows a level of timidity in PJ that is not evident in Mary in Luke 1. In the canonical text, Mary plays a fully active role as she goes "with haste" (1:39) and directly enters "the house of Zechariah" (1:40). In addition, once Mary is inside the home, she initiates the interaction by greeting Elizabeth.[73] In contrast, the Mary of PJ is not in a hurry, and she remains outside the home, indicating her presence simply by knocking on the door.

Step 2: From Blessing filled with Prophetic Promise to Priestly Blessing from Elizabeth and John

Luke 1:40–45	PJ 12.1–8
(4) 40 where she entered the house of Zechariah and **GREETED** Elizabeth [εἰσῆλθεν εἰς τὸν οἶκον Ζαχαρίου καὶ ἠσπάσατο τὴν Ἐλισάβετ].	(4) 4 She knocked on the door [ἔκρουσεν πρὸς τὴν θύραν];

72. Μετὰ σπουδῆς. This is not a common phrase in the LXX/NT: Exod 12:11; 1 Esd 2:25; 3 Macc 4:15; 5:24, 27; Ps 77:33; Wis 19:2; Ezek 7:11; Dan 10:7; Mark 6:24; Luke 1:39.

73. The succinct statement by the Roman architect and military engineer Vitruvius (*Arch.* 6.5.1) demonstrates the social norms regarding entry into private space: "When we have arranged our plan with a view to aspect, we must go on to consider how, in private buildings [*privatis aedificiis*], the rooms belonging to the family, and how those which are shared with visitors, should be planned. For, into the private rooms no one can come uninvited."

5) 41 **When Elizabeth heard** [ἤκουσεν … ἡ Ἐλισάβετ] Mary's **GREETING** [τὸν ἀσπασμόν], **THE CHILD** [τὸ βρέφος] **leaped** in her womb. And Elizabeth was filled with the Holy Spirit	(5) and **when Elizabeth heard** [ἀκούσασα ἡ Ἐλισάβεδ] she cast aside the **SCARLET** [τὸ κόκκινον] and ran to the door and opened it.
(6) 42 and exclaimed with a loud cry, "**BLESSED** are you among women, and **BLESSED** is the fruit of your womb.	(6) 5 And she **BLESSED** Mary and said,
(7) 43And **why has this happened to me, that the mother of my Lord comes to me?**	(7) **Why has this happened to me, that the mother of my Lord comes to me*?**
(8) 44 **For behold**, as soon as I heard the sound of your greeting, **THE CHILD** [τὸ βρέφος] **in my womb leaped** for joy [ἐσκίρτησεν ἐν ἀγαλλιάσει].	(8) **For behold, THAT WHICH IS IN ME** [τὸ ἐν ἐμοὶ] **leaped** [ἐσκίρτησεν] and **BLESSED** you."
45 And **BLESSED** is she who believed that there would be a fulfillment of what was spoken to her by the Lord."	

* A near verbatim twelve-word string from the Lukan account (the only difference is the location of the verb):

PJ 12.5, πόθεν μοι τοῦτο ἵνα ἡ μήτηρ τοῦ κυρίου μου ἔλθῃ πρὸς ἐμέ;
Luke 1:43, πόθεν μοι τοῦτο ἵνα ἔλθῃ ἡ μήτηρ τοῦ κυρίου μου πρὸς ἐμέ;

As the scene unfolds in both accounts, there are significant differences in the events that occur. After Mary knocks on the door in PJ 12.4a, Elizabeth casts aside the scarlet, runs to the door, opens it, and "blesses" Mary. The action with "the scarlet" is a likely reference to Elizabeth's own connection to the temple—evidence of priestly rhetorolect. In addition, her immediate "blessing" of Mary is imitative of the blessing of the priest when Mary first went to the temple as a three-year-old and the blessing when she took the scarlet and purple threads to the priest just before her visit to Elizabeth.

In addition, Elizabeth tells Mary that "that which is in her womb" leaped and "blessed" (εὐλόγησεν) her. This means that the repetitive texture of blessings on Mary includes not only blessings from the priest at the temple and a blessing from Elizabeth, the mother of John, but also a priestly blessing from the unborn John! It is noticeable in this context that there is no mention of Mary's child or other language that evokes a prophetic mode of discourse. The entire nature of the actions is priestly.

In the Lukan account of Mary's visit of Elizabeth, there are substantive prophetic aspects in the context of priestly blessings. When Mary enters the house "of Zechariah" and calls out a greeting to Elizabeth, the babe in Elizabeth's womb leaps and Elizabeth is filled with the Holy Spirit (1:41–42). The final event is clearly an activation of a prophetic topos woven into the Lukan corpus.[74] This topos also figures significantly in the Magnificat of Luke 1:46–55.[75] As the scene unfolds in Luke, blessings occur, and analysis of the nature of the "blessings" reveals that they are not uniformly focused on Mary, as they are in PJ. In Luke 1:41–55 the blessings are located on the lips of Elizabeth (1:42, 45), and they are enclosed by markers of prophetic discourse (1:41, 45b).[76] The object and the cause of these blessings are not uniform or explicit. In *Blessing 1* (1:42a) Elizabeth exclaims, "Blessed are you among women." Mary is described here as blessed, but the reason for her blessing is related to *Blessing 2* (1:42b), where the "fruit of her womb" is called blessed.[77] In *Blessing 3* (1:45) Elizabeth extols the one who believed in the fulfillment of things previously spoken by the Lord. Here, it is not immediately clear who this blessed figure is. In *Blessings 1* and *2*, Elizabeth uses the second person pronoun (σύ, σου) to connect the blessings to Mary, but in 1:45, the use of the impersonal third person construction makes uncertain a direct link between this blessing to Mary and/or her fruit. In other words, it could just as well be applied to Elizabeth as the "one who believed," thinking of the earlier account in Luke

74. See n. 27 above.

75. See the analysis of the Magnificat on pages 133–37 above.

76. Marker 1 (Luke 1:41): Elizabeth is filled with the Holy Spirit. Marker 2 (Luke 1:45b): Elizabeth describes the importance of belief in the words previously spoken by the Lord. There is one more possible instance of "blessing" in this section (both in PJ and Luke), spoken by Mary of her blessing (PJ 12.6, εὐλογοῦσιν; Luke 1:48, μακαριοῦσιν). However, this form of blessing is looking forward to Mary's future state of blessing while all other "blessings" point to something that has already occurred.

77. Bovon, *Luke 1*, 59.

1:24–25 regarding her confidence in what God has also done for her own situation.[78] On the other hand, it leads in Luke to Mary's pronouncement of a full-bodied "Magnificat" that "magnifies the Lord" for all that the Lord has done for her (1:46–49).

In PJ all of the details find their culmination in an ending that can initially be described as an omission of the Magnificat in Luke 1:46–55 by the author (see the table below).

Step 3: From Magnifying the Lord to Forgetting the Mysteries

Luke 1:46–55	PJ 12.6
(9) [46] And **Mary** said,	(9) [6] But **Mary** FORGOT
(10) "**MY SOUL MAGNIFIES** [μεγαλύνει] **THE LORD**, [47] and my spirit rejoices in God my Savior, [48] for he has looked with favor on the lowliness of his servant.	(10) the **MYSTERIES** that the archangel Gabriel had spoken to her and gazed at the sky and said,
(11) Surely, from now on **ALL THE GENERATIONS WILL BLESS ME** [μακαριοῦσίν με πᾶσαι αἱ γενεαί]; [49] for the mighty one has done great things for me, and holy is his name. [50]	(11) "**WHO AM I, LORD**, that **ALL THE GENERATIONS** OF THE EARTH **WILL BLESS ME** [πᾶσαι αἱ γενεαὶ τῆς γῆς εὐλογοῦσίν με]?"
His mercy is for those who fear him from generation to generation. [51] He has shown strength with his arm; he has scattered the proud in the thoughts of their hearts. [52] He has brought down the powerful from their thrones, and lifted up the lowly; [53] he has filled the hungry with good things, and sent the rich away	

78. NA[28] suggests an allusion to Gen 30:23. See Rusam, *Das Alte Testament*, 45.

> empty. [54] He has helped his servant Israel, in remembrance of his mercy, [55] according to the promise he made to our ancestors, to Abraham and to his descendants forever."

While in Luke Mary responds to the blessings by "speaking" (Luke 1:46, Καὶ εἶπεν Μαριάμ), in PJ Mary responds by "forgetting" (PJ 12.6, Μαριὰμ δὲ ἐπελάθετο). Given the preceding analysis, it should not be surprising that the Magnificat has been fragmented and scattered throughout various places in the story. That is to say, if priestly rhetorolect is indeed energizing the narrative, the Magnificat—a hymn filled with prophetic speech and words of remembrance—might be perceived to be dissonant with the rhetorical flow of PJ. It is striking that the only remaining vestiges that the author of PJ has left from the Magnificat concern the topoi of blessing and magnifying.[79] It is also noticeable that in PJ Mary is filled with "forgetting" rather than remembrance.

In the context of Mary's forgetting, there is one more detail that bears mentioning. On the heels of Mary's sudden spell of amnesia, the things that were spoken to her by the angel Gabriel are called "mysteries" (PJ 12.6). At first glance, it is difficult to ascertain the motive for the use of the term: why did the author call the things spoken by Gabriel "mysteries" (τὰ μυστήρια) when "words" (τὰ ῥήματα or οἱ λόγοι) would have sufficed? The term "mysteries" applied to a wide range of activities: the local cults for a particular city-state; initiations and purifications from wandering priests; and great international loci of pilgrimage such as that at Eleusis and Samothrace.[80] Despite the variety, all of these activities took place within the

79. In fact, these might even be called the least "prophetic" of all the words found in the Magnificat. There is the possibility of an allusion to Gen 30:13 (and to a lesser degree Mal 3:12), though in actual content, the circumstances are not the same. In Rusam's thorough analysis of allusions in the Magnificat (*Das Alte Testament*, 65–69), Luke 1:48b plays a very small role in the overall composition's recall of and allusions to the Hebrew Bible.

80. Sandra Blakely, "Toward an Archaeology of Secrecy: Power, Paradox, and the Great Gods of Samothrace," *Archeological Papers of the American Anthropological Association* 21 (2011): 52.

realm of ritual, and so it is not unexpected that the author of PJ would reinterpret the things spoken by Gabriel not as *prophecy* but as *mystery*.

The closing of the event is similar in both accounts, though the author of PJ has made the narrative flow better in grammatical terms (see the table below).[81]

Step 4: From Magnifying the Lord to Forgetting the Mysteries

Luke 1:56	PJ 12.7–8
(1) [56] **And Mary remained with her about three months** [Ἔμεινεν δὲ Μαριὰμ σὺν αὐτῇ ὡς μῆνας τρεῖς]	(1) [7] **And she stayed with Elizabeth for three months** (καὶ ἐποίησεν τρεῖς μῆνας πρὸς τὴν Ἐλισάβετ).
(2) and then **returned to her home** [καὶ ὑπέστρεψεν εἰς τὸν οἶκον αὐτῆς].	(2) [8] Day by day her own belly grew.
	(3) Mary then **returned to her home** [Μαριὰμ ἀπῆλθεν εἰς τὸν οἶκον αὐτῆς] **IN FEAR**, and **HID HERSELF** from the sons of Israel.
	(4) [9] She was sixteen when these **MYSTERIES** happened to her.

As mentioned above, since Mary is purported to be the speaker of the Magnificat in Luke 1:46–55, it would have been better to write "And *she* remained with *Elizabeth* about three months" (Ἔμεινεν δὲ σὺν Ἐλισάβετ ὡς μῆνας τρεῖς), rather than "And *Mary* remained with *her* about three months" (Luke 1:56). Though there is no Magnificat in PJ, Mary still speaks some words concerning her future state of blessedness (PJ 12.6). The author writes, "And *she* stayed with *Elizabeth* for three months" (PJ 12.7), adding the detail that Mary's stomach/womb was growing larger (PJ 12.8a).[82]

81. See the discussion on the grammar of Luke 1:56 above.

82. The verb ὀγκόω is unattested in the LXX/NT, although it is found once each

In each instance the author's final comments bring the narrative to an end, but the tone of the account reveals quite a different picture of the Mary of PJ and of Luke. In Luke, there is movement from fear (1:29–30) to praise, with a thoroughly positive picture of Mary in 1:46–55. In the closing of PJ, the reader encounters a different Mary: a sixteen-year-old woman who remained fearful (12.8, φοβηθεῖσα) "when these mysteries happened to her" (12.9).

It is important for us to explore this result by looking forward a bit in Mary's story in PJ. After Mary's visit to Elizabeth, things do not go very well for Mary. When Joseph comes home from his building projects and finds Mary pregnant (13.1), he accuses her of having "forgotten the Lord your God" (13.7). When he asks her where that which is "in her womb" came from, she responds that she does not know (13.10). After this, Joseph does not talk to Mary any more (14.1). When Annas the scholar comes to the house to ask why Joseph has not attended the assembly and observes that Mary is pregnant (15.3), Annas tells the high priest, and he sends temple assistants to bring her to the temple court along with Joseph (15.4–9). In this context, the high priest joins Joseph in accusing Mary of having "forgotten the Lord her God" after she has been raised in the holy of holies and fed by heavenly messengers (15.10–12). The shaming of Mary causes her to weep bitterly as she protests that she indeed has never had sex with any man (15.13). At this point both Mary and Joseph are forced to drink water of testing, but when they are sent into the wilderness they return unharmed (16.5–6). With this result, Joseph takes Mary back to his home "celebrating and praising the God of Israel" (16.8). Joseph's joy, however, does not produce hymnic praise to God. If it did, we might find fragments of Zechariah's hymnic praise after the birth of his son John in it, or we might even find some fragments of Mary's Magnificat in it. But like Mary, who does not praise God in a hymn like she does in the Lukan Magnificat, Joseph also does not praise God with even one poetic statement. Does this mean there are no other fragments of the Lukan hymns

in Revelation of Ezra 5.13 and T. Levi 6.9. In PJ it occurs 4×: 12.8; 13.1; 15.3, 8. It is also common in Greco-Roman literature (e.g., Euripides, *El.* 381; *Ion* 388; Xenophon, *Mem.* 1.2.25; Ps.-Aristotle, *Probl.* 966A; Ps.-Longinus, *Subl.* 28.2; Plutarch, *Stoic. rep.* 1043E; *De laude* 547E), though the use of ὀγκόω with γαστήρ is rare (a TLG search yields only Aesop, *Fab.* 47; Josephus, *Ant.* 1.257; Ps.-Galen, *Def. med.* 19.401 prior to the third century CE).

anywhere in PJ? We must look further to find the answer, and what we find may be a bit surprising.

2.3. Relocation of Topoi in the Benedictus: Protevangelium of James 23.1–9 and Luke 1:66–79

There is no account of the birth of John in PJ, so there is no immediately obvious place for a relocation of fragments of Zechariah's Benedictus (Luke 1:67–79) in this story that focuses on the births of Mary and Jesus, rather than on the births of John and Jesus. There is reference to the newborn son of Elizabeth and Zechariah, however, when Herod is looking for him with the intent of killing him. Might there be a fragment or two of Zechariah's Benedictus somewhere in the account of Herod's agents' looking for John?

As we look for a place where some fragments of Zechariah's Benedictus might appear in PJ, we need to look more closely at the context of Zechariah's hymn in Luke. We must recall that in Luke Zechariah is mute from the time of the appearance of the angel to him in the temple (1:20) until after John is born (1:57). At the time of his circumcision on the eighth day after the birth, when Elizabeth and Zechariah must have a name for the child, the expectation is to name the child Zechariah after his father (1:59). When Elizabeth asserts that his name should be John and people question her about it, they motion to Zechariah and he writes on a tablet, "His name is John" (1:63). At this point Zechariah regains his speech with praise to God (1:63), and this raises the question among the people: "What then will this child become?" (1:66). In answer to this question, "Zechariah was filled with the Holy Spirit and spoke prophetically" with the Benedictus (1:68–79).

Since, as stated above, there is no account of the birth of John in PJ, and also there is no circumcision event, there is no special occasion for people to ask Zechariah what John will become. But there is a question put to Zechariah about his son in PJ. When officers sent out by Herod find Zechariah "serving at the altar" (in the Jerusalem temple), they ask him, "Where have you hidden your son?" (23.1). This question provides an opening for PJ to include statements by Zechariah that reconfigure statements in the Benedictus from a prophetic to a priestly mode. The reconfiguration of Zechariah, his son John, and the Benedictus from prophetic promise to priestly death unfolds in three steps. The first step shows how PJ reconfigures Zechariah's prophetic function in Luke into an entirely priestly role (see table below). This emerges when Herod sends officers to him asking him where he has hidden his son John.

Step 1: From Prophetic to Priestly Zechariah

Luke 1:66–67	PJ 23.1–3
(1) [66] All who heard them pondered them and said,	(1) [1] Herod, though, kept looking for John [2] and sent officers to Zechariah **SERVING AT THE ALTAR** [ἐν τῷ θυσιαστηρίῳ] with this message for him:
(2) "What then will this **child** be?" For, indeed, **THE HAND OF THE LORD** was with him.	(2) "**WHERE** have you **HIDDEN YOUR SON?**"
(3) [67] Then his father Zechariah was **FILLED WITH THE HOLY SPIRIT** and spoke this **PROPHECY saying**:	(3) [3] But he answered them **saying, "I AM A MINISTER** [λειτουργός] of God, **ATTENDING** to his **TEMPLE**. How should I **KNOW WHERE MY SON IS?**"

Instead of responding to the question of Herod's officers in a prophetic mode, as in Luke, Zechariah responds to them in a priestly mode: "I am a minister [λειτουργός] of God, attending to the temple of the Lord [τῷ ναῷ κυρίου]. How should I know where my son is?" (23.3). This leads to the next step, where the agents report back to Herod what Zechariah has told them (see table below).

Step 2: From a Mighty Savior Who Saves from the Hand of All Who Hate to a Priest Whose Blood Is in the Hand of Herod

Luke 1:68–75	PJ 23.4–6
(4) [68] "**BLESSED** be the Lord God of **ISRAEL**, for he has looked favorably on his people	(4) [4] So the agents left and reported all this to Herod, who became angry and said, "Is

and redeemed them. 69 He has **RAISED UP A MIGHTY SAVIOR** for us in the **HOUSE OF HIS SERVANT DAVID**, 70 as he spoke through the mouth of his holy **PROPHETS** from of old, 71 that we would be **SAVED FROM OUR ENEMIES** and from **THE HAND** of all who hate us.	**HIS SON** going to rule over **ISRAEL**?"
(5) 72 Thus he has shown the mercy **PROMISED** to our ancestors, and has **REMEMBERED** his holy covenant, 73 the oath that he swore to our ancestor Abraham,	(5) 5 And he sent his agents back with this message for him: "Tell me the truth. **WHERE IS YOUR SON**?
(6) to grant us 74 that we, being rescued from **THE HANDS OF OUR ENEMIES**, might **SERVE** him without fear, 75 in holiness and righteousness before him all our days.	(6) Do you not **KNOW** that I have your **BLOOD IN MY HAND**? 6 And the officers went and reported this message to him.

When the agents return to Herod, he asks them, "Is his son going to rule over Israel?" (23.4). Zechariah's Benedictus in Luke essentially provides the answer to the question raised by Herod. In the first part of the Benedictus, Zechariah blesses the Lord God of Israel for raising up a mighty savior "in the house of his servant David" (1:69). As a result, Zechariah says, "we, being rescued from the hands of our enemies, might serve him without fear, in holiness and righteousness before him all our days" (1:73). In this part of the Benedictus Zechariah is speaking about Jesus (vv. 68–75); then in the last part he speaks about John (vv. 76–79). Taken together in PJ, Zechariah's answer to the agents and Herod's question about one who will rule over Israel "embody" the realities of Zechariah's Benedictus in Luke. But they embody them in a totally "priestly" context in PJ.

As the episode unfolds, PJ shifts the prophetic topos of the power of God to save us "from our enemies and from the hand of all who hate us" (Luke 1:71) to the priestly topos of sacrifice in the temple when the enemy has "your blood" in his "hand" (23.5). Throughout his responses to the officers, Zechariah embodies the "prophetic reality" of Luke 1:74–75 in a mode of "priestly sacrifice." He speaks "without fear" as a high priest in the temple who "serves" the Lord God in a manner prophesied by the Zechariah in Luke, namely, "in holiness and righteous before him in all his days" (Luke 1:74–75). This priestly embodiment of the prophetic promise, however, changes Zechariah from a prophetic speaker in Luke to a martyr for God in PJ. This leads to step 3 of the episode (see table below).

Step 3: From the Tender Mercy of God in the Breaking of Dawn to Innocent Priestly Blood at the Temple at Daybreak

Luke 1:76–79	PJ 23.7–9
(7) [76] And you, child, will be called the **PROPHET OF THE MOST HIGH**; for you will go before the Lord to prepare his ways, [77] to **GIVE KNOWLEDGE OF SALVATION** to his people by the **FORGIVENESS OF THEIR SINS.**	(7) [7] Zechariah answered, "I am a **MARTYR FOR GOD**. Take my **BLOOD**.
(8) [78] By the **TENDER MERCY OF OUR GOD,**	(8) [8] The Lord, though, will receive my spirit because you are shedding **INNOCENT BLOOD** at the entrance to the **TEMPLE** of the Lord."
(9) **the dawn** from on high **WILL BREAK** upon us,	(9) [9] And so **at daybreak** Zechariah was **MURDERED,**
(10) [79] to give light to those who sit in **DARKNESS** and in the **SHADOW OF DEATH,** to guide our feet into the way of peace."	(10) but the people of Israel **DID NOT KNOW** that he had been **MURDERED.**

In a deeply ironical way in PJ, Zechariah's response and Herod's question shift the mode of the episode from the prophetic hope of being saved from one's enemies to "serving" God through priestly death in God's temple when an enemy has them "in his hand." Instead of a focus on "the tender mercy of our God," the story shifts to the Lord's receiving of Zechariah's spirit when his innocent blood is shed at the entrance of the temple. This shifts the focus, in Luke, from "the dawn" of a new day that will bring a promising new era to Israel to a focus on the murder of Zechariah at daybreak in PJ. The new day brings murder rather than a promise of peace, but the people of Israel sit in darkness about this "shadow of death." They do not know Zechariah has been murdered.

The closings of the Zechariah stories respectively in Luke and PJ produce very different stories for the father of John. While Zechariah's prophetic words in Luke's Benedictus end with a hopeful statement concerning the coming light and peace for those who have been waiting for God to act in history, Zechariah in PJ experiences martyrdom at the hands of Herod's agents at the temple. The hand of the enemy has not been removed from him. Rather, he dies at the hand of officers sent by Herod. Through the act of the pouring of blood (PJ 23.7; 24.4), the reconfiguration of the role of Zechariah from prophet (Luke) to priest (PJ) is complete. In Luke's Gospel, Zechariah begins as a priestly figure and becomes a prophet filled with the Holy Spirit.[83] In PJ, Zechariah emerges as the high priest in 8.6–7 and remains tied closely to the temple to the end of his life. In Luke, then, the character of Zechariah travels from the role of a priest whom an angel punishes with muteness to the role of a prophet who promises great things both for Jesus and John. In PJ, the portrayal of Zechariah is much different. There is only a brief allusion to his muteness, in PJ 10.9–10, as the story moves through his claim not to know where his son is hidden to his death at the altar of the temple. Rather than functioning momentarily as a prophet and then disappearing from the story, as Zechariah does in Luke, Zechariah moves into the center of the story, and this leads us to the dramatic finish of PJ.

83. Luke 1:23 tells the reader that at a certain point in time, Zechariah's days of service in the temple have come to an end.

2.4. Relocation of Topoi in the Gloria: Protevangelium of James 24.1–11 and Luke 2:9–15

If it was a surprise to discover the close relation between the episode that leads to Zechariah's death and Zechariah's Benedictus in Luke, it may be even more surprising to find a relation between the episode in which the priests find out about the murder of Zechariah and the Gloria in Luke. This leads us to the next part of the story (see table below).

Step 1: From Glory and Fear in the Presence of an Angel of the Lord to Fear while Waiting to Glorify God in the Presence of Zechariah

Luke 2:9–15	PJ 24.1–11
(1) 9 Then an angel of the Lord stood before them,	(1) 1 At the hour of formal greetings the priests departed but Zechariah did not meet and bless them as was customary.
(2) and the **glory of the Lord** [δόξα κυρίου] shone around them,	(2) 2 And so the priests waited around for Zechariah, to greet him with prayer and to **glorify the Most High God** [δοξάσαι τὸν ὕψιστον θεόν].
(3) and they were very **afraid** [ἐφοβήθησαν φόβον μέγαν].	(3) 3 But when he did not show up, they all became **AFRAID** [ἐφοβήθησαν]. 4 One of them, however, summoned up his courage, entered the sanctuary, and saw dried **BLOOD** next to the Lord's **ALTAR**.

Comparative exegesis between the episode where the priests become aware of Zechariah's death and Luke 1–2 reveals that PJ relocates the topos of fear in the context of angels' glorifying of the Lord in the Gloria in Luke to fear that enters the priests as they come to "glorify the Most High God" with Zechariah in the early morning. In Luke, an angel appears before shepherds, with the glory of the Lord shining around them, and the shepherds become afraid. In PJ, the priests come to greet high priest Zechariah with prayer and glorify the Most High God, but when Zechariah does not appear, they become afraid. Apparently PJ presents a daily ritual of the priests where they came in the early morning to greet the high priest just as clients in Roman society greeted benefactors at the beginning of a day. Instead of glorifying the benefactor himself in PJ, priests would glorify the Most High God. This topos of human glorification of God is a repetitive texture throughout PJ, which could be understood to operate within a priestly mode of early Christian discourse.[84] In Luke 2:9 and PJ 24.3, both groups of characters (priests in PJ and shepherds in Luke) become fearful, though the cause is different. In the canonical text, it is due to the *presence* of a heavenly figure in their midst, while in PJ, it is due to the *absence* of their high priestly benefactor. While the topoi of fear and glorifying God in the episode in PJ point clearly to the Gloria in Luke, the presence of a voice that announces the murder of Zechariah is even more striking. This leads us to step 2 (see table below).

Step 2: From Promise by an Angel of Finding a Child to Announcement by a Voice that Zechariah Has Been Murdered

Luke 2:10–15	PJ 24.5–9
(4) [10] But **the angel said** [εἶπεν … ὁ ἄγγελος] to them,	(4) [5] And **a voice said** [φωνὴ λέγουσα],
(5) "**DO NOT BE AFRAID** [μὴ φοβεῖσθε]; for see—I am bringing you good news of great joy for all the people: [11] to you is born this day in the city of David a **SAVIOR**, who is the Messiah, the Lord. [12] This will be a sign for you: **YOU WILL FIND A CHILD** wrapped in bands of cloth and lying in a manger."	(5) "Zechariah has been **MURDERED! HIS BLOOD** will not be cleaned up until his avenger appears."

84. Cf. PJ 6.15; 14.7; 16.8; 25.3.

(6) [13] And suddenly there was with the angel a multitude of the heavenly host, praising God and saying, [14] "**GLORY TO GOD** in the highest heaven, and on earth **PEACE** among those whom he favors!"	(6) [6] When he heard this utterance he was **AFRAID** [ἐφοβήθη] and went out and reported to the **PRIESTS** what he had seen and heard.
(7) [15] When the angels had left them and gone into heaven,	(7) [7] And they summoned up their courage, entered, **and saw what had happened.**
(8) the shepherds said to one another, "Let us go now to Bethlehem and **see this thing that has taken place**, which the Lord has made known to us."	(8) [8] The panels of the **TEMPLE** cried out, and the priests ripped their robes from top to bottom [περιεσχίσαντο ἀπὸ ἄνωθεν ἕως κάτω]. [9] They didn't find a corpse, but they did find his **BLOOD**, now turned to stone.

After the angel appears to the shepherds in Luke, producing fear in them, the angel announces "a gospel of great joy" to them, namely, that they will find a child, who is a Savior Messiah, wrapped in bands of cloth and lying in a manger. Protevangelium of James reconfigures this scene into the presence of "a voice," which is obviously a "divine" voice,[85] that speaks to the priest who is sent into the sanctuary to find Zechariah. This "voice" (PJ 24.5, φωνή) announces the tragic murder of high priest Zechariah. When the priests summon the courage to enter the sanctuary to see the thing that had taken place (cf. Luke 2:15), they do not find a corpse but they find Zechariah's blood. What an alternative to finding a child lying in a manger! But one day the child in the manger would lie in a tomb after shedding blood on a cross. And as with Zechariah, people would be unable to find the body after it had been placed in a tomb. The ending of PJ presents a dramatic story of priestly sacrifice that places high priest Zechariah, father of John, in the foreground, rather than Jesus the Messiah Savior of

85. Speech coming forth from an unidentified φωνή occurs two other times, in PJ 11.2; 20.12. It occurs once on the lips of Elizabeth in PJ 22.7.

Israel. In PJ the words produce fear (PJ 24.6), like the fear the women have in Luke 24:5 when they do not find the body of Jesus. Protevangelium of James has turned the hymn of the Gloria in Luke 2:13–14 into a story of "not finding the body" similar to Luke 24:1–12.

The Gloria in Luke 2 sets the shepherds on a path of investigation, while the murder of Zechariah begins a series of events that moves to the final scene in PJ. First, the readers are told that "the panels of the temple cried out" (PJ 24.8, τὰ φατνώματα τοῦ ναοῦ ὀλόλυξαν), which echoes language found in Amos regarding the end of Israel as a geopolitical kingdom. In the prophetic text, the Lord solemnly declares, "The end has come upon my people Israel … and the panels of the temple will cry out" (Amos 8:2–3 LXX, τὸ πέρας ἐπὶ τὸν λαόν μου Ισραήλ … καὶ ὀλολύξει τὰ φατνώματα τοῦ ναοῦ).[86] This prophetic description of the end presents the end of Israel as a national entity. The event in PJ seems to enact in an especially dramatic way the movement from the prophetic rhetorolect in Luke to the priestly rhetorolect in PJ. In the events that lead from the birth of Mary to the birth of Jesus in PJ, the prophetic voice of the Lukan hymns has been silenced by a focus on priests and the temple.[87] But the focus on priests and the temple leads to a tragic death at the hand of enemies, just like the gospel accounts about Jesus. Is this a "priestly" overmapping of the "prophetic-apocalyptic" story of the life and death of Jesus in early Christianity? If so, why does it focus in this way on Zechariah, father of John? In this story, the voice of prophecy has been silenced by the death of a priest at the altar of the temple of the Lord.[88]

Second, the priests of the temple symbolically reenact what later occurs in the holy of holies in the Jerusalem temple when Jesus is crucified. In both Matthew and Mark, the readers are told that the curtain of the inner sanctum has been torn top to bottom.[89] Do the priests' ripping of their robes from top to bottom here in PJ take away the neces-

86. A TLG search yields Amos 8:3 LXX and PJ 24.8 as the only Greek texts prior to the early fifth century CE to describe the "panels" (φάτνωμα) of a "temple" (ναός), and therefore makes more likely the possibility that the author of PJ was aware of such language in Amos.

87. Cf. Amos 8:3, ἐπιρρίψω σιωπήν.

88. See the woe Jesus pronounces on this murder in Luke 11:51.

89. Matt 27:51, τὸ καταπέτασμα τοῦ ναοῦ ἐσχίσθη ἀπ᾽ ἄνωθεν ἕως κάτω εἰς δύο. Mark 15:38, τὸ καταπέτασμα τοῦ ναοῦ ἐσχίσθη εἰς δύο ἀπ᾽ ἄνωθεν ἕως κάτω. PJ 24.9, αὐτοὶ περιεσχίσαντο ἀπὸ ἄνωθεν ἕως κάτω.

sity of perpetuating the cultus in a context of the death of Jesus on the cross?[90] Is PJ presenting a narrative "hinge" from the story of Mary to the story of Jesus? Is there an implication here that Mary has grown up, Jesus has been born, and the rest of the story is to be found in Luke's Gospel (and the other canonical gospels) with their prophetic-apocalyptic rhetorolect? Or is there an implication here that priestly rhetorolect is ultimately more efficacious than prophetic-apocalyptic rhetorolect? Whichever it might be, the story in PJ is not quite over. The very final events do not occur until the priests report the murder of Zechariah to the people (see table below).

Step 3: From Telling about the Child to Reporting the Murder of Zechariah

Luke 2:16–18	PJ 24.10–11
(9) [16] So they went with haste and found Mary and Joseph, and **THE CHILD** lying in the manger.	(9) [10] They were **AFRAID** and went out and **REPORTED** to the people that Zechariah had been **MURDERED**.
(10) [17] **When** they saw this, **THEY MADE KNOWN** what had been told them about this child;	(10) [11] **When** all the tribes of the people **heard** this, they began to **MOURN**;
(11) [18] and all who **heard** it were **AMAZED** at what the shepherds told them.	(11) and they beat their breasts for three days and three nights.

In the final verses of the episode about the death of Zechariah, PJ reconfigures the topos of messengers relaying information that has been

---

90. Paul Foster claims that the veil to which Mary contributed (12.1) is the "very veil that will be ripped asunder at Jesus' death" ("The *Protevangelium of James*," in *The Non-Canonical Gospels*, ed. Paul Foster [London: T&T Clark, 2008], 123). At PJ 24.8, the priests rip "their own robes from top to bottom," which seems to be a clear reconfiguration of the "ripping of the temple curtain from top to bottom" in the canonical gospels. But note that Foster refers to Mary's "role in *weaving* the … veil" (123 [emphasis added]), when her activity is identified as spinning (10.6: νέω; 10.10: κλώθω), which is earlier in the process of textile production.

given to them. In Luke's Gospel, the report of the shepherds amazes those who hear it, while in PJ, all the people mourn for a prolonged period of time. The mood of the messengers is entirely different in PJ as the priests are still "afraid" (24.10, φοβηθέντες), while the shepherds "go with haste" in Luke 2:16 (σπεύσαντες). The hurried movement by the shepherds in Luke recalls an earlier episode with Mary, in which she went "with haste" (1:39, μετὰ σπουδῆς) to confirm the veracity of prophetic speech given to her. But this still is not the end. There is yet one more remarkable event before PJ comes to a close.

2.5. Relocation of Topoi in the Nunc Dimittis: Protevangelium of James 24.12–14 and Luke 2:25–35

The ending of PJ features a remarkable relocation of Simeon, who in Luke 2:25 was waiting to see the "consolation of Israel" before his death. Protevangelium of James 24.12 relocates the Simeon episode with its "unmistakable eschatological tenor"[91] to solve the issue of who will take over Zechariah's position as high priest in the *temple* (lit: "stand in the place of Zechariah"; τίνα ἀντ' αὐτοῦ στήσουσιν; 24.12) after he is killed. In Luke, Simeon functions as a prophet in the temple alongside the prophetess Anna (Luke 2:36–38). Thus Simeon stands within the prophetic tradition of waiting for God to act according to his promises. In PJ, Simeon is reconfigured from a prophet focused on the coming of Jesus to a high priest who succeeds high priest Zechariah, father of John, after Herod's officers kill him because Herod fears that John will become ruler of Israel. As this occurs, instead of being "dismissed in peace" from further activity in the story of God's work among his people, Simeon becomes the new high priest in the temple. A look at this reconfiguration of the Nunc Dimittis will bring the story of PJ to a conclusion (see table below).

---

91. Bovon, *Luke 1*, 100.

From Prophetic Simeon Filled with Holy Spirit to Priestly Simeon through the Falling of the Lot

Luke 2:25–35	PJ 24.12–14
(1) [25] Now there was a man in Jerusalem whose name was **Simeon**; this man was righteous and devout, looking forward to the consolation of Israel [παράκλησιν τοῦ Ἰσραήλ],	(1) [12] After three days, however, the priests deliberated about whom they should appoint to the position of Zechariah.
(2) and **THE HOLY SPIRIT RESTED ON HIM** [πνεῦμα ἦν ἅγιον ἐπ᾽ αὐτόν].	(2) [13] The lot fell to **Simeon.**
(3) [26] **It had been revealed to him by the HOLY SPIRIT that he would not see death before he had seen the Lord's Messiah** [κεχρηματισμένον ὑπὸ τοῦ πνεύματος τοῦ ἁγίου μὴ ἰδεῖν θάνατον πρὶν [ἢ] ἂν ἴδῃ τὸν χριστὸν κυρίου].	(3) [14] This man is **the one who was informed by the Holy Spirit that he would not see death until he may see the Messiah** in the flesh [ὁ χρηματισθεὶς ὑπὸ τοῦ ἁγίου πνεύματος μὴ ἰδεῖν θάνατον ἕως ἂν τὸν Χριστὸν ἐν σαρκὶ ἴδῃ].
(4) [27] Guided by the **SPIRIT**, Simeon came into the temple; and when the parents brought in **THE CHILD** Jesus, to do for him what was customary under the law,	
(5) [28] Simeon took him in his arms and praised God, saying, [29] "Master, now you are dismissing your servant in peace, according to your word; [30] for my eyes have seen your **SALVATION**, [31] which you have prepared in the pres-	

ence of all peoples, [32] a light for revelation to the Gentiles and for glory to your people Israel."

(6) [33] And the child's father and mother were amazed at what was being said about him. [34] Then Simeon blessed them and said to his mother Mary, "This child is destined for the falling and the rising of many in Israel, and to be a sign that will be opposed [35] so that the inner thoughts of many will be revealed—and a sword will pierce your own soul too."

Luke and PJ develop the character of Simeon in the context of the rhetorolects they foreground in relation to John and Jesus. In Luke 2:25b, Simeon is—as with many of the other Lukan characters in Luke 1–2—described as one on whom the Holy Spirit rests in relation to the child Jesus. In contrast, PJ solidifies Simeon's status as Zechariah's replacement as the high priest in the temple, as the lot falls in his direction, much as it did earlier with Joseph (PJ 9.7).[92]

Protevangelium of James significantly abbreviates the resource text in Luke 2:26–35 as it relocates and reconfigures the Nunc Dimittis. Since the character of Simeon now functions within the priestly rhetorolect of PJ,

92. This reconfiguration of Simeon from prophet to priest in the temple functions within this priestly rhetorolect that has taken over the narrative of PJ. Near the conclusion of Sirach (50:21), for example, the people fall down to receive blessings from the Most High in which everything has reached its fulfillment, but here at the end of PJ, there is a complete reversal of this event. The focus is not about wisdom in the temple, but a continuity of the priestly line. Cf. Vernon K. Robbins, "Bodies and Politics in Luke 1–2 and Sirach 44–50: Men, Women, and Boys," *Scriptura* 90 (2005): 824–38, reprinted in updated form in this volume, pages 41–63; Claudia V. Camp, "Storied Space, or, Ben Sira 'Tells' A Temple," in *"Imagining" Biblical Worlds: Studies in Spatial, Social and Historical Constructs in Honor of James W. Flanagan*, ed. David M. Gunn and Paula M. McNutt, JSOTSupp 359 (London: Sheffield Academic, 2002), 64–80.

there is no prophetic trajectory for him to follow in the recitation of the Nunc Dimittis as found in Luke 2:28–32, along with the prophetic words found in Luke 2:34–35.[93] In other words, as the new high priest, Simeon literally "stands in the place of Zechariah" (24.12) even in the way he functions within this new priestly environment. Just as Zechariah has been relocated from his prophetic environment to a priestly one in PJ with the result that he no longer speaks the prophetic words of the Benedictus, here Simeon becomes the high priest as successor to Zechariah and has no words of prophecy to proclaim to Mary and Joseph.[94] The fact that the author of PJ follows the words of Luke 2:26 rather closely in PJ 24.14 brings into sharper relief his rhetorical interest. The author was not unaware of the Lukan account; rather, he omits the Nunc Dimittis as part of his purposeful reconfiguration of Simeon within his narrative.

3. Conclusion

Careful analysis of the four Lukan hymns shows that prophetic rhetorolect stands in the foreground in Luke 1–2. The prophetic emphasis can be seen most clearly in how the characters operate within the narrative world of the first two chapters of Luke's Gospel: their concerns for their respective circumstances are understood in light of God's promises in the past along with their implications for the future. On occasion after occasion, the Holy Spirit acts as a divine force energizing the characters as prophetic figures who break forth in the well-known hymns commonly called the Magnificat, Benedictus, Gloria, and Nunc Dimittis. Comparative exegesis of Luke 1–2 and PJ shows that rather than simply omitting or being ignorant of these hymns from the Lukan resource text, the author of PJ shaped his narrative with a different rhetorical interest, namely, a priestly one. Within the story of PJ, the gravitational force of the temple produces a relocation of characters from their prophetic role in the Lukan narrative into a priestly mode of discourse. In PJ, these figures become less energized by the Holy Spirit and more energized by priestly blessing and service either in or in relation to the temple. The shift away from appealing to Israel's Scriptures as in Luke 1–2 contributes to this reconfiguration of the characters in PJ. Within the

93. See Rusam, *Das Alte Testament*, 78–85, for an analysis of all the scriptural allusions found in Luke 2:29–35.

94. It is interesting, however, that the midwife exclaims with a variation of Luke 2:30, 32, at the birth of Jesus in PJ 19.14; see Hock, *The Infancy Gospels*, 67n19.

priestly rhetorolect of PJ, there is no need to reach back to words spoken by the prophets in order to make sense of the present. Rather, the focus is on continuity in the service to the temple, ritual purity, and repeated blessings that animate the narrative world of PJ. The author of PJ, one who is well-versed in *progymnastic* training, has written the story of the birth of Mary and Jesus in a way that fits within his own priestly mode of discourse.

Since Adolf von Harnack, it has been typical to view PJ as demonstrating various strata of textual history, with a later redactor who has joined the pieces together.[95] One view claims three independent sources behind PJ: chapters 1–17 constitute "The Nativity of Mary"; chapters 18–21 "The Apocryphon of Joseph"; and chapters 22–24 "The Apocryphon of Zachariah."[96] Edouard Cothenet adds another reason internal to the narrative for positing these layers: "The differentiation of the documents proposed by A. von Harnack corresponds roughly to each of the apparent protagonists: Mary, Joseph, Zechariah."[97] Whatever the "original" independent text(s) may have been—if such things even existed—we are not convinced that fragmenting the text in this way helps us to understand the form and rhetoric of PJ.

In addition to the internal priestly rhetoric of the story in PJ, what might the implications be of its ending with an account of the death of high priest Zechariah, father of John? Many aspects of the account of Zechariah's martyrdom evoke an image of high priest Zechariah as the forerunner to Jesus's sacrificial death on the cross, which includes the shedding of his blood and the absence of his body. In effect, in PJ the high priest Zechariah, rather than his son John, is the forerunner of Jesus. Zechariah, rather than John, "prepares the way of the Lord" in PJ. Instead of John's death and burial (cf. Mark 6:14–29) functioning as the event that "points forward" to Jesus's death and burial, the death of the high priest Zechariah by the altar in the temple (PJ 24.1–9) points forward to Jesus's

95. Adolf von Harnack, *Geschichte der altchristlichen Litteratur bis Eusebius*, 2 vols. (Leipzig: Hinrichs, 1893–1904), 1:19–21; 2:598–603; Edouard Cothenet, "Le Protévangile de Jacques: origine, genre et signification d'un premier midrash chrétien sur la Nativité de Marie," *ANRW* 25.6:4258.

96. Cothenet, "Protévangile," 25.6:4258: "la Nativité de Marie … l'Apocryphum Josephi … l'Apocryphum Zachariae."

97. "La distinction des documents, proposée par A. von Harnack, correspondait en gros à chacun des protagonistes apparents: Marie, Joseph, Zacharie" (Cothenet, "Protévangile," 25.6:4259).

crucifixion, burial, and empty tomb. Important studies have explored the etiological basis of the martyrdom story on the misidentification of John's father Zechariah with the Zechariah of Luke 11:51 // Matt 23:35.[98] On the basis of the evidence that PJ was relocating and reconfiguring aspects of Luke 1–2 in the account of Zechariah's martyrdom, possibly one should view PJ 23.1–4 as a reconfiguration of Luke 9:7–9. Perhaps the author of PJ has redirected Herod's concern from Jesus in the Lukan episode to John while he was still a child. While the Lukan version focuses on the death of John, namely, "John I beheaded; but who is this about whom I hear such things?" (Luke 9:9), the PJ version presents Herod's concern about the newborn John as leading to the death of his father Zechariah: "Is his son [John] going to rule over Israel?" (PJ 23.4).

The overall effect of the ending of PJ, in relation to writings in the New Testament, is to present an account alternative to the argument in the Epistle to the Hebrews about the "heritage" of Jesus as "high priest who gave the perfect sacrifice once for all" (Heb 7:15–27; 9:11–14; 10:5–10). Instead of Jesus being "high priest after the order of Melchizedek," in PJ Jesus's high priestly forerunner is Zechariah, father of John. Does this mean that in PJ Jesus is "high priest after the order of Zechariah, father of John, and his successor Simeon"? It would seem so. But what exactly might this mean to some early Christians? Would this be some kind of significant "rebuttal" of the writer of the Epistle to the Hebrews? Or would it simply be another interesting version of Jesus's priestly heritage that would supplement other versions? Does it foster an interest in Jesus as *priest* over against that of Jesus as prophet? It will be interesting to see more research on this issue in Christian writings during the second through fifth centuries CE in particular.

---

98. Foster, "Protevangelium of James," 121; W. D. Davies and Dale C. Allison, *A Critical and Exegetical Commentary on the Gospel according to Saint Matthew*, 3 vols., ICC (Edinburgh: T&T Clark, 1989–1997), 3:317–19; H. T. Fleddermann, *Q: A Reconstruction and Commentary*, BTS 1 (Leuven: Peeters, 2005), 547.

Appendix 1: Similar and Different Words in the First Three Lukan Hymns

Content	To Zechariah	To Mary	To the Shepherds
Angel speaks	1:13a, **εἶπεν** δὲ πρὸς αὐτὸν **ὁ ἄγγελος**	1:30a, καὶ **εἶπεν ὁ ἄγγελος** αὐτῇ	2:10a, καὶ **εἶπεν** αὐτοῖς **ὁ ἄγγελος**
Command: "Do not fear"	1:13b, **μὴ φοβοῦ**	1:30b, **μὴ φοβοῦ**	2:10b, **μὴ** <u>φοβεῖσθε</u>
Reason 1: Relating to God	1:13c, διότι εἰσηκούσθη ἡ δέησίς σου*	1:30c, εὗρες γὰρ χάριν παρὰ τῷ θεῷ	2:10c, ἰδοὺ γὰρ εὐαγγελίζομαι ὑμῖν χαρὰν μεγάλην ἥτις ἔσται παντὶ τῷ λαῷ
Reason 2: Birth of a child	1:13d, καὶ ἡ γυνή σου Ἐλισάβετ γεννήσει υἱόν σοι	1:31a, καὶ ἰδοὺ συλλήμψῃ ἐν γαστρὶ καὶ τέξῃ υἱόν	2:11a, ὅτι ἐτέχθη ὑμῖν σήμερον σωτήρ
Reason 3: Identification of the son	1:13e, **καὶ καλέσεις τὸ ὄνομα αὐτοῦ** Ἰωάννην	1:31b, **καὶ καλέσεις τὸ ὄνομα αὐτοῦ** Ἰησοῦν	2:11b, ὅς ἐστιν χριστός
Rejoicing	1:14, καὶ ἔσται χαρά σοι καὶ ἀγαλλίασις καὶ πολλοὶ ἐπὶ τῇ γενέσει αὐτοῦ χαρήσονται		[see 2:10c]
"Greatness" of the son	1:15a, **ἔσται** γὰρ **μέγας** ἐνώπιον [τοῦ] κυρίου	1:32a, οὗτος **ἔσται μέγας**	

Status of the son	1:15b, καὶ οἶνον καὶ σίκερα οὐ μὴ πίῃ,καὶ πνεύματος ἁγίου πλησθήσεται ἔτι ἐκ κοιλίας μητρὸς αὐτοῦ	1:32b, καὶ υἱὸς ὑψίστου κληθήσεται καὶ δώσει αὐτῷ **κύριος** ὁ θεὸς τὸν θρόνον **Δαυὶδ** τοῦ πατρὸς αὐτοῦ	2:11c, **κύριος** ἐν πόλει **Δαυίδ**
Concerning Israel	1:16, καὶ πολλοὺς τῶν υἱῶν Ἰσραὴλ ἐπιστρέψει ἐπὶ κύριον τὸν θεὸν αὐτῶν	1:33a, καὶ βασιλεύσει ἐπὶ τὸν οἶκον Ἰακὼβ εἰς τοὺς αἰῶνας	[See 2:10c above]
Final remark	1:17, καὶ αὐτὸς προελεύσεται ἐνώπιον αὐτοῦ ἐν πνεύματι καὶ δυνάμει Ἠλίου, ἐπιστρέψαι καρδίας πατέρων ἐπὶ τέκνα καὶ ἀπειθεῖς ἐν φρονήσει δικαίων, ἑτοιμάσαι κατεσκευασμένον	1:33b, καὶ τῆς βασιλείας αὐτοῦ οὐκ ἔσται τέλος	

Note: * While there is no mention of "God" here, it is implied, as the subject of the passive εἰσηκούσθη must be God.

Part 3
Acts of John

Naked Divinity: The Transfiguration Transformed in the Acts of John

Jonathan M. Potter

1. Introduction

The transfiguration was a deeply meaningful story about Jesus that was variously retold in a wide spectrum of early Christian writings. Not only do the three Synoptic Gospels recall this episode, but also 2 Peter, both extant versions of the Apocalypse of Peter,[1] the Acts of Peter, and the Acts of John (AJohn).[2] While all of these compositions contain an episode that can be identified as "the transfiguration," in each case this extraordinary encounter with Jesus is (re)configured in ways that develop the themes of the host compositions and make sense within their conceptual worlds.

In the case of the Acts of John, the presence of a transfiguration account (or rather, as is shown below, transfigurations) is notable in itself, since the work lies ostensibly in the Johannine tradition and does in fact engage in characteristically Johannine discourse.[3] The Gospel of John (GJohn) notably

1. The Apocalypse of Peter survives "in full" (as we understand it) only in an Ethiopic version. There is also a significant Greek fragment found at Akhmim. Since the shorter Akhmim fragment does not correlate exactly with any portion of the Ethiopic version, the relationship between the two texts is complicated, and scholars have proposed various theories on their relationship. Furthermore, neither is related to the Coptic Apocalypse of Peter found later at Nag Hammadi. For a recent study of the Petrine transfiguration traditions (with comparatively very little discussion of AJohn), see Simon S. Lee, *Jesus' Transfiguration and the Believers' Transformation: A Study of the Transfiguration and Its Development in Early Christian Writings*, WUNT 2/265 (Tübingen: Mohr Siebeck, 2009).

2. Matt 19:1–8; Mark 9:2–8; Luke 9:28–36; 2 Pet 1:16–18; Apoc. Pet. (Ethiopic) 15–17; Apoc. Pet. (Akhmim) 1–20; Acts Pet. 20; AJohn 90–91.

3. Examples are given throughout this paper.

lacks a transfiguration episode, and indeed, many modern scholars of GJohn see a transfiguration narrative as theologically incompatible with Johannine Christology, since Jesus appears in light and glory throughout his earthly life, not one mere glimpse.[4] However, this was apparently not a problem for the communities that produced and read AJohn, who seem happy to combine Johannine traditions with a whole range of other traditions. Thus, at the broad level, the transfigurations in AJohn 90–91 (and beyond) fill what could have been (and still is) perceived as a lacuna in the Johannine tradition vis-à-vis the Synoptic tradition. But the transfigurations in AJohn are really much more than an attempt to fill a gap.

Acts of John is not a "gospel," nor is it an attempt to tell the full story of Jesus's life.[5] The section in which John recounts events from his experience with "the Lord"[6] (chs. 87–105, hereafter called "the Testimonies" for reasons described below) is highly selective and focuses on the mystery of the Lord's changing appearance (see the narrative frame that introduces the section in chs. 87–88 and concludes John's sermon in 103–5) and the gradual revelation of the Lord's true nature to John.[7] The first part of this section, which includes the transfigurations, recounts John's unsuccessful attempts to understand the Lord's true nature (88–93). Jesus then draws the disciples into the mystery of himself with the Hymn-Dance (94–96). Then when Jesus is taken to be crucified, John flees to the Mount of Olives, where the Lord appears to him and reveals the unity lying beneath the many forms and names the Lord assumed for the sake of humanity, as well as the paradoxical nature of his humanity and suffering (97–102).

In view of this overall context, it becomes clear that AJohn skillfully reconfigures the transfiguration by suppressing topoi present in the Synoptic

4. See, e.g., D. Moody Smith, *John*, ANTC (Nashville: Abingdon, 1999), 39.

5. Since "gospel" as a type or genre of literature is ill-defined, perhaps it would be more precise to say that AJohn is not a gospel in the same way that the canonical gospels are. But since neither the text itself nor any other ancient literature identifies it as a "gospel" (and the word εὐαγγέλιον, "gospel," never occurs in AJohn), it seems best not to refer to it as such. It does, however, contain gospel-like traditions about Jesus. "What" this section "is" will be discussed further below.

6. "The Lord" is by far the most common appellation for Jesus in AJohn; thus it seems to be the most appropriate way of referring to him in a discussion of this work. "Jesus" occurs relatively little. Next after "Lord" is "Christ." Combinations (Lord Jesus, etc.) are also frequent.

7. Note that since I use AJohn for Acts of John, and GJohn for Gospel of John, "John" alone always refers to the person John.

transfiguration that conflict with its understanding of the Lord, transforming topoi that the author understands differently, and introducing new topoi (some derived from other resources) that advance the broader interests of this work. The end result is a series of transfigurations that are only superficially similar to the Synoptic transfiguration, while serving a completely different function within the overall narrative and Christology of AJohn. In short, whereas the Synoptic transfiguration accounts are a one-time preresurrection glimpse of Jesus's glorified state and serve as further confirmation of his divine sonship and authority, "the transfiguration" in AJohn is just one instance among many where the Lord's changing appearance is experienced. Thus in AJohn, it is more accurate to speak of transfigurations occurring throughout Jesus's life. And whereas the Synoptic accounts seem to provide a glimpse of future reality, the AJohn transfigurations (and particularly the climactic one in the middle of AJohn 90) show the Lord as he always has been: divine and not *truly* human at all.

This essay proceeds as follows. First, I give a preliminary analysis of the transfiguration accounts in AJohn 90–91, focusing primarily on its narrative context in the Testimonies. Since the AJohn transfigurations in 90–91 have particular affinities with the version in Luke, I then examine the Lukan transfiguration, again focusing on narrative context and, more importantly in Luke, the overall function of this transfiguration account. Having situated both transfiguration accounts within their broader contexts, I then engage in a close comparative exegesis of AJohn 90–91 and Luke 9:28–36, showing how AJohn can be read as reconfiguring the Lukan account. If this study seems slow in focusing on AJohn 90–91, this reflects an effort to give full weight to the larger narrative unit and not to allow the parallels with the Synoptic Gospels to dictate the terms of the discussion.

2. Preliminary Analysis: The Transfiguration(s) in Acts of John

2.1. Text and Overview of Acts of John

Acts of John survives in incomplete form, and its manuscript tradition is complicated, to say the least.[8] There is a current consensus that chapters

8. For an overview of the text of AJohn, see J. K. Elliott's introduction in *The Apocryphal New Testament: A Collection of Apocryphal Christian Literature in an English Translation* (Oxford: Clarendon, 2005), 303–10.

1–17 included in the earlier edition of M. Bonnet[9] are not original, and that, rather, the original beginning has been lost.[10] The order of the extant material is also problematic (due to the fragmentary and disjointed nature of the manuscript tradition), but the order originally proposed by Knut Schäferdiek and followed by Eric Junod and Jean-Daniel Kaestli's critical edition appears to have gained solid support.[11] Since this order is radically different than the chapter numbers (which are based on Bonnet's old edition, but which have been retained by all scholars) would suggest, it is worth reviewing here. This also serves as a broad outline of the whole book.

Order and Outline of the Acts of John[12]

A. Missing beginning
B. 18–36: John travels to Ephesus and ministers there
C. Gap
D. 87–105: The Testimonies: John, while at Ephesus, recalls the mysterious nature of Christ
E. 37–55: End of first visit to Ephesus
F. Disputed (chs. 56–57)
G. 58–61: John's return to Ephesus (incident with the bedbugs)
H. 62–86: The stories of Drusiana and Callimachus
I. 106–115: The "Metastasis" (John's last days and death)

Even with the reconstruction shown in the outline above, the unity of the work is disputed.[13] While a case can be made that all the material listed

9. In R. A. Lipsius and M. Bonnet, eds., *Acta apostolorum apocrypha*, 2 vols. (Leipzig: Mendelssohn, 1891–1903), 2.1:160–216.

10. Elliott, *Apocryphal New Testament*, 304; Pieter J. Lalleman, *The Acts of John: A Two-Stage Initiation into Johannine Gnosticism*, SAAA 4 (Leuven: Peeters, 1998), 12–13, 15–17.

11. Knut Schäferdiek, "Johannesakten," in *Neutestamentliche Apokryphen in deutscher Ubersetzung II*, ed. Edgar Hennecke and Wilhelm Schneemelcher (Tübingen: Mohr Siebeck, 1964), 125–76; Eric Junod and Jean-Daniel Kaestli, *Acta Iohannis*, 2 vols., CCSA 1 (Turnhout: Brepols, 1983), which is the Greek text utilized in this study. On support for this order, see Lalleman, *Acts of John*, 25–27 (who disagrees on this matter); and Elliott, *Apocryphal New Testament*, 304, 310–11.

12. Based on Junod and Kaestli, *Acta Iohannis*, 1:98–100; and Elliott, *Apocryphal New Testament*, 304, 310–11.

13. It is disputed on both technical (the MS tradition) and conceptual/theological grounds (see Lalleman, *Acts of John*, 25–68).

above is "original," it must be kept it mind that this is speculative since not a single manuscript contains all of it (in any order). There is no hard evidence that AJohn ever circulated in this form. The Testimonies, chapters 87–105, do, however, survive in full (and in this order) in one manuscript ("C" in Junod and Kaestli), which contains *only* this material.[14] The only other fragments from this section are not found with other parts of AJohn. Thus there is no *manuscript* evidence tying this material to the rest of AJohn. In this essay (following most publications on AJohn), I assume significant affinity between the Testimonies and the surrounding material (hereafter, "the Acts"), but due to the problematic textual tradition, I only treat chapters 87–105 as "my text."[15] While I read the Testimonies with an eye to the rest of AJohn, my focus is on 87–105.

2.2. The Testimonies: Acts of John 87–105

Before focusing on the transfiguration episodes in 90–91, it is helpful first to look in greater detail at its context in the Testimonies. Chapter 87 begins in medias res, but there is enough to suggest what was happening in the immediate context: "Then those who were present inquired about the cause, and were especially perplexed because Drusiana had said, 'The Lord appeared to me in the tomb in the form of John and of a youth'" (AJohn 87; Elliott).[16] The perplexity created by Drusiana's experience of the Lord's multiple forms creates an opportunity for John to give what amounts to a sermon composed primarily of recollections or testimonies (88–102) that recall similar experiences from the time John spent with Jesus during his earthly ministry. The narrative frame, begun in 87 and 88, concludes the Testimonies in 103–5 with a call by John for his hearers to worship and abide in the Lord, and finally with a notice that John and others then departed.

---

14. See Junod and Kaestli, *Acta Iohannis*, 1:26–29, for a discussion of the manuscript tradition of chs. 87–105.

15. While 87–105 does not seem to be a self-contained work, judging from the way it begins in the middle of a story and refers to previously discussed narrative elements, as described below, the manuscript itself is not fragmentary, as the superscript and subscript indicate (given in Junod and Kaestli, *Acta Iohannis*, 1:189, 217). My assumption is that 87–105 was not composed as an isolated work, but that it came to be copied as such, for reasons unknown.

16. All AJohn translations follow Elliott, *Apocryphal New Testament*, unless otherwise specified.

The Testimonies themselves have a clear and logical arc: John begins with his first experience of Jesus, when Jesus called him and his brother James (AJohn 88), and he ends with the Lord's ascension.[17] In between, John recounts several occasions when he had glimpses of the Lord's fluctuating physical manifestations, and he then goes on to describe the climactic events just prior to and including the crucifixion. To help clarify the structure of the Testimonies, I have created an outline highlighting its opening-middle-closing texture.[18] Since I am focusing on the Twelve Testimonies (more on terminology below) concerning Jesus's physical form in the opening of the middle, I have numbered them T1–T12 for ease of reference.

Opening-Middle-Closing Texture for Acts of John 87–105

Opening:

O and M: 87: Perplexity surrounding Drusiana's vision of the Lord in two forms ("John"—i.e., old man—and a young man).
C: 88a: John will attempt to relate his own experience of the Lord's glorious form.

Middle:

Opening: O: 88b: John and James called by Jesus: James sees a child; John sees an attractive and cheerful man. Both perplexed. [Testimony = T1]
M: 89: (a) Soon after, John sees a bald-headed man with a thick beard; James sees a youth with a new beard. [T2]
(b) John tries to see him "as he was": never saw his eyes close. [T3]
(c) John sometimes saw a small and unattractive man, sometimes one "reaching to heaven." [T4]
(d) Sometimes Jesus felt "smooth and tender," sometimes "hard, like stone." John perplexed. [T5]
90: (a) John, James, and Peter see ineffable light while Jesus prays on mountain. [T6]

17. The Synoptic parallels with these events are discussed below in the section on reconfigurations.

18. For the concept of opening-middle-closing texture and its analysis, see Vernon K. Robbins, *Exploring the Texture of Texts: A Guide to Socio-Rhetorical Interpretation* (Valley Forge, PA: Trinity Press International, 1996), 19–21.

(b) Same three accompany Jesus to mountain. While Jesus prays, John sees Jesus's "naked divinity": an inhuman, radiant being reaching up to heaven. Then he turns and John sees a man of small stature who pulls John's beard and rebukes him for unbelief and inquisitiveness. [T7]
91: Peter and James, angry at John, ask with whom Jesus was speaking (apparently they heard two voices). John says to ask Jesus himself. [T8]
92: John, when he is supposed to be sleeping, sees and hears Jesus talking to someone, presumably himself in multiple forms. [T9]
93: (a) Sometimes Jesus felt "material and solid," sometimes "immaterial and bodiless." [T10]
(b) Jesus blesses/breaks bread, a small piece of which is satisfying, so disciples keep their own loaves. [T11]
(c) John sees no footprints. [T12]
C: John addresses audience again, speaks to encourage faith: the Lord's works are unutterable mysteries.
Middle: O: 94a Jesus instructs about the Hymn-Dance before his arrest.
M: 94b–95: Hymn-Dance
C: 96: Jesus teaches about himself, concludes dance.
Closing: O: 97: John flees to cave, which the Lord illuminates; the Lord speaks to him.
M: (a) 98: Cross of light; Lord speaks with voice only but no shape.
(b) 99: People will misunderstand.
c) 100: Flawed human nature: those who listen to his voice will become like him.
(d) 101: The paradox of the Lord's suffering.
C: 102: The Lord finishes teaching and then ascends. John laughs.

Closing:
O: 103: Call to worship the Lord properly: with the soul not the body.
M: 104: Conclusion of sermon: the Lord is no mere human but God. "Abide in him" and "you shall possess your soul indestructible."

C: 105: John departs with Andronicus and Drusiana after speaking to the brethren.

Although words of the μαρτυρ- family do not appear in the Testimonies, the overall function of the Testimonies is to bear witness to the Lord, and it is for this reason that I have chosen to designate this section using such a Johannine term.[19] Despite the lack of explicit language recalling the topos of bearing witness from GJohn,[20] it is hard to imagine more vivid witness "to the light" (cf. GJohn 1:7–8) than the testimonies that John shares with his Ephesian audience in AJohn 87–105. In AJohn 88, John specifically states the purpose of his sermon: "I will communicate to you those things whereof you are able to become hearers, that you may see the glory that surrounds him who was and is both now and forever." Thus John's goal is to share a glimpse of the Lord's glory, which is very much in line with what GJohn does (cf. GJohn 1:14: "we have seen his glory").[21] In the Testimonies, the intended result of this vision of the Lord's glory is to worship the Lord correctly, namely, by understanding his true divine nature (103, 104). In GJohn, seeing Jesus's glory leads to belief in him (GJohn 2:11), which is also the purpose of the testimony the author provides (19:35; 20:30–31). Although the Testimonies do not thematize the topos of belief the way GJohn does, there are a few key points where belief/unbelief toward Jesus is stressed (AJohn 90; 92), and a Johannine concept of belief in Jesus as accepting Jesus's true identity (in GJohn, as Son of God and Messiah; see esp. 20:31) certainly drives the conclusion to the Testimonies in AJohn 103–4, even if the word "belief" is not used. For all these reasons, the designation Testimonies seems apt for this collection of John's recollections to the Ephesians. The lack of some specific

19. Eric Junod, "Polymorphie du dieu sauveur," in *"Gnosticisme et monde hellénistique," actes du Colloque de Louvain-la-Neuve, 11–14 mars 1980*, ed. Julien Ries, Publications de l'Institut Orientaliste de Louvain 27 (Louvain-la-Neuve: Institut orientaliste, 1982), 38–46, seems to have been the first person to use the term "testimonies" (*témoignages*) in relation to AJohn. He uses the term only for the specific episodes in chs. 88–93, but while I also use the term for those same episodes (see further below), I also think the term accurately characterizes the entire section 87–105.

20. μαρτυρ- words occur forty-seven times in thirty-five verses in GJohn: 1:7, 8, 15, 19, 32, 34; 2:25; 3:11, 26, 28, 32, 33; 4:39, 44; 5:31, 32, 33, 34, 36, 37, 39; 7:7; 8:13, 14, 17, 18; 10:25; 12:17; 13:21; 15:26, 27; 18:23, 37; 19:35; 21:24. In at least two-thirds of these references, the object of the testimony is Jesus.

21. Δόξα, often translated "glory," is another key topos in GJohn.

Johannine terminology reflects the fact that while the Testimonies (and the rest of AJohn) dwell within a conceptual world that is still very much Johannine, they extend beyond it, having incorporated concepts and topoi from other resources.

2.3. Metamorphosis in the Twelve Testimonies of Acts of John 88–93

As the outline above (p. 186) shows, the transfiguration account occurs within a series of twelve Testimonies about the Lord in the opening of the middle (AJohn 88–93).[22] The "transfiguration" occurs in the very middle of this unit and actually comprises three Testimonies, numbered T6–T8 on the chart above. The Twelve Testimonies do not follow a linear progression from lesser to greater. Rather, the three Testimonies comprising "the transfiguration" (6–8) are central both in location and importance, and within these three, the middle Testimony, T7, is the most revealing, in that John here gains a glimpse of the Lord's "naked divinity."[23] The details of T7 make this clear, as is discussed below, but the centrality of this revelation is also implied by the greater detail of the narrative. The other eleven Testimonies are primarily short notices about a particular way that the Lord appeared, sounded, or felt, with little dialogue or narration of actions. T7, by contrast, goes into much greater detail and includes dialogue between John and Jesus (which none of the other eleven Testimonies contain).

But while the "Transfiguration Testimonies" (T6–T8) are of central importance, and especially T7, it is also important to note what is common to all the Twelve Testimonies. Each Testimony relates one or more examples of Jesus's changing form, or "metamorphosis."[24] The Testimonies relate not

---

22. Although this may be a bit of shameless numerology, I do find it interesting that there are *twelve* Testimonies. These twelve Testimonies could be read as a reconfiguration of the twelve disciples who witnessed Jesus's words and deeds (this is obviously speculative). Interestingly enough, I identified these Twelve Testimonies before having read Junod and Kaestli's presentation of the same material (Junod, "Polymorphie du dieu sauveur"; Junod and Kaestli, *Acta Iohannis*, 2:474–90; list on 2:475), and I came up with the same number and specific list of Testimonies. This suggests to me that this is a clear and intentional feature of the text, whether or not there is any significance to the number twelve.

23. On this point I cannot agree with Junod and Kaestli, *Acta Iohannis*, 2:475, who see a total lack of logic to the structure of the Testimonies other than a basic chronological framework: "La structure de l'ensemble du témoignage défie toute logique."

24. Terminology for the phenomenon of Jesus's changing physical form in AJohn

only changes in Jesus's appearance but also the way his body feels to the touch, and instances of his use of multiple voices (creating the effect of dialogue with himself). Although interacting with a variety of senses, these metamorphoses all relate to Jesus's having a multifarious physical, material existence. It should also be mentioned that, at times, John's descriptions of the Lord's changing and surprising physical manifestations will seem cryptic or even nonsensical—for example, when he "sees" the Lord having no shape but a voice alone above the cross of light (98).[25] But John makes clear from the very beginning of the Testimonies the impossibility of fully

---

remains problematic. The term "polymorphy" (and related forms) is often used in relation to AJohn, but Pieter J. Lalleman ("Polymorphy of Christ," in *The Apocryphal Acts of John*, ed. Jan N Bremmer, SAAA 1 (Kampen: Kok, 1995], 97–118) argues that the term should be limited to instances of multiple *simultaneous* forms (Fred Lapham, *An Introduction to the New Testament Apocrypha* [London: T&T Clark, 2003], 134, follows this definition). Lalleman considers polymorphy to be a subset of the wider phenomenon of metamorphosis or shape-shifting (see esp. "Polymorphy of Christ," 102–3). Thus he sees both metamorphosis and polymorphy as present in AJohn. His desire for precise terminology is admirable, but it does not seem to me that polymorphy, *when restricted to his strict definition* (i.e., only applies to *simultaneous* variations in form) is a useful category for AJohn, since Jesus's form is constantly changing, sometimes simultaneously different, other times not, and oftentimes it is simply not clear. The clearly polymorphic instances in AJohn (by Lalleman's definition) are not qualitatively different from those that cannot be identified as such, and they do not seem to serve a different function. Furthermore, Lalleman's attempt to rigidly define polymorphy leads him to interpret tendentiously to maintain this distinction, such as when he still counts the different ways Jesus "feels" in T5 (AJohn 89d) as polymorphic, claiming the change happened so quick it was as if simultaneous, even though there is no such indication in the text ("Polymorphy of Christ," 104). So to avoid confusion, I will abide by Lalleman's definition (even if I am not entirely convinced by his argument) and simply not use language of polymorphy, since I do see it as a distinct phenomenon in AJohn. Other terms for Jesus's changing appearance in AJohn have been suggested, but *metamorphosis* and *metamorphic* seem to adequately describe the changes of forms Jesus undergoes in these Testimonies. See also the remarks of Lee (*Jesus' Transfiguration*, 174–76), who surveys a range of views on this terminology. Lee agrees that Lalleman's definition is overly strict, and he thus uses the term *polymorphy* in a way that allows for both simultaneous and successive instances of metamorphosis.

25. In this case, one could explain this as an effect of the light, like when one looks at such a bright light that no form can be seen. While this is a plausible explanation for ch. 98, it should be noted that although the cross seems to be emitting light in this situation, there is no mention of light in association with the Lord "above" the cross; voice is the only attribute of the Lord in this case. Thus if the Lord's "form" is here obscured by light, it is the light of the cross, not his own light. Whatever the case, T10 (what

explaining everything: "I, indeed, am able neither to set forth to you nor to write the things which I saw and heard. Now I must adapt them to your hearing; and in accordance with everyone's capabilities I will communicate to you those things whereof you are able to become hearers" (88). This "inability to describe" is a topos repeatedly invoked in AJohn, and since it occurs in the transfiguration account, we will return to it later.

Recalling Drusiana's vision of the Lord in two forms—that of John, that is, an old man,[26] and of a young man (discussed above), the Testimonies begin with James and John seeing Jesus in two different forms (AJohn 88b).[27] Here James sees a child, while John sees an attractive and cheerful man (T1). Soon after, James and John again see two different forms; this time James sees a young man with a new beard, while John sees a bald-headed man with a thick beard (T2).[28] Seemingly both perplexed (88b) and yet curious, John tries to see Jesus "as he was" (89b), and what he notices is a particular detail rather than a whole new form: Jesus never seems to close his eyes (T3). John then makes the more general statement (89c) that sometimes the Lord appeared as a small and unattractive (or better, misshapen: δύσμορφος) man but other times as "one reaching to heaven" (T4).[29] Then, in 89d, John for the first time relates that Jesus's changing form extended beyond appearance: when they would recline together at a meal, John says that Jesus would take him "upon his breast," and when John held Jesus, his body sometimes felt "smooth and tender," perhaps as

something "immaterial and bodiless" feels like), discussed below, definitely describes an experience that exceeds human language and comprehension.

26. Cf. AJohn 27, where John's appearance is identified as that of an old man.

27. Chapter numbers from the Testimonies followed by a letter indicate the subdivisions given in the outline above (pp. 186–88).

28. In ancient Jewish and Greek culture, the beard was seen as a sign of manhood and maturity. By contrast, Roman men in the imperial period generally went clean shaven. See Colbow Gudrun and Hurschmann Rolf, "Beard," in *Brill's New Pauly: Antiquity*, ed. Hubert Cancik and Helmuth Schneider (Brill Online, 2012). The issue of beards will come up again in the transfiguration account.

29. This seems to be an expression for extraordinary height. See, e.g., T. Reu. 5.7: "And the women lusting in their minds after their forms, gave birth to giants, for the Watchers appeared to them as reaching even unto heaven" (R. H. Charles, *The Apocrypha and Pseudepigrapha of the Old Testament in English: With Introductions and Critical and Explanatory Notes to the Several Books*, 2 vols. [Oxford: Clarendon, 1913], 2:299).

one would expect of flesh.[30] But other times, it felt quite unlike flesh, rather "hard, like stone" (T5). The "transfiguration" accounts in 90–91 relate three forms of metamorphosis, which are discussed further below, but the basics are Peter, James, and John seeing in the Lord indescribable light (90a, T6), John seeing a radiant and inhuman Jesus reaching to heaven, who turns and becomes a small man (90b, T7), and Peter and James hearing multiple voices (91, T8). In 92, John hears the multiple voices conversing (T9). In 93a, John recalls a different pair of tactile sensations: sometimes Jesus was "material and solid" (like a body should be), but other times "the substance was immaterial and bodiless and as if it were not existing at all" (T10). One might ask what an "immaterial and bodiless" substance feels like, but we already know what John would say: he is unable to say adequately! T11, in 93b, is the only Testimony in this section that is not an actual occurrence of metamorphosis. Here Jesus blesses and breaks bread at a Pharisee's house, and the pieces he distributes are sufficient to satisfy the disciples. Although this does not seem to imply an instance of metamorphosis, it does convey Jesus's remarkable control over physical matter. Rather than showing another form Jesus assumed, it shows the *effect* of the metamorphic Jesus on the physical world. Viewed in this way, the final Testimony in this sequence then plays the role of opposite (opposite pairs are common in the Testimonies): John never saw Jesus leave footprints (93c, T12).[31] Thus sometimes, as with the bread, Jesus interacted with and had an effect on his physical environment, but other times he did not. To give a sense of all the different metamorphic phenomena John and the other disciples witnessed, I have created table 1 below.

30. The language here, ἀνακείμενον ἐμὲ ἐπὶ τὰ ἴδια στήθη ἐδέχετο, seems like an obvious allusion to the references in GJohn to the beloved disciple's reclining "at the breast" of Jesus (ἐπὶ τὸ στῆθος in GJohn 13:25; 21:20; cf. 13:23, ἦν ἀνακείμενος εἷς ἐκ τῶν μαθητῶν αὐτοῦ ἐν τῷ κόλπῳ τοῦ Ἰησοῦ).

31. Within T12 there is a curious statement that seems like it could be important, at least inasmuch as it recalls key Johannine language. John says, "I wished to see whether the print of his foot appeared upon the earth—**for I saw him raising himself from the earth**—but I never saw it" (93). Is this a significant statement, echoing, e.g., GJohn 12:32, or is it simply an awkward way of describing Jesus's manner of walking? The potential echo is weaker in Greek, since AJohn 93 uses ἐπαίρω, whereas GJohn uses ὑψόω.

Table 1. Jesus's Metamorphoses in Acts of John 88–93

	Visual Phenomena	Aural Phenomena	Tactile Phenomena
Ordinary	child (T1) young man (T2; cf. 87) attractive man (T1) bald man, thick beard (T2) small, ugly man (T4; T7?)		smooth and tender (T5) material and solid (T10)
Extraordinary	reaching to heaven (T4, T7) eyes never close (T3) light/radiance (T6, T7) inhuman (T7) no footprints (T12)	multiple voices (T8, T9)	hard like stone (T5) immaterial and bodiless (T10) (?) makes the bread satisfy everyone (T11)

As the table shows, Jesus's metamorphoses in the Testimonies comprise both ordinary and extraordinary phenomena, in terms of normal human experience and qualities. Naturally, the very fact of Jesus's changing form is extraordinary, but it is important to note that many of the individual phenomena are not normal human characteristics. While a great deal more could be said about the individual phenomena and their specific combinations, two broad observations must suffice. First, taken together, the continual flux in Jesus's physical embodiment illustrates one of the Testimonies' key theological claims: the Lord took on a variety of forms for the sake of humanity. This point is made most explicitly in the last section of the Testimonies' middle, where the Lord instructs John. There the Lord provides a long list of names by which the "cross of light" is at various times called (98). The Lord stresses to John the unity underlying this apparent diversity. The Lord's fluctuating form seems to be a physical manifestation of this diversity, all unified in the person of Jesus. Second, the extraordinary metamorphic phenomena point to the Lord's true nature as divinity. Although the two groups—ordinary and extraordinary—represent a fairly even balance numerically, the Testimonies place the accent on the extraordinary. This illustrates the teaching revealed more clearly to John when the Lord instructs John directly in the closing of the middle of the Testimonies. There John learns that Jesus's humanity is essentially illusory and not the Lord's true nature. This point is reiterated in John's closing to his sermon, after he has finished recounting the Testimonies proper. In order to show more clearly the priority placed on the Lord's divinity and the illusory nature of his humanity, we must now look in greater detail at the climactic metamorphic experience of John in the transfiguration account.

2.4. The "Transfiguration" Testimonies (Acts of John 90–91, T6–T8)

There are two reasons, or groups of reasons, for narrowing our focus on this specific cluster of Testimonies. First, these three Testimonies naturally belong together in that they all relate to experiences of Jesus's metamorphosis on the mountain where he would go to pray. John, James, and Peter are present in all three Testimonies, and this specific grouping only occurs in these three Testimonies. T7 and T8 refer to the same event, but from two different perspectives (T7 is John's perspective; T8 is that of Peter and James). Thus T6–T8 have a narrative unity. Furthermore, as mentioned above, this cluster of Testimonies lies prominently at the middle of the Twelve Testimonies. This first set of reasons for focusing on T6–T8 as a group is internal to the text.

The second reason for focusing on these specific Testimonies is purely heuristic: T6–T8 are clearly a reconfiguration of the Synoptic transfiguration account. But I cannot stress enough that while this parallel with the Synoptic Gospels sets these Testimonies apart from the others, within the Testimonies as a whole, the "Transfiguration Testimonies" (T6–T8) are not a unique and singular event like the transfiguration is in the Synoptics. It is clear from the depictions of metamorphosis throughout the Testimonies that, in AJohn, Jesus's physical form during his earthly life was constantly changing. Thus we might say that Jesus was always being transfigured. In some sense, earlier transfiguration traditions are probably the origin, or at least one of the roots of the metamorphic depiction of Jesus in AJohn and other early Christian literature. But the phenomenon of metamorphosis is endemic in the Testimonies, so when AJohn is considered on its own, there is no one event that could be singled out as "*the* transfiguration." Thus it is only in relation to the Synoptic Gospels that we can speak of a specific set of "Transfiguration Testimonies" in AJohn.[32] But the linguistic parallels between AJohn 90–91 specifically and the Synoptic transfiguration accounts are striking enough to warrant close examination.

Having discussed the narrative context of the "Transfiguration Testimonies" (AJohn 90–91, T6–T8), it is helpful to briefly discuss the main features of this subset of the Testimonies. A closer analysis of AJohn 90–91, noting parallels with and differences from other transfiguration traditions, is given below in the comparative exegetical section. Here the focus is on this unit's relationship to the rest of the Testimonies. I have created the outline below to highlight the opening-middle-closing texture of this section of AJohn.[33] This also bolsters the conclusion that these three Testimonies can be read together as a unit within the larger group of the Twelve Testimonies, which constitutes the opening of the middle of AJohn 87–105.

Opening-Middle-Closing Texture of Acts of John 90–91 (Elliott translation, modified)[34]

Opening

O: 90 (1) And at another time he took [παραλαμβάνει] me and James and (2) Peter to the mountain [εἰς τὸ ὄρος] where he was accustomed to pray [εὔχεσθαι],
M: and we SAW [εἴδομεν] (3) in him such LIGHT [φῶς] that it is not possible for a HUMAN [ἀνθρώπῳ] (4) who uses mortal [φθαρτῷ] speech to describe what it was like [οἷον ἦν].

Middle

O: Again in a similar way he led [ἀνάγει] (5) us three up to the mountain, saying: "Come with me." And we (6) went again, and we SAW [ὁρῶμεν] him at a distance praying [εὐχόμενον].

32. For this reason I enclose this phrase with quotation marks.

33. While in general I give only chapter numbers in references to AJohn, for the sake of close analysis of chapters 90–91 I provide line numbers based on Junod and Kaestli's critical Greek text, with minor adjustments. These line divisions are given in parentheses in the text in the outline. Note also that the words "the old man" in 91.4 are based on the conjectural γέρων (in place of γενόν from the manuscript) printed in Junod and Kaestli's edition. See the textual note in *Acta Iohannis*, 1:194.

34. Font guide: all caps = repetitive texture (see Robbins, *Exploring*, 8–9).

M: (a) (7) So I, because he loved me [ἐφίλει με], went to him quietly [ἠρέμα], as though he should not SEE me, (8) and stood [ἵσταμαι] LOOKING [ἀφορῶν] upon (9) his back.
(b) And I SAW [ὁρῶ] that he was not dressed in garments [ἱμάτια], (10) but WAS SEEN [ὁρώμενον] by us as naked, (11) and not at all like a MAN [ἄνθρωπον], and that his feet were whiter [λευκοτέρους] than snow, (12) so that the earth there was LIT [καταλάμπεσθαι] up by (13) his feet, and that his head touched to heaven, so that I was afraid [φοβηθέντα] (14) and cried out.
(c) And he, turning around, APPEARED [ὀφθῆναι] as a small [μικρόν] MAN [ἄνθρωπον], (15) and took hold of my BEARD and pulled it and said (16) to me: John, be not unbelieving but believing [μὴ γίνου ἄπιστος ἀλλὰ πιστός], and not inquisitive [περίεργος]. (17) And I said to him, "But what did I do, Lord?"
C: And I tell you, (18) brothers, I suffered such pain for thirty days at the place (19) where he took hold of my BEARD, that I said to him, (20) "Lord, if your playful tug has given me so much pain, (21) what if you had given me a beating?" So he said to me, (22) "Let it be your concern from now on not to tempt him who is not to be tempted [ἀπείραστον]."

Closing

O: 91 (1) But Peter and James were angry because I spoke with the Lord, (2) and beckoned to me to come to them (3) and leave [ἀπολιπῶν] the Lord alone.
M: And I went, and they both said to me: (4) The old man [γέρων] who was speaking with the Lord [τῷ κυρίῳ προσομιλῶν] on the top of the mount, who (5) was he? For we heard both of them speaking.
C: And I, when I considered (6) his great grace [τὴν πολλὴν χάριν αὐτοῦ], and his unity which has many faces [πολυπρόσωπον ἑνότητα], and his wisdom (7) which without ceasing looked upon us, said, (8) "This you shall learn if you ask him."

Acts of John 90 opens in a typical way for the Testimonies, simply stating that what he is about to relate took place "at another time" (90.1).

This is especially characteristic of the Twelve Testimonies (AJohn 88–93), in which there are only a few temporal indicators. Other than the general sense that this series of Testimonies is in chronological order (88 begins with the call of John, 94 indicates events before Jesus's arrest, and 98–102 relate events around the crucifixion), the Twelve Testimonies are strung together with vague connectors such as "sometimes," "again," and "another." Careful attention to the use of connecting phrases within 90–91 reveals that the three Testimonies (T6–T8) actually cover two separate occasions. The first Testimony (T6; 90.1–4) refers to one or more instances when John, James, and Peter saw ineffable light in Jesus when he was praying on a mountain. The next Testimony (T7; 90.4–22) begins "again in a similar way he led us...," indicating a separate but related occasion, which is further described from the perspective of Peter and James in the third Testimony of this series (T8; 91). Thus even within "the transfiguration" in AJohn, there are multiple transfigurations. And further, although not conclusive, T6 might even be read as implying that this appearance of light while Jesus was praying was a recurring event, since Jesus was accustomed to praying on that mountain.

For AJohn, this group of characters is interesting. John is of course ubiquitous, and he is two other times accompanied by his brother James (88b, 89). Peter, however, is only mentioned in this story (90.2 and 91.1) and once before in 88b, where he and his brother Andrew are called to follow Jesus. Andrew's presence is also notable since he is not only present but also one of the people to witness the Lord's changing form: he sees the light in Jesus in 90.3, and then he (along with James) seems to hear the Lord speaking with multiple voices in 91, although he does not realize they are both the Lord. Other than James, who is a witness on four occasions (T1, T2, T6, T8), the primary witness to the Lord's mysterious form is John, as we would expect in a work written from John's perspective. Furthermore, while James and Peter are present in all three episodes, it appears that only John witnessed the extraordinary form of Jesus in the central T7, since Jesus is praying at a distance, and John sneaks up behind him. Inasmuch as T7 is the central episode of the "Transfiguration Testimonies," John is thus the central witness to Jesus's mysterious form in both the "Transfiguration Testimonies" and the Twelve Testimonies as a whole.

As already noted above, the middle Testimony of this group (T7, 90.4–22) is probably the most important. It occupies a central position both within the "Transfiguration Testimonies" and within the Twelve

Testimonies as whole. At eighteen lines, it is easily the longest,[35] and greater narrative detail as well as the presence of actual dialogue with Jesus[36] lend increased prominence. These features suggest that we might read this central episode as the focal point of the Twelve Testimonies. If these Testimonies are especially important, and the middle one, T7, is still more significant, what then is the purpose of this? What christological claims do these particular Testimonies make? And how do these claims relate to other parts of the Testimonies?

Within the taxonomy of table 1 above, this cluster of Testimonies contains primarily extraordinary manifestations of the Lord. The first two Testimonies, T6 and T7, are purely visual phenomena. First, John, James, and Peter see indescribable light in Jesus (90.2–4), most likely while he is praying (this is not explicitly stated). In the following similar but more expansive episode, Jesus is praying by himself a little ways from the three disciples (90.6). When John sneaks up to catch a glimpse of Jesus unawares, he sees more than he bargained for. What John sees, I argue, is the most remarkable appearance of Jesus in these Twelve Testimonies, and it is a complex of multiple extraordinary visual phenomena. Like T4, the Lord again is enormous, "reaching to heaven" (90.13), and like T6, he again produces light—this time specifically from his feet, which are described as "whiter than snow" (90.11–13). But beyond these now familiar phenomena, there is something new: the Lord is not clothed, but naked, and as a result, he appears "not at all like a man." As the title of this paper suggests, this is not merely a statement about Jesus's wardrobe. Although this cluster of attributes itself suggests something like a theophany or at least a glimpse of an otherworldly being, we need to examine this more closely to appreciate the full import of what John has seen.

The specific collocation of removing garments and not appearing to be human is not found elsewhere in AJohn, nor are there any (other) metaphorical uses of language concerning garments. Although I have mostly reserved the use of comparative texts for the final section of this essay, an analog from the Gospel of Thomas will enable us to get to the point quickly here. In Gos. Thom. 37, Jesus says that to truly see him, they need to remove their garments and strip naked. Coupled with other logia such as 28, Gos. Thom. seems to present the concept that human nature

35. For comparison, T1 is eleven lines, and all the rest are less than ten lines long.

36. In the Twelve Testimonies, the Lord speaks briefly in T1, T6, and T9, but there is no actual dialogue—no conversation between Jesus and anyone else.

(specifically the body) is a garment that must be shed to attain enlightenment and oneness with the divine.[37] Other statements in AJohn do express the concept that the human body is dead and an impediment to spiritual development.[38] The illusory, nonessential nature of Jesus's human body is a major focus of the cross of light discourse (97–102) and the closing of John's sermon (113). In view of these facts, it seems likely that when John says he saw Jesus naked and appearing not at all human, AJohn is drawing on the topos of the human body as a garment.[39] Thus John sees the Lord as he really is—divine and not truly human. Perhaps it was curiosity that drove John to take a closer look after formerly seeing the ineffable light in Jesus while he was praying (T6). On that first occasion, however, I suspect it was only a glimpse of φῶς peeking through Jesus's σάρξ. This time, with σάρξ completely out of the way, John catches a glimpse of the Lord in all his glory, and his response is fear rather than curiosity.[40] And all of this from only Jesus's back![41] We can only imagine what would have happened had John seen his face.

The Lord's reaction (90.14–16) to John's terrified cry is to turn and face John, at which point Jesus now appears as a small man (cf. T4). Jesus then rebukes John with a word and a deed: he tugs John's beard[42] and urges him

37. Gospel of Mary 16 may be expressing a similar concept, although exactly what is meant by the "garment" there is less clear. For more on this topos in Gos. Thom. and Gos. Mary, see Vernon K. Robbins, "Questions and Answers in Gospel of Thomas," in *La littérature des questions et réponses dans l'Antiquité profane et chrétienne: de l'enseignement à l'exégèse: actes du séminaire sur le genre des questions et réponses tenu à Ottawa les 27 et 28 septembre 2009*, ed. M.-P. Bussières, IPM 64 (Turnhout: Brepols, 2013), 3–36, here 24–26; and Robbins, *Who Do People Say I Am*, 182, 211.

38. This is most vividly portrayed in the episode concerning a portrait painted of John, who says to the person who had the portrait made, "What you have done now is childish and imperfect: you have painted the dead picture of what is dead" (AJohn 29). Cf. AJohn 103: "Let us worship him not with any part of our body but with the disposition of the soul."

39. Whether or not this comes directly from Gos. Thom. is unimportant, but considering the other resonances of Gos. Thom. (discussed further below), a literary relationship is certainly possible.

40. Junod and Kaestli perfectly capture the relationship between these two transfigurations: "Il y a donc deux scènes de transfiguration, la première étant comme *éclipsée* par la seconde" *Acta Iohannis*, 2:482 (emphasis added).

41. The allusion here to Exod 33:18–23 is discussed below.

42. Based on preliminary research on the cultural significance of the beard (discussed briefly above), this is not the amusing gesture it would seem to be to modern

toward belief in place of unbelief and inquisitiveness.[43] Unfortunately for readers, Jesus gives no direct answer to John's question concerning what his offense had been, but we may suspect that Jesus already answered the question, and that John has difficulty either understanding or accepting it. The only thing Jesus says after this is "not to tempt him who is not to be tempted" (90.22). We thus have three elements by which to identify John's offense: unbelief, inquisitiveness, and temptation.[44] The charge of unbelief and inquisitiveness suggests that the Lord did not intend for John to catch a glimpse of his "naked divinity." John's inquisitiveness and its implicit unbelief are echoed in the next Testimony after the "Transfiguration Testimonies," T9 (AJohn 92), in which John tries to stay awake and watch Jesus. Even after Jesus tells John to go to sleep, he continues watching and listening while pretending to be asleep. Fortunately for John, and almost surprisingly for readers, Jesus does not tug John's beard or give him a beating (see 90.21)! What does happen is that one Jesus tells another that his chosen followers do not believe in him, and the other responds without surprise, noting that they are (merely) humans. This Testimony clarifies John's offense and Jesus's reaction on the mountain in T7 in two ways: John's curiosity is equated with unbelief, but Jesus's restraint in rebuking him (only a playful tug—90.20) derives from his understanding that as one thoroughly human and uninitiated, such behavior is expected. Perhaps this is why Jesus tolerates John's inquisitiveness throughout the Twelve Testimonies. It is only later that John truly comes to understand Jesus's identity, when the Lord willingly initiates the disciples into a kind of lesser mysteries in the Hymn-Dance (AJohn 94–96), and then initiates John alone into greater mysteries through the cross of light discourse (AJohn 97–102).[45]

The final Testimony of the "Transfiguration Testimonies," T8 (AJohn 91), relates the perspective of Peter and James on John's startling experience. First, they are angry that John spoke with the Lord (91.1). Perhaps

---

readers (or to me, at least!), but a very serious challenge to John's masculinity and maturity.

43. This line and Jesus's words to Thomas at the end of GJohn are compared below.

44. At present, I have been unable to determine with any precision what the nature of this temptation is. Robbins (*Who Do People Say I Am*, 210) acknowledges that it is confusing and suggests that the temptation is for Jesus "to simply take the form of God." It could also be related to Satan's temptation of Jesus in the wilderness.

45. For this understanding of these two initiations, see Lalleman, *Acts of John*, 52–66, and Robbins, *Who Do People Say I Am*, 221–22.

they object to John's interrupting Jesus in prayer, or perhaps they are a bit jealous. Whatever the case, they urge John to leave Jesus alone (91.2–3). When John comes back, we learn another reason they wanted John to come back: they heard Jesus talking to an old man and want to know who he was (4–5). Exactly what they witnessed is difficult to ascertain. They definitely heard two voices speaking (91.5), which suggests that they experienced Jesus's metamorphosis in the aural phenomenon of multiple voices, just as John does in the next Testimony (T9; AJohn 92).[46] Although John makes no mention of having heard the same thing (and he need not have, since the metamorphic Jesus is often experienced simultaneously in different ways), John did see Jesus in two different forms, and it seems most likely that James and Peter heard those two forms conversing.[47]

Having come to the end of the preliminary analysis of AJohn 90–91 and the Testimonies as a whole, several important features have emerged. This whole section of AJohn, which I have dubbed the Testimonies, is concerned with bearing witness to the mysterious form, nature, and identity of the Lord. The first section, the Twelve Testimonies (88–93), contains twelve episodes in which John bears witness to the constantly fluctuating physical form of Jesus. To borrow Synoptic language, Jesus in the Testimonies is constantly being transfigured. His body is constantly in flux, and he takes on both ordinary and extraordinary forms that are perceived visually, aurally, and tactilely. This diversity of form is the physical manifestation of the diverse names and roles the Lord assumed for the sake of humanity, as elucidated in the cross of light discourse (97–102). Yet in that discourse, the Lord reveals to John that there is unity beyond the diversity, and he describes this unity using language of both light (98) and *logos* (99). A further crucial point of this final discourse is that as light and *logos*, the Lord is primarily divine and his humanity, particularly his human body, was simply a form he took on temporarily (see especially 101). Coming back to the Twelve Testimonies, in the midst of Jesus's diverse forms, I argue that T7 is the one occasion when John saw the Lord's true, divine nature. John's final comment in T8, as he reflects on what he has just expe-

---

46. Given the fact that in T7, it is John who talks to Jesus, a less likely explanation, given the context and the point the John is making, is that they actually heard John talking to Jesus. But which one is the "old man"? Although tempting as a simple solution to the problem, this option really does not fit the context as well as that suggested above.

47. Lalleman, "Polymorphy of Christ," 105–6, supports this reading.

rienced in T7, expresses this well: "I considered his great grace, and his unity which has many faces [πολυπρόσωπον ἑνότητα]" (91.5–6). Thus, in the Testimonies of AJohn, Jesus's identity is primarily that of a God who takes on a variety of physical manifestations, both ordinary and otherwise.

3. The Lukan Transfiguration (Luke 9:28–36)

The Synoptic transfiguration accounts share many details in common, and we could compare AJohn 90–91 with all three Synoptic accounts (or *all* early Christian accounts, such as those listed above). However, I have selected Luke because a distinctively Lukan feature appears in the very beginning of the account in AJohn 90: Jesus goes to the mountain to *pray* (AJohn 90.2; Luke 9:28). But this does not mean I ignore the other Synoptic Gospels, since I read Luke itself as a reconfiguration of Mark. Focusing on Luke allows for a more manageable comparison. Before comparing AJohn and Luke, however, we first need to look at the Lukan transfiguration in its own context(s). As with the discussion of AJohn 90–91 above, my foci here are the main features of the Lukan transfiguration and its function and significance within the Gospel of Luke.

There is a long and still unresolved debate among source-critical scholars over the origin of the transfiguration story.[48] It would be unproductive to enter that discussion here, and it is sufficient to note that I am unconvinced by the argument that the transfiguration is a displaced resurrection account. Since I accept the essential validity of both Markan priority and the Two-Source Hypothesis, and since I am discussing the transfiguration in *Luke* specifically, for my purposes the "origin" of the transfiguration story is the Gospel of Mark.[49] Thus while I am uninterested here in pregospel sources, I *am* interested in how Luke reconfigures the transfiguration for his own purposes. As is shown below, analysis of Luke's redaction is a window into how he conceives of the transfiguration.

Before examining the specific features of the transfiguration narrative, we should first consider the placement of the transfiguration within the overall arc of Luke's story of Jesus. Although we could begin by looking just at Luke, for the sake of brevity I will begin this analysis with a parallel

48. See Adela Yarbro Collins, *Mark: A Commentary*, Hermeneia (Minneapolis: Fortress, 2007), 414–15, for a good Forschungsbericht.

49. Lee provides references for arguments that Luke has access to sources in addition to Mark (*Jesus' Transfiguration*, 109).

chart of the whole books of Luke and Mark, focusing on the position of the transfiguration within the overall works, as well as the specific sequence of episodes in which the transfiguration is embedded (table 2). Then, after comparing the placement of these transfiguration accounts, I compare the two in a parallel chart of the episodes themselves (table 3). Together these two comparisons show that the way Luke fits this episode into his overall story is reflected in specific editorial choices, and thus both a purely narrative approach and a redactional approach yield similar results.

Table 2. Parallel Opening-Middle-Closing Texture of Luke and Mark*

Gospel of Luke†	Gospel of Mark‡
OPENING (1:1–4:13/15): Beginnings O: Preface (1:1–4) M: Infancy Narrative (1:5–2:52) C: Preparation (3:1–4:13)	OPENING (1:1–13): Preparation O: "The beginning of the gospel…" (1:1) M: John and Jesus (1:2–11) C: The temptation (1:12–13)
MIDDLE (4:16–21:38): Jesus's Ministry	**MIDDLE (1:14–13:36) Jesus's Ministry and Death**
***Opening*: Galilean Ministry (4:14–9:50)** O: Jesus returns to Galilee/rejection at Nazareth (4:14–30)	*Opening*: Jesus's early ministry of healing and teaching brings followers, fame, and opponents (1:14–3:35)
M: Intertwined narrative of many healings and miracles with calling of disciples, teaching, and confrontations mixed in (4:31–8:56)	***Middle*: Jesus the Healer and Teacher (4–13)** O: Jesus teaches the kingdom in parables, heals many, continues to face opposition (4:1–8:26)
C: Discipleship and identity (9:1–50)	**M: Jesus's identity and mission revealed and misunderstood (8:27–10:52)**
O: Mission of the Twelve (9:1–17) (a) The Twelve sent out (9:1–6) (b) Herod perplexed (9:7–9) (c) The Twelve return, five thousand fed (9:10–17)	

M: Jesus's identity (9:18–36) (a) "Who do you say I am?" Peter: "The Messiah" (9:18–20) (b) Jesus's suffering and the nature of discipleship (9:21–27) **(c) The transfiguration (9:28–36)** C: The disciples misunderstand (9:37–50) *Middle*: Travel Narrative (9:51–19:27): Some Healing but Mostly Teaching	(a) "Who do you say I am?" Peter: "The Messiah" (8:27–30) (b) First passion prediction and the nature of discipleship (8:31–9:1) **(c) The transfiguration and the coming of Elijah (9:2–13)** (d) The disciples continue to misunderstand (9:14–50) (e) Teaching in Judea—disciples *still* don't understand (10) C: Activities and teaching in Jerusalem (11–13)
Closing: Jerusalem (19:28–21:38): Triumphal Entry; Full of Controversy, Ends with Apocalyptic Discourse	*Closing*: Jesus the Suffering Son of Man (14–15) O: Passion preparation (14:1–42) M: The suffering of the Son of Man: Jesus betrayed, arrested, tried, denied, handed over, beaten, mocked, and crucified (14:43–15:32) C: Death and burial of the Son of God (15:33–47)
CLOSING (22:1–24:53): Jesus's Passion and Exaltation O: Plot, last supper, final discussions, Gethsemane (22:1–22:38) M: Jesus's arrest, trial, crucifixion, death, and burial (22:39–23:56) C: Resurrection and ascension (24)	CLOSING (16): The Empty Tomb O: Three women visit the tomb (16:1–3) M: The empty tomb and the young man (16:4–7) C: The women flee is terror and amazement (16:8)

* The location of the transfiguration accounts is in bold.
† In this section, the OMC contours are entirely my own analysis, while in the identification of some of the smaller units I utilized Joel B. Green's outline in *The Gospel of Luke*, NICNT (Grand Rapids: Eerdmans, 1997), 25–29.

‡ In this section I was aided by Carl Holladay's outline in *A Critical Introduction to the New Testament: Interpreting the Message and Meaning of Jesus Christ*, expanded digital ed. (Nashville: Abingdon, 2005), 174–75.

As this table shows, the transfiguration in Luke occurs in a cluster of scenes concerned with Jesus's identity located in the middle of the closing of Luke's account of Jesus's Galilean ministry, which itself forms the opening of the middle of the Gospel of Luke. This whole closing section (9:1–50) of the Galilean ministry focuses on Jesus's identity and the nature of following him. The disciples' failure to understand these things is a theme running through this section and brought to a head just after the transfiguration. After this closing of the Galilean ministry, Luke proceeds to what many consider the "heart" of his gospel (and it is certainly the locus of much unique Lukan material): the Travel Narrative (9:51–19:27).

When we compare the narrative location of the transfiguration in Luke with its position in Mark, similarities and contrasts emerge. In terms of the progression of Jesus's Galilean ministry, the episode occurs in essentially the same place, at the end. The specific cluster of stories relating to Jesus's identity and discipleship is also very similar. In both gospels, the sequence of episodes is the same: (a) messianic declaration by Peter, (b) first passion prediction and the nature of discipleship, and (c) transfiguration, followed by further examples of the disciples' misunderstanding. Thus in relation to its immediate context, Luke is essentially following Mark. But when we "zoom out" further, some dissimilarity emerges. In Mark, the identity and discipleship cluster occurs in the very middle of the entire Gospel, and in many ways 8:27–9:13 (or even extended to 9:50) forms the central message of Mark: the messianic Son of Man had to suffer, and those who follow him will share in this suffering. In Mark 10 Jesus begins moving toward Jerusalem, and then in chapter 11, a mere two chapters after the transfiguration, Jesus enters Jerusalem, which starts the chain reaction leading to his death. By contrast, Luke's inclusion of the lengthy Travel Narrative (which is not so focused on Jesus's identity) has the overall effect of shifting the discipleship and identity cluster into the opening of the middle and distancing the transfiguration from the realization of Jesus's mission. This is not to say that the discipleship and identity material is unimportant; the Galilean ministry is still vital to Luke's story and in many ways sets up the rest of the Gospel. Nonetheless, the transfiguration and the surrounding discussion of Jesus's identity as suffering

Son of Man is not the *main* point of Luke's Gospel, nor is this Luke's main christological claim as it is for Mark.[50] What then does the transfiguration accomplish for Luke? To answer this, we need to delve into the details (table 3). This also helps us to address an issue that has become apparent already: while the transfiguration fits its immediate context in dealing with the issue of Jesus's identity, *what* does it actually say about Jesus? And how does this relate to the suffering Son of Man material preceding it?

Table 3. Parallel Opening-Middle-Closing Texture of the Transfiguration in Luke and Mark*

Luke 9:28–36 (my trans.)	Mark 9:2–13 (my trans.)
Opening O: 28 Now it happened [Ἐγένετο] that about (α) *eight days after* these sayings (β) Jesus took with him [παραλαβών] Peter and John and James, (γ) and he went up [ἀνέβη] to the MOUNTAIN [εἰς τὸ ὄρος] *to PRAY* [προσεύξασθαι].	Opening And (α) *after six days*, (β) Jesus took with him [παραλαμβάνει] Peter and James and John, (γ) and led them up [ἀναφέρει αὐτοὺς] to a *high* mountain [εἰς ὄρος ὑψηλόν] *alone* [μόνους], *by themselves* [κατ’ ἰδίαν].
M: 29 And it happened [ἐγένετο] that (δ) *while he was PRAYING*, the appearance *of his face* [τὸ εἶδος τοῦ προσώπου αὐτοῦ] was different [ἕτερον], (ε) and his clothes [ὁ ἱματισμὸς αὐτοῦ] were dazzling white [λευκὸς ἐξαστράπτων].	(δ) And he was transfigured [μετεμορφώθη] before them [ἔμπροσθεν αὐτῶν], 3 (ε) and his clothes [τὰ ἱμάτια αὐτοῦ] became [ἐγένετο] *exceedingly* [λίαν] dazzling white [στίλβοντα λευκά], *such as no fuller on earth is able* [*δύναται*] *to bleach them.*

50. In Luke the key passage for Jesus's identity is the rejection at Nazareth (4:14–30), which Luke moves forward to a crucial and programmatic position at the very beginning of his ministry. Rather than presenting Jesus as suffering Son of Man, it focuses Jesus's identity on being the Lord's anointed one who brings good news to the poor and captives. This understanding of Jesus's identity is especially shaped by Robbins, *Who Do People Say I Am*, 75–95.

C: 30 And *look! Two men* [*ἄνδρες*], *who were* (ζ) Moses and Elijah, (η) were speaking with him [συνελάλουν αὐτῷ]. 31 (θ) They appeared [ὀφθέντες] *in GLORY* [*ἐν δόξῃ*] *and were speaking* [*ἔλεγον*] *of his departure* [*τὴν ἔξοδον αὐτοῦ*], *which he was about to accomplish* [*πληροῦν*] *in Jerusalem.*

Middle

O: 32 *Now Peter and those with him were weighed down with sleep* [*βεβαρημένοι ὕπνῳ*]; *but since they had stayed awake, they saw* [*εἶδον*] *his GLORY and the two men who stood with him.*

M: (a.) 33 *And it happened that as they were leaving him* [*ἐν τῷ διαχωρίζεσθαι αὐτούς*], (ι) Peter said to Jesus, "*Master* [*Ἐπιστάτα*], it is good [**καλόν**] for us to be here; and let us make three tents, one for you, one for Moses, and one for Elijah"—(κ) not knowing [μὴ εἰδώς] *what he was saying* [*ὃ λέγει*].

(b.) 34 *But while he was saying these things*, (λ) a cloud came and began to overshadow them; (μ) *and they were frightened* [*ἐφοβήθησαν*] *as they entered the cloud.*

C: 35 (ν) Then a voice [**φωνή**] came [**ἐγένετο**] from the cloud, *saying*, "This is my Son, *the chosen one* [*ἐκλελεγμένος*]; listen to him!"

Closing

36 (ξ) When the voice had come [*ἐν τῷ γενέσθαι*], Jesus was found

Middle

4 And (ζ) ELIJAH *with* Moses [Ἠλίας σὺν Μωϋσεῖ] (θ) appeared [ὤφθη] *to them*, (η) and they were speaking with [ἦσαν συλλαλοῦντες] Jesus.

5 (ι) Then Peter said to Jesus, "*Rabbi*, it is good [**καλόν**] for us to be here; let us make three tents, one for you, one for Moses, and one for ELIJAH." 6 (κ) For he had not known [plup. ᾔδει] *what he should say* [*τί ἀποκριθῇ*], (μ) *for they became terrified* [*ἔκφοβοι*].

7 Then (λ) a cloud came overshadowing them, and (ν) a voice came [**ἐγένετο**] from the cloud, "This is my Son, *the Beloved*; listen to him!" 8 (ξ) And *suddenly, when they looked around, they saw no one any more,* but Jesus alone [**μόνον**] with them.

Closing

9 (ω) As they were coming down the mountain, he

[*εὑρέθη*] alone [**μόνος**]. And (ο) they kept silent [ἐσίγησαν], and in those days (π) *told no one* [οὐδενὶ ἀπήγγειλαν] anything of that which they had seen … [οὐδὲν ὧν ἑώρακαν].

ordered them to (π) *tell no one* [*μηδενί … διηγήσωνται*] about what they had seen [ἃ εἶδον διηγήσωνται], until after the Son of Man had risen from the dead. 10 So (ο) they kept the matter to themselves, questioning what this rising from the dead could mean.

[Note: the following verse, 37, mentions having come down from the mountain, but it clearly begins a new episode: "It happened that on the next day, (ω) having come down from the mountain, a great crowd met him."]

11 Then they asked him, "Why do the scribes say that ELIJAH must come first?" 12 He said to them, "ELIJAH is indeed coming first to restore all things. How then is it written about the Son of Man, that he is to go through many sufferings and be treated with contempt? 13 But I tell you that ELIJAH has come, and they did to him whatever they pleased, as it is written about him."

* Font guide: Greek letters in parentheses indicate corresponding/contrasting units of text; bold = exact agreement in wording (in a few instances I have marked phrases as exact agreement even though there are very minor, stylistic variations in wording [e.g., μίαν σοί in Luke for σοὶ μίαν], which are not a concern here); underline = closely similar wording; all caps = repetitive texture in one version (bold and all caps indicates exact agreement and repetitive texture in one version); italics = contrasting or distinctive elements between versions.

Despite narrating the same basic event, there are numerous differences and few verbatim agreements.[51] Here we can discuss only a few of

51. Matthew, by contrast, follows the Markan account much more closely.

the more important distinctive features of Luke's account.[52] Perhaps the most distinct feature of Luke's transfiguration occurs at the very beginning (O and M in the opening): Luke adds that Jesus went up to the mountain specifically *to pray* (9:28), and furthermore, the change in Jesus's appearance occurs while he is praying (9:29). This is a remarkable reconfiguration by Luke. Mark gives no reason for Jesus's ascent, but the fact that he *leads* (ἀναφέρει) the three disciples up the mountain suggests a certain intentionality: in Mark, it could be inferred that Jesus took the disciples there specifically so that they would see him transfigured. In Luke, Jesus does "take along" (παραλαβών) Peter, James, and John, as in Mark (there a finite verb is used), but the main verb (ἀνέβη) simply expresses that *Jesus* ascended the mountain, with prayer as the stated purpose. Rather than understand Luke's addition of prayer as simply a narrative expansion that explains Jesus's reason for going to the mountain, Jesus's prayer here should be read in the context of the topos of prayer as it is used throughout Luke, which, it turns out, is a significant and well-known motif. Not only is prayer generally emphasized,[53] but also when Jesus prays, things happen.[54] Prayer punctuates Jesus's ministry from beginning to end, and his constant practice of prayer is noted several times. His preferred places of prayer are deserted places (5:16), by himself (9:18), and, notably for us, on the mountain (6:12; 9:28, 29). Even more importantly, several key events are preceded by and implicitly precipitated by Jesus's prayer. Luke rewrites Jesus's baptism so that it is when he is praying *after* being baptized that heaven opens and the voice from heaven declares Jesus's divine sonship (Luke 3:21–22). In Luke alone, Jesus prays all night on the mountain

52. There is a great deal of scholarship on the transfiguration accounts, and the commentary tradition has produced ample analyses of the minute differences between accounts. For bibliography, see John Nolland, *Luke 1–9:20*, WBC 35A (Dallas: Word, 1989), 487–89; and François Bovon, *Luke 1: A Commentary on the Gospel of Luke 1:1–9:50*, trans. Christine M. Thomas, Hermeneia (Minneapolis: Fortress, 2002), 369. For a specific analysis of Matthew's and Luke's rewriting of the Markan transfiguration, see Lee, *Jesus' Transfiguration*, 92–127.

53. Προσεύχομαι and προσευχή are used twenty-two times in Luke, and to these we may add three uses of δέησις. In Luke 1:13, Zechariah's prayer for a child is heard. Anna is praised for her prayer in the temple (2:37). Furthermore, Jesus frequently teaches about prayer, e.g., "pray for those who abuse you" (6:28); the Lord's prayer (11:1–13); parable of persistent prayer (18:1–8); humble prayer (18:9–14); temple supposed to be a house of prayer (19:46); scribes pray hypocritically (20:47).

54. I thank Vernon Robbins for encouraging me to think about this so simply.

before calling the twelve disciples (6:12–16). In all three Synoptic Gospels, Jesus prays at Gethsemane for the "cup" to be removed and subsequently resigns himself to the will of God (Luke 22:39 and parr.). And while the intensive prayer scene of 22:43–44, in which Jesus prays in such anguish and earnestness that he sweats blood, is generally considered to be unoriginal,[55] whoever added it understood how important prayer was for the Lukan Jesus. Jesus's final act before dying is to commend his spirit to the Father (23:46). In view of all of this, we might ask whether Jesus's transfiguration in Luke could have come about in any other way.

We have already identified Jesus's identity as the central concern of the cluster of scenes of which the transfiguration is a part. What then does Luke's reconfiguration of the transfiguration say about Jesus? On the one hand, both transfiguration accounts provide a voice that literally answers the question of Jesus's identity: "This is my Son" (Luke 9:35; Mark 9:7). Thus Jesus's identity as Son of God is clearly emphasized in both accounts. But Luke reconfigures this in two ways. First, the fact that Jesus's prayer brings about his glorification (see below) is indicative of the close relationship Jesus has with the Father,[56] which is reiterated throughout the Gospel by the repeated depiction of Jesus in prayer. Second, whereas Mark says, "This is my Son, the beloved" (Mark 9:7, more closely echoing the baptismal voice from heaven; cf. Mark 1:11), Luke reads, "This is my son, *the chosen one*" (Luke 9:35). Thus while Mark's statement adds nothing new, Luke takes the opportunity to further develop the identity of Jesus. The "chosen one" probably looks back to Jesus's identification in 4:14–30 as the Lord's anointed one (Messiah), and this connection is confirmed in the crucifixion account, when the leaders mock him, saying, "He saved others; let him save himself if he is the Messiah of God, his chosen one!" (Luke 23:35).

The addition of "glory" is another striking Lukan reconfiguration that clarifies an important feature of the episode: what does Jesus's remarkable appearance signify? Jesus himself is nowhere else in either gospel described with a radiant appearance or clothing using the language employed here.[57] However, Luke introduces "glory" (δόξα) in reference to the appearance of Moses and Elijah (9:31), and it is also applied to Jesus in the following

55. Although it is undoubtedly ancient: Bruce Metzger, *A Textual Commentary on the Greek New Testament*, 2nd ed. (New York: United Bible Societies, 1994), 151.

56. Cf. Bovon, *Luke 1*, 375.

57. Collins, *Mark*, 416.

verse (9:32). The "glory" the three disciples see here is or at least includes the idea of radiant appearance.[58] More importantly, this is not an isolated occurrence of "glory." In Jesus's discourse just before the transfiguration (eight days before, according to 9:28), he says, "Those who are ashamed of me and of my words, of them the Son of Man will be ashamed when he comes in his glory and the glory of the Father and of the holy angels" (9:26). By carrying this concept of glory into the transfiguration, Luke makes clearer what could only be guessed at in Mark: the appearance of the transfigured Jesus is a glimpse of what the Son of Man will look like when he comes in glory. It is thus a kind of proleptic experience of the parousia. I suspect that Mark also has this in mind, but Luke makes the connection explicit. Later, in the apocalyptic discourse, this glorious figure is again mentioned: "Then they will see the Son of Man coming in a cloud with great power and glory" (Luke 21:27; cf. Mark 13:26).[59]

Yet Jesus's glory in Luke (unlike Mark) is not delayed until the parousia. In Luke 24, after Jesus's resurrection, he appears to two disciples on the road to Emmaus. They do not recognize him, and they know only of an empty tomb (they only know Mark!). Jesus then says, "Oh, how foolish you are, and how slow of heart to believe *all that the prophets have declared*! Was it not necessary that the Messiah should *suffer these things and then enter into his glory*?" (Luke 24:25–26 NRSV). This suggests that glory followed Jesus's suffering more immediately than just in the parousia. Having completed his prophetic mission, Jesus would then enter glory. I would suggest that this entering into glory takes place at the ascension, giving even deeper meaning to Acts 1:10, where the angels tell the disciples that Jesus will return in the same manner in which he was taken up. Thus Jesus would be glorious both following the completion of his earthly mission and when he comes again. This helps explain Luke's addition to the transfiguration in 9:31, where it says Jesus and his visitors were talking about his imminent ἔξοδος. Altogether this shows Luke engaging in a blended prophetic/apocalyptic discourse, in which Jesus is both a prophet on a mission from God and a divine figure who will come to earth at the end of time. This reconfiguration of the transfiguration serves to enhance both images of Jesus.[60]

58. So Bovon, *Luke 1*, 377.

59. Note that even the cloud (in the singular, as in 9:34) is present! Mark 13:26 has "clouds."

60. In speaking of prophetic and apocalyptic discourse, I specifically have in mind

4. Reconfigurations of the Lukan Transfiguration in Acts of John 90–91

Now that we have thoroughly examined the accounts of AJohn and Luke in their own contexts, it should already be clear that these are very different stories, despite some obvious similarities. Yet beyond the obvious "parallels," a careful comparison shows that AJohn 90–91 skillfully reconfigures the Synoptic transfiguration both by employing its own characteristic topoi and by drawing on other resource texts outside the Synoptic transfigurations. The end result, as we have seen above, is a centrally important Testimony to AJohn's conception of Jesus's identity and the nature of his life on earth. As noted above, I use Luke as my primary comparative text, but throughout I note other possible resource texts that AJohn may be utilizing. I have given Luke priority in this comparison because of the distinctive prayer topos employed in both accounts and to make the comparison manageable, but as the detailed analysis below shows, AJohn is probably working from multiple traditions and/or a blended/harmonized gospel tradition like the *Diatessaron*.[61]

A brief survey of the Synoptic parallels outside the "transfigurations" solidifies this last point. The call narrative (AJohn 88b) most resembles Matt 4:18–22 and Mark 1:16–20, in that Simon Peter and Andrew are called first, and then John and James. The call happens from Jesus on the shore, as in AJohn. But examination of the details shows blending. Overall, Luke's call narrative (5:1–11) is quite different: Jesus joins Simon in his boat (no mention of Andrew), leading to a miraculous catch of fish, which James and John (cf. 5:7, 10) help bring in. Then they all follow Jesus (5:11). Unlike Matthew, Mark, and AJohn, in Luke the call is not from the shore. But there is one detail that might suggest that AJohn is also incorporating the version in Luke: John says to James, "Because of our long watch that we kept at sea you are not seeing straight" (AJohn 88). This could recall Peter's

the "rhetorolects" identified by Vernon K. Robbins in "Conceptual Blending and Early Christian Imagination," in *Explaining Christian Origins and Early Judaism: Contributions from Cognitive and Social Science*, ed. Petri Luomanen, Ilkka Pyysiäinen, and Risto Uro, BIS 89 (Leiden: Brill, 2007), 161–95; and Robbins, *The Invention of Christian Discourse*, vol. 1, RRA 1 (Blandford Forum, UK: Deo, 2009).

61. A preliminary comparison with the *Diatessaron* itself was not, however, particularly insightful, either for the transfigurations or for the other Synoptic parallels in AJohn. It did not contain the same combinations of features from the four gospels that are evident in AJohn.

comment, unique to Luke 5:5, that "we" (which could be understood to include his partners, James and John) "have worked all night long."

While many of the details of the Lord's ascension in AJohn 102 are unique to it (John is the only witness), the very presence of an ascension and specifically the use of the aorist passive, ἀνελήφθη, strongly suggests Luke-Acts. Acts 1:2 and 11 use ἀνελήμφθη, which is probably the source for the use of the same word in the longer ending of Mark (16:19). Luke 24:51 gives a short account of the ascension, using the similar ἀναφέρω instead of ἀναλαμβάνω. While the ascension is considered a distinctively Lukan episode, we cannot discount the possibility that AJohn knows Mark with its longer ending. But AJohn's knowledge and use of Lukan resources is unambiguously affirmed in AJohn 93 (T11) by Jesus's having been invited to dinner at a Pharisee's house.[62]

Returning to the "Transfiguration Testimonies," we begin, as usual, with an opening-middle-closing chart, as seen in table 4.

Table 4. Comparative OMC Texture Chart*

AJohn 90–91 (Elliott, modified)	Luke 9:28–36 (my trans.)
Opening O: 90 (1) And at another time (α) he took [παραλαμβάνει] me and James and (2) **Peter** (β) **to the mountain [εἰς τὸ ὄρος]** where he used to (γ) pray [εὔχεσθαι],	Opening O: 28 Now it happened ['Εγένετο] that about eight days after these sayings (α) **Jesus** took with him [παραλαβών] Peter and John and James, and (η) he went up [ἀνέβη] (β) **to the MOUNTAIN** [εἰς τὸ ὄρος] (γ) to PRAY [προσεύξασθαι].
M: and (δ) we SAW [εἴδομεν] (3) in him such a (ε) LIGHT [φῶς] (ζ) that it is not possible for a MAN [ἀνθρώπῳ] (4) who uses mortal speech to describe what it was like.	M: 29 And it happened [ἐγένετο] that (θ) while he was PRAY-ING [ἐν τῷ προσεύχεσθαι], the appearance of (ι) his face [τὸ εἶδος τοῦ προσώπου αὐτοῦ] was different [ἕτερον], (κ) and his clothes [ὁ ἱματισμὸς αὐτοῦ] were

62. Cf. Robbins, *Who Do People Say I Am*, 211.

	(ε) dazzling [ἐξαστράπτων] (λ) white [λευκός].
	C: 30 And look! Two men [ἄνδρες], who were Moses and Elijah, were speaking with him [συνελάλουν αὐτῷ]. 31 (δ) They appeared [ὀφθέντες] in GLORY [ἐν δόξῃ] and were speaking [ἔλεγον] of his departure [τὴν ἔξοδον αὐτοῦ], which he was about to accomplish [πληροῦν] in Jerusalem.
Middle	Middle
O: Again in a similar way (η) he led [ἀνάγει] (5) us three (β) **to the mountain [εἰς τὸ ὄρος]**, saying: Come with me. And we (6) went again: and (δ) we SAW [ὁρῶμεν] him at a distance (θ) praying [εὐχόμενον].	O: 32 Now Peter and those with him were weighed down with sleep [βεβαρημένοι ὕπνῳ]; but since they had stayed awake, (δ) they saw [εἶδον] his GLORY and (ο) the two men who stood [συνεστῶτας] with him.
M: o: (7) Now I, because he loved me [ἐφίλει με], went to him quietly [ἠρέμα], as though he should not (δ) SEE me, (8) and stood [ἵσταμαι] (δ) LOOKING [ἀφορῶν] upon (9) (ι) his back:	M: (a.) 33 And it happened that as they were (ξ) leaving him [ἐν τῷ διαχωρίζεσθαι αὐτούς], Peter said to Jesus, "Master [Ἐπιστάτα], it is good [καλόν] for us to be here; and let us make three tents, one for you, one for Moses, and one for Elijah"—not knowing [μὴ εἰδώς] what he was saying [ὃ λέγει].
m: and (δ) I **SAW** (ὁρῶ) that he was (κ) not dressed in garments [ἱμάτια], (10) but (δ) WAS SEEN [ὁρώμενον] by us as naked, (11) and not at all like a MAN [ἄνθρωπον], and (ι) that his feet were (λ) whiter [λευκοτέρους]	(b.) 34 But while he was saying these things, a cloud came and began to overshadow them; and they (μ) were frightened [ἐφοβήθησαν] as they entered the cloud.

than snow, (12) so that (ε) the earth there was LIT up by (13) (ι) his feet, and that his head touched to heaven: so that I (μ) was afraid [φοβηθέντα] (14) and cried out,

c: and he, turning around, (δ) APPEARED [ὀφθῆναι] as a MAN [ἄνθρωπον] of small stature, (15) and took hold of my BEARD and pulled it and said (16) to me: John, (ν) **be not unbelieving but believing [μὴ γίνου ἄπιστος ἀλλὰ πιστός]**, and not inquisitive. (17) And I said unto him: But what have I done, Lord?

C: 35 Then a voice [φωνή] came [ἐγένετο] from the cloud, saying, "This is my Son, the chosen one [ἐκλελεγμένος]; listen to him!"

[John 20:27: (ν) **be not unbelieving but believing [μὴ γίνου ἄπιστος ἀλλὰ πιστός]**]

C: And I tell you, (18) brothers, I suffered such pain for thirty days at the place (19) where he took hold of my BEARD, that I said to him: (20) Lord, if your playful tug has given me so much pain, (21) what if you had given me a beating? And he said to me: (22) Let it be your concern from henceforth not to tempt him who is not to be tempted.

Closing
O: 91 (1) But Peter and James were angry because I spoke with the Lord, (2) and beckoned to me to come to them (3) and (ξ) leave [ἀπολιπῶν] the Lord **alone [μόνον]**.

Closing
36 When the voice had come [ἐν τῷ γενέσθαι], Jesus was found [εὑρέθη] **alone [μόνος]**. (ζ) And they kept silent [ἐσίγησαν], and in those days told no one [οὐδενὶ ἀπήγγειλαν] anything of that which they had seen … [οὐδὲν ὧν ἑώρακαν].

M: And I went, and they both said unto me: (4) (o) The old man [γέρων] who was <u>speaking with the Lord</u> [τῷ κυρίῳ προσομιλῶν] upon the top of the mount, who (5) was he? For we heard <u>both of them</u> speaking.

C: And I, when I considered (6) his great grace, and his unity which has many faces, and his wisdom (7) which without ceasing looked upon us, said: (8) This you shall learn if you ask him.

* Font guide: Greek letters in parentheses indicate comparable/contrasting units of text (the same letter may be used twice in one column if the wording is repeated); bold = exact agreement in wording; underline = closely similar wording; all caps = repetitive texture in one version (bold and all caps indicates exact agreement *and* repetitive texture in one version). Italics have not been employed to mark "distinctive" elements since these accounts are not as close as those in Mark and Luke.

Both episodes open in similar ways: Jesus takes[63] Peter, James, and John[64] up to a mountain,[65] where they see Jesus in an extraordinary way, involving language of light (AJohn 90.3) and shining (Luke 9:29: "dazzling"; no exact verbal parallels). This is shared with nearly *all* the transfiguration accounts (except the highly abbreviated account in 2 Peter) and seems to be a basic feature of "the transfiguration." Acts of John then immediately incorporates a distinctively Lukan topos: the mountain is where Jesus would go to *pray*. Not only does this parallel the specific pur-

63. While Luke has the same verb in a participial form, here AJohn uses the exact form as Mark: παραλαμβάνει.

64. As noted above, this is a unique combination of characters in AJohn. This heightens the sense that AJohn is incorporating a resource text. Notice, however, the exact reversal of the order: John, James, Peter.

65. Note the verbatim parallel εἰς τὸ ὄρος in AJohn 90.2, 4, and Luke 9:28. Mark 9:2 reads εἰς ὄρος ὑψηλόν.

pose of Jesus's visit to the mountain in Luke 9:28, but also the statement that it was Jesus's custom to pray there (90.2) echoes Jesus's earlier prayer on the mountain in Luke 6:12 (and cf. 5:16).

The light the three disciples see in Jesus during this first transfiguration (T6) is an enlightening reconfiguration that is characteristic of this section and the whole work. Neither Luke nor Mark uses φῶς in the transfiguration,[66] but light-language is present in Luke through expressions like "dazzling" (ἐξαστράπτω; cf. Mark 9:3) clothing (9:29), and even "glory" (9:31, 32) has a sense of luminosity here. Acts of John takes this and reconfigures it through his Johannine-influenced lens so that φῶς is explicitly mentioned, and it is not coming from his clothing but is *in* Jesus. Thus the three disciples *see* (GJohn 1:14: "We have seen his glory") the very essence of Johannine Christology: the Light-*Logos* become flesh (GJohn 1:14). But already in the opening of AJohn 90–91 we see still another topos being incorporated, that of the inability of human language to adequately describe Jesus (a point he reiterates in AJohn 93). This topos is vividly employed in Gos. Thom. 13, but even just judging from the other apocryphal transfiguration accounts (e.g., Apoc. Pet. [Akhmim] 7, 9; Apoc. Pet. [Ethiopic] 15; Acts Pet. 20), it became a meaningful way to talk about—or rather not to talk about!—the mystery of Jesus and his identity.[67]

The way AJohn distributes transfiguration material across two separate events and three Testimonies make the comparison less "clean" after this point. For while the opening of AJohn narrative ends with the inability topos, the opening of the Lukan account continues to further describe the extraordinary occurrences at the transfiguration. Some of this material is picked up in the second "Transfiguration Testimony," other bits have echoes in the closing, and some is simply omitted. What is interesting is that AJohn builds these two "Transfiguration Testimonies" on the two instances of prayer language in Luke 9:28–29, which there refer to one and the same event.

The middle of AJohn 90 begins much like the opening of his own account and the Synoptic account: Jesus again takes[68] the same three disciples up to the mountain. This time, however, Jesus goes off to pray

66. Only Matt 17:2 uses φῶς, as a description of Jesus's transfiguration clothes.

67. Cf. Robbins, *Who Do People Say I Am*, 211–12.

68. The word used here, ἀνάγει, is not in NA^{28} in any of the Synoptic accounts, but it is more like the ἀναφέρει of Mark 9:2 and Matt 17:1. Further, ἀνάγει *is* used in the D text, and a few others, of Matthew and Mark.

by himself a short distance away[69] (90.6). Although Jesus's prayer is not mentioned again in this episode, it is clearly "while Jesus was praying" (Luke 9:29) that John glimpses naked divinity. Thus again the Lukan prayer topos is employed,[70] and as in Luke, it is when Jesus is praying that "things happen." For the remainder of the middle and the closing, AJohn 90–91 is less dependent on the Synoptic transfiguration narratives, especially in terms of the basic sequence of events. Nonetheless, reconfigurations and relocations do occur, while the middle especially draws on other resource texts.

Both accounts (AJohn and Luke) describe a rich set of visual phenomena, and verbs of seeing are present in both.[71] Nonetheless, while there are basic similarities (light-language noted above; Jesus's appearance changes), AJohn certainly does not simply repeat the Synoptic metamorphosis itself. In Luke, the appearance of Jesus's face changes, his clothing is dazzling (9:28), and more broadly he has a visible glory that the disciples can see (9:32). Acts of John heightens this light imagery while incorporating several other extraordinary visual phenomena, which combine to scintillating effect. As already noted concerning the opening, there AJohn tweaks the light-language by explicitly stating that there was φῶς in Jesus. Now it is specifically his whiter-than-snow feet that shine so much that they illuminate the ground (Dan 7:9 and Rev 1:15 may be resources for this). Recalling T4, Jesus's head "touched to heaven" (90.13). In direct contrast with all three Synoptic accounts, in which Jesus's *clothes* shine (Luke 9:29; Mark 9:3; Matt 17:2; cf. Dan 7:9), the Lord here in T7 is completely naked! He is not wearing any garments, and thus any light he emits is *from himself*. This deliberate and explicit change only serves to confirm the conclusions about the central significance of this image of "naked divinity" discussed above. A surprising resource AJohn draws on is Exod 33:18–23. Whereas

69. This particular language echoes Jesus's prayer in the garden in Luke 22:41 and parallels.

70. While I have noted above how prayer is a distinctively Lukan topos, I should point out that a few manuscripts have in Mark 9:2, "while they [or "he" in some] were praying." Similar statements that *they* (but not *he*) were praying also occur in the *Diatessaron* 24.3–4, Apoc. Pet. (Ethiopic) 15, 17; Apoc. Pet. (Akhmim) 6. However, there are no manuscripts of Mark that include prayer in the earlier statement concerning why they went to the mountain (Luke 9:28; AJohn 90.2). So it is still seems likely that Luke is a resource for the prayer topos in AJohn.

71. Forms of ὁράω appear in Luke 9:31–32, while AJohn is replete with ὁράω forms in the opening through middle, at which point it is not used again in 90–91.

both Luke and Matthew describe a change in Jesus's *face* (and Matt 17:2 even describes it as "shining"), John does not see Jesus's face but only his *back*. For anyone familiar with the story of Sinai told in Exodus, this immediately recalls Moses's only being allowed to view the LORD's back. The effect of this allusion is to heighten the sense that this is a *theophany*, an appearance of God. This stands in contrast to the Synoptic accounts,[72] where Jesus's appearance is most like an angel or the apocalyptic Son of Man coming in the clouds (the literal cloud, present in the Synoptics, is also missing here!).

I have already noted the presence of Johannine φῶς in the opening, and John's Gospel again is an important resource in the middle. First, in 90.7, John's rationale for approaching Jesus when he was praying by himself is that "he loved me" (ἐφίλει με). This of course calls to mind the Beloved Disciple of GJohn (e.g., 20:2), whom tradition would go on to identify as the author of the Gospel and the disciple John himself. Then when Jesus turns and rebukes John (90.16), he does so with a verbatim quotation from GJohn 20:27. There the words were Jesus's rebuke of "doubting Thomas." This application of Jesus's rebuke of Thomas is actually very fitting because Thomas's desire to verify the evidence of Jesus's resurrection by touching his body is very much like John's continual quest in the Testimonies to figure out Jesus's nature and identity, including an instance of touching Jesus's body (T5; T10).

In both the middle and the closing, a reconfiguration of the characters is evident. John is obviously the main character of AJohn, and even in the Testimonies, which are centered on Christology, everything is told from John's perspective. Yet we should not let this obscure a fundamental reconfiguration of the Synoptic transfiguration that especially becomes clear in the climactic central "Transfiguration Testimony" T7. In the vast majority of early Christian transfiguration narratives, Peter is clearly the most prominent of the disciples present. In fact, if we set aside AJohn, the transfiguration appears to be a distinctly Petrine topos.[73] In Luke, for example, Peter actually says more than anyone else in the story, including the voice from heaven! In AJohn, Peter is still present, but he is pushed to the periphery as John takes center stage. Table 4 above vividly illus-

72. Bovon makes it very clear that the he understands the Lukan transfiguration this way: "'the different appearance' does not express Jesus' divine nature" (*Luke 1*, 375).

73. Thus Simon Lee, *Jesus' Transfiguration*, focuses on the transfiguration narratives (canonical and noncanonical) that center on Peter.

trates this. In Luke, Peter's primary role is in the middle, which opens with the statement that he and his companions saw Jesus's glory because they stayed awake. While his speech there about building booths is nothing worthy of commendation, the Petrine transfiguration tradition seems to have capitalized on his primary role in that form of the story. In AJohn 90, the middle is composed of T7 which centers on John's private encounter with Jesus. John quickly becomes the main witness to Jesus's form due to his special relationship with Jesus (based on the Beloved Disciple topos from GJohn), and he alone sees what I have argued is the most revealing of Jesus's physical manifestations.[74] Peter (along with James) only seems to experience an aural effect of this event: he hears two voices speaking, but he does not understand that they are both the Lord. Thus Peter is displaced as the major character, while his unflatteringly ignorant speech in the Synoptic account is retained, being relocated and reconfigured as a failure to recognize the Lord.[75]

While AJohn does incorporate in modified and heightened form some of the visual phenomena from the Synoptic transfiguration, it so reconfigures (and in some cases simply omits) so much of the purpose-defining elements of the transfiguration that it completely transforms the whole episode. Gone are the prophets Moses and Elijah. And more importantly, gone is *the* central event of the Synoptic transfiguration: the voice from heaven. In Luke, as I showed above, the divine voice authenticates and

74. There is a problem in the text here: "*I* saw that he was not dressed in garments, but he was seen [ὁρῶμενον] *by us* as naked, and not at all like a man" (90.9–10). This comes after the notice that John sneaked up on Jesus, so we would expect "was seen by me." Considering Peter and James's question in 91, they do not seem to have seen what John saw. I do not think the text is conveying the idea that all three disciples saw what John sees in 90.9–10. There are three options here: (1) the author made a mistake: this should be a last resort; (2) a copyist made a mistake: this is not implausible since there are no other manuscripts to compare, so it is not out of line to suggest an emendation, such as ΥΠΟΜΟΥ (ὑπό μου) for ΥΦΗΜΩΝ (ὑφ' ἡμῶν); (3) accept the text as is. I have already noted why it does not seem correct to understand "we" here as the same "we" in 90.5, i.e., John, James, and Peter. I suspect that the "we" here can be explained by analogy to the communal "we" in GJohn 1:14, 16; and 1 John 1:1–4 (cf. Smith, *John*, 58). When AJohn 90 relates a shocking experience of *seeing* Jesus in his true nature, it is almost as if John cannot help but slip into the paradigmatic discourse of GJohn 1:14: "The Word became flesh and lived among *us*, and *we* have seen his glory."

75. Perhaps GJohn 21:4–7 is a resource, where John rather than Peter recognizes Jesus on the shore.

reaffirms Jesus as the chosen Messiah and Son of God, while the visual phenomena provide a glimpse of his future glory. Bits and pieces of these elements are reconfigured. For example, in AJohn 91 Peter and James perceive two people on the mountain (presumably not including John), which is the faintest echo of the two men who appear in Luke 9:30. Furthermore, these same two disciples do hear talking, although they give no report of what was said nor call attention to the *voice* itself.

Overall, however, two of the three main elements of the transfiguration (Jesus's metamorphosis, the appearance of Moses and Elijah, and the voice from heaven) have all but disappeared, and the one that remains, the change in Jesus's appearance, has been completely reworked. Yet such significant reconfiguration is not surprising. The two elements that have nearly disappeared are closely tied to a prophetic/apocalyptic Jesus who is totally foreign to the precreation discourse of AJohn,[76] in which Jesus is not God's anointed one nor the coming Son of Man, but rather an unchangeable *Logos* who took on human form and flesh temporarily, and who is really to be identified with God. This Jesus needs no divine authorization or fatherly commendation because he is God and even "the Father" (AJohn 98).

5. Conclusions

In this comparison of transfiguration stories in AJohn and Luke, we have seen how both engage in reconfigurations of existing sources and resources. While they share a core of similar elements that identify both as "transfiguration stories," each one uses the transfiguration to develop their own distinctive presentation of the identity and nature of Jesus. This was evident first by reading these transfigurations within their own literary contexts and then by reading them in conversation with one another. This led to the conclusion that these stories are superficially similar, but really make different claims about Jesus. When Luke reconfigured the Markan transfiguration, he retained the Markan Son of Man who will come again

76. For a preliminary presentation of precreation discourse within the framework of emerging Christian rhetorolects, see Robbins, "Conceptual Blending," esp. 165, 176–84; and see also Robbins, "Precreation Discourse and the Nicene Creed: Christianity Finds Its Voice in the Roman Empire," *R&T* 18 (2012): 1–17. A fuller presentation by Robbins of precreation rhetorolect will be provided in the forthcoming second volume of *The Invention of Christian Discourse*.

in glory, while tweaking the story to show Jesus also as the chosen Messiah, the Son of God. The reconfiguration in AJohn's Testimonies is much more pronounced. Partaking in a very different mode of discourse, AJohn removes the prophetic/apocalyptic Son of Man and the authorizing attendants, and portrays the Lord in his true, precreation essence: not a human at all! Acts of John gives not a foretaste of the future but a glimpse of the timeless reality of the divine Light/*Logos*.

In a very real way, we have thus seen how AJohn blends Johannine and Synoptic discourse and Christology. In GJohn, Jesus is already/always "transfigured" and overall has a constant, unchanging identity. This stands in contrast to the Lukan Jesus, whose transfiguration there provides a glimpse of his postsuffering and parousia glory. When AJohn pulls the transfiguration into its own configuration of Johannine, precreation discourse, transfigurations—glimpses of Jesus's glory—become a constant feature throughout Jesus's life. But AJohn pushes beyond even Johannine discourse and lives in the world of writings like the Gospel of Thomas, in which the identity of Jesus cannot adequately be expressed with words. This aspect of AJohn is evident in the way Jesus's human flesh is revealed in the climactic transfiguration of T7 (AJohn 90) to be a garment, something that must be removed to see his real identity. In AJohn, Jesus is divine and not truly human, a *Logos* only temporarily and partially concealed in human flesh.

Christ as Cosmic Priest: A Sociorhetorical Examination of the Crucifixion Scenes in the Gospel of John and Acts of John

Thomas Jared Farmer

1. Introduction

In *De fuga et inventione*, Philo of Alexandria suggests that the high priest is a manifestation of the *logos*, the agent of divine wisdom through which God created and sustains the world (*Fug.* 108–112). In the Gospel of John (GJohn) and the Acts of John (AJohn), Christ has taken over the roles of redeemer and cosmic priest. The crucifixion scenes in the GJohn and the AJohn each present Christ as a divine mediator, who through his sacrifice on the cross helps to restore a fractured cosmos and bridge the chasm between God and humanity. In both cases, their respective authors blended language drawn from the Jewish wisdom tradition with contemporary philosophical discourse. This conceptual blending all takes place within a frame of reference that understands Christ's death in relation to the sacrificial system of the Hebrew Bible. The integration of these elements within a discourse determined by the cultural memory of a community steeped in Jewish ceremony gave rise to what Vernon K. Robbins refers to as a "priestly rhetorolect."[1] The presence of this priestly frame of

1. There are six such "rhetorolects" utilized in sociorhetorical criticism, in order to evaluate patterns of discourse. See Vernon K. Robbins, "Conceptual Blending and Early Christian Imagination," in *Explaining Christian Origins and Early Judaism: Contributions from Cognitive and Social Science*, ed. Petri Luomanen, Ilkka Pyysiäinen, and Risto Uro, BIS 89 (Leiden: Brill, 2007), 161–95; and Robbins, *The Invention of Christian Discourse*, vol. 1, RRA 1 (Blandford Forum, UK: Deo, 2009).

reference "introduces a conceptual hierarchy, with God at the top, humans at the bottom, and the priest and the material substance of the cosmos in a position of mediation between God and humans."[2]

The purpose of this essay is to provide a comparative exegesis of the crucifixion scenes in GJohn 19 and AJohn 98–101. As these two works narrate different events transpiring at two respective locations at the time of the crucifixion, however, there is minimal overlap in their actual sequential narratives. As a result, comparison will largely consist of evaluation of overlapping themes and topoi shared by the two works. In particular, I will focus on the degree to which each account depicts Jesus performing the role of cosmic priest. To demonstrate the narrative context of the crucifixion scenes in GJohn and AJohn, I will begin the discussion of each work with a brief outline and an overview of the composition as a whole.

2. The Crucifixion in the Gospel of John

2.1. Outline of the Gospel of John[3]

I. The Prologue (1:1–18)

II. The Book of Signs (1:19–12:50)
- a. The Beginning of Jesus's Ministry (1:19–51)
  - i. The First Testimony of John the Baptist (1:19–28)
  - ii. The Spirit Descends on Jesus (1:29–34)
  - iii. The First Disciples (1:35–51)
- b. The Cana *Inclusio* (2:1–4:54)
- c. The Feasts (5:1–10:42)
  - i. The Sabbath (5:1–47)
  - ii. The Passover (6:1–71)
  - iii. Sukkot (Tabernacles/Booths) (7:1–10:21)
  - iv. Hanukkah (Lights/Dedication) (10:22–42)
- d. The "Hour" (11:1–12:50)
  - i. The Raising of Lazarus (11:1–54)

2. Robbins, "Conceptual Blending," 181.

3. The contours of this outline roughly match the outline of GJohn given by Francis J. Moloney, *The Gospel of John*, SP 4 (Collegeville, MN: Liturgical Press, 1998), 23–24.

    ii. The Hour Has Come (11:55–12:36)
    iii. Close of Jesus's Ministry (12:37–50)

III. The Book of Glory (13:1–20:31)
  a. The Farewell Discourse (13:1–17:26)
  b. The Passion (18:1–19:42)
    i. The Garden (18:1–11)
    ii. Jesus's Appearance before "the Jews" (18:12–27)
    iii. Jesus before Pilate (18:28–19:16a)
    iv. The Crucifixion (19:16b–37)
    v. Jesus's Burial (19:38–42)
  c. The Resurrection (20:1–29)
    i. Events at the Tomb (20:1–18)
    ii. Events in the House (20:19–29)
  d. The Conclusion to the Gospel (20:30–31)

IV. The Epilogue
  a. Jesus at the Sea of Tiberias (21:1–14)
  b. The Restoration of Peter and the Death of the Beloved Disciple (21:15–24)
  c. The Second Conclusion to the Gospel (21:25)

2.2. Overview of the Gospel of John

There is a transparency in the relationship between the author of GJohn and its audience that is more readily apparent than in the case of the Synoptics.[4] John clearly knows his readers (GJohn 20:30–31) and assumes their prior knowledge of the events recounted in his narrative, as well as the symbols employed to interpret them (e.g., GJohn 1:1, 14; 6:32–59; 14:6). In addition, this high degree of symbolic language—matched with the general sectarian nature of much of the Gospel (e.g., GJohn 10:8; 14:6; 15:18–27; 16:2–4, 8, 20, 33; 17:13–19; cf. also 1 John 2:19)—makes it unlikely that the work was composed for evangelistic purposes (see GJohn 16:1).[5] Rather, the work appears to have been written to a community that

4. Biblical quotations are generally based on the NRSV, with occasional modifications for the sake of comparison.

5. Thus, making the present tense πιστεύητε a more likely reading of 20:31 than the aorist πιστεύσητε.

thought of itself as a loving and faithful remnant (GJohn 13:34–35) surrounded by hostile adversaries (GJohn 15:18; 16:33; cf. AJohn 100).[6]

Irony is a characteristic literary technique employed by the author of GJohn. As Luke Timothy Johnson recounts the story, "Characters are given lines that state the truth far beyond their own intentions … and the readers always know more than the characters in the narrative and can appreciate their words and actions at quite another level."[7] Thus the two tiers of knowledge created between the narrator/reader and the characters within the narrative itself serve to create an "insider" awareness concerning the relevance of the dense symbolic language expressed throughout GJohn (see, e.g., GJohn 3:2–21; 4:10–14; 8:28; 12:32–34).[8]

The overall structure of the book consists of four major sections. The Prologue (1:1–18) introduces the main themes and topoi explicated within the body of the narrative. The Book of Signs (1:19–12:50) details Jesus's public ministry. The Book of Glory (13:1–20:31) details Jesus's passion, death, and resurrection. The Epilogue (21:1–25) provides an explanation of the death of the Beloved Disciple, narrates the restoration of Peter, and provides a second conclusion to the Gospel.

2.3. Opening-Middle-Closing Analysis of the Crucifixion in the Gospel of John

Sociorhetorical interpretation treats texts as layered compositions whose multiple "textures" can only be drawn out by employing a variety of evaluative tools and methods. One means of evaluating the narrative structure of a given pericope is to divide (and subdivide) its sections in opening-

---

6. The distinctiveness of the use of language in GJohn has led many to see within it a kind of cryptolect or "antilanguage" that uses emic discourse (or insider-speak) to reinforce community identity and/or exclude outsiders. See Wayne Meeks, "The Man from Heaven in Johannine Sectarianism," *JBL* 91 (1972): 44–72; Bruce J. Malina, "John's: The Maverick Christian Group, The Evidence of Sociolingusitics," *BTB* 24 (1994): 167–82; and Bruce J. Malina and Richard Rohrbaugh, *Social-Science Commentary on the Gospel of John* (Minneapolis: Fortress, 1998).

7. Luke Timothy Johnson, *The Writings of the New Testament*, 3rd ed. (Minneapolis: Fortress, 2010), 472.

8. There are two tiers of awareness in AJohn as well between John and the great multitudes around the cross, who are outside of the mystery. However, this depiction lacks the Johannine sense of irony and never gives a voice in 98–101 to characters outside the mystery.

middle-closing (OMC) segments. This method of textual examination aids in determining both the logical flow of the narrative and in highlighting specific features and patterns of argumentation presented within the specific text.[9] The outline below represents the opening-middle-closing texture of the main sections and subsections of GJohn's crucifixion narrative. This is followed by analysis and interpretation of each of these opening, middle, and closing units.

Opening-Middle-Closing of the Crucifixion Scene in the Gospel of John[10]

Opening (19:16–37)
- O: The crucifixion of Jesus (19:16–18)
- M: Pilate's inscription (19:19–22)
- C: The division of Jesus's clothing (19:23–24)

Middle (19:25–30)
- O: Mary entrusted to the care of the beloved disciple (19:25–27)
- M: Jesus's thirst (19:28–29)
- C: Jesus's final words and death (19:30)

Closing (19:31–37)
- O: Judeans request that bodies be removed; Jesus's legs not broken (19:31–33)
- M: Blood and water flow from Jesus's pierced side (19:34–35)
- C: These things fulfilled Scripture (19:36–37)

Opening (19:16–37). In choosing the parameters for the opening of GJohn's crucifixion scene, the episodic nature of the narrative is brought to the foreground. As can be observed in the outline above, this first segment of John's crucifixion scene is easily divisible into three discrete parts: the

9. For a detailed description of textual (and textural) analysis in sociorhetorical criticism, see Vernon K. Robbins, *Exploring the Texture of Texts: A Guide to Socio-Rhetorical Interpretation* (Valley Forge, PA: Trinity Press International, 1996); and Robbins, *The Tapestry of Early Christian Discourse: Rhetoric, Society and Ideology* (London: Routledge, 1996). For opening-middle-closing texture specifically, see Robbins, *Exploring the Texture*, 19–21.

10. The letters *O*, *M*, and *C* in this chart designate the opening, middle, and closing subsections of the larger units of the text.

crucifixion of Jesus, Pilate's inscription, and the division of Jesus's clothing. These three scenes are separated from the middle by the transition words μὲν οὖν, "so much for," which sum up the section before the introduction of a new series of scenes at the beginning of the middle segment.

Some of the salient features of John's interpretation of the crucifixion can be observed through comparison with the scene's portrayal in the Synoptics. For example, the Synoptics have Simon of Cyrene carry the cross for Jesus (Mark 15:21; Matt 27:32; Luke 23:26). The Gospel of John, however, insists on making Jesus the master of his own fate even while bearing his own cross (καὶ βαστάζων ἑαυτῷ τὸν σταυρόν; cf. Gen 22:6). Alongside GJohn 19:18, the Synoptics record that the two men crucified with Jesus were thieves or bandits (cf. Isa 53:12), an element lacking in the Johannine account.[11] Likewise, John's Gospel is the only canonical gospel in which the other men crucified do not revile Jesus on the cross. In this and other senses, the Johannine crucifixion presents a more "dignified" death than in the Synoptics (though this is a point that should not be stressed too far, such that it obscures the implicit suffering in the scene). It is, therefore, possible that the brief description of the crucifixion (ὅπου αὐτὸν ἐσταύρωσαν) given in GJohn is an intentional move to shift attention away from the actual bloody execution of Jesus.[12] Indeed, Raymond Brown has noted that "all the Gospels are content with this laconic description without entering into gruesome details."[13]

The prominence of Christ's position in the center of the two crucified men (μέσον δὲ τὸν Ἰησοῦν) has been taken as an (ironic) fulfillment of Jesus's words in GJohn 12:32, that already on the cross Jesus was drawing people to himself.[14] Brown speculates that the gospels may be recalling Ps 22:17(16): "a company of evildoers encircle me."[15] As has already been noted, however, the two men are never specifically referred to as criminals in John's Gospel. In GJohn 19:19–22, Jesus is specifically executed as a

11. In AJohn the other two men are not mentioned. If you were to read AJohn by itself you would no doubt get the impression that Christ was crucified alone.

12. See Moloney, *Gospel of John*, 502.

13. Raymond E. Brown, *The Gospel according to John*, 2 vols., AB 29–29A (Garden City, NY: Doubleday, 1966–1970), 2:900.

14. See Thomas L. Brodie, *The Gospel according to John: A Literary and Theological Commentary* (New York: Oxford University Press, 1993), 545; see also Moloney, *Gospel of John*, 507.

15. Brown, *Gospel according to John*, 2:900.

(pretender) king. The irony of interplay between two kingdoms ties into regal imagery and the topos of kingship mentioned elsewhere in John's Gospel (e.g., 1:49; 3:5; 6:15; 7:42; 12:12–19; 18:33–39).

Concerning GJohn 19:23–24, Francis Moloney speaks metaphorically of the division of Jesus's outer garments and the preservation of his inner garment, saying, "There must be more to the focus on the fact that the inner garment of Jesus is not to be torn asunder. Is there something precious that belongs to Jesus whose unity must be maintained?" The focus on Jesus's tunic may point to a possible link with priestly garments, which would highlight Jesus's role as mediator.[16] If so this would place into even starker relief the imagery of sacrifice already implicit in the crucifixion scene.[17] In performing this restorative act with his sacrifice on the cross Jesus has reached the hour to which the whole narrative of John has been building (cf. 12:23; 13:1; 17:1).

Middle (19:25–30). The conceptual distance between 19:25a and 19:25b–30.[18] can be seen in the NRSV's inclusion of the transitional word "Meanwhile" in order to mark the space between the conclusion of one scene (indicated by the use of μὲν οὖν) and the beginning of a new scene (indicated by the use of δέ). The parameters of the middle reflect two discrete scenes: the trusting of the care of Mary to the Beloved Disciple, and the death of Jesus, which I have subdivided between the description of Jesus's thirst and his final words/death. This subdivision of the closing of the middle segment is marked in 19:30 by the transitional phrase ὅτε οὖν, "When therefore…."

The Gospel of John 19:25–27 witnesses a symbolic merging of the physical and spiritual families of Jesus.[19] In GJohn 19:28–29, Jesus drinks

16. For a defense of the identification of Jesus's tunic with the robes of the high priesthood, see John Paul Heil, "Jesus as the Unique High Priest in the Gospel of John," *CBQ* 57 (1995): 728–45. Though the strength of this particular point is a matter of debate, the argument has been made by Heil and others that a holistic reading of John's Gospel reveals an implicit understanding (and ironic depiction) of Jesus as high priest.

17. Cf. Exod 29:5; Rev 1:13; Philo, *Fug.* 110–112. See also Moloney, *Gospel of John*, 507; Brown, *Gospel according to John*, 2:908, 920–21; D. Moody Smith, *John*, ANTC (Nashville: Abingdon, 1999), 358.

18. Note that NA[28] (and some other editions and translations) ends v. 25 after ταῦτα ἐποίησαν and begins v. 26 with εἱστήκεισαν δέ (i.e., it begins v. 26 with what is 25b in the NRSV).

19. See Smith, *John*, 360; Brown, *Gospel according to John*, 2:1019–1026; Sjef van Tilborg, *Imaginative Love in John*, BIS 2 (Leiden: Brill, 1993).

the cup the Father had given him (cf. 18:11), and fulfills his role as obedient Son (e.g., 4:34; 5:19, 30, 36; 6:38; 7:18; 8:28–29, 55; 10:17–18, 37; 12:49–50). The presence of hyssop is another means of tying Jesus's death to the institution of the Passover (GJohn 12:1; 13:1; 18:28, 39; 19:14), his priestly role, and the significance that Jewish festivals no doubt carried for GJohn's audience (see Exod 12:22; Heb 9:18–20).[20] The Johannine sense of irony can again be seen here as Jesus, the source of living water (cf. GJohn 7:38), cries out in thirst.[21]

In GJohn 19:30, Jesus's final words on the cross denote fulfillment or completion. They pronounce the triumphant achievement of the task appointed to him by the Father (cf. 4:34; 5:36; 17:4).[22] In spite of the fact that Jesus's death in GJohn appears on the surface to be more triumphant, too sharp of a distinction should not be made between the death of Jesus here and in the Synoptics. For example, Alfred Loisy maintained that "the death of the Johannine Christ is not a scene of suffering, of ignominy, of universal desolation [as in the Synoptics]—it is the beginning of a great triumph."[23] This contrast, however, does not do justice to the implicit note of agony in the Johannine Jesus and in many respects exaggerates the element of defeat in the Synoptic scene. We may likewise reject the reading that suggests the moment of glorification was Jesus's handing over of his spirit while on the cross to the symbolic representatives of the church: Mary and the Beloved Disciple. For as Brown has noted, "If such an interpretation of 'he handed over the spirit' has any plausibility, we would stress that this symbolic reference is evocative and *proleptic*, reminding the reader of the *ultimate* purpose for which Jesus had been lifted up on the cross. In Johannine thought the actual giving of the Spirit does not come now but in xx 22 after the resurrection."[24]

The NRSV's translation of παρέδωκεν as "gave up" is misleading and is ultimately out of step with the thrust of the passage. It should instead

---

20. References to Jewish feasts/festivals in GJohn include Passover (2:13, 23; 4:45; 6:4; 11:55; 12:1; 13:1; 18:28; 18:39; 19:14), Booths (7:2), Hanukkah (10:22), and Sabbath (5:9).

21. Brown, *Gospel according to John*, 2:930.

22. Moloney, *Gospel of John*, 504.

23. Alfred Loisy, *Le quatrième évangile: les épîtres dites de Jean* (Paris: Nourry, 1921), 490. Quoted (and translated) by Brown, *Gospel according to John*, 2:930.

24. Brown, *Gospel according to John*, 2:930–31.

be rendered as "handed over" or "entrusted."[25] This fits well with GJohn's concern to portray Jesus as fully in control during the passion narrative.[26] The Gospel of John omits accompanying details from the account of Jesus's death: Jesus's outcries; darkness at noon (cf. Mark 15:33); the rending of the temple veil (cf. Mark15:38); the centurion's confession (cf. Mark 15:39; Luke 23:47). If John had been familiar with these elements within the passion narrative (apart from Jesus's painful outcries), it seems unlikely that he would have simply refrained from using them.

Closing (19:31–37). The parameters of the closing of the Johannine crucifixion narrative are perhaps the most difficult in this sequence to establish, because the end of each discrete section serves as an introduction to the next. The opening segment presents the concerns of the "Jews/Judeans" over the violation of ritual purity associated with allowing the condemned to remain on the cross into the Sabbath. This introduces the necessity that the legs of the condemned be broken in order to hasten death. This provides the transition to the middle segment, since Jesus was already dead and therefore it was not necessary for his legs to be broken. Instead, the middle segment describes how Jesus's side was pierced leading to an effusion of blood and water. This prompts an acknowledgment of the truth of this testimony, which serves as a transition to the closing segment. The closing segment quotes Scripture (providing a second testimony), which interprets the events of the opening and middle segments of the closing texture.

Concerning GJohn 19:34, John Chrysostom maintained that the blood and water represented the sacraments of baptism and Eucharist (cf. 7:37–39), which flowed from the side of Christ through his act of sacrifice.[27] It is through these sacraments that the continued presence of the absent Christ is renewed in the faithful community. While the imagery of blood and water flowing from Christ may not have been a consciously intended antidocetic element within the Gospel, the testimony that Jesus "really" had a body that died, was pierced, and emitted bodily fluids does serve as a corrective to those who would deny Christ's humanity. Brown notes that "in Johannine thought the drama of the cross does not end in

---

25. BDAG, 761–62; see also Moloney, *Gospel of John*, 508–9; Smith, *John*, 361–62; Brown, *Gospel according to John*, 2:910.

26. See Smith, *John*, 361.

27. John Chrysostom, *Homiliae in Joannem* 85.3 (*NPNF1* 14:317; PG 59:463).

the death but in a flow of life that comes from death: the death of Jesus is the beginning of Christian life."[28]

3. The Crucifixion in the Acts of John

3.1. Outline of the Acts of John[29]

I. From Miletus to Ephesus (18)

II. John's First Stay in Ephesus (19–36)
   a. John raises Lycomedes and Cleopatra from the dead (19–25)
   b. Lycomedes's friend paints a portrait of John (26–29)
   c. John preaches in a theater prior to the healing of a sick woman [absent from the text] (30–36)
   d. ****possibly narration of the healing of the woman*[30]
   e. ****possibly narration of the conversion of Andronicus*
      — *likely includes a narration of the raising of Andronicus and Drusiana (leading to the sermon given in 87–105)*

III. The Mysteries of the Polymorphic Christ (87–105)
   a. Drusiana recounts how the Lord appeared to her in a tomb in the form of a youth (87)
   b. John's testimonies (88–105)
      i. Episode 1 (88)—call narrative [Jesus revealed as both child and a man of cheerful countenance]
      ii. Episode 2 (89)
         1. Jesus revealed to John as bald-headed man with thick flowing beard; revealed to James as youth with new beard
         2. John never saw Jesus's eyes shut
         3. Revealed as both small unattractive man and as one reaching up to heaven

---

28. Brown, *Gospel according to John*, 2:913.

29. This outline is largely based on that of J. K. Elliott, *The Apocryphal New Testament: A Collection of Apocryphal Christian Literature in an English Translation* (Oxford: Clarendon, 2005), 310–11, but with increased detail added for the section of my focus, "III. Mysteries of the Polymorphic Christ (87–105)."

30. *** indicates gaps in the text or unoriginal material.

        4. Jesus's flesh revealed as both smooth/tender and hard as stone
    iii. Episode 3 (90–91)
        1. Jesus takes John, Peter, and James to a mountain and is revealed as light
        2. Jesus was dressed in garments but appeared naked with feet as white as snow
        3. Pulls John's beard in rebuke of his unbelief
        4. Peter and James's anger at John
    iv. Episode 4 (93)
        1. Jesus's body revealed as both material and immaterial
        2. The miraculous loaf of bread
        3. Jesus leaves no footprints
    v. Episode 5 (94–96)—the Hymn-Dance
    vi. Episode 6 (97–102)
        1. The Crucifixion
            a. John escapes to a cave at the Mount of Olives, where Jesus appears to him, lighting up the cave (97)
            b. The cross of light (98)
            c. The meaning of the cross (99)
            d. The multitude and Christ's oneness with the Father (100)
            e. The suffering [?] of the Logos (101)
            f. Jesus taken up (102)
        2. John's exhortation (103–105)
c. ****Stories taken from Pseudo-Abdias*
    i. *The broken gems*
    ii. *Rods and stones turned to gold and jewels*
d. ****Lazarus and Dives retold and explained*
e. ****Raising of Stacteus*
f. ****Aristodemus and the poisoned cup*
g. ****(stories in P.Oxy. 850)*
    i. *Zeuxis*
    ii. *John and the soldier*

IV. Conclusion of John's First Stay in Ephesus (37–55)
a. Destruction of the Temple of Artemis and the conversion of her followers (37–45)
b. Raising of the priest of Artemis (46–47)

  c. Story of the Parricide and the call to Smyrna (48–54)
  d. ***(56–57)
    i. *Including the stories of the healing of the sons of Antipatros, and the partridge*
    ii. *Probably stories concerning the characters referred to in 59 would have occurred in this gap*

V. Return to Ephesus (58–59) and the Obedient Bedbugs (60–61)

VI. John's Second Stay in Ephesus (62–86; 106–115)
  — Final reunion with the brethren; John's last act of worship; prayers and Eucharist; John's death (106–115)[31]

3.2. Overview of the Acts of John

The Acts of John is a collection of traditions surrounding the figure of the apostle John (identified with the Beloved Disciple of GJohn). The work itself contains numerous (and sometimes unrelated) stories including John's preaching; his insights into mysteries; miracle stories (including resurrections from the dead); a disturbing story in which John destroys the temple of the goddess Artemis; an amusing tale in which John successfully commands bedbugs to cease disturbing his sleep; and so on. Largely as a result of its content, it is difficult to determine the date and provenance of the composition. The material it preserves appears to come from several different sources—including folklore and pagan material—and has subsequently undergone numerous internal changes and redactions over the course of its history.

The original AJohn was most likely a late second-century production and may have originated in Egypt.[32] The earliest definite reference to the work is in Eusebius (*Hist. eccl.* 3.25.6), where it is listed among impious or heretical works (including other apocryphal Acts). Other attestations of the work can be found in Augustine (*Ep.* 237 to Ceretius), who recounts some ten lines of the Hymn of Christ; Innocent I (*Ep.* 6.7, PL 20:502); Turribius of Astorga (*Ep. ad Idacium et Ceponium* 5 [PL 54:693–95); and

31. Brown has noted the similarity between the death of Jesus in GJohn and the account of the death of John in AJohn (Brown, *Gospel according to John*, 2:910).

32. The introductory information provided here is primarily based on Elliott's introduction in *Apocryphal New Testament*, 303–11.

the *Virtutes Johannis* (in Pseudo-Abdias).[33] Though initially condemned as heretical and considered to be gnostic by nineteenth-century commentators, the orthodoxy of AJohn has more recently been a matter of dispute. Recent commentators such as Eric Junod and Jean-Daniel Kaestli have noted that there are differing Christologies in AJohn 87–93 and 94–102, 109, with the latter possibly representing interpolations from a Valentinian gnostic source sometime in the third century.[34] This being the case, there are significant portions of AJohn that are not themselves heterodox.

A complete text of the original AJohn has not survived. The text as we have it today exists only in fragmentary form and is the result of scholarly collations of Greek manuscripts dating from the tenth to the fifteenth centuries.[35] An ancient stichometry attributed to Nikephorus, the ninth-century patriarch of Constantinople, lists the length of the original AJohn as containing 2,500 stichoi. If this estimate is correct, this would make the original comparable in size to the Gospel of Matthew. The material comprising AJohn that we currently have consists of approximately 1,700 stichoi, meaning that roughly one-third of the original has been lost.[36] Ultimately, the shape of the original AJohn is impossible to determine, as there appears to have been numerous stories about John circulating in the early church that were eventually attached to AJohn in a rather indiscriminate manner. It is therefore difficult to separate original material from later interpolations in the text. Additionally, the presence of lacunae throughout the available manuscripts means that the overall structure, theology, and purpose of AJohn remain elusive. The proposed structure of the reconstructed text largely follows a series of sojourns of the apostle John to and from Ephesus: Miletus to Ephesus (18); John's First Stay in Ephesus (19–36); The Mysteries of Christ (87–105); Conclusion of John's First Stay in Ephesus (37–55); Return to Ephesus (58–59); and John's Second Stay in Ephesus (62–86; 106–115).

---

33. Additionally, Ceretius reports that the hymn circulated as an independent document among the Priscillianists (Augustine, *Ep.* 237 to Ceretius). This and the other attestations are given by Elliott, *Apocryphal New Testament*, 303.

34. See Eric Junod and Jean-Daniel Kaestli, *Acta Iohannis*, 2 vols., CCSA 1 (Turnhout: Brepols, 1983), 2:692–93.

35. Paul G. Schneider, "The Mystery of the Acts of John: An Interpretation of the Hymn and the Dance in Light of the Acts' Theology" (PhD diss., Columbia University, 1990), 8.

36. See Pieter J. Lalleman, *The Acts of John: A Two-Stage Initiation into Johannine Gnosticism*, SAAA 4 (Leuven: Peeters, 1998), 14–15.

3.3. Opening-Middle-Closing Analysis of The Crucifixion in the Acts of John

The context for the "crucifixion" discourse in AJohn can be found in chapter 97, which recounts how after the disciples have been initiated into the deeper mysteries through participation in the Lord's Hymn-Dance (94–96). John then flees the scene of Christ's passion[37] and goes to the Mount of Olives (97).[38] While John is hiding in a cave during Jesus's crucifixion, darkness comes over the whole earth at the sixth hour (cf. Matt 27:45; Mark 15:33; Luke 23:44). The Lord appears in the middle of the cave in a form that illuminates it (cf. PJ 19.2).[39] The Lord's voice reveals to John that he has compelled him to come to the mountain, so that he may "hear matters needful for a disciple to learn from his teacher and for a man to learn from his God" (AJohn 97; cf. Matt 17:1–11; Mark 2:12; Luke 9:28–36).

The Crucifixion in Acts of John: Opening (ch. 98)[40]

O:

> [98] Καὶ εἰπὼν ταῦτα ἔδειξέν μοι **σταυρὸν φωτὸς** πεπηγμένον καὶ περὶ τὸν **σταυρὸν** ὄχλον πολύν, μίαν **μορφὴν** μὴ ἔχοντα. Καὶ ἐν αὐτῷ ἦν **μορφὴ** μία καὶ ἰδέα ὁμοία. αὐτὸν δὲ τὸν κύριον ἐπάνω τοῦ **σταυροῦ** ἑώρων σχῆμα μὴ ἔχοντα ἀλλά τινα **φωνὴν** μόνον, **φωνὴν** δὲ οὐ ταύτην τὴν ἡμῖν συνήθη, ἀλλά τινα ἡδεῖαν καὶ χρηστὴν καὶ ἀληθῶς θεοῦ,

M:

> (a) λέγουσαν πρός με· Ἰωάννη, ἕνα δεῖ παρ᾽ ἐμοῦ ταῦτα **ἀκοῦσαι**· ἑνὸς γὰρ χρῄζω τοῦ μέλλοντος **ἀκούειν**.

---

37. This is an interesting choice given that GJohn places John (alone among the Twelve) at the foot of the cross.

38. The Mount of Olives is an appropriate place from John to "learn from his teacher/God" (cf. Matt 24; Mark 13; Luke 21).

39. This reference follows the chapter/verse divisions presented in Bart D. Ehrman and Zlatko Pleše, *The Apocryphal Gospels: Texts and Translations* (New York: Oxford University Press, 2011), hereafter abbreviated E-P.

40. The translation used is that of Elliott, *Apocryphal New Testament*, while the Greek is based on the critical edition of Junod and Kaestli, *Acta Iohannis*. Since the Greek text or translation may not be readily available to some readers, it seemed best to include it in full here.

(b) ὁ **σταυρὸς** οὗτος ὁ τοῦ **φωτὸς** ποτὲ μὲν **λόγος** καλεῖται ὑπ' ἐμοῦ δι' ὑμᾶς, ποτὲ δὲ **νοῦς**, ποτὲ δὲ **Ἰησοῦς**, ποτὲ **Χριστός**, ποτὲ **θύρα**, ποτὲ **ὁδός**, ποτὲ **ἄρτος**, ποτὲ **σπόρος**, ποτὲ **ἀνάστασις**, ποτὲ **υἱός**, ποτὲ **πατήρ**, ποτὲ **πνεῦμα**, ποτὲ **ζωή**, ποτὲ **ἀλήθεια**, ποτὲ **πίστις**, ποτὲ **χάρις**. Ταῦτα μὲν ὡς πρὸς ἀνθρώπους·
(c) ὃ δὲ ὄντως ἐστίν, αὐτὸς πρὸς αὐτὸν νοούμενος καὶ εἰς ἡμᾶς λεγόμενος, διορισμὸς πάντων ἐστίν· καὶ τὸν πεπηγμένον ἐξ ἀνεδράστων ἀνάγγη βιάβα καὶ ἐστίν· καὶ τὸν πεπηγμένον ἐξ ἀνεδράστων ἀνάγγη βιάβα καὶ **ἁρμονία σοφίας**· **σοφία** δὲ οὖσα ἐν **ἁρμονίᾳ**

C:

ὑπάρχουσιν **δεξιοὶ** καὶ **ἀριστεροί**, **δυνάμεις**, **ἐξουσίαι**, **ἀρχαὶ** καὶ **δαίμονες**, **ἐνέργειαι**, **ἀπειλαί**, **θυμοί**, **διάβολοι**, **Σατανᾶς** καὶ ἡ **κατωτικὴ ῥίζα**, **ἄφες τῶν γινομένων προῆλθεν φύσις**.

O:

[98] And having said this, he showed me a **cross** of **light** set up, and around the **cross** a great multitude which had no one **form**; and in the **cross** was one **form** and one likeness. And the Lord himself I saw above the **cross**, not having a shape, but only a **voice**, and a **voice** not such as was familiar to us, but a sweet and kind **voice** and one truly divine,

M:

(a) and it said to me: John, it is necessary that one man should **hear** these things from me, for I have need of someone who will **hear**.
(b) This **cross** of **light** is sometimes called **Word** by me for your sakes, sometimes **Mind**, sometimes **Jesus**, sometimes **Christ**, sometimes **Door**, sometimes **Way**, sometimes **Bread**, sometimes **Seed**, sometimes **Resurrection**, sometimes **Son**, sometimes **Father**, sometimes **Spirit**, sometimes **Life**, sometimes **Truth**, sometimes **Faith**, sometimes **Grace**. Thus it is called for the sake of humans.
(c) But in truth, as known in itself and as spoken to us, it is the marking off of all things and the uplifting and foundation of those things that are fixed but had been unstable, and the

> **harmony** of the **wisdom** and indeed the **wisdom** of the **harmony.**

C:

> But there are on the **right** and on the **left, powers, authorities, lordships** and **demons, operations, threatenings, wrath, devils, Satan,** and the **inferior root,** from which the **nature of the transient things proceed.**

Determining the parameters of the opening of AJohn (98) is more difficult than with GJohn, because much of the section under evaluation (98–102) represents direct speech, rather than a third person account of discrete episodes. I have chosen to mark the close of the description of the forms "from which transient things proceed" as the transition point to the middle (99–100), as the next paragraph serves as both a summation of the opening and a natural transition to a new series of descriptions. The opening can be subdivided between (O) the introduction of the cross of light; (M) (a) the necessity of the revelation, (b) the forms of representation; (C) and a description of contrary forms leading to transient things.

In AJohn 98, the "cross of light" (σταυρὸς φωτός) becomes the central organizing element in this portion of AJohn.[41] Its "one likeness and form" (μορφὴ μία καὶ ἰδέα ὁμοία) is contrasted with the great multitude, "which has no one form" (μίαν μορφὴν μὴ ἔχοντα). This contrast is hardly coincidental, and the interplay between "unity" and "diversity," and later between "likeness" and "unlikeness," demonstrates more than a passing familiarity with Platonic philosophy on the part of the author of the Acts of John.

For example, Middle Platonism[42] attempted to resolve the duality that traditional Platonism created by the polarity between the material world and the world of the "Forms." One means of resolving this tension was to postulate an essentially monistic universe of divine "Oneness," from which "Mind" (νοῦς) emanates and gives rise to multiplicity through its

41. In the Pauline corpus there are several references to objects that are said to be composed of/or refer to light: Rom 13:12 refers to "armor of light" (ὅπλα τοῦ φωτός); Eph 5:9 refers to "fruit of the light" (καρπὸς τοῦ φωτός); 2 Cor 11:14 refers to an "angel of light" (ἄγγελον φωτός).

42. Middle Platonism is the period of Platonic thought that bridges the work of Antiochus of Ascalon (ca. 125–ca. 68 BCE) and Plotinus (ca. 204–270 CE).

contemplation of the Forms. This interpretation of Platonism arose primarily through the influence of Stoicism,[43] which had maintained that the world had its ultimate origin in a fully transcendent "First Principle."[44] In the hierarchy created by the emanations from the "highest form" (the "Monad" [Τὸ Ἕν] or "God"), material bodies and elements connoting diversity carried with them necessarily negative connotations. Thus the description of the "great multitude" in AJohn as having "no one form" may indicate its distance from "the one likeness and form" revealed in the cross of light.[45]

Despite the fact that in chapter 97 John tells us that the Lord "stood" in the cave conveying some sense of corporeality, by chapter 98 he has become a mere voice (φωνὴν μόνον)[46] "without outward appearance"

---

43. See John Dillon, *The Middle Platonists, 80 B.C. to A.D. 220* (Ithaca, NY: Cornell University Press, 1977), 46. See also the discussion in Stephen Gersh, *Middle Platonism and Neoplatonism: The Latin Tradition*, 2 vols., PMS 23.1–2 (Notre Dame: University of Notre Dame Press, 1986), 1:370–79; see also Laurence W. Wood, *God and History: The Dialectical Tension of Faith and History in Modern Thought* (Lexington, KY: Emeth, 2005), 21–27.

44. I.e., the irreducible foundational proposition that serves as the basis for all other propositions. This is related to the τοῦ ἀγαθοῦ ἰδέα of Plato's *Republic* and perhaps also Parmenides's notion of the "One." Later it was developed by Augustine as *summum bonum* "the highest good" (Augustine, *De natura boni*). This is also similar to the teaching of Aristotle (*Physics* 8; *Metaphysics* 9) and subsequent peripatetic philosophy that the world derives from an "unmoved mover" (οὐ κινούμενον κινεῖ).

45. In the later writings of Plotinus, the goal of human life becomes "henosis" or mystical union with the "One." Henosis (ἕνωσις) is a Platonic concept that postulates a return of the forms to a state of unity in/with the source of all being. This concept, however, does not maintain that all diversity will simply be collapsed into a kind of "All-Oneness." Rather, as Werner Beierwaltes maintains, "The intention of *henosis-koinonia*-theory is accordingly in conceiving the Nous to strike a balance between unity and difference, allowing unity to be maintained in difference, identity despite distinction, and distinction despite identity. Unity as a sustained, correlative web of ideas and categories can only be conceived, if every individual in mutual participation and interpenetration … can preserve (σῴζειν, φυλάττειν) its particularity and peculiarity (οἰκεῖον, ἰδιότης)" (Werner Beierwaltes, "Nous: Unity in Difference," in *Platonism and Forms of Intelligence*, ed. John Dillon and Marie-Élise Zovko [Berlin: Akademie, 2008], 231–46). For subsequent use in Christian theology, see Ysabel de Andia, *Henosis: L'Union à Dieu chez Denys l'Aréopagite* (Leiden: Brill, 1996). This concept is expanded by subsequent Christian writers such as Evagrius of Pontus and Pseudo-Dionysius the Areopagite.

46. Φωνή is prominent in John's Gospel, as Jesus's followers are depicted as those

or "regular form" (σχῆμα μὴ ἔχοντα).[47] This representation is consistent, however, with both the polymorphic nature of the Lord's *appearances* in 87–102, as well as the Platonic concern for unity expressed in the "one form and likeness" of the cross of light. This is because, for Platonism, the concern is for unity in essence (not necessarily in representation). For example, in Plato's *Parmenides*, the character Socrates maintains that the properties of likeness and unlikeness are contrary, but not contradictory if the object in question is different in its relatedness (not its essence) to other properties (or different forms of "unlikeness"). This principle of "separation" can be demonstrated by the phrase "one among many." The same object can simultaneously possess properties of (and thus exist in) two separate and contrary categories. The categories are themselves matters of perspective and relatedness to other respective objects (128e–130a; cf. *Phaedo* 75c11–d2, 100b6–7; *Republic* 476b10, 480a11).

For the author of AJohn, the singularity of the "cross of light" serves as a unifying principle into which all the forms in which the Lord is represented become sublated. In much the same way that light refracted through a prism will be separated into constituent spectral colors, so too the various forms in which the Lord is represented are necessarily perspectival views of the "true light" and cannot fully encapsulate the completeness of his being. This section of AJohn has little room for the irony characteristic of GJohn. Rather, AJohn seeks to lay bare the mysteries through an explication of the events of the crucifixion. Perhaps more than anywhere else in this section of AJohn, the language of GJohn looms large in the predications used to describe the cross of light "for the sake of humans" (Word, Mind,[48] Jesus,[49] Christ, Door, Way, Bread, Seed, Resurrection, Son, Father, Spirit, Life, Truth, Faith, and Grace) (see table below).

---

who listen to his and/or the divine voice (GJohn 1:23; 3:29; 5:25, 28, 37; 10:3–5, 16; 11:43; 12:37).

47. This calls to mind the condemnation of the Jews/Judeans in GJohn 5:37–38, in which Jesus says that they have "never *heard his* [the Father's] *voice or seen his form*, and [they] do not have his word abiding in [them], because [they] do not believe him who he has sent." Here John hears a voice and sees one form and likeness in the cross.

48. Mind (νοῦς), does not have a strong correlation with GJohn but as we have seen carries with it Platonic resonances. Mind does appear as a structural element in the Gospel of Mary, another work with strong Platonic elements.

49. Ποτὲ δὲ Ἰησοῦς is excluded from the Greek text of Junod and Kaestli, *Acta Iohannis*.

Topoi Associated with the "Cross of Light" in AJohn	Corresponding Verses in GJohn
Bread	6:32–59
Word/Logos	1:1, 14
Christ	1:17, 41; 4:25–26, 29; 7:26–31; 9:22; 10:24–26; 11:27; 17:3; 20:31
Door	10:7–8
Way	14:6
Seed (σπόρος)	see 12:24 (κόκκος τοῦ σίτου)
Resurrection	6:54; 11:25
Son	1:34, 49, 51; 3:13–18, 36; 5:19–27; 6:27, 40, 53, 62; 8:28, 35–36; 9:35; 11:4, 27; 12:23, 34; 13:31; 14:13; 17:1; 19:7; 20:31
Father	1:14, 18; 2:16; 3:35; 4:21, 23; 5:17–23, 26, 36–37, 43, 45; 6:27, 32, 37, 40, 44–46, 57, 65; 8:16, 18–19, 27–28, 38–42, 49, 54; 10:15–18, 25–38; 11:41; 12:26–28, 49–50; 13:1–3; 14:2, 6–13, 16, 20–31; 15:1, 8–10, 15–16; 23–26; 16:3, 10, 15–17, 23–32; 17:1, 5, 11, 21, 24–25; 18:11; 20:17, 21
Spirit	1:32–33; 3:5–8, 34; 4:24; 7:39; 14:17, 26; 16:13; 19:30; 20:22
Life	1:4; 3:15–16, 36; 4:14; 5:24–29, 39–40; 6:27, 33–35, 40, 63, 68; 8:12; 10:28; 11:25; 14:6; 17:2–3
Truth	1:14, 17; 5:33; 8:32; 14:6, 17; 15:26; 16:13; 17:17, 19; 18:37–38
Faith	1:7, 12; 2:22–23; 3:15–16, 18, 36; 4:41–42, 53; 5:24, 38, 46; 6:29, 35, 40, 47, 69; 7:31, 38–39; 8:24, 30–31; 9:35–38; 10:37–38, 42; 11:25–27, 40–48; 12:36–46; 13:19; 14:1, 10–12; 16:27, 30; 17:8, 20–21; 19:35; 20:8, 25, 29, 31
Grace	1:14, 16–17

It is interesting that Father, Son, Spirit, (Jesus), and Christ appear to be bounded by the figure of the cross in AJohn. Might this convey the notion that it is only through participation in the cross that these other signifiers have their meaning, so that Jesus only becomes Son, Door, Way, and so on through his acceptance of the cross? Likewise, it is interesting which Johannine elements are *not* reproduced in AJohn. For example, Jesus's role as Paschal Lamb is absent (GJohn 1:29, 35; 19:36; cf. Exod 12:10; 12:46; Num 9:12). The absence of this element is especially baffling given the strong resonances of the priestly rhetorolect elsewhere in AJohn. Also missing are the kingship elements (GJohn 1:49; 3:5; 6:15; 7:42; 12:12–19; 18:33–39; 19:19–22) and the image of Jesus as the good shepherd who lays down his life for his sheep (GJohn 10:11, 14–15).

Just as there are variegated forms through which one can pass to the true light of eternal unity, there are likewise elements that underlie and perpetuate disharmony and evanescence. The list in AJohn 98 demonstrates some familiarity with the Pauline corpus, as there are clearly resonances between Paul's epistles and the language employed by the author of AJohn. For example, "on the right and on the left" (δεξιοὶ καὶ ἀριστεροί)[50] (see 2 Cor 6:7), "powers" (δυνάμεις), "authorities" (ἐξουσίαι), "lordships" (ἀρχαί), "demons" (δαίμονες), "operations" (ἐνέργειαι), "threatenings" (ἀπειλαί), "devils" (διάβολοι), "Satan" (Σατανᾶς), "the inferior root" (ἡ κατωτικὴ ῥίζα) (cf. Rom 2:8; 11:16, 18; 15:12; Gal 5:20; Eph 1:19; 3:7; 4:31; 6:9, 12; 2 Cor 12:20; Phil 3:21; Col 1:29; 2:12; 3:8; 2 Thess 2:9, 11; 2 Tim 3:3). Many of the words used are characteristic of Paul, and their use within the New Testament is restricted to the Pauline Epistles.

The Crucifixion in Acts of John: Middle (chs. 99–100)

O:

(a) [99] οὗτος οὖν ὁ σταυρὸς **ὁ διαπηξάμενος τὰ πάντα λόγῳ καὶ διορίσας τὰ ἀπὸ γενέσεως καὶ κατωτέρω, εἶτα καὶ εἰς πάντα πηγάσας·**
(b) οὐχ οὗτος δέ ἐστιν ὁ **σταυρὸς** ὃν μέλλεις ὁρᾶν **ξύλινον** κατελθὼν ἐντεῦθεν· οὔτε ἐγώ εἰμι ὁ ἐπὶ τοῦ **σταυροῦ**, ὃν νῦν

50. Similar expressions appear in Matt 6:3; 20:21, 23; 25:33; Mark 10:37, but from the context would suggest a Pauline reference. Likewise, the phrase derives from Isa 54:3, but as there are few explicit references to the OT in AJohn, a NT citation is much more probable.

οὐχ ὁρᾷς ἀλλὰ μόνον φωνῆς ἀκούεις. ὃ οὐκ εἰμὶ ἐνομίσθην, μὴ ὢν ὃ ἤμην ἄλλοις πολλοῖς ἀλλ' ὅ τι με ἐροῦσιν ταπεινὸν καὶ οὐκ ἐμοῦ ἄξιον.
(c) ὡς οὖν ὁ τόπος τῆς ἀναπαύσεως οὔτε ὁρᾶται οὔτε λέγεται, πολλῷ μᾶλλον ὁ τούτου κύριος οὔτε ὀφθήσομαι.

M:

[100] ὁ δὲ περὶ τὸν σταυρὸν μονοειδὴς ὄχλος ἡ κατωτικὴ φύσις ὑπάρχει. Καὶ οὓς ὁρᾷς ἐν τῷ σταυρῷ, εἰ καὶ μίαν μορφὴν οὐκ ἔχουσιν, οὐδέπω τὸ πᾶν τοῦ κατελθόντος συνελήφθη μέλος. ὅταν δὲ ἀναληφθῇ ἄνθρωποι φύσις καὶ γένος προσχωροῦν ἐπ' ἐμὲ φωνῇ τῇ ἐμῇ πειθόμενον, ὃν νῦν ἀκούω με σὺ τοῦτο γενήσεται, καὶ οὐκέτι ἔσται ὃ νῦν ἔστιν. ἀλλ' ὑπὲρ αὐτῶν ὡς κἀγὼ νῦν·

C:

(a) μέχρι γὰρ μήπω ἴδιόν μου λέγεις ἑαυτὸν τοῦτο οὐκ εἰμὶ ὅ εἰμι· ἐὰν δέ με **ἀκούσῃς**, ἀκούων καὶ σὺ μένε ὡς κἀγώ, ἐγὼ δὲ ὃ ἤμην ἔσομαι, ὅταν σὲ ὡς ἐγὼ παρ' ἐμαυτῷ· παρὰ γὰρ τοῦ τοῦτο εἶ.
(b) τῶν οὖν πολλῶν, ἀμέλει καὶ τῶν ἔξω τοῦ μυστηρίου, καταφρόνει· γίνωσκε γάρ με ὅλον παρὰ τῷ πατρὶ καὶ τὸν πατέρα παρ' ἐμοί.

O:

(a) [99] This **cross**, then, is that which has **united all things by the Word, and marked off things transient and inferior, and then compacted all into one**.
(b) But this is not **the cross of wood** which you will see when you go down there, neither am I he who is on the **cross**, whom now you do not see, but only hear a voice. I was reckoned to be what I am not, not being what I was to many others: but they will call me something else which is vile and not worthy of me.
(c) Therefore, just as the place of rest is neither seen nor spoken of, much less shall I, the Lord of this place, be seen or spoken of.

M:

[100] Now the multitude around the cross which is the lower

> nature is not of one form; and those whom you see in the cross, do not have one form. That is because every member of him who came down has not yet been gathered together. But when the human nature is taken up, and the race which comes to me in obedience to my voice, then he who now hears me shall be united with it and shall no longer be what it is now, but shall be above them, as I am now.

C:

> (a) For as long as you do not call yourself mine, I am not that which I was. But if you **hear** me and hearken to me, then you shall be as I am, and shall be what I was, when I have you with myself. For from this you are.
> (b) Therefore, ignore the many, and despise those who are outside the mystery! Know that I am wholly with the Father, and the Father with me.

The middle (99–100) provides insights into the nature of the crucifixion itself. Moving concentrically from the establishment of the cross as the unification point, the Lord's explanation incorporates notions of mystical union with the "one" through obedience to God's voice. The middle can be divided between sections: (O) (a) marking the cross of light as the unification point of all things, (b) introduction of the bilocation of the Lord during his crucifixion, (c) the establishment of the ineffability of the Lord's true essence;[51] (M) the disunity of humanity and the promise of *henosis* to those who are obedient; (C) (a) the different perspective of the Lord's essence gained through obedience, (b) confidence in the faith that the Lord is one with the Father. When compared with the middle of the crucifixion account in GJohn (19:25–30), an interesting point of comparison may be seen: as the cross marks the point of unification in AJohn, it also becomes the place of the unification of Jesus's earthly and spiritual

51. The significance of the "place of rest" mentioned here is difficult to determine. A possible (though admittedly tenuous) link can be made (at least evocatively) with a statement in the Gospel of Thomas. In Gos. Thom. 2 (P.Oxy. 654.5–9), "Jesus says, 'Let the one who seeks not cease seeking until he finds; and when he finds he will be amazed, and when he has been amazed, he will rule, and when he has ruled, *he will rest*'" (translation E-P).

families in GJohn (symbolized by the giving of Mary over to the care of the Beloved Disciple).

This cross, which here becomes the locus of meaning, is not "the cross of wood," the historical event as it were, but rather meaning is invested in the ahistorical "Logos event" whose spiritual significance transcends both time and location. The bilocation of Jesus in this narrative (dying on the cross while at the same instant speaking to John) appears to hold in tension proto-orthodox and docetic Christologies, fitting comfortably in neither. Unlike the canonical gospels, which more clearly point to the physical suffering of Jesus, or the Gospel of Judas (56–58),[52] which clearly points to a nonsuffering divine Jesus, the suffering of Jesus in AJohn appears more ambiguous. He suffers, but he does not suffer! This apparent equivocation, as we will recall, points us to the author's latent Platonic tendencies and the multifarious ways in which positional objectivity affects interpretation. For example, from a non-Christian perspective, the physical suffering of Jesus (indeed, the entire historical event as denoted by the "cross of wood") could be seen as ultimately insignificant (from the relative scope of history). For the Christian, however, the cross is the central event in the history of the cosmos.

In this respect, while Jesus *did indeed suffer*, he *did not suffer* what "they say" he suffered (namely, a painful and ignominious death). Rather, if we could merely see the truth, as John does, we would see in the death of Jesus "simultaneously" the squalid execution of a peasant preacher and the transcendent act of God. In that case we might laugh at (cf. AJohn 102) or "despise those outside the mystery" (100), who view the pitiful scene, not recognizing its true (if hidden) importance. The cross is thus a prism that refracts the true light in various shades; perception is a matter of positioning oneself, so to speak. This change in perspective giving rise to a new view of an object can be characterized as a parallax.[53]

Nevertheless, while Jesus suffers and does not suffer, he is also simultaneously the one on the cross and not the one on the cross. In this way, the *real* person of Jesus, his transcendent divinity, is not harmed (here the christological balance tips more toward the docetic). Therefore, while he endured suffering, his divine essence remained unharmed. Indeed, the

52. The chapter divisions follow E-P.

53. A parallax is the "apparent difference" in an object when viewed from separate lines of sight. Thus an object may "appear" to change or exhibit differing characteristics when viewed from separate perspectives.

Lord's true divine essence is the mystery AJohn seeks to express in the statement, "know that I am wholly with the Father and the Father with me."[54]

The Platonic language expressed earlier reappears in AJohn 100: "Now the multitude around the cross which is the lower nature is not of one form." Here, however, the author of AJohn introduces the notion that this lower "human nature" will be "gathered together" (συνελήφθη) and "taken up" (ἀναληφθῇ). Those who are obedient to the Lord's voice will be united with him and "shall no longer be what it is now, but shall be *above* them." This image of being (from) "above" has clear resonances with GJohn. The word used here, however, is ὑπέρ rather than the familiar Johannine word ἄνωθεν. It becomes a clear theological position of the author of this portion of AJohn that obedience to God and faith in the Lord causes a change in perspective, which eventuates in *henosis* with the unifying source of all being.

The Crucifixion in Acts of John: Closing (ch. 101)

O:

> [101] οὐδὲν οὖν ὧν μέλλουσιν λέγειν περὶ ἐμοῦ ἔπαθα· ἀλλὰ καὶ τὸ πάθος ἐκεῖνο ὃ ἔδειξά σοι καὶ τοῖς λοιποῖς χορεύων μυστήριον βούλομαι καλεῖσθαι. ὃ γὰρ εἰ σὺ ὁρᾷς τοῦτο ἐγώ σοι ἔδειξα· ὃ δέ εἰμι τοῦτο ἐγὼ μόνος οἶδα, ἄλλος οὐδείς.

M:

> (a) τὸ οὖν ἐμὸν ἐαΐμε ἔχειν, τὸ δὲ σὸν δι' ἐμοῦ ὁρᾶν, ἐμὲ οὐδείς. τὸ οὖν ἐμὸν ἐαΐμε ἔχειν, τὸ δὲ σὸν δι' ἐμοῦ ὁρᾶν, ἐμὲ δὲ ὄντως ὁρᾶν, οὐ ἔφην ὑπάρχειν ἀλλ' ὃ σὺ δέ νυ γνωρίζειν συγγενὴς ὤν.
>
> (b) ἀκούεις με παθόντα καὶ οὐκ ἔπαθον, μὴ παθόντα καὶ ἔπαθον· νυγέντα καὶ οὐκ ἐπλήγην· κρεμασθέντα καὶ οὐκ ἐκρεμάσθην· αἷμα ἐξ ἐμοῦ ῥεύσαντα καὶ οὐκ ἔρευσεν· καὶ

54. Cf., e.g., GJohn 1:1, 18; 4:26; 5:18; 6:20, 35, 46, 48; 8:12, 24, 38, 58; 9:5, 38; 10:7, 11, 14–15, 30–33, 38; 11:25; 13:19; 14:6–14; 15:1, 5, 24; 16:15. I take Jesus's absolute "I AM" (Εγώ εἰμι) statements as intentional allusions to Exod 3:14, ἐγώ εἰμι ὁ ὤν (אֶהְיֶה אֲשֶׁר אֶהְיֶה), and thus as implicit identifications of Christ with YHWH. For a brief discussion of John's usage, see Elizabeth Harris, *Prologue and Gospel: The Theology of the Fourth Evangelist*, JSNTSup 107 (Sheffield: Sheffield Academic, 1994), 130–54.

ἁπλῶς ἃ ἐκεῖνοι λέγουσιν περὶ ἐμοῦ ταῦτα μὴ ἐσχηκέναι, ἃ δὲ μὴ λέγουσιν ἐκεῖνα πεπονθέναι.

C:

τίνα δὲ ἔστιν αἰνίσσομαί σην· οἶδα γὰρ ὅτι συνήσεις. νόησον οὖν με **λόγου** αἴνεσιν, **λόγου** νύξι, **λόγου** αἷμα, **λόγου** τραῦμα, **λόγου** ἐξάρτησιν, **λόγου** πάθος, **λόγου** πῆξιν, **λόγου** θάνατον· καὶ οὕτως χωρίσας ἄνθρωπον λέγω. τὸν μὲν οὖν πρῶτον **λόγον** νόησον, εἶτα κύριον νοήσεις, τὸν δὲ ἄνθρωπον τρίτον καὶ τὸ τί πέπονθεν.

O:

[101] Therefore I have suffered none of the things which they will say of me: that suffering which I showed to you and to the rest in the dance, I wish it to be called a mystery. For what you are, you see that I showed you; but what I am, that I alone know, and no one else.

M:

(a) Let me, therefore, keep that which is mine, and that which is yours you must see through me. As for seeing me as I am in reality, I have told you this is impossible unless you are able to see me as my kinsman.

(b) You hear that I suffered, yet I did not suffer; that I suffered not, yet did I suffer; that I was pierced, yet I was not wounded; hanged, and I was not hanged; that blood flowed from me, yet it did not flow; and, in a word, those things that they say of me I did not endure, and the things that they do not say those I suffered.

C:

Now what they are I will reveal to you for I know you will understand. Perceive in me the slaying of the **Logos**, the piercing of the **Logos**, the blood of the **Logos**, the wounding of the **Logos**, the hanging of the **Logos**, the passion of the **Logos**, the nailing of the **Logos**, the death of the **Logos**. And so I speak, discarding manhood. Therefore, in the first place think of the **Logos**, then you shall perceive the Lord, and thirdly the man, and what he has suffered.

The closing (101) is perhaps the most enigmatic section we have examined. It can be divided into three segments, with the middle segment subdivided into two sections: (O) the (non)suffering of Jesus is a mystery, and he alone knows his true nature; (M) (a) seeing the Lord as he is is impossible, unless you see him as a kinsman, (b) the Lord suffered and yet did not suffer; (C) introduction of the Logos as a means of understanding the Lord's suffering. When compared with the closing of GJohn's crucifixion narrative (19:31–37), several interesting elements may be seen, as shown in the table below.

Similar Elements in the Closings of the Crucifixion Narratives

Gospel of John 19:31–37	Acts of John 101
"Instead one of the soldiers pierced his side with a spear" (v. 34) and "they looked upon him who they have pierced" (v. 37)	"the piercing of the Logos," "the nailing of the Logos,"
"and blood and water came out" (v. 34)	"the blood of the Logos," "the wounding of the Logos"
"When they came to Jesus [they] saw that he was already dead" (v. 33)	"Perceive in me the slaying of the Logos," "the death of the Logos"

Despite the fact that the Logos has already been taken up as just another form that is to be understood in relation to the cross of light, it here becomes an integral component to understanding the suffering of the Lord. If we were simply making judgments with respect to number of occurrences, the word *logos* would not seem to figure all that prominently in the Fourth Gospel. In fact, within the entirety of GJohn's narrative, the author only employs this enigmatic use of the term *logos* in two verses—both in the prologue (1:1 [3×], 14). Nevertheless, the term clearly carries significance for GJohn disproportionate to its actual number of occurrences. The elements most contiguous throughout the various uses of the term in GJohn and other ancient literature convey the notions of "rationality" and "purpose" (especially as it relates to the creation and ordering of the cosmos). Therefore, no matter its ultimate point of reference, in designating Jesus as God's Logos, the authors of

GJohn and AJohn both interpret him in some sense "as the divine clue to the structure of reality."[55]

In attempting to understand the use of *logos* in this passage, it will be beneficial briefly to examine its use in Philo. As a Middle Platonist, Philo accepted the notion of a transcendent first principle (which he identified with God) as well as an active and demiurgic force (the *logos*). For Philo, God can be characterized as both ὁ ὤν (the "Being"; *Mos.* 1.75) and νόος (the "Mind"; *QG* 2.62). The *logos* is to be identified with God's "reason" or "speech" that serves as "the mediating principle between divine transcendence and the material world."[56] Philo distinguishes between the role of the *logos* before the act of creating the cosmos (*antemundane*) and its role in creating and sustaining the cosmos (*mundane*; *Mos.* 2.127).[57] He defines the *logos*—in its antemundane stage—as the most general of the forms/ideas (τὸ γενικώτατον and τί),[58] or the typos of the forms/ideas (*Migr.* 18).[59] In its mundane stage, the *logos* becomes the active and efficient cause of the cosmos (τὸ δραστήριον αἴτιον; *Opif.* 8).[60] The forms/ideas, therefore, serve as the patterns for the creation of the phenomenal world, according to which the demiurgic *logos* fashions the universe (*Opif.* 16; *Her.* 156; *Migr.* 6; *Cher.* 127). Philo refers to the *logos* as the "firstborn" or first "created being" (*Deus* 31) and God's divine wisdom (*Her.* 199; cf. Prov 8).

Returning to the narrative of AJohn, therefore, it becomes clearer why the Lord has told John that his ultimate nature (his divine essence) is beyond human comprehension. This is why it would be impossible for those of the lower nature to understand him if he were not revealed to us

55. Jaroslav Pelikan, *Jesus through the Centuries: His Place in the History of Culture* (New York: Harper & Rowe, 1985), 58; also 57, 59–70.

56. Amy-Jill Levine, "Visions of Kingdoms: From Pompey to the First Jewish Revolt," in *The Oxford History of the Biblical World*, ed. Michael D. Coogan (New York: Oxford University Press, 2001), 376.

57. See Charles A. Anderson, *Philo of Alexandria's Views of the Physical World*, WUNT 2/309 (Tübingen: Mohr Siebeck, 2011), 144.

58. Philo, *Det.* 118; *Leg.* 2.86; 3.175; *Opif.* 25.

59. Philo, *Leg.* 3.96; *Cher.* 127; *Prov.* 1.23. See discussion in Robert M. Berchman, *From Philo to Origen: Middle Platonism in Transition*, BJS 69 (Chico, CA: Scholars Press, 1984), 28. For a discussion of Plato's concept of the ideas, see W. D. Ross, *Plato's Theory of Ideas* (Oxford: Clarendon, 1951); Plato, *Parm.* 129–135; *Theaet.* 184–186, *Phileb.* 14–18.

60. See also Philo, *QE* 2.68; *Fug.* 110, 112; *Her.* 188, 119, 130.

in the form of a "kinsmen" (συγγενής). His humanity points to his divinity. The Lord as priest and Logos sustains the cosmos, standing as mediator between humanity and divinity, making possible the return to unity with God through the sacrifice of the cross. The lack of resurrection accounts in AJohn means that the glorification of the Lord is synonymous with the crucifixion. The two events cannot be decoupled, because in this priestly frame it is the suffering of the Logos (the moment of sacrifice) at which the cosmos is restored.

4. Conclusion

Since there is no narrative of the resurrection or postresurrection appearances in AJohn, the crucifixion represents the central moment of the Lord's glorification. This is because it is through Jesus's death that all the various forms of the universe are brought into harmony through the Lord's mediating sacrifice. While all of the canonical gospels narrate the crucifixion scene, AJohn removes the reader from the actual scene almost entirely. In contrast to the canonical gospels, AJohn depicts Jesus bilocationally, as being on the cross, while also speaking to John in a cave at the Mount of Olives. These texts could thus be read in tandem with AJohn, providing an explanation of the significance of the events narrated within GJohn's crucifixion scene. Of central importance for the author of AJohn is the figure of the "cross of light" as the organizing principle that suffuses all other representations of Jesus with meaning. The variegated forms in which the cross of light is depicted are demonstrative of the dichotomy between the "one and the many" or between the "higher and the lower natures" of creator and created as understood in various forms of Platonism.

There is similarity in function between the "cross of light" here and the Logos in GJohn. Indeed, as we have seen, the Logos returns as the second most important structural principle in the narrative and dominates the last section of the closing of the crucifixion scene in AJohn (101). The connection between the Logos and elements of priestly, precreation, and wisdom rhetorolects is apparent in several places in AJohn 98–101. In particular, there is a recurring connection with the Lord's function as priest and his role as cosmic mediator.

Part 4
Response Essays

Response: Luke and the Protevangelium of James

Ronald F. Hock

1. Introduction

Most volumes of essays, even if they contain several engaging and insightful contributions, nevertheless often lack any overarching coherence. The present collection of seven essays by Vernon Robbins and his students at Emory University, however, manages to do both, and to do so very well. The essays not only provide many insights but also gain in coherence by focusing on a small group of texts and by analyzing those texts with the same interpretive methodology. The texts include Luke-Acts and John as well as two apocryphal texts, the Protevangelium of James and the Acts of John, and the methodology is Robbins's ever-developing sociorhetorical interpretation.

The first two essays, by Robbins, focus on Luke-Acts, especially the birth stories of Luke 1–2, whereas the next three, by Christopher Holmes, Mandy Hollman, and Michael Suh and Robbins, deal with the Protevangelium of James (PJ). Given my own efforts some years ago regarding this gospel,[1] I welcome the opportunity to reenter the discussion of interpreting this apocryphal gospel and so will restrict my comments to the essays on this gospel as well as to those on one of its resource texts, Luke 1–2. I leave the final two essays on the Acts of John by Jonathan Potter and Jared Farmer to the other respondents.

1. Ronald F. Hock, *The Infancy Gospels of James and Thomas*, ScholBib 3 (Santa Rosa, CA: Polebridge, 1995), 2–81.

2. Sociorhetorical Interpretation of Luke-Acts

2.1. Early Christian Rhetorolects

Robbins's lead essay, "Priestly Discourse in Luke and Acts" (pp. 13–40 above) is appropriately placed in the lead-off position since it introduces the sociorhetorical method of interpretation used throughout the volume. Accordingly, a brief summary of this method will precede an analysis of the substance of the essay. "Priestly discourse" is a term that belongs to a larger conceptual approach to early Christian literature that Robbins and other scholars have developed since the mid-1990s. This approach begins with the assumption that early Christianity is a new form of Judaism. Within this context Christianity produced its own distinctive discourse. Early Christian discourse, in Robbins's analysis, is a blend of six distinct rhetorolects: wisdom, prophetic, apocalyptic, precreation, miracle, and priestly. A rhetorolect, he says, is "a form of language variety or discourse identifiable on the basis of a distinctive configuration of themes, topics, reasonings, and argumentations."[2] Rhetorolects have two dimensions, a rhetography or a graphic pictorial narration, and a rhetology, or a belief-argumentation that supports the narration. In addition, rhetography itself has two parts, a background narrative that informs the foreground narrative of the text. In the case of Christian rhetography the background narratives come from Old Testament storylines that inform the foreground narratives of Jesus and his followers. The sources of Christian rhetology are the belief-argumentations from Judaism and the broader Hellenistic culture that support the Christian narratives. Depending on historical circumstances, any of the six rhetorolects can emerge as dominant or be pushed into the background. In the texts investigated in this volume the authors tell their Christian stories in terms of prophetic or priestly rhetorolects. The priestly rhetorolect, given its centrality throughout the volume, is discourse about temples, altars, priests, and worship assemblies where priests offer sacrifice, prayers, and blessings in the belief that such offerings will provide beneficial exchanges between God and humans.

Identifying distinct rhetorolects in the development of early Christian discourse is very attractive and well worth pursuing. But three com-

2. Vernon K. Robbins, "The Dialectical Nature of Early Christian Discourse," *Scriptura* 59 (1996): 356. Quoted above in Robbins, "Priestly Discourse in Luke and Acts," 15.

ments suggest themselves. First, while background storylines of Christian rhetography are illustrated with specific Old Testament texts for each rhetorolect, Christian rhetology remains vague, a point I return to later. Second, the concept of rhetography with its background and foreground narratives seems similar to what Dennis MacDonald and his students have called mimesis with its hypotexts and hypertexts. Of special interest, while Robbins and the other authors in this volume assume Old Testament texts as background narratives, MacDonald and his students argue that the Homeric epics are the hypotext or background narratives for significant portions of the gospels and Acts. Engagement of these two similar but opposing approaches to the background storylines of early Christian discourse should prove fruitful.[3] Third, while the term "rhetorolect" is central to the other essays in this volume, the terms "rhetography" and "rhetology" do not appear. The consequence is that while rhetography receives extensive, if implicit, treatment, rhetology is neglected, a neglect I will address at the end.

Turning to the substance of Robbins's essay, he presents a clear, comprehensive, and insightful discussion of Luke-Acts that demonstrates a pervasive priestly rhetorolect in this two-volume work. Robbins is initially intrigued by the opening scene of Luke's Gospel in which the priest Zechariah offers incense in the temple (1:9). Such a scene is unique in the gospels and leads Robbins to ask whether this priestly scene has any significance beyond the first chapter for Luke's story about Jesus as a whole and even for the Christian movement as presented in Acts. As it turns out, much in every way, to borrow a Pauline phrase. And, in fact, such a priestly rhetorolect is unique among the gospels.

But we are getting ahead of ourselves. The remainder of the essay is an analysis of the many ways priestly rhetorolect informs the whole of the Lukan narrative. The first two chapters, which will be important for the later essays on the Protevangelium of James, can illustrate Luke's priestly rhetorolect. I have already mentioned the foreground narrative of Zechariah offering incense in the temple, but there are also hints of Old Testa-

3. See, e.g., Dennis R. MacDonald, *The Homeric Epics and the Gospel of Mark* (New Haven: Yale University Press, 2000). See also Dennis R. MacDonald, ed., *Mimesis and Intertextuality in Antiquity and Christianity* (Harrisburg, PA: Trinity Press International, 2001); and especially the essays that posit Homeric influence on Jewish texts, by MacDonald ("Tobit and the Odyssey," 11–40) and by George W. E. Nickelsburg ("Tobit, Genesis, and the *Odyssey*: A Complicated Web of Intertextuality," 41–55).

ment background stories in that Zechariah is identified as belonging to the priestly order of Abijah (1:5), who was a grandson of Aaron, the founder of the priesthood (Exod 28; Lev 8), and if the reference to Abijah was too subtle, Zechariah's wife, Elizabeth, being called a descendant of Aaron makes the priestly connection obvious. The priestly rhetorolect continues when Zechariah's first words after regaining his speech are to bless God (1:64) and shortly thereafter to say that his son John would forgive the people their sins (1:77)—blessing and forgiving being part of priestly rhetorolect.

Mary is identified as a relative of Elizabeth (1:36) and so likewise a descendant of Aaron, and later, when Mary visits her, Elizabeth blesses her (1:42). In addition, after Jesus is born, his mother and father take him to the temple and offer a sacrifice of purification (2:22), following the dictates of Leviticus (Lev 12:8). And while at the temple Simeon takes Jesus in his arms and blesses God (2:28) and later blesses Jesus's parents (2:34). At age twelve Jesus returns to the temple and engages the teachers there (2:46–47). In short, this abbreviated summary of priestly rhetorolect in Luke 1–2 shows that John's and Jesus's births are both narrated in a context of priestly places, actors, and actions.

Robbins continues his analysis through the rest of Luke and even Acts, and while it is not necessary to go into detail, the pervasiveness of priestly rhetorolect continues. His conclusions that the surprising frequency of Jesus's praying (e.g., Luke 5:16; 6:12; 9:18, 28; 22:41–42), his advising on prayer (11:2–4; 17:22; 20:47), and his offering of forgiveness (5:20 and 7:48–50) are all priestly activities are especially noteworthy. At the end Jesus looks forward to his disciples' performing priestly functions by offering repentance and forgiveness of sins to all nations (24:47) and then blesses them (24:50). After the ascension the disciples are found in the temple continually blessing God (24:53). Despite all this priestly discourse, Robbins notes that Jesus's death surprisingly is not seen as sacrificial, as it is in Mark 10:45 and Matt 20:28.

In Acts the priestly rhetorolect continues although blended with miracle, prophetic, and apocalyptic rhetorolects. Still, at the beginning of Acts there is priestly rhetorolect as the disciples pray together in the upper room (Acts 1:13–14), pray about a replacement for Judas (1:25), pray after Pentecost (2:42), and pray everywhere as they go from Jerusalem to Rome (e.g., 4:23–26; 6:4, 6; 8:15, 22; 9:11;10:2, 30; 12:5; 13:3; 27:29). Besides praying, there is an emphasis on priestly forgiveness of sins through belief in Jesus and the ritual of baptism (2:38; 5:31; 10:43; 13:38; 26:18). Indeed, baptism becomes the "priestly" ritual of a devout life instead of priestly blood sacrifice and thus becomes the way Christians receive the priestly benefit of forgiveness of sin.

This is just a summary of some of the priestly rhetorolect in Acts, but it is sufficient to show that it is a significant part of discourse in Acts, and we are in debt to Robbins's comprehensive analysis of priestly rhetorolect in Luke-Acts. One question kept nagging at me, however, as the impressive amount of evidence for priestly rhetorolect was presented: how do we explain the prevalence of this priestly rhetorolect? Is there a historical circumstance to prompt Luke's overlaying this rhetorolect on his sources like Mark, Q, and his *Sondergut*? I would like to see some further reflection and research to come up with an explanation.

2.2. Corporeal Semantics

The second essay is also by Robbins, "Bodies and Politics in Luke 1–2 and Sirach 44–50: Men, Women, and Boys" (pp. 41–63 above), which appeared in an earlier form in *Scriptura* 90 (2005): 724–838. This essay also has a methodological part as well as a substantive one. In this essay Robbins introduces corporeal semantics. He starts off with an interesting point: "humans give meaning to the world outside of them by using terms related to their bodies" (p. 42). This point is nicely illustrated by a quotation from Giambattista Vico, a portion of which should suffice: "Thus, head for top or beginning; the brow and shoulders of a hill; the eyes of needles and of potatoes; mouth for any opening; the lip of a cup or pitcher; the teeth of a rake, a saw, a comb; the beard of wheat; the tongue of a shoe…." (p. 42).

Robbins next tries to incorporate this new approach with sociorhetorical interpretation. Such an incorporation is possible, he says, because "the analysis [in this essay] is grounded in a sociorhetorical presupposition that bodies are essential participants in the creation of meaning in a text" (p. 43). Robbins expands his definition of early Christian discourse accordingly. In the previous essay he said: "Christians blended six major 'rhetorical dialects' together during the first two centuries CE as they created early Christian discourse: wisdom, prophetic, apocalyptic, precreation, miracle, and priestly."[4] Now, with a nod to corporeal semantics, he says: "Early Christian discourse blended six different types of 'Christian body'

4. Robbins, "Priestly Discourse," 14–15.

together through the medium of six different rhetorolects: wisdom, miracle, prophetic, priestly, precreation, and apocalyptic."[5] He says further: "Each rhetorolect blends 'locations' in the world with the human body in distinctive ways. In addition, it blends the human body with 'locations' in the world" (p. 44).

With this emphasis on body it is not surprising that the word "body" or "bodies" appears frequently in the following analysis of Luke 1–2—indeed, nearly fifty times. And yet, I am not sure how much this emphasis on body enhances the analysis. A few examples will illustrate what I mean. What insight is gained when Robbins writes, "Their bodies [i.e., Zechariah and Elizabeth's] functioned in unity as they enacted the most honorable deeds of priestly heritage" (p. 46) that is not present if he were to write "Zechariah and Elizabeth functioned in unity as they enacted…"? Or: what is gained when we read "Zechariah's male body is invested 'politically' with authority to move 'closer' to the presence of God" (p. 48) that would be lost if he had written "Zechariah's priestly status is invested 'politically' with authority…"? And on occasion something seems to be missing by using the word "body," as in this sentence: "When the messenger speaks, he tells him to remove the fear that has overwhelmed his body" (p. 52), for the sense of this encounter requires us to assume that the fear engendered by Gabriel's message wholly overwhelmed Zechariah, in both body and soul. Similarly, something is lost when the word "bodies" is used in this sentence: "An … event occurs during the incense offering that transmits a special kind of blessing into the bodies of two interrelated priestly people" (p. 52), for the conception of John is really a blessing in the "lives" of Zechariah and Elizabeth. Finally, the use of "body" in contemporary English idiom sometimes means "corpse," as might occur to someone when reading this sentence: "'Priestly' holiness transfers from the context of the temple to the bodies of both John the Baptist and Jesus" (p. 60). Thinking of such an idiom is avoided if Robbins had simply said, "'Priestly' holiness is transferred to both John the Baptist and Jesus." The same could be said of calling Simeon and Anna "temple-bodies" (p. 60). To sum up, even though Robbins uses the word "body" to emphasize the physical relocation of priestly blessing from the temple to the household of Zechariah and Elizabeth—and rightly so—the point would just as easily be made

5. Robbins, Bodies and Politics," 44.

with other language, which can thus avoid the unnecessary, misleading, or even humorous uses of "body."

Now if the use of corporeal semantics has not added significantly to the analysis of Luke 1–2, this in no way means that Robbins's analysis is not first-rate. A number of important insights arise simply from his close and perceptive reading of the text in terms of sociorhetorical interpretation. Again, a few examples will suffice. Luke begins his gospel with two names, King Herod of Judea and the priest Zechariah (1:5). Herod appears nowhere else in the gospel and is dealt with here in only eight Greek words, whereas Luke uses fifty-four words just to narrate the priestly attributes of Zechariah and his wife Elizabeth in the immediate context (1:5–7), thereby suggesting that Luke opens his gospel with a priestly rather than a political rhetorolect. This suggestion is confirmed when Robbins notes that Zechariah and Elizabeth's living righteously "before God" (1:6) shows that they give priority to the commandments of God rather than to the decrees of Herod. In addition, Robbins is probably correct, though I had not thought of it, when he says that Luke's readers' cultural knowledge would have lead them to expect that Zechariah and Elizabeth would have a child despite their advanced years.

Also, Robbins makes excellent use of the elaborate and idealized description of the high priest Simon in Sir 50:1–21 in order to contrast the ordinary priest Zechariah offering incense in the temple with Simon's important role in city and temple including his appearance and actions before the assembled people with its wisdom rhetorolect of a double blessing.

The insights continue. Robbins emphasizes that blessing (εὐλογεῖν) is the special gift of a priest and adds that glorifying (δοξάζειν) is what nonpriestly people do, footnoting ten passages in Luke for confirmation. For example, the people of Nain, when Jesus raised the widow's son, were seized with fear and kept glorifying (ἐδόξαζον) God (7:16). Robbins makes perceptive use of the benediction in Sir 50:22–24, comparing it to Zechariah's blessing of John after his circumcision (Luke 1:68–79). Robbins cites at least five verbal parallels and concludes that Zechariah has taken the temple blessing and relocated it in the hill country of Judea. Robbins also senses a shift from the previous priestly discourse to kingly language in the annunciation to Mary (1:26–38) and draws several more parallels from the description of Simon in Sir 50.

Mary's following visit to Elizabeth's house, however, witnesses the return of priestly rhetorolect (1:39–56). Robbins says that the blessings of Mary and her unborn child by Elizabeth (1:42) turn Elizabeth into a priest.

Her evoking "all women" in the blessing ritualizes Mary's status as a person "favored by God" (cf. 1:28, 30) and so turns her house into a house of God. Elizabeth's next blessing, in the third person singular, seems to envision a congregation of people at Elizabeth's house, and Elizabeth's joyful speech and Mary's subsequent Magnificat in the Judean hill country (1:46–55) recall the shouting, trumpeting, and singing in the midst of blessings at the Jerusalem temple (cf. Sir 50:16–21). In short, according to Robbins, the powers of God have moved outside the temple and a woman has become a mediator of God's blessings. Finally, Robbins has drawn attention to the important role that the temple plays at both the beginning of the Gospel and again at the end—from Zechariah offering incense and Joseph and Mary taking the infant Jesus for the purifying sacrifice (2:21–24) and later a twelve-year-old Jesus (2:41–51) to years later when Jesus returns to the temple where his prophetic wisdom is heard by the people (19:45–48) and where after his ascension his followers are found and, in priestly fashion, blessing (εὐλογοῦντες) God (24:53). This sampling of insights should be enough to underscore the value of Robbins's sociorhetorical interpretation of Luke 1–2.

3. Sociorhetorical Interpretation of Protevangelium of James

After Robbins's two essays on Luke 1–2, we have three essays that appropriately follow in that they deal in one way or another with the Protevangelium of James (PJ), whose contents often draw on Luke 1–2. A general comment is in order at the beginning. Scholarship on PJ has not advanced much recently, to judge from the bibliography in the recent edition by Bart Ehrman and Zlatko Pleše, compared to mine.[6] Accordingly, the appearance of these three essays is especially welcome and deserving of our attention.

3.1. Mary as Blessed Mother

The first of these essays, by Christopher T. Holmes, "Who Am I to Be Blessed? Mary as Blessed Mother in the Protevangelium of James" (pp.

6. See Bart D. Erhman and Zlatko Pleše, *The Apocryphal Gospels: Texts and Translations* (New York: Oxford University Press, 2011), 37–38; and Hock, *Infancy Gospels*, 78–79. But add now Lily C. Vuong, *Gender and Purity in the Protevangelium of James*, WUNT 2/358 (Tübingen: Mohr Siebeck, 2013) (non vidi).

67–101 above) has three major sections. The first sets the context for Mary's visit to Elizabeth in Luke 1:39–56 and PJ 12.2–3, whereas the second is seemingly the focus of the essay, a careful comparative exegesis of Mary's visit to Elizabeth in Luke and PJ, but this exegesis really serves as the jumping off point for the third section, as Mary's visit ends with her asking, "Who am I that all the women of earth should bless me?" (12.2).[7] The third section is a survey of the topos of blessing as a way of understanding more precisely the nature of Mary's blessedness that is raised by her question.

Holmes opens with a comparison of the context for the visit in each gospel. In the case of Luke he notes that the accounts of the births of John and Jesus have a number of similarities, but the one that interests him most is the number of features that identify a prophetic rhetorolect—ten features in all—that are scattered throughout Luke 1–2. There are, to be sure, some features of priestly rhetorolect, but they are subsumed under the prophetic, such as the setting of the temple that is used as a platform for prophetic rhetorolect.

In the case of PJ the author does not narrate the birth of John and so does not mention Zechariah and Elizabeth (until much later in the narrative). Instead, he opens with a different story, one about Joachim and Anna, the birth of their daughter Mary and on to her childhood in the temple and her removal to Joseph's house. Thus Mary, not John, becomes the forerunner of Jesus. But not only have the characters and their stories changed; so has the rhetorolect—from Lukan prophetic to PJ's priestly, that is, where ritual actions benefit God in a manner that activates divine benefits for humans. The temple is the first space for activating such benefits, and PJ begins and ends in the temple.

But Holmes notes a subtle shift in first space as the activation of divine benefits moves from the temple to Mary, who becomes a "moving temple." For example, Mary's birth, he says, activates divine benefits for Joachim and Anna. In some sense, yes, but what really activates Joachim and Anna's benefits are their prayers of supplication that are heard by God, who sends an angel to inform each that Anna will conceive (4.1–2). Presumably, after her birth Joachim continues to receive forgiveness via sacrifices at the temple. In other words, the temple has not moved.

7. [Note that *all* references to PJ throughout this response essay use the references numbers from Ehrman and Pleše, while the original essay by Suh and Robbins used the reference numbers from Hock, *Infancy Gospels*.—eds.]

Holmes next turns to the parallel accounts of Mary's visit to Elizabeth and analyzes them according to the schema opening-middle-closing. In the opening Holmes argues against the traditional chapter divisions of PJ by assigning 12.1 to the previous story about Mary returning her threads to the temple and receiving the priest's blessing (12.1). Her visit to Elizabeth begins at 12.2. The argument is thorough and perceptive, noting, for example, that the priest's blessing rounds out a cycle of priestly blessings (6.2 and 7.2) and is ironic in that the same priest will later accuse her (15.3), whereas Elizabeth's blessing at opening the door to Mary is by a nonpriest and a woman besides. Also, the syntax of 12.2 parallels that of Luke 1:39. The middle, despite some literal agreements, differs from Luke in a number of ways. In Luke Elizabeth blesses Mary on hearing her greeting, whereas in PJ Elizabeth drops her scarlet thread, runs to the door, opens it, and then blesses Mary. In both accounts the unborn John leaps up (Luke 1:41, 44; PJ 12.2), but in PJ he also blesses Mary (12.2). This blessing, parallel with the third blessing in Luke (1:45), is not spelled out, and Holmes finds that significant since the Lukan blessing speaks of belief and fulfillment, features of prophetic rhetorolect. Other omissions are noted. Luke says that Elizabeth was filled with the Holy Spirit before she blesses Mary and the unborn child, but PJ drops the reference to the Holy Spirit, consistent with a priestly rhetorolect, and drops the blessing of Mary's unborn child completely, although here Holmes does not suggest any reason for the omission.

As the middle section continues Holmes senses a change not only in length but also in tone. At the beginning of the Magnificat in Luke Mary rejoices in response to Elizabeth's blessings and consequently magnifies the Lord and is confident that all generations will bless her (1:46–48). Not only does PJ omit the Magnificat (Luke 1:46–54), but also the joy and confidence expressed by Mary in Luke are replaced by a tone of forgetfulness and confusion in PJ, suggested by the indicative blessing of Luke 1:48 being turned into a question in PJ: "Who am I, Lord, that all the women of earth will bless me?" (12.2).

The closing of Mary's visit to Elizabeth has both Luke and PJ mentioning a stay of six months and a return home (Luke 1:56; PJ 12.3), but PJ adds several other details: her ever-increasing belly, her fear of returning home, her desire to hide herself from the sons of Israel, and her age of sixteen (PJ 12.3). Holmes explains these additions by saying that PJ is interested elsewhere in Mary's pregnancy, such as both Joseph and Annas the scribe observing Mary's by now very obvious condition (13.1; 15.1).

More important to Holmes, however, is Mary's confusion in PJ—it's all a mystery to her—which leads him to seek to resolve the confusion by asking a question that refers back to the title of his essay: Why, indeed, is Mary to be blessed by all the women of the earth? The answer, he claims, is to be found in the nature of Mary's blessedness, which leads Holmes to do an extensive analysis of the topos of blessing in Luke and PJ.

Holmes approaches this question at first with a lexical analysis and then discusses the topos of blessing in PJ by rehearsing the entire story and interpreting it at the same time. He first charts the frequency of ten words in Luke and PJ that indicate praise and blessing and finds several significant differences in usage. For example, both gospels share some words in particular that deserve special treatment, including glory/glorify (δόξα/δοξάζειν), bless (εὐλογεῖν), and magnify (μεγαλύνειν). Luke, Holmes says, uses glory/glorify twenty-two times and does so in a theocentric way in which Jesus is the instrument that brings about glorifying God (with one exception, where the people glorify Jesus for his teaching [4:15]). Protevangelium of James's usage—six times but at the same rate as Luke since PJ is only one-fourth the length of Luke—is also theocentric, but now Mary is the instrument that prompts glorifying God, such as Mary's parents glorifying God because she did not turn back after arriving at the temple (8.1). Holmes highlights one other usage. In PJ 24.1 the priests are waiting to greet Zechariah in order to glorify God, but of course the priests will continue to wait since Zechariah has been murdered. Holmes notes that the priests are in effect powerless to activate divine benefits. This powerlessness confirms the changing role of the temple in PJ in that benefits occur in proximity to Mary, not to the temple.

Magnifying and especially blessing are more frequent in PJ and reflect the gospel's priestly rhetorolect. Blessing (εὐλογία/εὐλογεῖν) occurs seventeen times in PJ—at more than seven times Luke's rate—and so receives extensive treatment. The first occurrences of blessings concern Anna and, Holmes perceptively notes, allude to the first blessings in the LXX: "And God blessed [ηὐλόγησεν] them, saying 'Increase and multiply'" (Gen 1:22, 28). In other words, blessing is tied to producing offspring, as is clear when Anna, while lamenting her childlessness in her garden, prays: "God of my Fathers, bless [εὐλόγησον] me and hear my prayer, just as you blessed [εὐλόγησας] the womb of Sarah and gave her a son, Isaac" (2.4). Later, she is informed that her prayers have been answered, and when Joachim returns from his supplications in the desert, Anna exclaims: "Now I know that the Lord God has blessed [εὐλόγησεν] me greatly. This widow is no longer a widow and I, once childless, am now pregnant" (4.4).

Blessings continue but now in regard to Mary. Joachim celebrates Mary's first birthday with a feast that includes the chief priests and priests. When Joachim presents her to the priests, they bless (ηὐλόγησαν) her: "God of our fathers, bless [εὐλόγησον] this child and give her a name which will be on the lips of future generations forever" (6.2), and when he shows her to the chief priests, they also bless her: "Most high God, watch over this child and bless [εὐλόγησον] her with the ultimate blessing, one which cannot be surpassed" (6.2).

Holmes notes that these blessings continue the priestly rhetorolect of PJ. He also says that the blessings may be related to Anna's earlier actions: her turning Mary's bedroom into a holy precinct (ἁγίασμα) and giving her undefiled daughters of the Hebrews to amuse her (6.1). This connection allows Holmes to suggest that Mary is depicted as a sacred vessel or sacred space and the priests as passing on a priestly function to her. But this connection is not convincing. Anna's actions in the light of her vow to give her offspring to God (cf. 4.1) are thus preparatory to Mary's eventual service in the temple. The feast is thus a new event in Mary's life and has more to do with her surviving her first year as well as allowing Anna to get vindication from her earlier humiliation: "Who will announce to the sons of Reubel that Anna has a child at her breast?" (6.3).

Holmes also has an intriguing suggestion about the priests' blessing that asks for Mary's name to last for all generations. He relates this blessing to a similar blessing made to Abraham in which God says: "I will make you into a great nation, I will bless [εὐλογήσω] you, I will magnify your name [μεγαλύνω τὸ ὄνομά σου], and you will be blessed [ἔσῃ εὐλογητός]" (Gen 12:2). Holmes notes that key terms in this blessing appear in Mary's blessings—"name" here and 7.2; "magnify" in 7.2; and "name," "magnify," and "be blessed" in 12.1. In other words, just as Abraham activates divine benefits as a father, so Mary will do as a mother. The suggestion is worth consideration, but the point of Abraham's blessing was to be the father or better the ancestor of innumerable offspring, whereas Mary is to be the mother of only one, the son of God.

Holmes also comments on the second or high priests' blessing and specifically on the troublesome combination of phrases "the ultimate blessing" (ἐσχάτη εὐλογία) and "one that cannot be surpassed" (ἥτις διαδοχὴν οὐκ ἔχει). He correctly understands that the phrases should be understood together, emphasizing, as he puts it, "the utter singularity of the blessing spoken upon Mary. It is the highest 'rank' of those blessings that precede it, and there will be no equivalent blessing in the future" (p. 92). Holmes looks to the Old and New Testaments for parallels to this language and comes up empty. But what we have here is encomiastic language learned during progymnasmatic training. For example, in one of Libanius's sample encomia he says of Alexander the Great: "Alexander, king of Macedonia, was greatly admired and filled both continents with his accomplishments and so far surpassed both his predecessors and his successors that he has never yielded first place."[8] I will discuss later the importance of the encomium for PJ, but for now I would suggest "no *greater* blessing in the future," not "equivalent blessing," suggested to Holmes perhaps by Ehrman and Pleše's rendering "equal to none."

The next blessing of Mary occurs when she is taken to the temple at age three. Anna had vowed to give her child to God, and Joachim and Anna make good on that vow (7.1–2). On arrival Mary is welcomed by a priest, who kisses her and blesses her: "The Lord God has exalted your name among all generations. In you the Lord will disclose his redemption to the people of Israel during the last days" (7.2). Once again, as Holmes observes, the blessing is again said by a priest, and it stresses Mary's name and all generations, but there are new features: the blessing takes place in the temple, the priest kisses her and adds a future orientation in which Mary will play a role in the redemption of Israel during the last days. In addition, the language of the sentence preceding the blessing parallels that of Simeon, whose mention of salvation (equivalent to redemption) connects Jesus (who was in Simeon's arms at the time) to Mary (Luke 2:28). Holmes then argues that the last days refer to the end of Mary's pregnancy, an interpretation that, he says, receives confirmation at the time of the birth of Jesus when the midwife says: "Salvation has been born to Israel" (19.2). This interpretation, however, makes sense to the reader but not to the priest, a three-year-old girl, and the others present (7.2–3). At any rate, Holmes astutely notes that Mary's dancing at the altar, being fed by angels, and being loved by all (7.2–8.1) represent the high point of her childhood.

Mary stays in the temple until she reaches maturity at age twelve, when her fortunes begin to change (8.2). The priests are at a loss about what to do with her and eventually with divine advice remove her from

8. See Ronald F. Hock and Edward N. O'Neil, *The Chreia in Ancient Rhetoric*, 3 vols. (Atlanta: Society of Biblical Literature, 1986–2012), 2:141.

the temple and hand her over to a guardian, the widower Joseph (8.2–9.2). Joseph soon leaves her—"abandoned" is too strong a rendering of καταλείπειν since Joseph trusts to the Lord to protect her (9.3). While alone Mary is soon summoned with other virgins to spin thread for the temple curtain (10.1–2), a role Holmes regards as a demotion since she is just one of many virgins given this task and so becomes indistinguishable from them. But it is not clear that her fortunes really change. She leaves the temple with divine approval, Joseph's absence protects her from innuendo, and spinning thread ensures that while in Joseph's house she is engaged in virtuous work. Her virtue is further indicated when she hears a voice while getting water and then dashes back home and resumes her spinning (11.1).

It is in this virtuous posture of a Mary who is as pure as ever that the annunciation takes place. Gabriel's message is shorter but similar to Luke's (PJ 11.2; cf. Luke 1:30–33), but Mary's response, Holmes says, differs considerably from Luke's. In the latter Mary is concerned how she can conceive when she has not had sex with any man (Luke 1:34), but in PJ Mary says, "Will I give birth the way women usually do?" (11.2). In other words, Mary is now concerned with the way in which she will become a mother. Gabriel then says that she is to name him Jesus, for he will save his people from their sins (11.3), a message taken from Joseph's dream in Matthew's account (Matt 1:21) and a message, Holmes astutely adds, that underscores Mary's instrumentality in salvation mentioned in the priest's blessing in the temple (7.2). This Matthean tradition also identifies Mary's ultimate blessing as being chosen to be the mother of the son of the Most High.

Mary's final blessing occurs when she finishes her spinning and takes her threads to a priest, presumably the same priest, Holmes suggests, who had blessed her when she was taken to the temple at age three (cf. 6.2), a blessing that thus forms an *inclusio* with the earlier priestly ones. In any case, the priest accepts her threads and then blesses (εὐλόγησεν) her: "Mary, the Lord God has magnified your name [ἐμεγάλυνεν τὸ ὄνομά σου] and so you will be blessed [ἔσῃ εὐλογημένη] by all the generations of the earth" (12.1). Holmes sees in this blessing narrative irony. The priest blessed her for completing her work of spinning thread, but the reader, knowing about the annunciation, knows that she will be blessed by all because of her coming labor in giving birth. Holmes adds that the clause "you will be blessed" also echoes the promise to Abraham in Gen 12:2 (ἔσῃ εὐλογητός).

This selective if detailed summary of Holmes's essay should underscore how thoroughly and perceptively he has read PJ. He has correctly noted the change from Luke's prophetic rhetorolect in Luke 1–2 to PJ's priestly discourse in the comparable chapters. He rightly focuses on the visit of Mary to Elizabeth's house and senses an important issue about the presentation of Mary in this incident. This issue is encapsulated in Mary's question "Who am I to be blessed?" And the analysis of the topos of blessing to answer this question results in her identity and being blessed by God not only because of Mary's purity but also because of her role as the mother of the Son of God, the ultimate blessing indeed.

3.2. Mary as Sacred Vessel

The second essay to deal with PJ is "Temple Virgin and Virgin Temple: Mary's Body as Sacred Space in the Protevangelium of James" by Meredith Elliott Hollman (pp. 103–28 above). This essay maintains the quality of the preceding one in that we have the same thoroughness, detail, and consequent insight here as well. Hollman opens her essay with several orienting assumptions that will guide the subsequent analysis of her focal passage, Mary's dedication at the temple (7.1–8.1). Her first assumption is correct: the purpose of PJ is to answer the questions of who Mary was and why she of all the young women in Israel was selected by God to be mother of the Son of God.

Her second assumption is that Mary is obviously the central character of PJ and accordingly divides the story using the opening-middle-closing texture of analysis with Mary in the title of each section: Mary's Early Life (1.1–8.1), Mary's Trials as the "Virgin of the Lord" (8.2–16.3), and Mary as Virgin Mother (17.1–24.4). This division makes sense. There is, for example, a certain symmetry in that each section has roughly the same number of chapters and the sections deal with these stages of Mary's life. But that is not all there is to PJ in terms of content, and that extra content has to do with the literary form of PJ. To speak first of content: the opening, which is about Mary's early life, does not narrate her birth until 5.2, and even her conception is not narrated until 4.1. Likewise, the closing, which is about Mary as Virgin Mother, does not include the annunciation of Gabriel, which is in the middle section (11.2), and while the closing does narrate the virgin birth, Mary drops out of the narrative at 22.1. In other words, her absence at either end means that other characters play important, if not central, roles in the story—Joachim and Anna at the beginning and

Elizabeth and Zechariah at the end. Their roles and stories have an important function in the form of PJ. As I have argued previously, the form of PJ is that of an encomium, a familiar form that was learned during the study of progymnasmata.[9]

Hollman does recognize that "Protevangelium of James may even be described as an encomium of Mary" and cites some of its parts in a footnote. She does not, however, build on that recognition, but it may be of help here. The structure of an encomium of a person (πρόσωπον) contains these sections: ethnicity, upbringing and skills, deeds, comparison, and epilogue. Two of these sections are relevant here. The ethnicity section includes nationality, homeland, ancestors, and parents, whereas the comparison section compares the subject of the encomium with others of equal or greater virtue. Accordingly, the reason why Mary does not appear from the very beginning is because an encomium of her would appropriately include narratives about her parents, Joachim and Anna (chs. 1–5), as well as references to her ancestors, Abraham, Sarah, and Isaac (1.3; 2.4) and to her homeland of Israel (1.1–3). Similarly, a comparison with other virtuous persons would also appear at the end of an encomium, and here, of course, we have a comparison of the courageous actions of Elizabeth and Zechariah to protect John's life (chs. 23–24).

To be sure, this explanation of the narratives about Joachim and Anna at the beginning and about Elizabeth and Zechariah at the end does not really affect Hollman's central analysis of Mary's dedication at the temple, but the structure of an encomium does get at the rhetology of PJ, as I will explain at the end. That Mary of all young women in Israel was justifiably chosen by God to bear his son gains conviction as the author of PJ moves through the sections and contents of an encomium.

The third assumption is also correct when Hollman says that "Protevangelium of James … pushes the topos of virginity further" than Luke. The latter uses virgin (παρθένος) three times and PJ nine times, but what is more, while Luke uses the word in its usual sense and is concerned only

9. See my *Infancy Gospels*, 15–20. Admittedly, the earlier view that PJ is an apology for Mary against attacks from Jews and others continues in the analysis of Erhman and Pleše. They contend that I view PJ as "driven exclusively by biographical concerns" (see *Apocryphal Gospels*, 34). But I accept occasional apologetic concerns, as reflected, for example, in the priest's exoneration of Joseph and Mary after the water test (16.1–3). In contrast, encomiastic content and structure appear throughout the gospel and make it an encomium of Mary (see *Infancy Gospels*, 15–16).

with Mary's conception, PJ goes beyond Luke by asserting Mary's virginity even after birth, which is explicit in the midwife's confession to Salome: "A virgin has given birth" (19.3).

The last assumption or perhaps a theme that is introduced here is the characterization of Mary as being passive and silent, so much so that Mary functions like a sacred vessel, pure to be sure, but also empty, ready to receive and impart divine blessing. I will have occasion to challenge this characterization below, but for now I simply say that PJ is an encomium of a person (πρόσωπον), not of an object (πρᾶγμα), since PJ follows the structure of an encomium of a person.

The center of Hollman's essay is an analysis of the dedication of Mary at the temple (7.1–8.1), which she divides up in opening-middle-closing fashion. The emphasis of the analysis is an investigation of the background storyline that informs the foreground narrative about Mary. Thus Joachim and Anna's taking Mary to the temple recalls the story of Hannah and Samuel (1 Sam 1:21–2:11) and, more generally, the topos of an exceptional child dedicated to God from birth.

The similarities, she notes, are many. Both children are miraculously conceived, both are promised to serve God at the temple, both sets of parents wait until their child is old enough to leave home, both discuss when that time has come, and so forth. But there are also some differences. Both Joachim and Anna care for Mary, while Samuel is the prime responsibility of Hannah. This difference is nicely apparent, as Hollman quotes, using italics, Hannah's husband saying "may the Lord establish the word of *your* mouth" (1 Sam 1:23), whereas Joachim talks of the need "to fulfill the promise *we* made" (PJ 7.1). Anna is far more obsessive in preserving Mary's purity, and once at the temple Mary presumably never sees her parents again, whereas Hannah visits Samuel yearly (1 Sam 2:19–20). The account in 1 Samuel ends with Samuel ministering, whereas Mary is being ministered to, cared for like a dove and fed from the hand of an angel (PJ 8.1). Finally, in 1 Samuel the focus is on the faith of Hannah, but in PJ it is on the purity of Mary so that she is an acceptable gift to God. In short, the story in 1 Samuel was a resource text for PJ but not a source text suggesting literary dependence with specific verbal correspondences.

So far so good, but Hollman follows up this comparison with a further difference between Samuel and Mary. Samuel immediately begins assisting the priest Eli, a few years later he receives the word of the Lord, and eventually he becomes a leader in Israel, suggesting a person who was active and vocal. In contrast, Hollman asserts, Mary is remarkably passive and silent. The word "passive" is repeated several times in the following analysis to describe Mary: Anna and the undefiled daughters of Israel are responsible for her purity (6.1), Joachim and Anna decide when she is taken to the temple (7.1–2), the priests decide that she should be handed over to Joseph (9.1–3), and Joseph does not ask Mary about how she should be enrolled in Bethlehem (17.1).

Mary's silence is also emphasized. She is silent throughout chapters 6–10 and speaks only eight times in chapters 11–17 and then only briefly. In chapter 11, when she is on her own in Joseph's house and encounters Gabriel, she speaks for the first time, responding to the announcement that she will conceive with a question (11.2) and responding again to Gabriel's further information with a statement of acquiescence (11.3). Then at Elizabeth's house she responds to Elizabeth's and the unborn John's blessings and asks why she should be so blessed (12.2). Because of her pregnancy, Mary has to defend her virtue to Joseph (13.3) and to the high priest (15.3). She speaks for the last times en route to Bethlehem, once when she must explain to Joseph why she alternately laughs and laments (17.2) and again when she asks to be taken down from the donkey in order to give birth (17.3).

Hollman's emphasis on Mary's passivity and silence leads her to characterize her with the metaphor of sacred vessel. It also allows her to reanalyze Mary's dedication at the temple in terms of a second topos, the topos of the relocation of sacred space and specifically in terms of the relocation of the ark of the covenant. The reason for doing so is that the structure of the dedication story, she says, is similar to stories of the three major movements of the ark before it was taken by Nebuchadnezzar. Five Old Testament passages treat these movements (Exod 39–40; 1 Chr 15–16 and 2 Sam 6; 2 Chr 5–7 and 3 Kgdms 8), and Hollman detects a common pattern in narrating the movement and organizes this pattern according to opening-middle-closing. She then argues that the story of dedicating Mary, now a sacred vessel, can be organized according to the pattern of moving the ark. There are some surprising commonalities in the two patterns, in particular the closing of the middle section, which has the glory of God descending on the ark's new home and the grace of God pouring down on Mary in the closing of the middle section of PJ.

But the analysis falls short of conviction. For one thing the pattern has a general logic to it quite apart from the Old Testament precedents: preparing to move something, moving it, and setting it up in a new location, and if the object is religious, there would be various processions and rituals and signs of divine approval. In addition, the dedication of Mary in the temple does not follow the pattern as closely as Hollman presents it. In the opening section there are no preparations, no assembly, no start of the procession. In the middle the comparison is closer since Mary arrives in a procession with her parents and the undefiled daughters of the Hebrews whose torches add a ritualistic touch. Mary also receives divine grace, and the entire house of Israel rejoices in her, but in the closing there is no blessing, as that occurs in the middle, and there is no mention of the return of the procession of the undefiled daughters. Joachim and Anna do rejoice and praise God, but they too are forgotten before reaching home as attention reverts to Mary and her care in the temple.

Even if Hollman's comparison of the movements of the ark and Mary is not as close as her tables suggest, there are some aspects of this pattern that show up later, as in Salome's burning hand as punishment for doubting that a virgin has given birth (20.1) being modeled on Uzzah's punishment during David's moving the ark (2 Sam 6:6–7). But the thrust of the argument is to characterize Mary as an object being moved—here to the temple, then to Joseph's house, then toward Bethlehem. Indeed, Hollman concludes that Mary's "body becomes the 'tabernacle' on which the grace of God comes to rest" (p. 128).

This presentation of Mary as a temple, Hollman adds, implies a critique of the actual temple. To be sure, PJ was written long after the destruction of the temple, even if "James" never mentions this fact. But "James" could not mention the destruction because he was ostensibly writing shortly after the death of Herod (25.1). Still, Hollman contends, PJ portends the temple's destruction as seen in Zechariah's blood from his murder that has been turned to stone (23.3; 24.3). And yet the story does not end with the priests in disarray, their robes torn from top to bottom, and the people grieving for Zechariah, for Simeon is soon selected by lot to replace Zechariah, and the temple would then have continued to function as before (24.4).

It seems that for all the careful, perceptive, and insightful reading of PJ in the light of Old Testament background narratives, there is a basic misreading of Mary's overall role in the story as passive and silent and hence rather more like an object, a sacred object, and finally as a tabernacle or temple in competition with the actual temple in providing divine benefits. The passivity and silence, however, pertain more to the earliest years of her life than later. We do not expect children to be their own agents even at age three, when Mary goes to the temple. But as the years pass she becomes more active and vocal. The years from three to twelve are not narrated, but given her role at age twelve to help in the spinning of thread for the temple curtain, we can assume that during those years she had learned the adult skill of carding wool and spinning it into thread. In any case, when assigned this task she could do it. She then goes about this task responsibly, completes her part of the spinning, and gives her threads to the priest (12.1). While spinning thread she goes out for water, and when she hears a male voice, she acts in such a way as to avoid compromising her virtue by running back home and resuming her spinning (11.1). She acts to avoid rumors once when she returns from Elizabeth's by hiding herself from the sons of Israel (12.3). Later, when it is time to give birth, she does so without the aid of a midwife (19.2), and soon after she acts courageously to protect her infant son Jesus from Herod by hiding him in a manger (22.2).

Besides agency Mary also becomes more vocal. Again, early on we expect her to be silent, obeying her mother and father's decisions without objection (6.1; 7.2) and perhaps also the priests when they seek a guardian for her (8.2; 9.1). But once on her own she speaks clearly and forcefully. She asks a natural question about how she could give birth without knowing a man (11.2) and then complies piously with Gabriel's instructions: "May it happen to me as you have said" (11.3). Later, when first Joseph and then the priests learn that she is pregnant and assume the worst, Mary speaks up and defiantly defends her innocence (13.3; 15.3).

In short, because of the vow Anna made to give her child to the Lord, she took special precautions to ensure Mary's purity until her dedication at the temple. Her purity is assured while in the temple, but once out of the temple Mary makes every effort to protect her purity so that she can be the one to give birth to the Son of God and even after his birth to act with courage to protect the life of her infant son. Accordingly, Mary becomes in PJ the subject of an encomium about a praiseworthy πρόσωπον.

3.3. Protevangelium of James and Luke's Prophetic Hymns

The third and final essay on PJ once again maintains the high quality of the others and even adds a dash of detection. The essay is "From Prophetic Hymns to Death at the Altar: Luke 1–2 and Protevangelium of James" by Michael K. W. Suh and Vernon K. Robbins (pp. 129–77 above). And as in the previous essays the authors do a comparative exegesis but with a twist, for the four hymns in Luke 1–2—the Magnificat (1:46–56), the Benedictus

(1:67–79), the Gloria (2:14), and the Nunc Dimittis (2:28–32)—have no comparable passages in PJ, and here is where the detection comes in. To be sure, the hymns are not taken over whole in PJ, but that does not mean that the author of PJ did not use them in some way. Luke 1–2 is PJ's resource text, and since he was doing more than supplementing the Lukan story, it is possible that portions of the hymns as well as their contexts are used in the course of PJ's narrative in order to serve his own agenda.

To test this possibility the authors first review the four hymns. They predict how the rest of Luke will unfold in terms of God's past and future actions for his people so that we are dealing with a prophetic rhetorolect. Robbins has argued in his earlier essays that there is also a priestly rhetorolect operative in Luke 1–2, but that it is subsumed under the prophetic. The authors point out that the author of PJ might have picked up on the minor key of priestly rhetorolect and emphasized it in his own narrative, as we have seen in the two previous essays.

In any case, these four hymns, categorized more precisely as declarative psalms of praise, have a structure of (1) introductory praise, (2) motive clause(s) as the basis for the praise, and (3) amplification to round out the hymns. In addition, they fit in with a storyline of promise, fulfillment, and praise (i.e., the hymns) in Luke 1–2. But the fit is not always perfect since some of the hymns fit awkwardly in their immediate setting, an awkwardness that might have prompted the author of PJ to relocate them, and relocate them, as we will see, he did.

Each hymn receives a short analysis of its context and content. For example, the Magnificat is one hymn that interrupts the flow as some scholars see the verse before the Magnificat (1:45) connecting nicely to the verse after it (1:56), and there is the additional problem of who spoke the Magnificat, Mary or Elizabeth. The manuscripts favor Mary, but the narrative itself favors Elizabeth. A thorough discussion comes down in favor of Mary. The content of the hymn is prophetic with its story of God's people from Abraham's promise all the way forward to the present and future. The authors also point out that in the initial verses (1:46–49) Mary is prominent, but in the following ones she recedes in favor of God's actions toward his people (1:50–55).

The second hymn, the Benedictus, is also prophetic as it concerns Zechariah who, though a priest, nevertheless is filled with the Holy Spirit and speaks as a prophet (ἐπροφήτευσεν; 1:67). The hymn regards his son John as a prophet of the Most High who will prepare the way for the Lord (1:76). The authors also note that when Mary initially reacts with incredulity to

Gabriel's message (1:29), she is blessed by Elizabeth (1:42), but when Zechariah reacts similarly (1:18), he is cursed (1:20).

The third and briefest hymn, the Gloria, is only one verse (2:14), is spoken by angels, and continues the prophetic rhetorolect. The context speaks of an angel telling shepherds of the birth of a savior, the Davidic Messiah, which is the ultimate of prophetic fulfillment (2:11). Then follows an angelic announcement to the shepherds with the familiar "Glory to God in the highest" and the promise of peace (2:14).

The fourth hymn, the Nunc Dimittis, is by Simeon and contains both priestly and prophetic rhetorolect. The context refers to Jesus's parents fulfilling the law as well as to the temple setting (2:27) and thus indicates a priestly discourse, but Simeon's waiting for the consolation of Israel (2:25) and his being guided by the Holy Spirit to go to the temple (2:27) introduce prophetic discourse, as do the words of the hymn itself, such as his speaking of salvation and repeating the word "Israel" (2:30, 32).

The authors round out their discussion by identifying four similarities in the Lukan hymns that reflect a prophetic rhetorolect: they have the Holy Spirit move the characters into action; they have as the first space of political discourse a geopolitical kingdom; they contain the word group σωτηρ-; and they hearken back to Israel's Scriptures.

The authors now turn to PJ and briefly summarize its priestly rhetorolect as seen in the prominent role of the temple, the ritual practices of sacrifice and purity concerns, the dedication of Mary to the temple, and the priestly blessings of Mary. How then did the author of PJ read the Lukan hymns through the lens of a priestly rhetorolect? The hymns are omitted, to be sure, but why were they, and were even parts of them used? Now the detection of traces of these hymns in PJ begins.

The Magnificat (Luke 1:46–56). Toward the end of Mary's visit to Elizabeth (Luke 1:36–56) Mary responds to Elizabeth's blessings (1:42–44) with the Magnificat (1:46–55). In contrast, in PJ's telling of the visit (PJ 12.1–3) Mary responds to the blessings by forgetting the mysteries told her by Gabriel and then asking a question about why she should be blessed (12.2). It looks as if the omission is complete. Perhaps not. The authors contend that PJ includes the first word of the Magnificat: "I magnify" (μεγαλύνω; Luke 1:46) and does so precisely before Mary visits Elizabeth, that is, in the priest's blessing of her when she has turned in her spinning and when the priest says: "Mary, the Lord God has magnified [ἐμεγάλυνεν] your name" (12.1). What is more, the word becomes a repetitive texture in PJ as it is used three other times (5.2; 7.2; and 19.2). Apparently, the remainder of the Magnificat was too much for PJ's priestly agenda, and so he replaced it with the word "mysteries" (μυστήρια; 12.2), itself rather ritualistic and so priestly. In other words, at least a small, very small, portion of the Magnificat is taken up in PJ, but also repeated.

The Benedictus (Luke 1:67–79). This hymn, which is sung by Zechariah at the circumcision and naming of John (Luke 1:66–79), has no obvious place in PJ since the story of John's conception and birth is replaced by that of Mary. Its omission would therefore make sense. Nevertheless, Zechariah appears at the end of PJ in the context of his efforts to hide the whereabouts of his infant son from Herod's agents (23.1–3). Might fragments of this hymn be taken up here? The authors think so and proceed in four steps. First, Zechariah's prophetic role in Luke—being filled with the Holy Spirit and prophesying (Luke 1:67)—is reconfigured into a priestly one as he is introduced as a minister of God attending to his temple (PJ 23.1). Second, when Herod's agents report back that Zechariah did not answer their question, Herod responds by asking "Is his son going to rule over Israel?" (23.2). The authors contend that the author of PJ took Herod's concern about John becoming a ruler from the Benedictus, where Zechariah speaks of raising up a savior in the house of David (Luke 1:69). Third, Zechariah's prophetic hope that the power of God would save his people from their enemies (1:71) is turned into priestly discourse with Zechariah's talk of martyrdom and innocent blood being shed in the temple (PJ 23.3). Fourth, the authors become rather subtle when claiming that the prophetic dawn (ἀνατολή) of a new eschatological era in the Benedictus (Luke 1:78) is hinted at in Zechariah's being murdered around dawn (περὶ τὸ διάφαυμα; 23.3).

This argument is certainly intriguing, and there is no doubt that the prophetic Zechariah in Luke has become a priestly figure and even moves into the center of the latter part of the story in PJ, but there is precious little linguistic connection between the two passages, so that Herod's concern about a political rival could easily have come from Matt 2:16, and even where there are synonyms, such as references to dawn in both, it should be noted that there is a textual problem at this point in PJ. Some manuscripts do not read διάφαυμα, but διάφραγμα ("partition"), which, even if secondary, suggests that some scribe connected the murder more to location, in the light of Matt 23:35, than to the time of day in the Benedictus.

The Gloria (Luke 2:14). This briefest of hymns (Luke 2:14) is spoken to the shepherds in the field at the time of the birth of Jesus (2:8–15), and since this episode does not appear in PJ, there is no place for this hymn either. But not so fast. The authors look to the story in PJ that follows the murder of Zechariah (24.1–4). It is here that the priests learn of Zechariah's death, and it is here that the authors see the Gloria being used. The authors point to lexical parallels. In Luke an angel appears to the shepherds and the glory of the Lord (δόξα κυρίου) shown around them so that they became afraid (ἐφοβήθησαν; 2:9). Likewise, after Zechariah's death the priests wait around the temple to greet Zechariah and glorify the most high God (δοξάσαι τὸν ὕψιστον θεόν), and when Zechariah does not show up, they too became afraid (ἐφοβήθησαν; 24.1–2). In other words, the topos of glorification and fear experienced by the shepherds has been relocated to the priests at the temple as they await Zechariah. Indeed, the topos of glorification is a repetitive texture and part of a priestly mode of discourse (see also 6.3; 14.2; 16.3; and 25.1). Another lexical parallel is the use of τὸ γέγονος, or "what has occurred." In Luke the shepherds head into Bethlehem to see "this thing that has occurred" (τὸ ῥῆμα τοῦτο τὸ γέγονος; 2:15), whereas in PJ the priests when they venture to the murder scene see "what has occurred" (τὸ γέγονος; 24.3). Finally, the authors contrast the endings of these two accounts: the shepherds find a baby lying in a manger (Luke 2:16), whereas the priests find only the blood of Zechariah and the walls of the temple crying out (PJ 24.3), which recalls Amos 8:3 and so the end of prophecy, Israel, and the temple. Quite a contrast: good news in Luke versus doom in PJ.

Nunc Dimittis (Luke 2:28–32). The last of the four hymns in Luke is in the temple and is sung by a man named Simeon. He had been looking for the consolation of Israel and was assured by the Holy Spirit that he would not die before seeing the Messiah (2:25–26). When the infant Jesus is taken there in accordance with the purification laws of Moses, the Spirit guides Simeon to the temple, where he meets Joseph and Mary and takes Jesus into his arms (2:27–28) and then praises God with a prophetic hymn (2:29–32). Protevangelium of James has no equivalent scene, but Simeon does appear at the end of PJ when the priests, after mourning the death of Zechariah, choose his replacement by lot, which falls to Simeon, who now becomes high priest (24.3). In short, not only does Simeon have a new place in the story, but the prophet Simeon of Luke has also been reconfigured as a priest in PJ, and so the hymn is no longer appropriate. The character is used, if reconfigured, but the Nunc Dimittis is omitted.

After reviewing the authors' careful detective work in this essay it becomes clear that the usual view, that the author of PJ omitted the four hymns of Luke 1–2, is overstated. Instead, the author used the contexts and contents of the hymns but only if they could be reconfigured to conform to his priestly agenda. Especially noteworthy is that three of the hymns from the beginning chapters of Luke are used in the last chapters of PJ—two in relation to Zechariah and one in relation to Simeon. The authors conclude by paying special attention to Zechariah, who is turned into a high priest in PJ and who pays for protecting his son with his life. The authors go on to allege a correspondence between the deaths of Zechariah and Jesus. In fact, the correspondence is even more striking since not only is Zechariah murdered but also his body is not found (24.3). In effect, "the high priest Zechariah, rather than his son John, is the forerunner of Jesus. Zechariah … 'prepares the way of the Lord' (cf. Luke 1:76)" (p. 174).

This correspondence, however, fails to convince because it runs afoul of the encomiastic form of PJ. As stated earlier, the last major part of the encomium of a person is a comparison (σύγκρισις) in which the subject of the encomium is compared to others of equal or greater virtue. In other words, Zechariah's actions are designed to be compared to those of Mary, not of Jesus. Zechariah's courage in protecting his son (and Elizabeth's fleeing with John to escape the soldiers out to kill him [22.3]) highlight and reaffirm the virtues of Mary—her efforts to maintain her purity and her courage in protecting the infant Jesus.

4. Conclusion

At the outset I said that I welcomed the opportunity that these essays provided after some years to reengage in the interpretation of this infancy gospel, and that opportunity has been more than rewarded, as these essays have given me new and more profound understandings of both Luke 1–2 and PJ, thanks to the care, thoroughness, and insights contained in all five of the essays reviewed here. I especially appreciated the conceptual framework of rhetorolects in understanding the development of Christian discourse, and I am impressed with the insights that a comparative exegesis can provide both at the level of shifts in rhetorolect from Luke to PJ and in the countless individual insights that appear on every page and so enhance our appreciation of PJ's narrative.

I have also learned that a rhetorolect has both a rhetography and a rhetology. Throughout these essays the rhetography of Luke and PJ receives extensive analysis, but rhetology has been largely ignored even though it is also important for understanding what makes a narrative convincing. At several points in my comments I have emphasized that PJ is an encomium of Mary. Now I want to emphasize that this literary form from the broader Hellenistic culture is what provides PJ's rhetology. The fame and piety of Mary's ancestors and parents, the divine intervention in her conception, her careful upbringing at home and in the temple, her adult skill of spinning thread, her virtues of purity and courage, and the comparison of her virtues with those of Elizabeth and Zechariah—all these features of Mary's life in PJ derive from the structural conventions of composing an encomium. By following these conventions the author of PJ has not only praised Mary but also done so compellingly in the minds of his first readers.

Response: The Gospel of John and the Acts of John

Susan E. Hylen

The final two essays of this volume continue the analysis of early Christian texts using sociorhetorical criticism. These authors focus on the Acts of John (AJohn), a second-century Greek text that survives in fragments. This work recounts the miracles and teachings attributed to the apostle John, including John's experiences of Jesus. Jonathan Potter focuses on AJohn 87–105, and in particular on the transfiguration of Jesus in AJohn 90–91.[1] He compares AJohn with Luke's transfiguration story (Luke 9:28–36), drawing attention to its similarities while also bringing out the distinctive perspective of AJohn. Thomas Jared Farmer's essay analyzes AJohn 98–101 and draws on Johannine discourse and Platonic thought to shed light on this essential passage of AJohn.[2] Taken together, the two essays are a welcome addition to scholarship on the Acts of John, and they especially illuminate important features of AJohn 87–105, a segment in which much of the distinctive character of the work becomes visible.

Each of these essays raises the difficult question of the relationship between John's Gospel (GJohn) and the Acts of John. The relationship of AJohn to GJohn is suggested through the title and main character, but it is by no means straightforward. Some scholars have suggested that AJohn is anti-Johannine in its perspective.[3] The essays by Potter and Farmer bring to light a number of different ways GJohn and AJohn intersect, and this

1. Jonathan M. Potter, "Naked Divinity: The Transfiguration Transformed in the Acts of John," pp. 181–222 above.

2. Thomas Jared Farmer, "Christ as Cosmic Priest: A Sociorhetorical Examination of the Crucifixion Scenes in the Gospel of John and Acts of John," pp. 223–50 above.

3. See, e.g., Hans-Josef Klauck, *The Apocryphal Acts of the Apostles: An Introduction*, trans. Brian McNeil (Waco, TX: Baylor University Press, 2008), 17, 36; Charles E. Hill, *The Johannine Corpus in the Early Church* (Oxford: Oxford University Press, 2004), 263.

response tries to further the conversation by drawing out the nuances of their arguments. I will attend to each author's approach to this problem, returning also to the essay by Meredith Hollman, who likewise notes Johannine imagery in the Protevangelium of James.[4]

1. The "Testimonies" of the Acts of John

Jonathan Potter's analysis of the Acts of John is an insightful example of sociorhetorical criticism. He sheds light on an important segment of this text, the transfiguration of Jesus in AJohn 90–91. His careful analysis of Luke aids his discussion about the relationship of AJohn to other sources.

Potter begins with an exploration of AJohn 87–105, a section he refers to as "the Testimonies." He accepts the idea that AJohn 88b–93 is a series of twelve testimonies, but he also argues that the larger section of the text should be read alongside the Johannine idea of "testimony," bearing witness to Christ's glory and his divine nature. Although Potter's primary focus is on AJohn 88b–93 and on 90–91 in particular, his reading situates this section within its literary context in a way that makes sense of the author's larger aims.

Potter's work is a good example of the usefulness of Vernon Robbins's method of studying a passage's opening-middle-closing texture. Potter divides AJohn 87–105 into three initial sections, then subdivides each portion again. He divides the Twelve Testimonies once more, yielding a central section, AJohn 90–91, which Potter understands as central to the message of the text. This section echoes Synoptic stories of Jesus's transfiguration, but the author has significantly reworked the material to convey his message. Potter's approach helps him to unpack that message for the reader in a fruitful way.

The main idea that becomes clear in Potter's reading is that the transfiguration known from the gospels is not a singular moment of Jesus's ministry in AJohn, but is instead its defining feature. In AJohn 87–105, Jesus is always transfiguring or changing shape. The opening and middle sections include multiple occasions in which John describes Jesus's changing form. At times, Jesus appears to two people, each of whom sees him in a different form (88, 89). In other moments, John narrates different ways

4. Meredith Elliott Hollman, "Temple Virgin and Virgin Temple: Mary's Body as Sacred Space in the Protevangelium of James," pp. 103–28 above.

Jesus has appeared (89, 90) or felt (89, 93) to him, and one instance in which Jesus seems to appear as two people conversing with one another (92). This polymorphous nature of Jesus is a central concern of AJohn and its Testimonies. As a whole, the Testimonies witness to Jesus's continual changes in appearance and physical state.

These changes underscore the idea that what is most essential about Jesus is his divine nature, which exceeds any single physical or human form. Potter also arrives at this conclusion through his discussion of opening-middle-closing texture, because the central moment of the Twelve Testimonies (90–91) is John's vision of Jesus's "naked divinity" (90b). John sees Jesus "naked and not at all like a man," a revelation of Jesus's essential divinity. By peeling back the layers of text in this way, Potter arrives at core features of the text that he persuasively shows to be central to the author's larger concerns. In this case, Potter's use of opening-middle-closing texture contributes something to the former division of the text into twelve testimonies, and it clarifies the subject of the passage.

Potter then turns to an analysis of Luke's transfiguration scene. His goal in the essay is to discuss the use of Luke in AJohn, but to do so Potter recognizes that he must present a compelling claim about Luke's own agenda or purpose. The inclusion of this material probably adds more to Potter's argument than is really necessary for the reader, but his thoroughness also leaves the reader with few questions.

Potter has two important conclusions about Luke's transfiguration. First, Luke's emphasis on the importance of prayer and on Jesus as one who prays is carried through the transfiguration scene. Unlike Mark, Luke specifies Jesus's purpose in going up on the mountain with three disciples: to pray (Luke 9:28). Furthermore, Potter underscores the effectiveness of prayer in Luke: "when Jesus prays, things happen" (p. 209). Jesus's prayer on the mountain is thus not incidental to the account but an integral part of the events that follow.

A second conclusion is that Luke tells the transfiguration story as a vision of Jesus's glory. Again, this is language that only Luke includes: "since they had stayed awake, they saw his glory" (9:32). Like the Old Testament mountaintop encounters of God's glory, Luke tells the story of the transfiguration as one in which the disciples see the glory of God in Jesus.

These conclusions are important as Potter turns back to AJohn and its use of Luke. Potter capably shows how AJohn also understands prayer as the context in which the transfiguration occurs. In this text, Jesus also takes three disciples "to the mountain where he used to pray" (90). Through his prior analysis, Potter establishes AJohn's reliance on Luke with this reference to prayer. However, Potter does not go on to elaborate reasons why AJohn might include Luke's prayerful Jesus. This is the only instance of Jesus's prayer in AJohn. And while John also prays (AJohn 43, 85–86), it does not seem an important theme of the work. Thus Potter raises an interesting question in identifying AJohn's use of Luke that is worthy of further study.

According to Potter, AJohn's transfiguration may also be understood as a vision of God's glory. The word "glory" frames the beginning of the section in which Jesus's forms become visible. John tells the others he will tell them things he has seen and heard, "that you may see the glory that surrounds him" (AJohn 88). Although the word "glory" does not appear in the transfiguration of AJohn 90, the light imagery and John's vision of Jesus's "back" suggest to Potter that AJohn is creatively reworking Luke's transfiguration account. It may help to clarify that the imagery of Jesus's "back" is not a detail Luke includes but echoes the Old Testament story of Moses' vision of God's glory. Moses is not allowed to look at God directly, only from behind (Exod 33:18–23). With the inclusion of this detail, AJohn shows awareness of the Exodus tradition as well as of Luke's transfiguration account. It incorporates important themes from both in its testimony to Jesus's changing form.

Potter's essay opens up some important questions for further research. Although he attends more closely to the Gospel of Luke, Potter makes a number of claims about the relationship of the Acts of John to the Gospel of John. I summarize his findings here before returning to the subject again at the end of this response.

First, Potter connects the idea in AJohn of Jesus's consistently changing nature to John's notion of Jesus's divinity being visible throughout the Gospel. As Potter notes, there is no transfiguration scene in GJohn, which is consistent with GJohn's understanding that Jesus's glory is present throughout his life. From the beginning, the narrator indicates, "we have seen his glory" (1:14). Jesus's glory is visible in his signs (2:11), and he frequently makes revelatory statements about himself. In the Farewell Discourse, he states that God both has glorified and will glorify him (13:31). From this and other details of GJohn, many scholars conclude with Potter that Jesus's divine nature is manifest throughout the Gospel, and not simply in a singular moment like the transfiguration. What is interesting is that GJohn and AJohn share a sense of Jesus's consistent divine nature, yet they represent that nature in very different ways, so that for AJohn,

Jesus's transfiguration is an essential scene and one that is reiterated in other experiences of Jesus.

Second, Potter connects the light imagery of AJohn's transfiguration to GJohn's image of Jesus as light (GJohn 1:4–5; 8:12; 9:5). Although he points out that Luke also has a good deal of light imagery in the transfiguration scene, the use of the word φῶς ("we saw in him such light"; AJohn 90.2–3) suggests a Johannine connection. This is perhaps strengthened by Potter's inference that in AJohn, Jesus's clothing does not shine (cf. Luke 9:29), but he emits light from himself. This idea that Jesus essentially is light, when glimpsed in his naked divinity, Potter connects to the Johannine metaphor of Jesus as light.

Third, Potter notes two additional linguistic connections to GJohn: the identification of John as a disciple Jesus loves (AJohn 90.7; cf. e.g., GJohn 13:23; 20:2) and the quotation of Jesus's words to Thomas in GJohn 20:27 (AJohn 90.16). In each case the language is so similar in vocabulary and usage that there seems to be a direct borrowing from GJohn. The first identifies John with the Beloved Disciple (as did much of Christian tradition) and carries forward the importance of Jesus's love as a defining characteristic. The second quote attributes to John an experience of disbelief that is similar to Thomas's. The allusion adds nuance to the kind of objection Jesus has to John in AJohn's transfiguration scene.

Just as Potter has given careful attention to Luke's transfiguration account, so also additional attention could enhance our understanding of the connection between GJohn and AJohn. Potter's capable work with Luke provides an example of how one might proceed with GJohn, although the difficulty with GJohn is that there is no single passage like the transfiguration that can become the focus of comparison. As Potter shows, a number of disparate elements of GJohn are present in AJohn, and they are employed for different ends.

2. Cross and Crucifixion in the Gospel of John and the Acts of John

Jared Farmer's analysis of the Acts of John includes a direct comparison with the Gospel of John. He examines the crucifixion scene of the Gospel (19:16–37) and the cross-language of AJohn 98–101. Like Potter, Farmer also approaches these texts using sociorhetorical interpretation. In particular, he examines opening-middle-closing texture, and he looks for evidence of priestly rhetorolect in both passages. What is most fruitful in the essay is Farmer's discussion of social and cultural textures in his use of Platonic categories to shed light on AJohn 98–101.

Farmer begins with an examination of GJohn 19:16–37. Although he organizes his analysis according to his division of the text into opening, middle, and closing textures, his insights are not directly tied to these divisions, as Potter's were. Instead, they come from other modes of analysis. Most of Farmer's insights about the opening texture come through comparison of GJohn with the Synoptic Gospels. He notes, for example, that GJohn has Jesus carry his own cross (GJohn 19:17; cf. Matt 27:32; Mark 15:21; Luke 23:26), that the men crucified with Jesus are not bandits (GJohn 19:18; cf. Matt 27:38; Mark 15:27; Luke 23:32), and that no one reviles Jesus on the cross (cf. Matt 27:39; Mark 15:29; Luke 23:35–39). Farmer rightly concludes that GJohn characterizes Jesus as master of his own death.

In two instances, Farmer finds evidence of priestly rhetorolect in GJohn. First, he relates Jesus's seamless tunic, for which the soldiers cast lots (19:24), to "priestly garments" (p. 229). The word "tunic" (χιτών) is also used in the LXX to describe priestly clothing (e.g., Exod 28:4, 39–40; Lev 6:10), yet it is also a general term for clothing. For example, the same word describes the clothing of Tamar (2 Sam 13:18) and the leaders of the Assyrian army (Jdt 14:19). In the New Testament, the word is used for the clothes of the high priest (Mark 14:63) but also of any believer (e.g., Matt 5:40). It is possible there is a reason to see Jesus's tunic as a specific allusion to priestly garments. However, Farmer does not specify one, and the argument remains to be made that this portion of the narrative expresses a priestly concern.

Similarly, Farmer argues that the introduction of hyssop in GJohn 19:29 points to Jesus's "priestly role" (p. 230). The introduction of hyssop is a strange feature of GJohn's story, because hyssop is a somewhat floppy plant that was not a likely choice for raising a wet sponge to Jesus's lips. The unsuitability of the hyssop for this task raises the question of whether GJohn expects the reader to connect the hyssop to the other Passover imagery of the crucifixion account. In Exod 12:22, hyssop is used to mark the doors of the homes of the Israelites with the blood of the Passover offering. There are other uses of hyssop in the Old Testament—in particular, the use by a priest for the cleansing of leprosy (Lev 14:4, 6, 49, 51)—but these have little apparent connection to GJohn's crucifixion scene. The quantity of other Passover allusions in the narrative makes the connection to Exodus the most plausible.

However, Farmer gives little attention to the meaning of the allusion. In Exodus, hyssop marks the lintels of the Israelites' doorways to protect from the destroyer. In GJohn, someone uses hyssop to lift a sponge to Jesus's lips. Following the logic of the Passover narrative, the reader might thereby conclude that the hyssop marks Jesus as an Israelite, or evokes the idea of God's protection from the angel of death. But Farmer's idea that the allusion puts Jesus in a "priestly role" is much less obvious, for the marking with hyssop in Exodus is not the role of a priest per se, but a role taken on by one of the participants in the meal. How or if hyssop was used in Passover celebrations in the time of Jesus is unknown.

By incorporating elements of festival observance, GJohn's use of Passover imagery may raise a subject of priestly concern, and thus be considered part of GJohn's priestly rhetorolect. But the function of that imagery requires a more nuanced explanation: it does not necessarily make Jesus a priest. Farmer's work poses a useful reminder that priests had various responsibilities and concerns. An analysis of priestly rhetorolect should include attention to the specific issue at hand—prayer, purity, various kinds of sacrifice—and the ways they were perceived and practiced in antiquity.

Farmer makes a real contribution in his use of Platonic categories to understand AJohn 98–101. He identifies as an important theme of this passage the idea that the cross has "one form and likeness," while the multitude around the cross does not (AJohn 98, 100). Farmer connects this language to the idea from Middle Platonism of a singular divine that gives rise to multiplicity. He also connects this idea to the "cross of light," which has many names or aspects, though in its essence it is one thing.

Farmer goes on to relate this same idea to the language of AJohn 101: "I suffered not, yet I did suffer." Just as an object may appear different from different angles, so also the divine nature is unchanging, yet its appearance is manifold. Farmer's use of philosophical concepts sheds light on the purpose of AJohn 98–101. The text upholds the unity of the divine, although it may appear in a multitude of different ways when viewed from various angles.

Farmer also addresses Philo's concept of the *logos* to good effect. Like other Middle Platonists, Philo uses the *logos* as a mediating figure, the rational principle through which divine reason is made known to humankind. As Farmer argues, this may help to explain why Christ is both known and unknowable in AJohn (90, 93). The *logos* is manifest to humans, yet its essential nature is divine and thus hidden from view or inexpressible in human terms. The earlier essay by Potter also noted this language, describing it as an inclusion of a topos from the Gospel of Thomas. Farmer's analysis adds to this topic by suggesting a common philosophical background in which a mediating figure is required for humans to access knowledge that is otherwise beyond their grasp. His discussion provides a framework that gives continuity to this section of AJohn (98–101).

In the final paragraphs of his essay, however, Farmer moves to a discussion of this mediating Christ as a priestly figure. This shift again raises questions about the definition of priestly rhetorolect. The mediating role of the *logos* is a function of its divine nature. The *logos* emerges from the divine and shares in God's divine reason yet can manifest or communicate that reason to humankind. This seems very different from the priest's role as "mediator." The priest tries to affect the human/divine relationship from the human side, while the *logos* emerges from the divine side. To equate the role of *logos* with that of priest seems to generalize what counts as "priestly" to an extent that it may no longer be useful.

In his discussion of the many-sidedness of the cross and *logos*, Farmer notes the great overlap with Johannine language. Many of GJohn's multiple metaphors for Jesus are included here as facets of the cross of light: Word, Door, Way, Bread, Resurrection, Son, Father, Spirit, Life, Truth, and Faith. Although many of these words are used in other gospels, they have a particular Johannine resonance. Door, Way, Bread, Resurrection, Life, and Truth are used in GJohn's distinctive "I am" sayings, while other terms (e.g., Father, Son) frequently convey Jesus's relationship to God. Although another of these terms, "seed" (σπόρος), is not used in John's Gospel, its presence among these other Johannine terms may evoke the parable of the "grain [κόκκος] of wheat" (GJohn 12:24), which GJohn uses as one way to elaborate the meaning of Jesus's death. Although other New Testament texts have a closer connection in terms of vocabulary, the meaning is not related to the cross. For example, Mark uses scattered seed (σπόρος) as a metaphor for the reign of God (Mark 4:26), while in Luke the seed is the word of God (Luke 8:5). The Gospel of John's grain of wheat seems closest conceptually without using the same terminology. As a whole, the list of metaphors bears a distinctive Johannine imprint. I turn in the next section to a thematic discussion of this and other elements of AJohn that incorporate or reconfigure John's Gospel.

3. The Use of the Gospel of John by the Acts of John

These essays provide an opportunity to consider the ways a text like the Acts of John uses or incorporates material from the Gospel of John. The authors give a number of examples of the ways the later writing uses the

Gospel. Sometimes AJohn evokes GJohn through a strong linguistic connection, but at other times the connection is more conceptual in nature. Many of the proposals suggest a highly creative appropriation of the Gospel. Below I give examples from the essays of Potter and Farmer, and also briefly discuss Hollman's essay in this volume on the Protevangelium of James. These essays suggest a wide variety of uses of GJohn within these other early Christian texts.

A number of the allusions the authors identify are based on a direct linguistic connection between the texts. For example, Jesus's words in AJohn "be not unbelieving but believing" (90) directly quote GJohn 20:27. The words are addressed to John in AJohn and to Thomas in the Gospel. Nevertheless, Potter sees a correspondence between the purpose of the saying in each case: "This application of Jesus's rebuke of Thomas is actually very fitting because Thomas's desire to verify the evidence of Jesus's resurrection by touching his body is very much like John's continual quest in the Testimonies to figure out Jesus's nature and identity, including an instance of touching Jesus's body" (pp. 219). For Potter, the context of the saying in GJohn sheds light on the meaning of the passage in AJohn. The reader draws on the familiar story from GJohn in order to understand Jesus's somewhat confusing response to John's vision of the transfiguration. From this perspective, the quotation evokes the disciple's curiosity and desire to see, a desire the text equates with disbelief.

Similarly, Hollman discusses Joseph's invitation to the midwife, "come and see" in PJ 19.1. This language echoes the invitation of Jesus to two disciples in GJohn 1:39, and of Philip to Nathanael (GJohn 1:47). The Greek is not precisely the same in any of the three instances, including the two in GJohn, but as Hollman points out, the theme of "seeing and believing" that occurs in the midwife's encounter reinforces the importance of the same Johannine themes. The passage in PJ draws on GJohn's stories of disciples who looked for physical or visual confirmation prior to belief, and presents the midwife and Salome as characters in this same lineage. Like the example from Potter's essay, the allusion suggests the importance of the background story in GJohn, and validates its perspective by using this language in a similar way.

Many of the other allusions to GJohn in AJohn have a linguistic basis but are altered to such an extent that it is not clear in what sense one can use the context of the Gospel to inform the use of the term in AJohn. As Farmer points out, the list of terms in AJohn 98 draws heavily from GJohn's vocabulary. However, in AJohn, the terms are all aspects of the "cross of light," a phrase that is not found in GJohn. In the Gospel, many of the terms are metaphors for Jesus, and each has its own particular context—often with an extended discussion—that shapes its meaning. The Acts of John transfers this Johannine vocabulary to a new context. As Farmer notes, "The 'cross of light' becomes the central organizing element in this portion of AJohn" (p. 238). Word, Bread, Door, Way, and so forth now circle around and illuminate this central idea.

Farmer's conclusion, that the cross of light "suffuses all other representations of Jesus with meaning" (p. 250) suggests a very different relationship to GJohn than the earlier examples from Potter and Hollman. In the former cases, the Gospel and its context added meaning to the alluding text. In this latter example, the new relationship forged between GJohn's metaphors and the cross of light may become an alternative way of understanding the Gospel. Instead of activating the Gospel message as a part of the alluding text, these examples may impose new meaning on the Gospel, or supersede the Gospel message.

A third kind of intersection between these texts is more conceptual in nature than linguistic. One example is Potter's assertion that AJohn and GJohn share a sense that Jesus's nature is unchanging. This observation stems from a prominent difference between the texts rather than a similarity: the absence of a transfiguration scene in GJohn and the presence of many transfigurations in AJohn lead Potter to acknowledge the consistency of Jesus in each work. This is an astute observation, but it evokes further questions about the nature of the connection between GJohn and AJohn. Jesus's unchanging nature is quite different in AJohn than in GJohn. In AJohn, on the one hand, it is more that Jesus's form is constantly changing, because his divine nature cannot be contained in any one human state. In the Gospel, on the other hand, Jesus exceeds normal human abilities in his foreknowledge of events and people (e.g., 2:24–25; 13:1) and in his apparent control over his death. In this way he manifests divine qualities, yet his form is not a prominent part of the story.

Similarly, Hollman's comparison of the tabernacle in GJohn and PJ asserts a shared conception rather than a common vocabulary. She compares the light and cloud imagery at Jesus's birth in PJ 19 to GJohn's statement that the *logos* "became flesh and dwelt [or "tabernacled," ἐσκήνωσεν] among us" (GJohn 1:14). In PJ as in GJohn, Jesus is portrayed as the tabernacle, where God's glory may be visible to humans. Instead of quoting GJohn, PJ puts concepts together in a similar constellation to suggest something about Jesus's (and Mary's) identity.

Another scholar whose work suggests this kind of connection is Harold Attridge, who argues that AJohn expresses the Johannine notion that gazing on the cross of Jesus has a salvific effect.[5] The Acts of John takes up a central understanding in the Gospel, that the cross is a revelatory event that must be understood by believers, and builds on that understanding to communicate its message. The message is not the same, nor is it made with Johannine vocabulary. But AJohn embraces central theological ideas that the Gospel proposes.

These examples point to a creative reconfiguration of material from John's Gospel. Moreover, each one suggests a deep acceptance of at least part of the metaphorical worldview GJohn creates. The authors may assume that the presentation of Jesus in this way will be known and accepted by their readers. It requires no explanation or direct quotation from an authoritative source. This approach clearly places value on the earlier writing, while leaving plenty of room for the Gospel to be retooled for the author's own purposes.

Thus the essays of this book point to a variety of relationships between GJohn and AJohn or PJ. In doing so, they embody what I see as a positive step forward out of the constraints of the historical-critical method. This traditional approach has shaped many of the discussions of the relationship between these texts. The method tends to assume there is a direct lineage between texts, and a development that is traceable based on elements within the texts themselves. In this vein, interpreters often speak of a "Johannine trajectory" into which they situate a work like AJohn.[6] They tend to conclude either that AJohn is "Johannine," or that it is "anti-Johannine." Yet as Attridge writes, "Such a judgment does not do full justice to the appropriation of the key Johannine motifs of the Acts nor to the ways in which the Acts appears to wrestle with a fundamental Johannine

5. See Harold W. Attridge, "The Acts of John and the Fourth Gospel," in *From Judaism to Christianity: Tradition and Transition. A Festschrift for Thomas H. Tobin, S.J., on the Occasion of His Sixty-Fifth Birthday*, ed. Patricia Walters (Leiden: Brill, 2010), 255–65.

6. See, e.g., Jean-Daniel Kaestli, "Le Mystère de la croix de lumière et le johannisme," *Foi et Vie* 86, no. 5 (1987): 35–46; Helmut Koester, *History and Literature of Early Christianity*, vol. 2 of *Introduction to the New Testament* (Philadelphia: Fortress, 1982), 196–98; Pieter J. Lalleman, *The Acts of John: A Two-Stage Initiation into Johannine Gnosticism*, SAAA 4 (Leuven: Peeters, 1998), 110–23. Hill raises excellent questions about the idea of a Johannine "trajectory," only to conclude that the work represents an "anti-Johannine" trajectory. See Hill, *Johannine Corpus*, 262–63.

affirmation, that the crucifixion of Jesus was a revelatory event that needed to be understood and internalized by believers."[7] The acknowledgment of varieties in AJohn's use of GJohn complicates the decision to place the text in a camp that either favors or rejects the Gospel.

Sociorhetorical criticism opens up other possibilities, because the aim is not simply to trace a lineage between texts, but to explore the manifold texture of texts. In doing so, this approach can help us to see the variety that exists within a single work. As a result, the method raises new questions about the ways one Christian text employed another. One need not simply conclude that a text like AJohn is either Johannine or anti-Johannine. Instead, attention to the multiple connections and relationships between texts, alongside analysis of social and cultural factors, may eventually yield a new understanding of the possible ways Christian writings overlap and intersect. These essays mark a welcome step in that direction.

7. Attridge, "Acts of John," 265.

Rhetorical Discourses in Gospel of John and Acts of John: A Response

L. Gregory Bloomquist

Two of the chapters in this collection concern rhetorical analysis of material found in the Acts of John (AJohn) with a view to its relation to the Gospel of John (GJohn). My response seeks to develop further the sociorhetorical interpretation used to analyze these two texts, AJohn and GJohn.

Sociorhetorical interpretation (SRI) has shown itself to be useful for rhetorical interpretation. It has done so primarily through the use of two sets of strategies for interpretation. The first set of strategies, developed in the last decades of the twentieth century, concerns the analysis of *textures*. As I have suggested, building on Vernon Robbins's initial insights concerning the textures, this set of strategies really falls into three categories: (1) analysis of the innertexture of texts (e.g., analysis of regularly recurring vocabulary; of narrative characters and settings; of resulting topoi that are regularly drawn on for texts; the opening-middle-closing of a text, which provides the framework for understanding a text or a scene),[1] (2) analysis of the intertexture (e.g., analysis of the way the text reflects interactions in the social world, of ways the text reflects specific, local [cultural] references, of indexes of oral-scribal materials),[2] and finally (3) analysis of ideological texture (e.g., ways the material from the previous two textures is creatively reconfigured to address transformed or transformative ways of addressing novel situations, based on the assumption that few texts are written simply to "mirror" existing realities).[3] By attending to the textures,

1. This is the material covered by Robbins in Vernon K. Robbins, *Exploring the Texture of Texts: A Guide to Socio-Rhetorical Interpretation* (Valley Forge, PA: Trinity Press International, 1996), 7–39.

2. This is the material covered by ibid., 40–94.

3. While this is the material of ibid., 95–131, I have expanded on this particular

rather than by starting with either the literary device of historical-critical genres or the socioscientific analysis of cultures or historical movements, scholars can begin to assess the rhetorical shape that a text purports to provide for envisioning perceived and proposed realities.[4]

The second set of strategies, associated with SRI since the mid-2000s, involves several notions that develop analysis of ideological texture as I have understood it. By means of this second set of strategies Robbins has further grounded textural analyses in the way rhetorical performance seeks to create (rhetorically, "to invent") new realities.[5] Here Robbins has found the need to create a lexicon suitable for such an analysis. By "rhetorolect," Robbins understands rhetorical speech used in conventionally recognizable ways by local users who wittingly or unwittingly employ rhetorical topoi that are well known throughout, say, a large area (e.g., in the Mediterranean world).[6] Robbins adds that rhetorolects are also developed argumentatively in the form of "rhetology," a more deductive kind of argumentation that employs particular rhetorolects to argue in local, nonuniversal ways or are developed in the form of what Robbins calls "rhetography," where argumentation employs visually compelling topoi in particular local ways.[7] In other words, topoi can be developed in so-called logical ways ("topological") or in pictographic ways ("topographical"). Each of

set of strategies in L. Gregory Bloomquist, "Paul's Inclusive Language: The Ideological Texture of Romans 1," in *Fabrics of Discourse: Essays in Honor of Vernon K. Robbins*, ed. David B. Gowler, L. Gregory Bloomquist, and Duane F. Watson (Harrisburg, PA: Trinity Press International, 2003), 165–93.

4. For a similar attempt to discuss "apocalyptic discourse," see L. Gregory Bloomquist, "Methodological Criteria for Apocalyptic Rhetoric: A Suggestion for the Expanded Use of Sociorhetorical Analysis," in *Vision and Persuasion: Rhetorical Dimensions of Apocalyptic Discourse*, ed. Greg Carey and L. Gregory Bloomquist (St. Louis: Chalice, 1999), 181–203.

5. Thus the title of Robbins's magnum opus, Vernon K. Robbins, *The Invention of Christian Discourse*, vol. 1, RRA 1 (Blandford Forum, UK: Deo, 2009).

6. The initial discussion of "rhetorolect" dates from Vernon K. Robbins, "The Dialectical Nature of Early Christian Discourse," *Scriptura* 59 (1996): 353–62, http://www.religion.emory.edu/faculty/robbins/SRS/vkr/dialect.cfm. I have suggested that this large-scale, conventional deployment is actually akin to a "rhetorical language" with new, local uses of those "languages" in smaller regions of that world (e.g., Galilee within the broader Mediterranean world) actually becoming home to "rhetorolects." I have recently expanded on this notion in forthcoming essays.

7. Robbins, *Invention*, 16–17. See, too, his redefinitions of such words as "topology" and "topography"; Robbins, *Invention*, 16.

these forms of argumentation, along with the specific topoi employed, give a particular shape to the rhetorical discourse or "rhetorolect."

In the most recent discussions, rhetography has begun to appear as the key notion for "rhetorical force," a foundational assertion for any rhetorical analysis but used in SRI to identify the way a cultural and social reality is constructed through the text. This is not surprising since, according to Robbins, "rhetography" means "the features of a spoken or written communication that evoke a picture (graphic image) in the mind of a hearer or reader,"[8] or, as he later elaborated, "the progressive, sensory-aesthetic, and/or argumentative texture of a text ... that invites a hearer/reader to create a graphic image or picture in the mind that implies a certain kind of truth and/or reality."[9] Rhetography, which is about getting at "the picture an argument evokes,"[10] is central because it accords best with how humans process, communicate, and accept information.[11]

Though both AJohn and GJohn would require a full sociorhetorical interpretation to do justice to their individual parts, I will limit my remarks in this response to the two chapters in this book that engage a central component of AJohn and to the relevant discussion from GJohn that both authors invoke.

Furthermore, since even those limitations would lead me to a response that transgresses the boundaries of space provided, I will limit my remarks to the way the material of AJohn and GJohn interweave the characteristics of what Robbins has called priestly discourse into both texts. This is especially important for my engagement with Thomas Jared Farmer's article, which helpfully attempts to navigate the rhetorical discourses present in AJohn and GJohn and, in doing so, highlights priestly discourse. As will become clear, however, this discussion also helps to illuminate aspects of Jonathan Potter's article, which, even though it covers some of the same material as Farmer's, does not mention "priestly discourse."

---

8. Vernon K. Robbins, "Rhetography: A New Way of Seeing the Familiar Text," in *Words Well Spoken: George Kennedy's Rhetoric of the New Testament*, ed. C. Clifton Black and Duane F. Watson (Waco, TX: Baylor University Press, 2008), 81–106.

9. Robbins, *Invention*, xxvii.

10. Ibid., 17.

11. On this point, see my "Methodology for Rhetography and Visual Exegesis of the Gospel of John" (RRA/Sawyer Seminar in the Context of the Mellon Foundation Sawyer Seminar Program: Visual Exegesis: Images as Instruments of Scriptural Interpretation and Hermeneutics, Emory University, September 16, 2013).

1. Priestly Discourse

According to Robbins, priestly rhetorical discourse concerns sacrificial life performed for the purpose of beneficial exchange between God and humans. Defined as such, this might almost be described as the quintessential socioreligious discourse, for surely sacrificial life is a foundational element of religious practices as evidenced in ancient human settlements around the world[12] and in transformed ways in religious cultures today.[13] It is hardly unique to the Mediterranean world, much less to specific regions of the Mediterranean world.

But Robbins suggests that priestly rhetorical discourse can be identified more specifically than that, for in its argumentation it blends the social experiences associated with temples and other places of worship with reasoning about priestly agents, sacrificial agents, and special benefits that God can bring into the lives of humans. Thus priestly discourse can be identified by the particular, cultural experiences of particular, Mediterranean peoples that are associated with particular settings, particular agents (sacrificers, sacrificed, and recipients of benefits), and particular, perceived benefits, as well as particular (argumentative) forms in which these elements are blended. In other words, while priestly discourse does have a more generic form that is characteristically found throughout the Mediterranean world, it also has particular rhetorolectical instantiations, and it is these latter that we find in unique ways in both AJohn and GJohn.

---

12. Walter Burkert, *Greek Religion*, trans. John Raffan (Cambridge: Harvard University Press, 1985), 10–15. While it may be true that Robbins came to some understanding of priestly rhetorolect on the basis of Jewish practices alone (so Farmer, pp. 223 above, drawing from Vernon K. Robbins, "Conceptual Blending and Early Christian Imagination," in *Explaining Christian Origins and Early Judaism: Contributions from Cognitive and Social Science*, ed. Petri Luomanen, Ilkka Pyysiäinen, and Risto Uro, BIS 89 [Leiden: Brill, 2005], 161–95), it seems to me much more likely that Robbins has in actual fact drawn this rhetorolect and its description from the broader understanding of Mediterranean religious practices, including those from the Greco-Roman religious practices, which seems to have led him to his initial understanding of this discourse form as suffering-dying in Robbins, "Dialectical Nature."

13. Peter L. Berger, *Pyramids of Sacrifice: Political Ethics and Social Change* (New York: Basic Books, 1974; repr., Garden City, NY: Anchor, 1976).

2. Priestly Discourse Material in Gospel of John

In my own work on the Gospel of John, I have identified the following cases in which some form of priestly discourse is present: 1:19, 29 (cf. 36); 2:13–23; 3:14–17; 4:19–24; 5:14; 6:30–65; 7:14, 28, 32, 45–48; 8:20, 59; 10:11–18 (cf. 28), 23; 11:47, 49, 50–52, 55–57; 12:3–8, 24–25, 32; 14:18–31; 15:13; 17:14, 22, 26; 18:3, 10, 13–16, 19–24, 26, 35; 19:6, 15, 21.[14] These passages fall into three distinct but related categories.

First, there is material that refers to those involved in priestly activity as it is known within Judaism, either as practiced prior to 70 CE or in retrospect as found in, say, later rabbinic texts that reflect on or echo priestly activity prior to 70 CE. Material in GJohn that refers to those involved in priestly activity and thus also narrational texture characters with a role in priestly discourse can be found in passages that contain the term ἱερεύς (once: 1:19) and the term ἀρχιερεύς (frequently: 11:49, 51; 18:10, 13–16, 19–24, 26, 35; 19:6, 15, 21). The latter is also used in 7:32, 45–48; 11:47–53; 18:3 together with φαρισαῖος, a term that we might not initially consider "priestly." In fact, however, the suggestion of a connection between "high priest" and "Pharisee" as narrational characters in GJohn was suggested some time ago by Judith Lieu, who cautioned that in GJohn, unlike the Synoptics, the Pharisees are regularly associated with priestly personnel.[15]

Second, there is material that refers to the place or setting of priestly activity, be it spatially or temporally, again with the same caveat as in the first category. Material that refers to the place or setting of priestly activity and thus may serve as a likely setting for priestly discourse is found related to the word ἱερόν, by which is always understood the temple in Jerusalem (2:13–23; 5:14; 7:14, 28; 8:20, 59; 10:23; 11:56; 18:20), as well as the discussion of proper worship in Jerusalem or on the sacred mount of the Samaritans in 4:19–24.[16]

Third, there is material that may or may not refer to the setting or people normally understood to be involved in priestly activity but that, by the setting, or the language, or by some other indicator, appears to indicate

---

14. In this study, I will not enter into the question of the single or multiple authorship of John's Gospel.

15. Cf. in addition to the verses cited 1:24; 3:1; chs. 7–9 passim; 11:46, 57; 12:19, 42. See Judith Lieu, "Temple and Synagogue in John," *NTS* 45 (1999): 51–69.

16. A fuller, sociorhetorical interpretation of GJohn would require us to look also at the role of "synagogue" in John, given the connection of this place with the "Pharisees."

the presence of some kind of priestly discourse as identified above. Material that may or may not refer to the setting or people normally understood to be involved in priestly activity but that does involve the dynamics noted in Robbins's definition of priestly discourse can be found in 1:29, 36; 3:14–17; 6:30–65; 10:11–18 (cf. 28); 12:3–8, 24–25, 32; 14:18–31; 15:13; 17:14, 22, 26. I include in this category material that mixes and reconfigures one or more of the first two categories. This material is limited to the end of GJohn 11 and to chapter 12.

As is clear from the material of categories 1 and 2, priestly discourse in GJohn is consistently present, either implicitly or explicitly, in relation to the temple in Jerusalem and to the personnel related to the temple, including the Pharisees. As we shall see, this has direct implications not only for the material in category 3 but also for the whole of John's Gospel, which in fact is overshadowed by the Jerusalem temple and its personnel, and thus in fact finds its entire rhetorical display to be shaped by the priestly rhetorolect that takes shape in this gospel. The absence from AJohn of priestly rhetorolect in relation to the temple or to temple personnel (my categories 1 and 2) signifies a dramatic divergence from the rhetorical presentation found in GJohn; however, questions remain whether there is other priestly rhetoric in AJohn (e.g., of type 3), and if so whether it is in any other way connected to GJohn, and if so how?

3. Reconfigured "Priestly Discourse"

The Gospel of John gives extensive evidence of a reconfiguration of priestly discourse (my category 3). Admittedly, it is not easy to discern this discourse since the evidence does not come to us through explicit references to priestly personnel or temple space or time. Yet through the employment of phrases and imagery that can be understood as related to elements of mediation with a view to redemption or reconciliation of a person or people to God—for example, "lamb of God" (1:29, 36), "serpent" (3:14), "bread from heaven" (especially 6:31, 32), "shepherd" (chapter 10 passim), as well as a cluster of references to sacrificial giving in 12–17—we can discern some specific topoi of "priestly discourse."

If this is so, however, then priestly discourse is pervasive throughout the Fourth Gospel. Stated otherwise, we might say that priestly discourse pervades the imagery of the Johannine "passion," since unlike the Synoptic "passion" account, the passion of Jesus is not limited in GJohn to the end of Jesus's life: it is something that takes place from the first appearance of the Word become flesh and occurs throughout the Word's presence in the realm of the flesh. The picture of the passion of Jesus as GJohn paints it shows the events narrated in the final chapters of GJohn not as the start of the passion of Jesus but as the culmination of a passion that began in the first chapter.[17]

For example, it is not surprising to find multiple examples of reconfigured priestly discourse throughout GJohn 12–17, in addition to 18–19, especially in the many references to self-sacrifice (12:3–8, 24–25, 32; 14:18–31; 15:13; 17:14, 22, 26). Thus a text like GJohn 15:13 ("Greater love has no man than this, that a man lay down his life for his friends") can be seen to have primarily to do with the effect of priestly exchange on its recipients. Read in relation to the topoi of GJohn 10, a chapter that in many ways prefaces the private teaching that begins in 12–17, as well as in relation to the chapter that concludes that private teaching (GJohn 17), and there in particular to the priestly handing over of the word (17:14), the glory (17:22), and the knowledge of God's name as benefits of the priestly sacrifice, it becomes clear that priestly discourse in GJohn, as in many early Christian texts, had a clear goal: How is someone to share in Jesus as sacrifice/sacrificed in the promised benefits, and what are those benefits?[18] One could easily multiply these examples throughout the first nine chapters of the Gospel.

In sum, we see significant clues of a profound reconfiguration not just of the social language of priesthood but also of the more narrowly identifiable rhetorolect associated with the Second Temple Jewish experience of priestly activity, space, and speech. The Gospel of John presents a reconfiguration of priestly rhetorolect identifiable through indexes of

---

17. The presentation is very helpfully set forth in Josep Oriol Tuñí, "Pasión y muerte de Jesús en el cuarto evangelio: Papel y significación," *RCT* 1 (1976): 394.

18. See Carl Schneider, *Geistesgeschichte des antiken Christentums*, 2 vols. (Munich: Beck, 1954), 1:215. According to René Girard, this process continues in our history: "The process which is unfolding as history openly and visibly now to a vast number of people, and this process is the same thing as the coming of the Paraclete. When the Paraclete comes, says Jesus, he will bear witness to me, he will reveal the significance of my death as an innocent person, the significance of every death of an innocent person, from the foundation of the world to the world's ending. Those who come after Christ will therefore bear witness, like him, less by their words and beliefs than by their becoming martyrs, by dying in the manner of Jesus himself" ("History and the Paraclete," *Ecumenical Review* 35 [1983]: 16). A significant element of this echoing is picked up in AJohn.

priestly discourse and related topoi; however, it is important to note that these topoi are not used along lines of normal cultural expectation within Second Temple Judaism, that is, in relation to personnel, place, and time. True, there *is* cultural intertexture, but in GJohn it is ideologically configured so as to function not so much as a vehicle for existing topoi but as a means of establishing a new significance for the old topoi. Thus through the use of cultural intertexture relating to a locally accepted understanding of sacrifice, the nature of a *true* sacrifice and beneficial exchange becomes evident in GJohn, as opposed to the *seemingly* beneficial exchange familiar culturally to those who can be identified as sacrificer and sacrificed and limited to those authorized places of sacrifice, a seeming exchange that, as we would see in a fuller analysis of priestly discourse in GJohn, has actually become its sinister and oppressive dark side.

4. Argumentative Strategies in the Priestly Discourse Material of the Gospel of John

In terms of the rhetorical argumentative use of these topoi, it seems quite clear that much of the priestly discourse in John's Gospel follows rhetographical outlines rather than rhetological ones. This is clearly true for the primary priestly agents and their setting (categories 1 and 2): no argument is made that "these priests are doing this because…" or "that this is a temple means that it is…." But even in the case of those reconfigured priestly references in which Jesus or other sacrificers or sacrificed are the subject or object, the argumentation is still rhetographical rather than rhetological. For example, John provides no logical argumentation of the kind "Jesus is the Lamb of God because…," only the "indexical" "behold"[19] and then the "unpacking" of that image throughout the rest of the Gospel.

But this seems counterintuitive to what we expect from priestly discourse. For is it not more likely that priestly discourse will ensure the accuracy of beneficial exchange by logical arguments, such as "this heifer is appropriate for this sacrifice, because…" or "this sacrifice is invalid, because…" or "if you do *x*, then *y* will follow"? Priestly discourse is much

19. GJohn 1:29 in the mouth of John the witnesser. For the philosophical problem presented by "indexicals," see John Perry, *The Problem of the Essential Indexical and Other Essays*, rev. and expanded ed. (Stanford, CA: CSLI, 2000). In fact, a significant number of "rhetographical" statements throughout John's Gospel appear to take the form of "indexicals," such as the "I am" statements.

more likely to be in the form of a "gnostic-manipulationist" cultural response to life, that is, a response shaped "by a rigorous and disciplined ritual introduced into a person's or community's life."[20] Yet that is not what we find in John's Gospel, at least for the most part. Here, then, is yet another aspect of the Gospel's reconfiguration of priestly discourse.

Ironically, where we *do* find such rhetological argumentation is in the only self-expressive action of the named "priests" in John's Gospel: "it is better that one man [i.e., Jesus] die than that the people perish" (11:50). It is a statement that builds on the broadly held understanding of vicarious or sacrificial in Jewish oral-scribal materials prior to Jesus.[21] However, it also raises an interesting problem: as W. H. C. Frend notes, for the logic of sacrificial suffering of a person to work (e.g., for someone to die) "as a vicarious sacrifice on behalf of his people" (see 2 Macc 7:37) and thus to stay God's wrath (see 2 Macc 7:38), logically the victim would have to be innocent in God's eyes.[22] Surely the priests have not concluded that Jesus is innocent! More likely, John is here, as he does elsewhere, ironically depicting a character or characters speaking truth unwittingly, here even providing a priestly logical rationale for their assertion as one would expect from "true" priestly discourse.

The Gospel of John's single but ironic rhetological speech here, in the mouths of those who are clearly not Jesus's disciples and who will actually oversee his sacrifice, serves another purpose as well: it confirms the primacy of a rhetographical approach to Jesus on the part of those who *are* his faithful and beloved disciples, including the Gospel's author, and it hints at what the approach will be of those who will stand opposed to this

---

20. Bryan R. Wilson, "A Typology of Sects," in *Sociology of Religion: Selected Readings*, ed. Roland Robertson (Baltimore: Penguin, 1969), 361–83; Robbins, *Exploring*, 72–75.

21. O'Neill cites 2 Macc 7; 4 Macc 1:11; 6:27–29; 17:21–22; T. Jos. 19.11; T. Benj. 3.1, 6–8; 1QS 8:6, 10; 9:4; CD 14:19; Apoc. El. 3.33; Josephus, *J.W.* 5.419, and references to the blood of the temple (b. Giṭ. 57b; b. Sanh. 96b; y. Taʿan. 69a) and the Aqedah of Isaac (Frg. Tg. and Tg. Neof. Gen 22). See J. C. O'Neill, "Did Jesus Teach That His Death Would Be Vicarious as Well as Typical?" in *Suffering and Martyrdom in the New Testament: Studies Presented to G. M. Styler by the Cambridge New Testament Seminar*, ed. William Horbury and Brian McNeil (Cambridge: Cambridge University Press, 1981), 15.

22. W. H. C. Frend, *Martyrdom and Persecution in the Early Church: A Study of a Conflict from the Maccabees to Donatus* (Garden City, NY: Anchor, 1967), 45–46.

"author of life." It is an approach that AJohn both adopts and elaborates significantly but in ways that are profoundly different from GJohn.

5. Acts of John and Gospel of John

Potter and Farmer's chapters take us into the material of AJohn 87–105. This material has long been recognized as entirely distinct from the rest of the material in AJohn, even though it is often found today located textually at the central, physical point of the text.[23] In fact, the material found in 87–105 is so distinct from the rest of the material in AJohn that it is even a question as to how or whether it forms part of AJohn understood as a whole. Chapters 87–105 exist in a single, extant manuscript (C) from the fourteenth century, though it is also known in some form from the documents purporting to record the activities and decisions of the Council of Nicaea in 787 CE, at which AJohn, apparently including 87–105, was condemned.[24]

Thus a first noteworthy point for what follows is that the discussion of rhetorical discourses in AJohn concerns only 87–105. This is important because the rhetorical discourse found in the rest of AJohn is entirely different in a crucial way. The material of AJohn with the exception of 87–105 is characterized by miracle rhetorolect; 87–105, however, is not. Thus, in AJohn, excepting 87–105, we find regular occurrences of (a) a problematic situation, (b) a miracle, and (c) teaching regarding the significance of the miracle. This miracle discourse found in AJohn is comparable to any number of pericopes found in the canonical Synoptic traditions and in the Acts of the Apostles. True, unlike the material in the Synoptics and Acts, in AJohn the miracle situation often involves some form of sexual impurity and the teaching that follows involves an ascetic approach that suggests a way of counteracting future sexual error. As such, the extensive story of Drusiana that either follows on after the material of 87–105 or that directly precedes it and leads into it is characteristic. In this regard, it is very much of the same kind of tradition of miracle rhetorolect that we find in, say, the Acts of Paul and Thecla or Acts of Peter. But the main

23. Whether it is central physically is disputed. See the discussion in Potter.

24. Farmer's comment (p. 235) that roughly one-third of the original of AJohn has been lost (because in the ninth century Nikephorus lists its length as 2,500 stichoi while we only have 1,700 stichoi) must be reframed since what Nikephorus knew as AJohn may not have been the original form of the text.

point here is that there is a connection of the material in AJohn outside of 87–105 to the Synoptics, Acts, and various apocryphal Acts; there is, however, no connection whatsoever with the material of GJohn, even to the limited miracle discourse that we find in the Gospel.[25]

In contrast, AJohn 87–105 is rhetorical material of a completely different kind from that found elsewhere in AJohn, and it does appear to have at least some connection with what we find in GJohn as well as to gnostic texts.[26] However, there is another problem that faces those who wish to use the material of AJohn 87–105, and that is that this material is not homogeneous: on the one hand, we find visionary, gospel-like material (87–93 and 97–105); on the other, we find a kind of liturgical and hymnic performance (94–96). Additionally, the material of 87–93, though visionary and gospel-like, is different from that of 97–105. In sum, even within this body of material, we need to make clear what it is we are looking at and what kind of rhetorical discourse is present in those component parts. This very complex text, then, creates significant problems for analysis. Nevertheless, Potter and Farmer are both right to point to opening-middle-closing texture analysis as an important sociorhetorical approach to getting at the separate component parts (e.g., as in Potter's attempt to identify the opening 87–88a, middle 88b–102, and closing 103–105). Yet, while I agree on

25. There are significant exceptions to this assertion. For example, miracle discourse can be found in the wedding at Cana (GJohn 2), the healing of the paralytic (GJohn 5:1–15), the walking on water and the multiplication of the loaves (GJohn 6), the healing of the man born blind (GJohn 9), and the raising of Lazarus (GJohn 11), two of which—GJohn 5:1–15 and GJohn 9—lead to significant discourses by Jesus—GJohn 5:16–47 and GJohn 10, respectively. And, like the Synoptics, they do not propose any kind of moral, ascetic teaching. However, in contrast to the Synoptics, Acts, and the apocryphal gospels as well as AJohn, the miracles found in GJohn are platforms for continued elucidation of the figure of Jesus, a figure delineated against the backdrop of culturally identifiable priestly culture. Furthermore, the miracles of AJohn are fundamentally at odds with the miracles of GJohn, including the resurrection account in GJohn, by their enormous detail concerning an event. In contrast to the mystery and enigma that pervades GJohn, the resurrection appearances in AJohn are overly revealing. Richard Pervo, commenting on the resurrection accounts in AJohn, aptly notes: "The *AcJn* will concede nothing in the matter of strange resurrection stories" (Richard I. Pervo, "Johannine Trajectories in the *Acts of John*: Hommage à Helmut Koester," *Apocrypha* 3 [1992]: 54).

26. As Pervo noted some years ago, it is the material of 87–105 alone of all the material of AJohn that justifies the traditional claim that AJohn arose in some classically gnostic milieu ("Johannine Trajectories," 48).

the importance of discerning opening-middle-closing texture,[27] I find it difficult to endorse the textures discerned by either Potter or Farmer. The problem is that the material found within the broad parameters of chapters 87–105 is both fragmentary, probably interpolated and perhaps multiply interpolated, and of awkward composition, such as the very passage that Potter is interested in, 90–91.[28] Given the text-critical problems associated with this portion of AJohn and in the absence of any explicit guidelines or method that either Potter or Farmer give us for determining a sociorhetorical opening, middle, or closing, I found both of their suggestions for the outlines of opening-middle-closing texture to be largely impressionistic.[29] The problem is of course not unique to Potter and Farmer, nor is it unique to texts beset by text-critical problems.[30] The Society of Biblical Literature's Rhetoric of Religious Antiquity group, a group devoted to the scholarly refinement and use of sociorhetorical interpretation, is aware of the need for greater methodological rigor in identifying opening-middle-closing texture and will be addressing this issue in the future.

In terms of rhetorolects, the material we find in 87–93 and 97–105 appears primarily and broadly (in spite of differences) to be rhetorically the kind of visionary material that Tim Beech described as mantic discourse,[31] by which Beech means "Judeo-Christian apocalyptic discourse and Greco-Roman oracular discourse," while the so-called Hymn of Christ (94–96) combines mantic discourse with a very particular kind of discourse that Robbins at one point called "ritual,"[32] a broader, social category that includes priestly rhetorolect.[33] I believe there is value in starting with these two broad categorizations of the material. Discuss-

27. Robbins, *Exploring*, 19.

28. It is, for example, very difficult to see how Potter might justify 90.1–4a as opening material and why the break to middle material occurs at 4b.

29. The attempt to ground opening-middle-closing texture in lexical identifiers is helpful, but again the specific rationales for the lexica that were chosen as identifiers are missing in the chapters under consideration.

30. I have generally found that only semiotic analysis shows a strong methodological interest in or even an ability to establish the text in terms of its opening-middle-closing portions.

31. Timothy Beech, "A Socio-Rhetorical Analysis of the Development and Function of the Noah-Flood Narrative in *Sibylline Oracles* 1–2" (PhD diss., Saint Paul University, Ottawa, Canada, 2008).

32. Robbins, *Invention*, 1:494.

33. This is likely true, since a fundamental aspect of priestly rhetorolect is proper

ing the material of 94–96 as ritual discourse is helpful because both the material we find in 94–96 and priestly rhetorolect as a discourse mode share some elements, but what we find in 94–96 is certainly not like all priestly rhetorolect and most certainly not like any that we find in GJohn. Similarly, while the mantic discourse of AJohn 87–93 and 97–105 shares some similarities with elements of a kind of visionary material that we find in GJohn, it only vaguely resembles GJohn understood as a whole. For example, the topoi and their social-cultural context are completely different: where GJohn is immersed in the cultural world of Jesus's Judean-Jerusalem context and of the Jewish Scriptures insofar as they relate to that world, AJohn evidences no real connection of any kind to the Jewish Scriptures or to the Judean-Jerusalem context of GJohn.[34] And since, as we have seen, the rhetorical discourse of GJohn requires it be understood in those contexts, AJohn must then be seen to represent an almost complete departure from the rhetorical presentation of GJohn, making use of relatively few amenable elements from the Gospel. Thus there is a significant challenge here for anyone who would draw clear conclusions concerning the intertextual use of GJohn material in AJohn or even attempt to show related rhetorical strategies. There are, however, some that can be identified, as Potter and Farmer do.

6. The Transfiguration Scene in the Acts of John

Building to a limited extent on the outstanding work of Simon Lee,[35] Potter suggests the indebtedness of AJohn to Synoptic transfiguration accounts, with special focus on Luke, and with some occasional reconfiguration of material that we find in GJohn.[36] Thus Potter observes that the Synoptic-like transfiguration account given in AJohn actually contains interesting elements of Johannine language, in particular the language concerning the revelation of "glory" (e.g., 1:14) and the theme of "light." He also observes

---

ritual, in fact, a kind of gnostic-manipulationist mode in which the proper wording, gestures, movement, etc. ensures the desired outcome.

34. Pervo makes this point as well ("Johannine Trajectories," 48).

35. Simon S. Lee, *Jesus' Transfiguration and the Believers' Transformation: A Study of the Transfiguration and Its Development in Early Christian Writings*, WUNT 2/265 (Tübingen: Mohr Siebeck, 2009).

36. Potter is quick to note the absence of any transfiguration account in John's Gospel.

that the literary form of the "Testimonies" in the transfiguration account in AJohn seems to have some Johannine roots. Finally, he points to elements of Johannine phraseology in the central story itself as well as the identification of "John" with the disciple "whom Jesus loved" and the Thomasine rebuke that in AJohn Jesus renders against John, not Thomas (AJohn 90.16).

Given this interesting but admittedly limited evidence for any more extensive interaction with material from the Gospel of John itself, however, I find Potter's final conclusion overdrawn: "In a very real way, we have thus seen how AJohn blends Johannine and Synoptic discourse and Christology" (222). True, there are Johannine elements, as he points out; however, these are clearly quite limited, and overall the AJohn account is clearly less Johannine than it is Johannine. Moreover, even some of the Johannine elements that Potter detects do not so much derive from GJohn but from the later tradition regarding the Gospel and other Johannine materials. For example, that the narrative character "John" is central to the narrative of the AJohn transfiguration account depends not so much on the *narrational texture* of GJohn, in which "John" plays a minimal role, but on the tradition that associates John son of Zebedee, one of those who in the Synoptic account accompanied Jesus on the mountain, with the Gospel's Beloved Disciple, who does play a significant role, even as the putative author of the Gospel. The Fourth Gospel, however, nowhere makes the claim that the Beloved Disciple is "John," though by the time of the writing of AJohn the church had.[37]

It seems to be likely, then, that it is this later, church tradition, more than GJohn, that AJohn is dependent on. This does not invalidate a sociorhetorical study of AJohn of course, but it raises a very important question for Potter's study: Is AJohn engaging *intertexturally* with GJohn or with some other text or texts in which these Johannine materials have already been made use of? True, AJohn does seem to be reconfiguring in some way the topoi that are drawn from GJohn, but only in the same way that a homily on GJohn, preached centuries later than the Gospel itself, would do by looking at GJohn through already highly reconfigured optics.

37. Farmer himself slips on this point when he asserts that GJohn "places John (alone among the Twelve), at the foot of the cross" (236 n. 37). Of course, what the text says is that it is "the disciple whom Jesus loved" (GJohn 19:26) who is there with Jesus's mother.

This is the very point that makes Farmer's exploration of the Middle Platonic reinterpretation of GJohn so important.

As such, a major question for Potter will now be to explore the ways in which AJohn may be drawing the Johannine topoi not from GJohn but from early Christian traditions that have already blended elements of Johannine, Synoptic, and other early Christian discourse material. We will find these texts, for example, analyzed by Lee. And perhaps not surprisingly, they bear a striking resemblance to the Acts of John, namely, Acts of Peter and Apocryphon of John. So, we have at least two possibilities: AJohn may or may not be creative *intertexturally* with material from GJohn. These two questions—is AJohn creative intertexturally primarily with material from GJohn, or is it creative primarily with texts that have already significantly reconfigured material from GJohn—lead us to still other questions: Did AJohn draw oral-scribally from canonical biblical materials like GJohn—which is the only view envisioned by Potter—or also or even exclusively from texts like Acts of Peter or even materials like the *Diatessaron*?[38] Did the latter (i.e., Acts of Peter or the *Diatessaron*) draw from AJohn, or portions thereof? Did one or the other of these draw on a third source? Could the parallel material in any of these texts come from any other sources, or could it even overlap coincidentally? Now, of course, and thanks to Potter's study, we can raise these questions!

Second, as noted, the material of the AJohn transfiguration account seems to me to be an excellent example of some form of mantic discourse that is associated specifically with the kind of seer that is represented paradigmatically by Jesus and derivatively by John. This kind of discourse is clearly evident in GJohn. As such, the question that Potter's presentation needs to ask is: How does mantic discourse found in both AJohn—both outside of the section 87–105 and inside it![39]—and in GJohn reconfigure the Synoptic transfiguration account material? This question will be relevant whether AJohn is creative or derivative, whether it is working directly with the Synoptic texts or with GJohn or whether it is using an already-existing blend that it has only modestly transformed. I look forward to subsequent essays that will focus more specifically on AJohn and the con-

38. Potter offers this suggestion, though in a footnote he then discounts the possibility.

39. One implication of Pervo's essay ("Johannine Trajectories") is that the language *of* the miracles in AJohn when spoken by the apostle John *is* the language of GJohn's Jesus.

ceptual blendings that it promotes in light of the specific discourse(s) present in it, and among which I am convinced mantic discourse dominates.

Finally, and as is clear from my comments above, in my mind Potter's essay actually reveals not so much the incorporation of GJohn and its own rhetorical force into AJohn but rather the amazing distance between the two texts. While that distance is most obvious in the large body of miracle discourse material outside of AJohn 87–105, even in the case of the transfiguration account the distance between the two texts is noteworthy. But, this is not just true of the Transfiguration account in AJohn because elsewhere in AJohn, where the rhetorical presentation outlined in my previous sections is crucial for understanding GJohn, AJohn has a completely different rhetorical force. To illustrate that continuing distance, I turn to Farmer's material.

7. The Crucifixion Scene in the Acts of John

As is clear from the above presentation concerning the Gospel of John, the crucifixion scene in GJohn clearly interweaves a form of priestly rhetorolect into its narrative drama. It does *not* do so, however, by presenting Christ as high priest, whether that be explicitly as he is presented in Hebrews or implicitly through a subtle interweaving of categories and their ideological reconfiguration. Farmer is right to note in AJohn a highlighting of Jesus's control. Farmer is also right, however, to note that that control is not so much over the physical context of the crucifixion itself but over the perception of it by observers. It is not surprising to find significant elements of a priestly, gnostic-manipulationist approach to Jesus in this text. These are not, however, contrary to Farmer's assertion, presentations of Jesus as high priest, something that I believe to be only presented ironically in GJohn. That Jesus's undergarment was seamless and not torn does not help us see that this was actually or typologically a high-priestly tunic.[40] The mention of "hyssop" does not indicate Jesus's priestly role. More ironically, the reference to Jesus carrying his own cross in relation to Isaac carrying the fire and the wood for his sacrifice (cf. Gen 22:6), which has suggested to some that Jesus is fully in control of his fate, is not helpful: Isaac is clearly not in control of his destiny but clueless as to the outcome of the events

40. Only the reference to Philo, *Fug.* 111–112 seems useful.

that await him at the hands of his father.[41] In sum, Jesus as high priest is probably not a topos that is central to the priestly rhetoric of GJohn, even though Jesus as configurer of reality *is* central to AJohn. In contrast, Jesus as sacrifice is central to the priestly discourse that infuses GJohn, and this is absent from AJohn.

Yet most of the features in GJohn highlighted in Johannine priestly discourse are absent from AJohn, including the absence of any reference to the paschal lamb, which, as Farmer notes, is a reference that the author almost assuredly would have known from his own Christian context. But this absence, I would underscore, is more than just "an" absence: it is the absence of the fundamental rhetograph around which GJohn paints its picture of the Word in the realm of the flesh.[42] The distance between the two rhetorical presentations could not be greater.

Furthermore, a sociorhetorical approach to both GJohn and AJohn, with special attention to the rhetorical discourses at work in each, reveals matters that are otherwise ignored. An illustration can be found in attention to a word that is regularly passed over in commentary, namely, παρέδωκεν (GJohn 19:30). Farmer suggests that "we may … reject the reading that suggests the moment of glorification was Jesus's handing over of his spirit while on the cross to the symbolic representatives of the church: Mary and the Beloved Disciple" (p. 230). Fair enough, but he does not then indicate either why he rejects this reading or what the word does then mean. Yet a sociorhetorical interpretation of the Johannine crucifixion scene suggests that Jesus is not only the paschal sacrifice but also that, as such, and in contrast with the Synoptic depiction, he is that sacrifice precisely at the hands of those who take the lives of the lambs, namely, the temple personnel. Enigmatically and, yes, ambiguously, the Gospel actually says this syntactically when in GJohn 19:16 the narrator states that Pilate "handed over" (παρέδωκεν) Jesus to "them" (αὐτοῖς) to be crucified. Now, read in light of the Synoptic account, "them" here is normally understood to be the soldiers of Pilate's guard; however, in GJohn 19:15 the immediate referent for "them" in 19:16 does not refer to any soldiers, nor to any Jewish crowd, but

41. On the other hand, Isaac's father Abraham *would* be performing a kind of priestly activity analogous to the high priest.

42. A fuller sociorhetorical interpretation of GJohn will also reveal that the apparent cosmic dimensions of the Gospel's depiction are not so much cosmic in a contemporary or even in a Platonic mode but are actually the dimensions of the "world" of Second Temple Judaism, with the temple as the cardinal center of that "world."

only to the high priests: ἐκραύγασαν οὖν ἐκεῖνοι· ἆρον ἆρον, σταύρωσον αὐτόν. λέγει *αὐτοῖς* ὁ Πιλᾶτος· τὸν βασιλέα ὑμῶν σταυρώσω; ἀπεκρίθησαν *οἱ ἀρχιερεῖς*· οὐκ ἔχομεν βασιλέα εἰ μὴ Καίσαρα.[43] Verse 16, then, must be understood as Pilate's acquiescence to "them," that is, to the high priests with the action of crucifixion suggesting that they are the ones to fulfill the task: Τότε οὖν παρέδωκεν αὐτὸν *αὐτοῖς* ἵνα σταυρωθῇ. Παρέλαβον οὖν τὸν Ἰησοῦν (emphasis added). Thus the rhetorical force of GJohn's discourse—not the historical reality of the crucifixion event—builds on the priestly discourse of categories 1 and 2 above that sees the priests as being the ones who will take the sacrifice to the place of sacrifice, which in this case will not be the taking of the paschal lambs to the temple but rather the taking of *the* paschal lamb to Golgotha. True, the soldiers (19:16) take Jesus and crucify him (v.18), but the entire episode (19:16–30) is overseen by the priestly personnel (cf. 19:31), who interject during the actual crucifixion only that the description of the deed is wrong (19:20–22).

As such, it is to this same "them" that the verb in 19:30 likely also points. While immediate syntax might suggest that the object of the verb is the soldiers of 19:29, analysis of repetitive texture reveals the extensive use of the word παρέδωκεν: 6:64, 71; 12:4; 13:2, 11, 21; 21:20; as well as the extensive use in the arrest and crucifixion sequences: 18:2, 5, 30, 35, 36; 19:11, 16 (a verse cited by Farmer); and finally 19:30. Commentary and translations are consistent in its meaning everywhere, considering it to be a moment of arrest, betrayal, and so on. Everywhere, that is, except for 19:30. While it is not impossible that 19:30 is the one, exceptional use of the word throughout John, I find it very strange that the word is not understood in 19:30 to have the same rhetorical force that it has everywhere else in John, namely, to be handed over to be punished or killed, especially in light of who those whom GJohn considers to be the overseers of Jesus's death, namely, the temple personnel. Accordingly, is it not more likely that John 19:30 suggests that in the end, the sacrifice expired, an end that was desired and fulfilled by his sacrificers?[44] This death is a full, nondocetic death, as much a real death as that of the paschal lamb but like that death signifying something more than just the death of a being. In the

---

43. Emphasis added. The meaning of the subject of the third person plural verb at the start of v. 15 depends on the meaning of the reference immediately prior to v. 15 in v. 14, namely, τοῖς Ἰουδαίοις.

44. It may also mean simply that the soldiers have done their duty, but that seems unnecessarily to impoverish the otherwise rich, rhetographic use of this verb in John.

case of the slaughter of the paschal lamb, it can only be followed by the consumption of the paschal lambs at the meal that follows, something that John again ironically and, yes, ambiguously, and now also in a sinister way envisions as about to happen that same evening in homes adjacent to the temple with a purity and security guaranteed by the ones responsible for the spiritual benefits to the community (19:31). Yet for John the paschal lambs, once a symbol of freedom, are so no longer, since there has now been a greater, final slaying of the paschal lamb that takes away the world's sin.[45]

In contrast to this clearly rhetographically rich though dark depiction in John, what we find in AJohn are topoi that promote a vision of a priestly Jesus who is very much in control, even above the fray. These topoi include those "royal" topoi that are admittedly present to some extent in the Johannine crucifixion. The reason for this presence is compellingly made by Farmer when he points to the resonances of Middle Platonism in the material found in the crucifixion scene in AJohn. These resonances account for elements of the lexicon used in AJohn, including lexica drawn from GJohn or traditions derived from GJohn, as well as for the relative absence of material drawn more from Jewish Scriptures and culture and for a uniquely hieratic form of priestly discourse in AJohn, a form that is completely missing in GJohn. What is shown in AJohn is a revealer who as revealer provides a kind of redemptive guidance to humans. The revealer, in this case Jesus, is the one who takes away human blindness—or better said, human inability to see beyond appearances (see GJohn 7:24)—and gives humans in the person of John knowledge that all physical appearances are relative.[46] For this reason, polymorphy is primarily intended to be a directive concerning the proper place of relativism of perspectives in the material world, a relativism that contrasts with the essential unity of the divine. This kind of thinking is, as Farmer notes well, very much at

45. A fuller sociorhetorical analysis of John's Gospel reveals that "world" is not to be understood in a kind of cosmic, geocentric way, but rather culturally as the center of the Judean, Jerusalem-based world, namely, the sphere of meaning that finds its center in the temple. Jesus's sacrifice removes the stain that the temple has become, one that keeps Israel separate from God rather than atoned for with and by God.

46. I believe that it is less likely the case that AJohn depicts a narrative in which "through Jesus's death … all the various forms of the universe are brought into harmony through the Lord's mediating sacrifice," as Farmer suggests in his conclusion (p. 250), and much more likely that Jesus's death represents the height of the relativization of all physical (i.e., earthly) realities.

home in Middle Platonism. And though not absent from GJohn (again see 7:24), this still does not overcome the stark contrast between the rhetorical force of GJohn's crucifixion scene and that of AJohn.[47]

8. Analytical Conclusions

The depiction of Jesus in the Gospel of John, while built around events that differ dramatically from those of the Synoptic Gospels, comes close to the depiction found at the ground level of the extant Synoptic tradition in Mark. In that earliest of the Synoptic Gospels, Jesus is depicted as the one who, through his prophetic rejection by the Jewish leadership in the form of the Roman-appointed temple leadership and his resulting death with their full complicity, will inaugurate the end of time in the coming of the Son of Man, coming in the clouds of judgment over Jerusalem as he once was depicted as coming in the clouds of judgment over Babylon. In John's Gospel, the temple and its leadership are also the target of Jesus's intention; however, John's Gospel rhetorically displays an even more oppressive landscape against which the topography and topology of the narrative will play out: from the beginning of his earthly incarnation, the Word has been on trial not by the Roman overlords but by the personnel of the house of God. It is they, not the Romans, who seek to understand, who cannot understand, and who in the end will slay the paschal lamb, thus sealing the doom of their "world" but in doing so also opening the door to the sheep of God's wider flock. The rhetorical force of John's depiction is indeed forceful, rhetographically grounded in images that, while not recitations of the Jewish Scriptures for the most part, echo them and recontextualize

---

47. I believe that Farmer could actually have shown more clearly that AJohn is using certain topoi from GJohn or traditions drawn from GJohn, while at the same time reconfiguring the more physical force of those topoi as they are employed in the Gospel itself. For example, in AJohn 98 and 99 we find the following words being used: διαπηξάμενος, διορίσας, πηγάσας. It is true that these words can mean, as Farmer has it, "united," "marked off," and "compacted" respectively, all words that have a Middle Platonic value, and used as such in AJohn. However, etymologically, each of these words is actually more fundamentally related to the physical events of crucifixion as shown in John: "pierced or transfixed," "to have a line drawn through it," and "gushing forth" respectively. In other words, has the author of AJohn taken words that relate directly to the physical aspects of the crucifixion scene in John's depiction but then reconfigured them for a more philosophical meaning?

and reconfigure them for a new day.[48] To do so, GJohn employs priestly rhetorolect both as it would be understood culturally and also as ideologically reconfigured to present a new sacrifice taken by old hands.

Acts of John is a text that knows the Johannine tradition, though probably not just GJohn or even perhaps GJohn at all. But whether it knows GJohn or a tradition that itself draws on GJohn and that has developed over decades, it is clear that AJohn contains a few elements that are found in the rhetorical fabric of GJohn. The ones that it does contain—especially outstanding, rhetographical components that are associated with the "cross of light," including topoi such as Bread, Word, Door, Way, Resurrection, Son, Father, Spirit, Life, Truth, Faith—are topoi that have probably been picked up widely by the burgeoning Christian intellectual system, even ignoring the rhetorical force of the ground from which they were originally drawn, namely, GJohn. In doing so, AJohn, like so much of developing Christian discourse, presents a form of mantic discourse based in a Greco-Roman discourse of priestly, mediated visions, while employing some now disconnected Johannine topoi. In fact, a closer reading of AJohn thanks to these two essays reveals not first of all intertextural links of AJohn to GJohn but the distance between the rhetorical discourse that is prominent in the Gospel and the way that discourse is so profoundly reconfigured and in fact distant in AJohn. True, there is a connection through the topoi. But that connection is one that, as sociorhetorical interpretation would suggest, now needs to be traced through the mediated tradition of Christian intellectual reflection on Scripture, one that began within decades of the start of the Christian movement and that led to the invention of Christian discourse. It is that invention whose story is still being written. Sociorhetorical interpretation to this point has focused primarily on the biblical texts themselves. These two essays help us now to see the promise but also the challenges that SRI needs to confront as it moves into the ways those biblical texts have been so profoundly reconfigured, leading to the formation of new rhetorolects within Christian discourse.

Finally, these two essays also reveal how important it is to develop SRI not just in terms of its initial exploration of textures—what I call the first stage of SRI—but also now in light of the full panoply of resources available to SRI in this new millennium. Unfortunately, most SRI work is still

48. Farmer's concluding remarks concerning the significance of "priestly, precreation, and wisdom rhetorolects" in both GJohn and AJohn is forced given the minor role that he actually assigns to any discussion of rhetorolects.

being done as if the fuller exploration of insights from cognitive science and conceptual metaphor theory were not entirely relevant. If anything, these essays demonstrate how important it is today that a full SRI analysis not simply entertain the issues of textural analysis as we did in the 1990s. Future studies of AJohn must explore the new horizons available to us, what shape the conceptual blending takes in the varied strata of materials that make up this rich text, what rhetorolects are blended and how we can demonstrate that to be the case, what "anchors" help ground the "frames" within which the putative reader of the text is being invited to read the text, what metaphors are created through narrative action and voices, and so on. These and many other questions raised by SRI in this new millennium need to be on the horizon of all future SRI essays. These two essays helpfully point us to the new grounds where these questions will now be posed as students of SRI continue to push the boundaries of early Christian discourse and its invention.

Bibliography

Alter, Robert. *The Art of Biblical Poetry.* New York: Basic Books, 1985.

Anderson, Charles A. *Philo of Alexandria's Views of the Physical World.* WUNT 2/309. Tübingen: Mohr Siebeck, 2011.

Andia, Ysabel de. *Henosis: L'union à Dieu chez Denys l'Aréopagite.* Leiden: Brill, 1996.

Attridge, Harold W. "The Acts of John and the Fourth Gospel." Pages 255–65 in *From Judaism to Christianity: Tradition and Transition. A Festschrift for Thomas H. Tobin, S.J., on the Occasion of His Sixty-Fifth Birthday.* Edited by Patricia Walters. Leiden: Brill, 2010.

Barrett, C. K. *A Critical and Exegetical Commentary on the Acts of the Apostles.* 2 vols. ICC. Edinburgh: T&T Clark, 1994–1998.

Beech, Timothy. "A Socio-Rhetorical Analysis of the Development and Function of the Noah-Flood Narrative in *Sibylline Oracles* 1–2." PhD diss., Saint Paul University, Ottawa, Canada, 2008.

Beierwaltes, Werner. "Nous: Unity in Difference." Pages 231–46 in *Platonism and Forms of Intelligence.* Edited by John Dillon and Marie-Élise Zovko. Berlin: Akademie, 2008.

Benko, Stephen. "The Magnificat: A History of the Controversy." *JBL* 86 (1967): 263–75.

Berchman, Robert M. *From Philo to Origen: Middle Platonism in Transition.* BJS 69. Chico, CA: Scholars Press, 1984.

Berger, Peter L. *Pyramids of Sacrifice: Political Ethics and Social Change.* New York: Basic Books, 1974. Repr., Garden City, NY: Anchor, 1976.

Berger, Peter L., and Thomas Luckmann. *The Social Construction of Reality: A Treatise in the Sociology of Knowledge.* Garden City, NY: Doubleday, 1967.

Blakely, Sandra. "Toward an Archaeology of Secrecy: Power, Paradox, and the Great Gods of Samothrace." *Archeological Papers of the American Anthropological Association* 21 (2011): 49–71.

Blank, Sheldon H. "The Death of Zechariah in Rabbinic Literature." *HUCA* 12–13 (1937–1938): 327–46.

Bloomquist, L. Gregory. "Methodological Criteria for Apocalyptic Rhetoric: A Suggestion for the Expanded Use of Sociorhetorical Analysis." Pages 181–203 in *Vision and Persuasion: Rhetorical Dimensions of Apocalyptic Discourse*. Edited by Greg Carey and L. Gregory Bloomquist. St. Louis: Chalice, 1999.

———. "Methodology for Rhetography and Visual Exegesis of the Gospel of John." RRA/Sawyer Seminar in the Context of the Mellon Foundation Sawyer Seminar Program: Visual Exegesis: Images as Instruments of Scriptural Interpretation and Hermeneutics. Emory University, September 16, 2013.

———. "Paul's Inclusive Language: The Ideological Texture of Romans 1." Pages 165–93 in *Fabrics of Discourse: Essays in Honor of Vernon K. Robbins*. Edited by David B. Gowler, L. Gregory Bloomquist, and Duane Watson. Harrisburg, PA: Trinity Press International, 2003.

Boring, M. Eugene. *Mark: A Commentary*. NTL. Louisville: Westminster John Knox, 2006.

Boring, M. Eugene, Klaus Berger, and Carsten Colpe, eds. *Hellenistic Commentary to the New Testament*. Nashville: Abingdon, 1995.

Bovon, François. *Luke 1: A Commentary on the Gospel of Luke 1:1–9:50*. Hermeneia. Minneapolis: Fortress, 2002.

———. *Luke 3: A Commentary on the Gospel of Luke 19:28–24:53*. Hermeneia. Minneapolis: Fortress, 2012.

Brodie, Thomas L. *The Gospel according to John: A Literary and Theological Commentary*. New York: Oxford University Press, 1993.

Brown, Peter. *The Body and Society: Men, Women, and Sexual Renunciation in Early Christianity*. New York: Columbia University Press, 1988.

Brown, Raymond E. *The Birth of the Messiah: A Commentary on the Infancy Narratives in the Gospels of Matthew and Luke*. Updated ed. New York: Doubleday, 1993.

———. *The Gospel according to John*. 2 vols. AB 29–29A. Garden City, NY: Doubleday, 1966–1970.

Buth, Randall. "Hebrew Poetic Tenses and the Magnificat." *JSNT* 21 (1984): 67–83.

Camp, Claudia V. "Storied Space, or, Ben Sira 'Tells' a Temple." Pages 64–80 in *"Imagining" Biblical Worlds: Studies in Spatial, Social and Historical Constructs in Honor of James W. Flanagan*. Edited by David M. Gunn and Paula M. McNutt. JSOTSup 359. London: Sheffield Academic, 2002.

Charles, R. H. *The Apocrypha and Pseudepigrapha of the Old Testament in English: With Introductions and Critical and Explanatory Notes to the Several Books*. 2 vols. Oxford: Clarendon, 1913.

Cohen, Shaye J. D. "Menstruants and the Sacred in Judaism and Christianity." Pages 273–99 in *Women's History and Ancient History*. Edited by Sarah Pomeroy. Chapel Hill: University of North Carolina Press, 1991.

Collins, Adela Yarbro. *Mark: A Commentary*. Hermeneia. Minneapolis: Fortress, 2007.

Cothenet, Edouard. "Le Protévangile de Jacques: origine, genre et signification d'un premier midrash chrétien sur la Nativité de Marie." *ANRW* 25.6:4252–69.

Danker, Frederick W., Walter Bauer, William F. Arndt, and F. Wilbur Gingrich. *Greek-English Lexicon of the New Testament and Other Early Christian Literature*. 3rd ed. Chicago: University of Chicago Press, 2000.

Davies, W. D., and Dale C. Allison. *A Critical and Exegetical Commentary on the Gospel according to Saint Matthew*. 3 vols. ICC. Edinburgh: T&T Clark, 1988–1997.

deSilva, David A. "The Invention and Argumentative Function of Priestly Discourse in the Epistle to the Hebrews." *BBR* 16 (2006): 295–323.

Dillon, John. *The Middle Platonists, 80 B.C. to A.D. 220*. Ithaca, NY: Cornell University Press, 1977.

Dillon, Richard J. "The Benedictus in Micro- and Macrocontext." *CBQ* 68 (2006): 457–80.

Ehrman, Bart D., and Zlatko Pleše. *The Apocryphal Gospels: Texts and Translations*. New York: Oxford University Press, 2011.

Elliott, J. K., ed. *The Apocryphal New Testament: A Collection of Apocryphal Christian Literature in an English Translation*. Oxford: Clarendon, 2005.

———. "The Protevangelium of James." Pages 48–67 in *The Apocryphal New Testament: A Collection of Apocryphal Christian Literature in an English Translation*. Edited by J. K. Elliott. Oxford: Clarendon, 2005.

Farris, Stephen. *The Hymns of Luke's Infancy Narratives: Their Origin, Meaning and Significance*. JSNTSup 9. Sheffield: JSOT Press, 1985.

Fauconnier, Gilles. *Mental Spaces: Aspects of Meaning Construction in Natural Language*. Cambridge: Cambridge University Press, 1994.

Filson, Floyd V. "How Much of the New Testament Is Poetry?" *JBL* 67 (1948): 125–34.

Fitzmyer, Joseph A. *The Gospel according to Luke (I–IX): Introduction, Translation, and Notes*. AB 28. Garden City, NY: Doubleday, 1981.

———. *The Gospel according to Luke (X–XXIV): Introduction, Translation, and Notes*. AB 28A. Garden City, NY: Doubleday, 1985.

Fleddermann, H. T. *Q: A Reconstruction and Commentary*. BTS 1. Leuven: Peeters, 2005.

Foskett, Mary F. *A Virgin Conceived: Mary and Classical Representations of Virginity*. Bloomington: Indiana University Press, 2002.

Foster, Paul, ed. *The Non-Canonical Gospels*. T&T Clark Biblical Studies. London: T&T Clark, 2008.

———. "The *Protevangelium of James*." Pages 110–25 in *The Non-Canonical Gospels*. Edited by Paul Foster. T&T Clark Biblical Studies. London: T&T Clark, 2008.

Freedman, David Noel. "Pottery, Poetry, and Prophecy: An Essay on Biblical Poetry." *JBL* 96 (1977): 5–26.

Frend, W. H. C. *Martyrdom and Persecution in the Early Church: A Study of a Conflict from the Maccabees to Donatus*. Garden City, NY: Anchor, 1967.

Gersh, Stephen. *Middle Platonism and Neoplatonism: The Latin Tradition*. 2 vols. PMS 23.1–2. Notre Dame: University of Notre Dame Press, 1986.

Girard, René. "History and the Paraclete." *Ecumenical Review* 35 (1983): 3–16.

Glancy, Jennifer A. *Corporal Knowledge: Early Christian Bodies*. Oxford: Oxford University Press, 2010.

Gowler, David B., L. Gregory Bloomquist, and Duane F. Watson, eds. *Fabrics of Discourse: Essays in Honor of Vernon K. Robbins*. Harrisburg, PA: Trinity Press International, 2003.

Green, Joel B. *The Gospel of Luke*. NICNT. Grand Rapids: Eerdmans, 1997.

Gudrun, Colbow, and Hurschmann Rolf. "Beard." In *Brill's New Pauly: Antiquity*. Edited by Hubert Cancik and Helmuth Schneider. Brill Online, 2012.

Gunkel, Hermann. *The Psalms: A Form-Critical Introduction*. Translated by Thomas M. Horner. Philadelphia: Fortress, 1967.

Harnack, Adolf von. *Geschichte der altchristlichen Litteratur bis Eusebius*. 2 vols. Leipzig: Hinrichs, 1893–1904.

Harris, Elizabeth. *Prologue and Gospel: The Theology of the Fourth Evangelist.* JSNTSup 107. Sheffield: Sheffield Academic, 1994.

Heil, John Paul. "Jesus as the Unique High Priest in the Gospel of John." *CBQ* 57 (1995): 728–45.

Hill, Charles E. *The Johannine Corpus in the Early Church.* Oxford: Oxford University Press, 2004.

Hock, Ronald F. *The Infancy Gospels of James and Thomas: With Introduction, Notes, and Original Text Featuring the New Scholars Version Translation.* ScholBib 3. Santa Rosa, CA: Polebridge, 1995.

Hock, Ronald F., and Edward N. O'Neil. *The Chreia in Ancient Rhetoric.* 3 vols. Atlanta: Society of Biblical Literature, 1986–2012.

Holladay, Carl R. *A Critical Introduction to the New Testament: Interpreting the Message and Meaning of Jesus Christ.* Expanded Digitial Edition. Nashville: Abingdon, 2005.

Jay, Nancy B. *Throughout Your Generations Forever: Sacrifice, Religion, and Paternity.* Chicago: University of Chicago Press, 1992.

Johnson, Luke Timothy. *The Writings of the New Testament.* 3rd ed. Minneapolis: Fortress, 2010.

Johnson, Mark. *The Body in the Mind: The Bodily Basis of Meaning, Imagination, and Reason.* Chicago: University of Chicago Press, 1987.

Junod, Eric. "Polymorphie du dieu sauveur." Pages 38–46 in *"Gnosticisme et monde hellénistique," actes du Colloque de Louvain-la-Neuve, 11–14 mars 1980.* Edited by Julien Ries. Publications de l'Institut Orientaliste de Louvain 27. Louvain-la-Neuve: Institut orientaliste, 1982.

Junod, Eric, and Jean-Daniel Kaestli. *Acta Iohannis.* 2 vols. CCSA 1–2. Turnhout: Brepols, 1983.

Kennedy, George A. *Progymnasmata: Greek Textbooks of Prose Composition and Rhetoric.* WGRW 10. Atlanta: Society of Biblical Literature, 2003.

Klauck, Hans-Josef. *The Apocryphal Acts of the Apostles: An Introduction.* Translated by Brian McNeil. Waco, TX: Baylor University Press, 2008.

Knox, W. L. *The Sources of the Synoptic Gospels.* 2 vols. Edited by Henry Chadwick. Cambridge: Cambridge University Press, 1953.

Koester, Helmut. *History and Literature of Early Christianity.* Vol. 2 of *Introduction to the New Testament.* Philadelphia: Fortress, 1982.

Lakoff, George, and Mark Johnson. *Philosophy in the Flesh: The Embodied Mind and Its Challenge to Western Thought.* New York: Basic Books, 1999.

Lalleman, Pieter J. *The Acts of John: A Two-Stage Initiation into Johannine Gnosticism*. SAAA 4. Leuven: Peeters, 1998.

———. "Polymorphy of Christ." Pages 97–118 in *The Apocryphal Acts of John*. Edited by Jan N. Bremmer. SAAA 1. Kampen: Kok Pharos, 1995.

Lapham, Fred. *An Introduction to the New Testament Apocrypha*. London: T&T Clark, 2003.

Lee, Simon S. *Jesus' Transfiguration and the Believers' Transformation: A Study of the Transfiguration and Its Development in Early Christian Writings*. WUNT. 2/265. Tübingen: Mohr Siebeck, 2009.

Levine, Amy-Jill. "Visions of Kingdoms: From Pompey to the First Jewish Revolt." Pages 466–514 in *The Oxford History of the Biblical World*. Edited by Michael D. Coogan. New York: Oxford University Press, 2001.

Liddell, Henry George, Robert Scott, Henry Stuart Jones. *A Greek-English Lexicon*. 9th ed. with revised supplement. Oxford: Clarendon, 1996.

Lieu, Judith. "Temple and Synagogue in John." *NTS* 45 (1999): 51–69.

Limberis, Vasiliki. *Divine Heiress: The Virgin Mary and the Creation of Christian Constantinople*. New York: Routledge, 1994.

Lipsius, R. A., and M. Bonnet, eds. *Acta apostolorum apocrypha*. 2 vols. Leipzig: Mendelssohn, 1891–1903.

Loisy, Alfred. *Le quatrième évangile: les épîtres dites de Jean*. Paris: Nourry, 1921.

Louw, Johannes P., and Eugene A. Nida, eds. *Greek-English Lexicon of the New Testament: Based on Semantic Domains*. 2nd ed. Accordance electronic edition, version 4.0. New York: United Bible Societies, 1989.

MacDonald, Dennis R. *The Homeric Epics and the Gospel of Mark*. New Haven: Yale University Press, 2000.

———, ed. *Mimesis and Intertextuality in Antiquity and Christianity*. Harrisburg, PA: Trinity Press International, 2001.

———. "Tobit and the Odyssey." Pages 11–40 in *Mimesis and Intertextuality in Antiquity and Christianity*. Edited by Dennis R. MacDonald. Harrisburg, PA: Trinity Press International, 2001.

Malina, Bruce J. "John's: The Maverick Christian Group, The Evidence of Sociolinguistics." *BTB* 24 (1994): 167–82.

———. *The New Testament World: Insights from Cultural Anthropology*. Rev. ed. Louisville: Westminster John Knox, 1993.

Malina, Bruce J., and Richard Rohrbaugh. *Social-Science Commentary on the Gospel of John*. Minneapolis: Fortress, 1998.

Meeks, Wayne. "The Man from Heaven in Johannine Sectarianism." *JBL* 91 (1972): 44–72.

Metzger, Bruce. *A Textual Commentary on the Greek New Testament*. 2nd ed. New York: United Bible Societies, 1994.

Miles, Jack. *God: A Biography*. New York: Knopf, 1995.

Moloney, Francis J. *The Gospel of John*. SP 4. Collegeville, MN: Liturgical Press, 1998.

Nolland, John. *Luke 1–9:20*. WBC 35A. Dallas: Word, 1989.

Nickelsburg, George W. E. "Tobit, Genesis, and the *Odyssey*: A Complicated Web of Intertextuality." Pages 41–55 in *Mimesis and Intertextuality in Antiquity and Christianity*. Edited by Dennis R. MacDonald. Harrisburg, PA: Trinity Press International, 2001.

Nutzman, Megan. "Mary in the Protevangelium of James: A Jewish Woman in the Temple?" *GRBS* 53 (2013): 551–78.

Oakley, Todd V. "Conceptual Blending, Narrative Discourse, and Rhetoric." *Cognitive Linguistics* 9 (1998): 331.

O'Neill, J. C. "Did Jesus Teach That His Death Would Be Vicarious as Well as Typical?" Pages 9–27 in *Suffering and Martyrdom in the New Testament: Studies Presented to G. M. Styler by the Cambridge New Testament Seminar*. Edited by William Horbury and Brian McNeil. Cambridge: Cambridge University Press, 1981.

Patillon, Michel, and Giancarlo Bolognesi, eds. *Aelius Théon: Progymnasmata*. Collection des universités de France Série grecque 376. Paris: Belles Lettres, 1997.

Pelikan, Jaroslav. *Jesus through the Centuries: His Place in the History of Culture*. New York: Harper & Row, 1985.

Pellegrini, Silvia. "Kindheitsevangelien." Pages 2:886–902 in *Antike christliche Apokryphen in deutscher Übersetzung*. Edited by C. Markschies and J. Schröter. 2 vols. Tübingen: Mohr Siebeck, 2012.

———. "Das Protevangelium des Jakobus." Pages 2:903–929 in *Antike christliche Apokryphen in deutscher Übersetzung*. Edited by C. Markschies and J. Schröter. 2 vols. Tübingen: Mohr Siebeck, 2012.

Penner, Todd C. *In Praise of Christian Origins: Stephen and the Hellenists in Lukan Apologetic Historiography*. ESEC 10. New York: T&T Clark, 2004.

Perry, John. *The Problem of the Essential Indexical: And Other Essays*. Rev. ed. Stanford, CA: CSLI, 2000.

Pervo, Richard I. *Acts: A Commentary*. Hermeneia. Minneapolis: Fortress, 2009.

———. "Johannine Trajectories in the Acts of John: Hommage à Helmut Koester." *Apocrypha* 3 (1992): 47–68.

Pietersma, Albert, and Benjamin G. Wright, eds. *A New English Translation of the Septuagint: And the Other Greek Translations Traditionally Included under That Title.* New York: Oxford University Press, 2007.

Quarles, Charles L. "The *Protevangelium of James* as an Alleged Parallel to Creative Historiography in the Synoptic Birth Narratives." *BBR* 8 (1998): 139–49.

Robbins, Vernon K. "Conceptual Blending and Early Christian Imagination." Pages 161–95 in *Explaining Christian Origins and Early Judaism: Contributions from Cognitive and Social Science.* Edited by Petri Luomanen, Ilkka Pyysiäinen, and Risto Uro. BIS 89. Leiden: Brill, 2007.

———. "The Dialectical Nature of Early Christian Discourse." *Scriptura* 59 (1996): 353–62. http://www.religion.emory.edu/faculty/robbins/SRS/vkr/dialect.cfm.

———. *Exploring the Texture of Texts: A Guide to Socio-Rhetorical Interpretation.* Valley Forge, PA: Trinity Press International, 1996.

———. *The Invention of Christian Discourse.* Vol. 1. RRA 1. Blandford Forum, UK: Deo, 2009.

———. "Making Christian Culture in the Epistle of James." *Scriptura* 59 (1996): 341–51.

———. "Precreation Discourse and the Nicene Creed: Christianity Finds Its Voice in the Roman Empire." *R&T* 18 (2012): 1–17.

———. "Questions and Answers in Gospel of Thomas." Pages 3–36 in *La littérature des questions et réponses dans l'Antiquité profane et chrétienne: de l'enseignement à l'exégèse: actes du séminaire sur le genre des questions et réponses tenu à Ottawa les 27 et 28 septembre 2009.* Edited by M.-P. Bussières. IPM 64. Turnhout: Brepols, 2013.

———. "Rhetography: A New Way of Seeing the Familiar Text." Pages 81–106 in *Words Well Spoken: George Kennedy's Rhetoric of the New Testament.* Edited by C. Clifton Black and Duane F. Watson. SRR 8. Waco, TX: Baylor University Press, 2008.

———. "Socio-Rhetorical Interpretation." Pages 192–219 in *The Blackwell Companion to the New Testament.* Edited by David E. Aune. Oxford: Blackwell, 2010.

———. "Sociorhetorical Interpretation of Miracle Discourse in the Synoptic Gospels." Pages 17–84 in *Miracle Discourse in the New Testament.*

Edited by Duane F. Watson. Atlanta: Society of Biblical Literature, 2012.

———. "The Socio-Rhetorical Role of Old Testament Scripture in Luke 4–19." Pages 81–93 in *Z Noveho Zakona / From the New Testament: Sbornik k narozeninam Prof. ThDr. Zdenka Sazavy*. Edited by Hana Tonzarova and Petr Melmuk. Prague: Vydala Cirkev ceskoslovenska husitska, 2001.

———. *The Tapestry of Early Christian Discourse: Rhetoric, Society and Ideology*. London: Routledge, 1996.

———. *Who Do People Say I Am? Rewriting Gospel in Emerging Christianity*. Grand Rapids: Eerdmans, 2013.

Ross, W. D. *Plato's Theory of Ideas*. Oxford: Clarendon, 1951.

Rusam, Dietrich. *Das Alte Testament bei Lukas*. BZNW 112. Berlin: de Gruyter, 2003.

Ruthrof, Horst. *The Body in Language*. London: Cassell, 2000.

Schäferdiek, Knut. "Johannesakten." Pages 125–76 in *Neutestamentliche Apokryphen in deutscher Ubersetzung II*. Edited by Edgar Hennecke and Wilhelm Schneemelcher. Tübingen: Mohr Siebeck, 1964.

Schneider, Carl. *Geistesgeschichte des antiken Christentums*. 2 vols. Munich: Beck, 1954.

Schneider, Paul G. "The Mystery of the Acts of John: An Interpretation of the Hymn and the Dance in Light of the Acts' Theology." PhD diss., Columbia University, 1990.

Shore, Bradd. *Culture in Mind: Cognition, Culture, and the Problem of Meaning*. New York: Oxford University Press, 1996.

Simons, Robert. "The Magnificat: Cento, Psalm or Imitatio?" *TynBul* 60 (2009): 25–46.

Smid, Harm Reinder. *Protevangelium Jacobi: A Commentary*. Assen: Van Gorcum, 1965.

Smith, D. Moody. *John*. ANTC. Nashville: Abingdon, 1999.

Stempvoort, Pieter A. van. "The Protevangelium Jacobi: The Sources of Its Theme and Style and Their Bearing on Its Date." Pages 410–26 in *Studia Evangelica III*. Edited by F. L. Cross. TUGAL 88. Berlin: Akademie, 1964.

Strelan, Rick. *Luke the Priest: The Authority of the Author of the Third Gospel*. Burlington, VT: Ashgate, 2008.

Tannehill, Robert C. "The Magnificat as Poem." *JBL* 93 (1974): 263–75.

———. *The Narrative Unity of Luke-Acts: A Literary Interpretation*. 2 vols. Philadelphia: Fortress, 1986.

———. *The Shape of Luke's Story: Essays on Luke-Acts.* Eugene, OR: Cascade, 2005.

Thaden, Robert H. von, Jr. *Sex, Christ, and Embodied Cognition: Paul's Wisdom for Corinth.* ESEC 16. Blandford Forum, UK: Deo, 2012.

Tilborg, Sjef van. *Imaginative Love in John.* BIS 2. Leiden: Brill, 1993.

Tuñí, Josep Oriol. "Pasión y muerte de Jesús en el cuarto evangelio: Papel y significación." *RCT* 1 (1976): 393–419.

Vico, Giambattista. *The New Science of Giambattista Vico.* Ithaca, NY: Cornell University Press, 1968.

Vorster, Johannes N. "Construction of Culture through the Construction of Person: The *Acts of Thecla* as an Example." Pages 447–57 in *The Rhetorical Analysis of Scripture: Essays from the 1995 London Conference.* Edited by Stanley E. Porter and Thomas H. Olbricht. JSNTSup 146. Sheffield: Sheffield Academic, 1997.

Vorster, Willem S. "The Protevangelium of James and Intertextuality." Pages 262–75 in *Text and Testimony: Essays on New Testament and Apocryphal Literature in Honour of A. F. J. Klijn.* Edited by T. Baarda, A. Hilhorst, G. P. Luttikhuizen, and A. S. van der Woude. Kampen: Kok, 1988.

Vuong, Lily C. *Gender and Purity in the Protevangelium of James.* WUNT 2/358. Tübingen: Mohr Siebeck, 2013.

Watson, Duane F., ed. *Miracle Discourse in the New Testament.* Atlanta: Society of Biblical Literature, 2012.

Westermann, Claus. *The Praise of God in the Psalms.* London: Epworth, 1966.

Wilson, Bryan R. "A Typology of Sects." Pages 361–83 in *Sociology of Religion: Selected Readings.* Edited by Roland Robertson. Baltimore: Penguin, 1969.

Wood, Laurence W. *God and History: The Dialectical Tension of Faith and History in Modern Thought.* Lexington: Emeth, 2005.

Zwiep, Arie W. *Judas and the Choice of Matthias: A Study on Context and Concern of Acts 1:15–26.* WUNT 2/187. Tübingen: Mohr Siebeck, 2004.

Contributors

L. Gregory Bloomquist is Professeur titulaire / Full Professor in the Faculté de Théologie / Faculty of Theology at Université Saint-Paul / Saint Paul University in Ottawa, Ontario, Canada.

Thomas Jared Farmer is a doctoral student in Philosophy of Religion and Theology at Claremont Graduate University in Claremont, California.

Ronald F. Hock is Professor Emeritus of Religion at the University of Southern California in Los Angeles, California.

Meredith Elliott Hollman is a doctoral student in New Testament in the Graduate Division of Religion at Emory University in Atlanta, Georgia.

Christopher T. Holmes is a doctoral candidate in New Testament in the Graduate Division of Religion at Emory University in Atlanta, Georgia.

Susan E. Hylen is Associate Professor of New Testament at Candler School of Theology at Emory University in Atlanta, Georgia.

Jonathan M. Potter is a doctoral student in New Testament in the Graduate Division of Religion at Emory University in Atlanta, Georgia.

Vernon K. Robbins is Professor of New Testament and Comparative Sacred Texts in the Department and Graduate Division of Religion at Emory University in Atlanta, Georgia.

Michael K. W. Suh is a doctoral student in New Testament in the Graduate Division of Religion at Emory University in Atlanta, Georgia.

Ancient Sources Index

Hebrew Bible/Septuagint

Genesis
1–3 15
1:2 121
1:22 87, 263
1:28 87, 263
2:24 46
3–8 16
4 20
6:4 91
9:4 22
11:30 138
12 5, 92, 101
12:1 120
12:2 83, 91–92, 99, 264, 266
14 20
14:18–19 60
15 145
18 134
18:11 138
18:14 134
22:6 228, 306
22:18 92
30:13 LXX 85
30:13 157
30:23 156

Exodus
3:11 LXX 80
3:14 246
4:14–16 53
4:30 53
7:1 53
7:2 55
12:10 242
12:11 153
12:22 230, 284
12:46 242
13:2 22, 26
13:12 22, 26
13:15 22, 26
13:21–22 121
16:9–10 53
19:6 46
24:8 33
25:7 89
26:31–37 148
27:21 127
28 20, 256
28:1–43 45
28:4 284
28:39 284
28:40 284
29:4 127
29:5 229
33:18–23 199, 218, 277
34:15–16 22
38:8 113
39–40 116, 119, 270
39:32 116
39:33–43 116
39:43 117
40:1–15 116
40:9–15 117
40:16–33 116
40:30–31 116
40:34–35 116, 125
40:36–38 117, 120–21

Leviticus
1:1 127
3:17 22
4:17 148
4:20 24
4:31 24
4:35 24
5:6 24
5:16 24
5:18 24
6:10 284
8 20, 256
12:1–8 22
12:8 26, 256
13–14 22
14:4 284
14:6 284
14:49 284
14:51 284
16:2 148
16:8–9 34
17–18 22
17:3–18:30 22
19:26 22

Numbers
1:1 127
3:10 LXX 148
3:26 LXX 148
4:8 148
6:1–21 22
6:23–27 60
8:10–11 36
9:12 242
10:33–36 121
14:44 121
16:2 91
17:1–11 123
18:15–16 27
24:17 85
27:22–23 36

Deuteronomy
12:16 22
12:26–27 22
18:21–22 52
21:5 53
34:9 36

Joshua
2:18 148
3:1–4:18 121

Judges
13:5–7 LXX 138

1 Samuel
1–2 109
1:21–23 108
1:21–2:11 5, 107, 110, 269
1:22–24 26
1:23 108, 269
1:24–2:10 108
1:25 LXX 27
2:1–10 20, 109, 137
2:11 109–10
2:12–17 114
2:19–20 108, 269
2:20 60
2:22 108, 113–14
3–5 122

1 Kingdoms
2:11 110
2:18 110

2 Samuel
6 116, 270
6:3–6 125
6:6–7 53, 126, 271
6:12–17 125
7:12–14 124
7:14 123
7:18 80, 124
7:29 124
9:8 80
13:18 284

1 Kings
7:1–24 17

8 116
18:27 147

3 Kingdoms
8 270

2 Kings
6:32–37 17
19:21 147

1 Chronicles
15–16 116, 119, 270
15:1–15 116
15:15 118
15:25–29 116
15:25–16:1 125
16:1 116
16:2–36 117
16:4–42 117
16:43 117
17:1–6 121
17:6 121–22
17:16 80
18:17 92
22:19 89
24–25 34
24:10 21, 45
24:19 21, 45
28:10 89
29:14 80

2 Chronicles
3:14 148
5–7 116, 119, 270
5:1–4 116
5:4–8 125
5:5–10 116
5:7–8 118
5:11–14 116
6 123
6:1–42 117
6:18–21 127
7 117
7:1–3 125
7:1–4 116
7:4–9 117
24:20–22 149
26:11 92
28:7 92
36:16 147

Job
22:19 147
29:10 85

Psalms
2:4 LXX 147
21:8 LXX 147
22:17 228
34:16 LXX 147
40:3 LXX 85
50:20 142
71:17 LXX 85
77:33 LXX 153
79:7 LXX 147
88:18 142
105:8–13 120
114:1–2 120
143:15 LXX 85

Proverbs
1:30 147
8 16
11:12 147
12:8 147
15:4 LXX 136
15:5 147
15:20 147
23:9 147

Song of Songs
6:9 85

Isaiah
3:12 85
6:1–13 54
7:14 97
8:14–15 61
9:5–6 LXX 142
9:16 85

Isaiah (*cont.*)
37:22 147
51:17 61
53:7–8 39
53:12 228
54:3 242
56:5 91
61:1–2 131
66:1–2 23

Jeremiah
1:4–5 138
6:13–15 LXX 61
18:16 148
20:7 147
23:20 95
31:31 33

Ezekiel
7:11 153
8:17 147
20:35 120
22:5 91
23:3 91
41:1–42:12 51
44:2 148

Daniel
7:9 218
10:7 153
10:12 52
10:14 95
10:15 52
10:16 52, 54

Hosea
2:14 120

Joel
4:17 148

Amos
8:2–3 LXX 168
8:3 LXX 168
8:3 276

Micah
2:13 148
5:3–4 LXX 142

Zechariah
2:15 148

Malachi
3:12 85, 157
3:15 85

Judith
8:16 131
11:21 91
11:23 91
12:14 80
14:19 284

Wisdom of Solomon
2:16 85
6:4 131
9:13 131
18:1 85
19:2 153

Sirach
11:28 85
24 16
24:13–22 49
25:7 85
25:23 85
31:9 85
37:24 85
44–50 3, 49
45:6–22 49
45:7 85
45:15 55
46:1 92
48:8 92
50 50, 55–56, 60, 62
50:1 56
50:1–21 49, 259
50:4 56, 61
50:5 49–50
50:5–8 49

50:6 55
50:7 56
50:9 50
50:10 49
50:11–13 50
50:14–17 50, 56
50:16–21 58, 260
50:17–21 52
50:18 50
50:19 51, 56–57
50:20 51–52, 55–56
50:20–21 25
50:21 51, 55–56, 172
50:22 55–57
50:22–24 55, 259
50:23 57
50:24 55, 57

1 Maccabees
7:34 147
10:72 80

2 Maccabees
4 299
4:29 92
7 299
7:37–38 299
14:26 92

1 Esdras
1:47–49 147
2:25 153

3 Maccabees
4:15 153
5:24 153
5:27 153

4 Maccabees
1:10 85
1:11 299
6:27–29 299
16:9 85
17:21–22 299
18:13 85

New Testament

Matthew
1:21 98, 266
2:1 45, 120
2:3 45
2:7 45
2:12–13 45
2:15 45
2:16 45, 275
2:19 45
2:22 45
3:17 97
4:1–11 97
4:4 93
4:18–22 212
5:40 284
6:3 242
6:22 42
7:13 148
8:1–4 28
13:11 79
14:1 45
14:3 45
14:6 45
16:7–8 134
17:1 217
17:1–11 236
17:2 217–19
19:1–8 181
20:21 242
20:23 242
20:28 33, 94, 256
21:25 134
23:35 175, 275
24 236
25:33 242
27:2 99
27:31 99
27:32 228, 284
27:38–39 284
27:45 236
27:51 148, 168

Mark
1:1–13 203
1:11 210
1:13 71
1:14–13:36 203
1:16–20 212
1:40–45 28
2:6 134
2:8 134
2:12 236
4–13 203
4:1–8:26 203
4:11 79
4:26 286
6:14–29 174
6:24 153
8:27–30 204
8:27–9:13 205
8:27–10:52 203
8:31–9:1 204
9:2 216–18
9:2–3 206
9:2–8 181
9:2–13 204
9:3 217–218
9:4–9 207
9:7 210
9:10–13 208
9:14–50 204
9:50 205
10 204–205
10:24 93
10:37 242
10:45 33, 94, 256
11 205
11–13 204
13 236
13:26 211
14–15 204
14:1–42 204
14:43–15:32 204
14:44 99
14:53 99
14:63 284
15:16 99
15:21 228, 284
15:27 284
15:29 284
15:33 231, 236
15:33–47 204
15:38 148, 168, 231
15:39 231
16:1–8 204
16:19 213

Luke
1 70, 140
1–2 49, 67–69, 87, 100, 129, 130–34, 136–40, 143–47, 149, 165, 172–73, 175, 253, 258, 259–61, 267, 272–73, 276–77
1–4 70
1:1–4 45, 203
1:1–4:15 203
1:5 21, 23, 25, 44–46, 87, 137, 149, 256, 259
1:5–7 46, 52, 70, 259
1:5–24 70
1:5–25 24, 68, 137
1:5–2:40 70
1:5–2:52 203
1:5–4:13 68
1:6 23–24, 46–48, 259
1:7 137
1:8 47, 137
1:8–9 47
1:8–10 47, 59
1:8–20 71
1:8–21 20
1:8–23 60
1:9 47, 57, 60, 255
1:10 24, 47–48, 51
1:12 138
1:12–14 52
1:13 24, 71, 209
1:13–15 176
1:13–17 140
1:13–20 149
1:15 23, 56–57, 60, 136
1:15–17 177

1:16–17 69, 144
1:18 53, 138, 274
1:19 53, 56, 138
1:19–20 138
1:20 53, 69, 160, 274
1:21–22 60
1:21–25 138
1:23 54, 164
1:24–25 54, 156
1:26–27 56
1:26–38 25, 57, 68, 74, 80, 97, 133, 138, 140, 259
1:26–39 142
1:26–56 139
1:27 25, 56, 104, 140
1:28 57, 97, 134, 260
1:29 93, 98, 133–34, 138, 274
1:29–30 159
1:30 57, 133, 260
1:30–32 176
1:30–33 140, 266
1:30–38 98
1:31 57, 133
1:31–33 134, 142
1:32 140
1:32–33 69, 133, 144, 177
1:32–35 25
1:34 98, 104, 134, 138, 266
1:35 26, 57, 59–60, 98, 133–34
1:35–37 138
1:36 25, 57, 74, 133–34, 150, 256
1:36–56 137, 274
1:37 134
1:38 96
1:39 57, 73–74, 133, 151, 153, 170, 262
1:39–45 87
1:39–55 75
1:39–56 67–68, 73, 81, 259, 261
1:40 57–58, 77, 153
1:40–42 75
1:41 25, 57, 60, 77, 136, 144, 155, 262
1:41–42 134, 155
1:41–45 154
1:41–55 155
1:42 25, 57, 62, 77, 78, 82, 86, 90, 155, 256, 259, 274
1:42–44 274
1:42–45 68
1:43 57, 69, 74, 154
1:43–50 76
1:44 58, 78
1:45 58, 82, 86, 135, 137–38, 155, 262, 273
1:45–46 137
1:45–55 144
1:45–56 136
1:46 26, 82–83, 135–37, 150–51, 157, 274
1:46–47 144
1:46–48 79, 262
1:46–49 156, 273
1:46–53 156
1:46–54 79, 262
1:46–55 20, 58, 68, 131, 133–34, 136–37, 155, 156, 158, 260, 274
1:46–56 272, 274
1:47 135, 141, 145
1:48 25–26, 79, 82, 85, 124, 135, 144, 150, 155, 157, 262
1:49 69, 135, 144
1:49–53 144
1:49–54 79
1:50 135
1:50–55 273
1:51 135
1:51–53 61
1:51–55 77, 144
1:52–53 135
1:54 135, 136
1:54–55 69, 144, 157
1:55 135, 136
1:56 80, 137, 158, 262, 273
1:57 160
1:57–66 68, 71, 139
1:58 82–83
1:59 160
1:59–63 68
1:59–66 23
1:63 160

Luke (*cont.*)
1:64 24, 54–55, 62, 82, 86, 256
1:66 160
1:66–67 161
1:66–79 275
1:67 55, 57, 136, 139, 144, 273, 275
1:67–79 68, 131, 136–37, 139, 142, 160, 273, 275
1:68 24, 33, 55, 62, 139, 144, 161
1:68–74 144
1:68–75 161
1:68–79 142, 144, 160, 259
1:69 69, 140, 145, 161, 275
1:69–75 139, 144, 161
1:70 139
1:71 145, 163
1:72 55, 57, 139
1:73 139, 161
1:74 69
1:74–75 55, 163
1:75 24
1:76 139, 273, 277
1:76–77 144
1:76–79 139, 161, 163
1:77 24, 145, 256
1:78 55, 57, 275
1:78–79 144
1:79 55
1:80 68, 71
2 139–40, 168
2:1–7 80, 140
2:1–20 68
2:4–7 120
2:8–15 275
2:9 82, 165–66, 276
2:10 82, 141
2:10–11 142, 176
2:10–12 166
2:11 69, 141, 144–45, 177, 274
2:12 140
2:13 82, 83–84, 140
2:13–14 32, 168
2:13–15 167
2:14 82–83, 131–32, 141–42, 144, 273–75
2:15 167, 276
2:16 170, 276
2:16–18 169
2:17 56
2:20 32, 55, 82–84, 140
2:21 26, 59, 68
2:21–24 260
2:22 22, 26, 59, 71, 143, 256
2:22–24 59
2:22–28 143
2:23 22, 26–27, 59, 60, 143
2:24 22, 26–27, 40, 59, 143
2:25 60, 69, 143, 170, 172, 274
2:25–26 276
2:25–27 143
2:25–31 171
2:25–36 70
2:26 60, 144, 173
2:26–35 172
2:27 27, 59, 60, 143, 274
2:27–28 276
2:28 27, 60, 62, 82–83, 86, 94, 256, 265
2:28–32 131, 173, 273, 276
2:29 60, 69, 144
2:29–32 68, 144, 276
2:29–3:35 173
2:30 95, 144–45, 173, 274
2:30–31 60
2:31–32 144
2:32 60, 82–83, 94, 143–44, 173, 274
2:32–35 172
2:33 60
2:34 27, 60, 62, 82, 86, 256
2:34–35 173
2:36–37 114
2:36–38 170
2:37 27, 60, 209
2:38 33, 68
2:39 27, 59, 61, 143
2:40 68
2:41–51 71, 260
2:41–52 62
2:46 62
2:46–47 27, 256

2:47 62
2:52 71
3:1 45
3:1–3 24
3:1–4:13 203
3:6 145
3:8 24
3:12 63
3:15 134
3:19 45, 56
3:21 29, 34
3:21–22 36, 209
3:21–23 62
3:36 22
3:40 61
3:47–48 27
4:1–13 62
4:6 82, 83
4:14–30 203, 206, 210
4:14–9:50 203
4:15 32, 55, 82–83, 263
4:16 56
4:16–30 131
4:16–21:38 203
4:18 28, 63
4:18–19 62
4:31–8:56 203
5:1–11 212
5:5 213
5:7 212
5:10–11 212
5:14 22, 28
5:16 29, 209, 217, 256
5:17 17
5:20 31, 256
5:21–22 134
5:24 31
5:25 55, 82–83
5:25–26 32
5:26 55, 82–84
5:28 56
5:30 31
5:32 32
6:12 29, 209, 217, 256
6:12–16 210
6:19 17
6:20–22 82, 86
6:28 32, 82, 86, 209
6:30 56
6:37 31
7:11–17 17
7:16 17, 32, 55, 82–84, 259
7:23 82, 86
7:30 131
7:35 56
7:37–38 31
7:47 31
7:48–50 31, 256
8:3 45
8:5 286
8:10 79
8:13 30
8:37 56
9:1–17 203
9:1–50 203, 205
9:7 45
9:7–9 175, 203
9:9 45, 175
9:10–17 203
9:16 82, 86
9:18 29, 209, 256
9:18–36 204
9:21–27 204
9:26 82–83, 211
9:28 202, 209, 211, 216–18, 256, 281
9:28–29 206, 213, 217
9:28–36 181, 183, 204, 236, 279
9:29 209, 216–18, 283
9:29–35 29
9:30 221
9:30–35 214
9:30–36 207
9:31 82, 83, 210–11, 217
9:31–32 218
9:32 56, 211, 217–18, 281
9:34 211
9:35 210, 215
9:36 215
9:37 208
9:37–50 204

Luke (*cont.*)
9:38 82
9:51–19:27 204–5
10:23 82, 86
10:26 143
10:29–35 29
10:32 56
11:1 209
11:1–4 29
11:2–4 256
11:4 32
11:27–28 82, 86
11:34 42
11:34–36 43
11:35 56
11:51 168, 175
12:27 82–83
12:37–38 82, 86
12:43 82, 86
13:1 40
13:13 32, 55, 82–83
13:15 71, 86
13:31 45
13:35 82
14:10 82
14:14–15 82, 86
16:8 84
16:14 147
16:16–17 143
17:4 32
17:11–19 29
17:14 22
17:15 32, 55, 82–83
17:15–16 28
17:18 29, 82–83
17:22 30, 256
17:26–27 22
18:1 30
18:1–8 209
18:2 30
18:3–8 30
18:9–10 30
18:9–14 209
18:11–12 30
18:14 30
18:43 32, 55, 82–84
19:1–10 28
19:9 145
19:11–27 28
19:28–21:38 204
19:37 82–83, 140
19:37–38 32
19:38 82, 86, 142
19:45–48 260
19:46 27, 209
20:1–38 63
20:1–21:38 27
20:2 28
20:17–18 61
20:22–26 28
20:47 31, 209, 256
21 236
21:1–2 28
21:12 99
21:24 61
21:27 82–83, 211
21:36 31
22:1–38 204
22:1–24:53 204
22:20 33
22:27 33
22:32 29
22:39 210
22:39–23:56 204
22:40 29
22:41 218
22:41–42 29, 256
22:43–44 30, 210
22:44–46 30
22:66 99
22:66–71 71
23:7–8 45
23:11–12 45
23:15 45
23:26 99, 228, 284
23:32 284
23:34 32, 36
23:35 147, 210
23:35–39 284
23:44 236

23:45 148
23:46 36, 210
23:47 32, 55, 82–84, 231
24 204, 211
24:1–12 168
24:5 168
24:7 45
24:21 33
24:24 143
24:25–26 211
24:26 82–83
24:30 82, 86
24:44–53 62
24:47 32–33, 39, 256
24:50 82, 256
24:50–51 32, 86
24:51 82, 213
24:53 32–33, 63, 82–83, 256, 260

John
1:1 225, 241, 246, 248
1:1–5 126
1:1–18 224, 226
1:4 241
1:4–5 283
1:7–8 188
1:9 126
1:14 105, 126–27, 188, 217, 220, 225, 241, 248, 282, 288, 303
1:15 188
1:16 220
1:16–17 241
1:17 241
1:18 241, 246
1:19 188, 295
1:19–51 224
1:19–12:50 224, 226
1:23 240
1:24 295
1:29 242, 295–96, 298
1:29–34 224
1:32 188
1:32–33 241
1:34 188, 241
1:35 242
1:35–51 224
1:36 295–96
1:39 287
1:41 241
1:47 287
1:49 229, 241–42
1:51 241
2 301
2:1–4:54 224
2:11 188, 282
2:13 230
2:13–22 122
2:13–23 295
2:16 241
2:21 127
2:23 230
2:24–25 288
2:25 188
3:1 295
3:2–21 226
3:5 229, 242
3:5–8 241
3:11 188
3:13–17 295
3:13–18 241
3:14–17 296
3:15–16 241
3:26 188
3:28 188
3:29 240
3:32–33 188
3:34–36 241
4:10–14 226
4:14 241
4:19–24 295
4:19–26 122
4:20–21 29
4:21 241
4:23–26 241
4:26 246
4:29 241
4:34 230
4:39 188
4:42 141
4:44 188

John (*cont.*)
4:45 230
5:1–15 301
5:1–47 224
5:1–10:42 224
5:9 230
5:14 295
5:15 43
5:16–47 301
5:17–23 241
5:18 246
5:19 230
5:19–29 241
5:25 240
5:26 241
5:28 240
5:30 230
5:31–34 188
5:36 188, 230
5:36–37 241
5:37 188, 240
5:37–38 240
5:39 188
5:39–40 241
5:43 241
5:45 241
6 301
6:1–71 224
6:4 230
6:15 229, 242
6:20 246
6:27 241
6:30–35 295
6:30–65 296
6:31 296
6:32 225, 241, 296
6:32–59 241
6:33–35 241
6:35 246
6:37 241
6:38 230
6:40 241
6:44–46 241
6:46 246
6:47 241
6:48 246
6:53–54 241
6:57 241
6:59 225
6:62 241
6:64 308
6:65 241
6:69 241
6:71 308
7–9 295
7:1–10:21 224
7:2 230
7:7 188
7:14 295
7:18 230
7:24 309–310
7:26–31 241
7:28 295
7:31 241
7:32 295
7:37–39 231
7:38 230
7:38–39 241
7:39 241
7:42 229, 242
7:45–48 295
8:12 246, 283
8:13–14 188
8:16 241
8:17–18 188
8:18–19 241
8:20 295
8:24 241, 246
8:27–28 241
8:28 226, 241
8:28–29 230
8:30–31 241
8:35–36 241
8:38 246
8:38–42 241
8:49 241
8:54 241
8:55 230
8:58 246
8:59 295

9	301
9:5	246, 283
9:22	241
9:35–38	241
9:38	246
10	296–97, 301
10:3–5	240
10:7	246
10:7–8	241
10:8	225
10:11	242, 246
10:11–18	295–96
10:14–15	242, 246
10:15–18	241
10:16	240
10:17–18	230
10:22	230
10:22–42	224
10:23	295
10:24–26	241
10:25	188
10:25–38	241
10:28	295–96
10:30–33	246
10:37	230
10:37–38	241
10:38	246
10:42	241
11	296, 301
11:1–12:50	224
11:4	148
11:4–27	241
11:25	241, 246
11:25–27	241
11:27	241
11:40–48	241
11:41	241
11:43	240
11:46–53	295
11:49	295
11:50	299
11:50–52	295
11:51	295
11:55	230
11:55–57	295
11:55–12:36	225
11:56–57	295
12–17	296–97
12:1	230
12:3–8	295–97
12:4	308
12:12–19	229, 242
12:17	188
12:19	295
12:23	229, 241
12:24	241, 286
12:24–25	295–97
12:26–28	241
12:32	192, 228, 295–97
12:32–34	226
12:34	241
12:36–46	241
12:37	240
12:37–50	225
12:42	295
12:49–50	230, 241
13:1	229–30, 288
13:1–3	241
13:1–17:26	225
13:1–20:31	225–26
13:2	308
13:11	308
13:19	241, 246
13:21	188, 308
13:23	192, 283
13:25	192
13:31	241, 282
13:34–35	226
14:1–2	241
14:6	225, 241
14:6–14	241, 246
14:10–12	241
14:13	241
14:16–17	241
14:18–31	295–97
14:20–31	241
14:26	241
15:1	241, 246
15:5	246
15:8–10	241

John (cont.)
15:13 295–97
15:15–16 241
15:18 226
15:18–27 225
15:23–26 241
15:24 246
15:26–27 188
16:1–4 225
16:3 241
16:8 225
16:10 241
16:13 241
16:15 246
16:15–17 241
16:20 225
16:23–32 241
16:27 241
16:30 241
16:33 225–26
17 297
17:1 229, 241
17:3 241
17:4 230
17:5 241
17:8 241
17:11 241
17:13–19 225
17:14 295–97
17:14–16 120
17:20–21 241
17:22 295–297
17:24–25 241
17:26 295–297
18–19 297
18:1–11 225
18:1–19:42 225
18:2 308
18:3 295
18:5 308
18:10 295
18:11 230, 241
18:12–27 225
18:13–16 295
18:19–24 295
18:23 188
18:26 295
18:28 230
18:28–19:16 225
18:30 308
18:33–39 229, 242
18:35 295, 308
18:36 308
18:37 188
18:39 230
19 224
19:6 295
19:7 241
19:11 308
19:14 230, 308
19:15 295, 307–8
19:16 307–8
19:16–18 227
19:16–30 308
19:16–37 225, 227, 283–84
19:17 284
19:18 228, 284, 308
19:19–22 227–28, 242
19:20–22 308
19:21 295
19:23–24 227, 229
19:25–30 227, 229, 244
19:26 229, 304
19:28–29 227, 229
19:29 284, 308
19:30 227, 229–30, 241, 307–8
19:31 308–9
19:31–33 227
19:31–37 227–48
19:33 248
19:34 231, 248
19:34–35 227
19:35 188, 241
19:36 242
19:36–37 227
19:37 248
19:38–20:29 225
20:2 219, 283
20:8 241
20:17 241

20:19–29 225
20:21 241
20:22 230, 241
20:25 241
20:27 215, 219, 283, 287
20:29 241
20:30–31 188, 225
20:31 188, 225, 241
21:1–14 225
21:1–25 226
21:4–7 220
21:15–24 225
21:20 192, 308
21:24 188
21:25 225

Acts
1:2 213
1:6–7 34
1:8 35
1:9 34
1:10 211
1:11 213
1:12–14 34
1:13–14 34, 256
1:25 34, 256
1:26 34
2 62
2:4 136
2:17–21 34
2:23 131
2:34–35 38
2:36 34–35, 39
2:38 35, 38–39, 256
2:42 35, 256
2:47 32, 140
3:1–10 35
3:8 32, 140
3:9 32
3:13 32
3:24 20, 23
4:5 35
4:8 136
4:21 32
4:23–26 35, 256
4:31 35, 136
5:31 37, 141, 256
6:4 36, 256
6:6 36, 256
6:9 37
6:13–14 26, 37
7:8 22
7:35 33
7:38 120
7:39 21, 40
7:41–42 21, 40
7:43 21
7:44 127
7:44–46 21
7:47 23
7:48 23, 38
7:49 38
7:49–50 23
7:59–60 36
8:4–25 29
8:15 36, 256
8:17 36
8:19 36
8:22 256
8:26–40 29
8:27 29
8:32 39
8:35 39
8:38–39 39
9:11 36, 256
9:12 36
9:17 36, 136
9:22 36
9:40 36
10:2 36, 256
10:9–10 36
10:24 36
10:30 36, 256
10:31 36
10:43 37, 256
11:5 36
11:18 32
12:5 37, 256
12:12 37
12:23 32

Acts (cont.)
13:3 36, 256
13:9 136
13:20 20, 23
13:23 141
13:36 131
13:38 37, 256
13:39 37, 38
13:48 32
14:23 36
15:1 22, 38
15:5 22, 38
15:20 38
15:20–21 22
15:21 38
15:29 22, 38
16:3 22, 37
16:13 37
16:16 37
16:25 36
18:18 22, 37
19:6 36
20:16 37
20:27 131
20:36 36
21:20 32
21:20–21 38
21:20–26 22, 37
21:21 22
21:23 38
21:25 22, 36, 38
21:26 38
21:27–29 37
21:28 27, 37
22:17 37
24:27 92
26:18 37, 256
27:29 37, 256
28:8 36
28:10 36

Romans
2:8 242
7:11 148
8:32 33
11:16 242
11:18 242
13:12 238
15:11 140
15:12 242

1 Corinthians
2:1 79
15:3 33

2 Corinthians
5:14–15 33
6:7 242
11:14 238
12:20 242

Galatians
3 92
3:15–16 92
5:20 242

Ephesians
1:9 79
1:19 242
2:11–22 122
3:7 242
4:31 242
5:9 238
6:9 242
6:12 242

Philippians
3:20 120
3:21 242

Colossians
1:26 79
1:29 242
2:12 242
3:8 242

2 Thessalonians
2:9 242
2:11 242

1 Timothy
3:16 79

2 Timothy
3:3 242

Hebrews
1:2 95
4:8–11 123
5:7 29
6:19 148
7:15–27 175
8:5 127
9:3 148
9:11–14 175
9:12 33
9:18–20 230
9:21 127
10:1 122
10:5–10 175
10:12 39
10:20 148
11:4 148
11:8 120
11:13 123
11:13–16 120
11:39–40 120, 123
12:11 148
12:15 148
13:10 127

James
5:11 85

1 Peter
1:1–5 120
1:17 120
2:5 42
2:18 120
2:24 39
3:18 33

2 Peter
1:16–18 181

1 John
1:1–4 220
2:19 225

Revelation
1:13 229
1:15 218
7:15 127
12:12 127
13:6 127
19:5 140
21:3 127
21:22 122

Other Ancient Sources

1QS (Rule of the Community)
8:6 299
8:10 299
9:4 299

Acts of John
1–36 184
18–36 232, 235
27 191
29 199
37–55 184, 233, 235
43 282
46–47 233
48–54 234
56–57 184, 234
58–59 234–35
58–61 184
60–61 234
62–86 184, 234–35
85–86 282
87 182, 185–86, 232
87–88 301
87–93 235, 301–3
87–102 240
87–105 8, 182, 184–85, 188, 195, 232, 235, 279–80, 300–302, 305–6
88 182, 185–86, 191, 197, 212, 232, 280, 282

Acts of John (*cont.*)
88–93 8, 182, 188–89, 193, 197, 201, 280
88–102 185, 301
89 186, 190–91, 197, 232, 280–81
90 183, 186, 188, 192, 196, 202, 217, 220, 222, 281–82, 285, 287
90–91 181–83, 185, 192, 195, 197, 201–2, 212, 217–18, 233, 279–81, 302
90.1 196
90.1–4 197, 213, 302
90.1–6 195
90.2 197, 202, 216–18
90.2–3 283
90.2–4 198
90.3 197, 216
90.3–3.3 215
90.4 216, 302
90.4–22 197
90.5 220
90.5–11 214
90.6 198, 218
90.7 219, 283
90.7–91.8 196
90.9–10 220
90.11–13 198
90.12–91.3 216
90.13 198, 218
90.14–16 199
90.16 219, 283, 304
90.20–22 200
91 187, 197, 200, 221
91.1 195, 197, 200
91.2–5 201
91.5–6 202
92 187–88, 200–201, 281
93 187, 192, 213, 217, 233, 281, 285
94 187, 197
94–96 182, 200, 233, 236, 301–3
94–102 235
95–96 187
97 187, 233, 236, 239
97–102 182, 199–201, 233
97–105 301–3
98 187, 190, 193, 201, 221, 233, 236–39, 242, 285, 287, 310
98–101 224, 226, 250, 279, 283–86
98–102 197, 238
99 187, 201, 233, 310
99–100 238, 242–44
100 187, 226, 233, 245–46, 285
101 187, 201, 233, 246–48, 250, 285
102 187, 213, 233, 245
103 199
103–104 188
103–105 182, 185, 233, 301
104 187–88
105 188
106–115 184, 234–35
109 235
113 199

Acts of Peter
20 181, 217

Aesop, *Fables*
47 159

Apocalypse of Elijah
3.33 299

Apocalypse of Peter (Akhmim)
1–20 181
6 218
7 217
9 217

Apocalypse of Peter (Ethiopic)
15 217–18
15–17 181
17 218

Aristotle, *Metaphysics*
9 239

Aristotle, *Physics*
8 239

Augustine, *Epistles*
237 234–35

Babylonian Talmud, Giṭṭin
57b 299

Babylonian Talmud, Sanhedrin
96b 299

Babylonian Talmud, Ta'anit
69a 299

CD (Damascus Document)
14:19 299

Diodorus Siculus
18.7.7 134

Dionysius Thrax, *Fragments*
43.2 147

Euripides, *Electra*
381 159

Euripides, *Ion*
388 159

Eusebius, *Historia ecclesiastica*
3.25.6 234

Fragmentary Targum
Gen 22 299

Gospel of Judas
56–58 245

Gospel of Mary
16 199

Gospel of Thomas
2 244
13 217
28 198
37 198

Hesiod, *Theogony*
960 131
993 131

Hippocrates, *De morbis*
7.1.123 147

Homer, *Odyssey*
16.402 131

Innocent I, *Epistles*
6.7 234

Irenaeus, *Adversus haereses*
1.7.2 101
1.18.2 127
3.11.8 11, 40, 132

John Chrysostom, *Homiliae in Joannem*
85.3 231

Josephus, *Jewish Antiquities*
1.257 159
2.120 134
20.228 127

Josephus, *Jewish War*
5.2–5.3 113
5.6 113
5.419 299

Justin, *Dialogue with Trypho*
127.3 127

Mishnah, Yoma
5:1 48

Philo, *De cherubim*
127 249

Philo, *De fuga et inventione*
108–112 223
110 249
110–112 229
111–112 306

Philo, *De fuga et inventione* (cont.)
112 249

Philo, *De migratione Abrahami*
6 249
18 249

Philo, *De opificio mundi*
8 249
16 249
25 249

Philo, *De providentia*
1.23 249

Philo, *De vita Mosis*
1.75 249
2.127 249

Philo, *Legum allegoriae*
2.86 249
3.96 249
3.175 249

Philo, *Questiones et solutiones in Exodum*
2.62 249
2.68 249

Philo, *Quis rerum divinarum here sit*
119 249
130 249
156 249
188 249
199 249

Philo, *Quod deterius potiori insidari soleat*
118 249

Philo, *Quod Deus sit immutabilis*
31 249

Plato, *Parmenides*
128e–130a 240
129–135 249

Plato, *Phaedo*
75c11–d2 240
100b6–7 240

Plato, *Philebus*
14–18 249

Plato, *Republic*
476b10 240
480a11 240

Plato, *Theaetetus*
184–186 249

Plutarch, *De laude ipsius*
547E 159

Plutarch, *De Stoicorum repugnantiis*
1043E 159

Protevangelium of James
1 146
1–4 70
1–5 268
1–12 4, 74
1–17 174
1.1 E-P 70, 72
1.1–3 E-P 268
1.1–8.1 E-P 103, 267
1.1–8.3 Hock 7
1.2 E-P 73
1.2 Hock 146
1.3 E-P 70, 268
1.5 Hock 146
1.8 Hock 146
2–4 87–88, 91
2.4 E-P 70, 88, 113, 263, 268
2.6–7 Hock 146
2.9 Hock 146
3.1 E-P 80
3.3 E-P 82, 88
3.3–8 Hock 147
4 71
4.1 E-P 108, 110, 264, 267
4.1 Hock 148

4.1–2 E-P 71, 261
4.2 Hock 148
4.4 E-P 82, 88, 264
5 70–71
5.2 E-P 82–83, 267, 274
5.8 Hock 151–52
6 88, 90, 93–94
6–7 70
6–10 112, 270
6–12 88, 99
6.1 E-P 71, 88, 89, 109, 118, 264, 270, 272
6.1–3 E-P 103
6.1–8.1 E-P 110
6.2 E-P 74, 81–82, 84, 88, 90, 92, 99–100, 123, 262, 264, 266
6.3 E-P 80, 82, 84, 89, 100, 264, 276
6.3–4 Hock 148
6.7 Hock 25, 148
6.9 Hock 25, 148
6.15 Hock 166
7 79, 81, 88, 93, 95, 97
7.1 E-P 93, 108, 113, 118, 269
7.1–2 E-P 71, 265, 270
7.1–8.1 E-P 5, 103, 105–7, 109–10, 115, 117, 119, 125, 267, 269
7.1–8.1 Hock 127
7.1–9.11 Hock 114
7.2 E-P 81–82, 88, 91, 93–95, 98, 109, 111, 118–19, 123, 262, 264–66, 272, 274
7.2–3 E-P 108, 265
7.2–8.1 E-P 265
7.3 E-P 95, 109, 111, 118–19
7.3–8.1 E-P 119
7.7 Hock 6, 26, 148, 151
7.7–8 Hock 152
7.10 E-P 119
8–10 123
8.1 E-P 71, 82, 84, 108, 109–11, 118–19, 263, 269
8.1–2 E-P 109
8.2 E-P 71, 95, 100, 113, 265, 272
8.2 Hock 148
8.2–9.2 E-P 266
8.2–16.3 E-P 104, 267
8.3 E-P 71
8.3–9 Hock 149
8.3–9.3 E-P 96
8.4 Hock 7
8.6–7 Hock 164
9.1 E-P 104, 105, 272
9.1–3 E-P 270
9.2 E-P 80
9.2–3 E-P 113
9.3 E-P 96, 119, 266
9.7 Hock 172
10.1 E-P 96, 104, 123
10.1–2 E-P 266
10.1–10 Hock 148, 151
10.1–12.1 E-P 96
10.2 E-P 71, 96
10.6 Hock 169
10.6–10 Hock 151
10.8–10 Hock 149
10.9–10 Hock 164
10.10 Hock 169
11 75, 79, 88, 97, 270
11–16 70
11–17 112, 270
11.1 E-P 82, 97, 266, 272
11.1–2 E-P 81
11.1–3 E-P 115
11.1–12.3 E-P 104
11.2 E-P 79, 95, 98, 126, 266–67, 270, 272
11.2 Hock 167
11.3 E-P 91, 97–99, 119, 125, 266, 270, 272
11.6 Hock 112
11.9 Hock 112
12.1 E-P 74–75, 79, 81–82, 88, 91, 93, 99–100, 115, 262, 264, 266, 272, 274
12.1 Hock 150–51, 169
12.1–2 Hock 150
12.1–3 E-P 74, 274
12.1–9 Hock 137
12.2 E-P 68, 73–79, 81–82, 88, 113, 124, 261–62, 270, 274–75

Protevangelium of James (cont.)
12.2 Hock 6, 26, 152–53
12.2–3 E-P 67, 70–71, 74–75, 81, 87, 115, 261
12.3 E-P 78, 80–81, 262, 272
12.3 Hock 151, 153
12.4 Hock 153–54
12.5 Hock 154
12.6 Hock 112, 155–58
12.7–8 Hock 158
12.8–9 Hock 159
13.1 E-P 80, 104, 262
13.1 Hock 159
13.1–14.1 E-P 113
13.1–16.3 E-P 104
13.2–3 E-P 115
13.3 E-P 270, 272
13.7 Hock 159
13.8 Hock 112
13.10 Hock 112, 159
14 112
14–15 71
14.1 E-P 80
14.1 Hock 159
14.2 E-P 82, 84, 276
14.7 Hock 166
15 75
15–16 100
15.1 E-P 262
15.1–16.2 E-P 113
15.2 E-P 80, 104
15.3 E-P 115, 262, 270, 272
15.3 Hock 159
15.4 E-P 78, 80, 82
15.4–12 Hock 159
15.13 Hock 112, 159
16 97, 112
16.1 E-P 104
16.1–3 E-P 268
16.3 E-P 82, 276
16.5–6 Hock 159
16.8 Hock 159, 166
17 112
17–20 125
17–21 70
17.1 E-P 270
17.1–24.4 E-P 104, 267
17.2 E-P 71, 125, 270
17.3 E-P 112, 120, 125, 270
17.9 Hock 112
17.10 Hock 112
18–21 174
18.1 E-P 125
18.2 E-P 119
18.2–20.4 E-P 104
19 288
19.1 E-P 126, 287
19.2 E-P 73, 82–83, 95, 98, 101, 123, 125–26, 236, 265, 272, 274
19.3 E-P 104, 269
19.3–20.1 E-P 104
19.14 Hock 152
19.40 Hock 173
20 119
20.1 E-P 126, 271
20.3–4 E-P 126
20.12 Hock 167
21.1 E-P 74
21.1–23.3 E-P 113
21.1–24.4 E-P 104
22 70, 112
22–24 174
22.1 E-P 267
22.2 E-P 115, 272
22.3 E-P 71, 277
22.7 Hock 167
23–24 70–71, 268
23.1 E-P 71, 275
23.1 Hock 160
23.1–3 E-P 275
23.1–3 Hock 161
23.1–4 Hock 175
23.1–9 Hock 160
23.2 E-P 71, 275
23.3 E-P 271, 275
23.3 Hock 161
23.4 Hock 161–62, 175
23.5 Hock 163
23.5–6 Hock 162
23.7 Hock 164

23.7–9 Hock 163
23.7–24.12 Hock 149
24.1 E-P 82, 84, 263
24.1–2 E-P 276
24.1–3 Hock 165
24.1–4 E-P 276
24.1–9 Hock 174
24.1–11 Hock 165
24.2 E-P 85
24.3 E-P 85, 271, 276–77
24.3 Hock 166
24.4 E-P 271
24.4 Hock 164
24.5 Hock 166–67
24.5–9 Hock 166
24.6 Hock 168
24.6–9 Hock 167
24.8 Hock 168–69
24.9 Hock 168
24.10 Hock 170
24.10–11 Hock 169
24.12 Hock 170, 173
24.12–14 Hock 171
24.14 Hock 173
25 70
25.1 E-P 82, 84, 271, 276
25.1–4 E-P 104
25.2 E-P 82
25.3 Hock 166

Pseudo-Aristotle, *Problems*
966A 159

Pseudo-Galen, *Medical Definitions*
19.401 159

Pseudo-Longinus, *On the Sublime*
28.2 159

Revelation of Ezra
5.13 159

Sibylline Oracles
1.171 147

Socrates Scholasticus, *Historia ecclesiastica*
7.32 115

Strabo, *Geography*
14.1.4 131

Targum Neofiti
Gen 22 299

Tatian, *Diatessaron*
24.3–24.4 218

Testament of Benjamin
3.1 299
3.6–3.8 299

Testament of Joseph
19.11 299

Testament of Levi
6.9 159

Testament of Reuben
5.7 191

Testament of Simeon
4.9 134

Turribius of Astorga, *Epistula ad Idacium et Ceponium*
5 234

Vitruvius, *On Architecture*
6.5.1 153

Xenophon, *Memorabilia*
1.1.15 159

Personal Names Index

Aaron 20–21, 23, 25, 27, 34, 45–47, 49, 53–54, 57, 123, 256
Abel 20
Abijah 21, 23, 45–47, 256
Abraham 13, 20, 22, 53, 70, 91–92, 99, 101, 120, 122, 134–36, 138–39, 145–46, 264, 266, 268, 273, 307
Adam 22
Alexander the Great 265
Allison, Dale C. 94, 175
Alter, Robert 132
Anderson, Charles A. 249
Andia, Ysabel de 239
Andrew 197, 212
Andronicus 188
Anna 4, 26–27, 60, 68–70, 73, 80, 88–90, 93–94, 100, 105, 107–8, 110, 113–14, 117–19, 122, 146–48, 151, 170, 209, 258, 261, 263, 264–65, 267–72, 276
Annas 24, 159, 262
Antiochus of Ascalon 238
Aristotle 239
Athanasius 115
Attridge, Harold W. 289–90
Augustine 239
Barrett, C. K. 22
Beech, Timothy 302
Beierwaltes, Werner 239
Benko, Stephen 137
Berchman, Robert M. 249
Berger, Klaus 49
Berger, Peter L. 43, 294
Beyer, H. 90
Blakely, Sandra 157
Blank, Sheldon H. 149
Bloomquist, L. Gregory 9, 14, 292–93
Bolognesi, Giancarlo 130
Bonnet, M. 184
Boring, M. Eugene 49, 94
Bovon, François 131, 136–37, 139–41, 143, 155, 170, 209–11, 219
Brodie, Thomas L. 228
Brown, Peter 101
Brown, Raymond E. 131, 135, 139–40, 228–32, 234
Burkert, Walter 294
Buth, Randall 132
Caiaphas 24
Cain 20
Camp, Claudia V. 49, 58, 172
Charles, R. H. 191
Cohen, Shaye J. D. 72, 96
Collins, Adela Yarbro 202, 210
Colpe, Carsten 49
Cornelius 36, 37
Cothenet, Edouard 98, 101, 174
Daniel 52, 54
David 20–23, 25, 56, 116, 119, 121–26, 140, 142, 162
David 271, 275
Davies, W. D. 94, 175
Derrida, Jacques 41
deSilva, David A. 18
Dillon, John 239
Dillon, Richard J. 132
Dionysius the Pseudo-Areopagite 239
Drusiana 185–88, 191, 300
Ehrman, Bart D. 67–68, 81, 89, 101, 103, 109, 112, 147–48, 236, 260–61, 265, 268

Eleazar 36
Eli 108, 113–14, 122, 269
Elijah 16–17, 29, 131, 138, 210, 220–21
Elisha 16–17, 131
Elizabeth 3–5, 21, 23–25, 44–48, 51–52, 54–59, 61–62, 67–71, 73–75, 77–78, 80–81, 86–89, 99–100, 113, 115, 124, 133–39, 149, 152–55, 158–60, 167, 256, 258–62, 267–68, 270, 272–77
Elliott, J. K. 67, 69, 101, 129, 147–48, 183–85, 195, 232, 234–36
Evagrius of Pontus 239
Farmer, Thomas Jared 8–9, 253, 279, 283–88, 293, 300–307, 309–11
Farris, Stephen 131–33, 136–37, 141
Fauconnier, Gilles 44
Filson, Floyd V. 132
Fitzmyer, Joseph A. 25–27, 30, 32–33, 45, 57
Fleddermann, H. T. 175
Foskett, Mary F. 67, 79, 89, 95–96, 98, 101, 104–5, 113–14
Foster, Paul 67, 81, 169, 175
Freedman, David Noel 132
Frend, W. H. C. 299
Gabriel 24–25, 53, 55–57, 75, 78, 97, 133–35, 138–40, 153, 157–58, 258, 266–67, 270, 272, 274
Gersh, Stephen 239
Girard, René 297
Glancy, Jennifer A. 72, 96
Gowler, David B. 14
Green, Joel B. 204
Gudrun, Colbow 191
Gunkel, Hermann 132
Hannah 20, 26–27, 107–10, 137, 269
Harnack, Adolf von 174
Harris, Elizabeth 246
Heidegger, Martin 41
Heil, John Paul 229
Herod Agrippa II 37
Herod the Great 4, 44–48, 70–71, 84, 112–13, 149, 160–62, 164, 170, 175, 259, 271–72, 275
Hill, Charles E. 279, 289
Hock, Ronald F. 9, 25, 89, 105, 112, 129, 147–48, 173, 253, 261, 265
Holladay, Carl R. 205
Hollman, Meredith Elliot 5, 7, 9, 253, 267–71, 280, 287–88
Holmes, Christopher T. 4, 5, 9, 115, 124, 253, 260–67
Husserl, Edmund 41
Hylen, Susan 9
Irenaus 2
Isaac 88, 107, 139, 263, 268, 306–7
Isaiah 16, 54
James, Brother of Jesus 38
James, Son of Zebedee 29, 186–87, 191–92, 194, 197–98, 201, 209, 212, 216, 220–21
Jay, Nancy B. 58
Jepthah 107
Jeremiah 16
Jesus 3–40, 42–45, 57–63, 68–73, 79–80, 83–86, 92–101, 112, 115, 120, 123–27, 130–35, 139–43, 149–52, 160–64, 167–75, 181–250, 254–66, 272–90, 296–310
Joachim 4, 25–26, 70, 72–73, 84, 88, 93, 100, 105, 107–8, 110–11, 113, 117–19, 122, 146–47, 261, 263–71
John the Baptist 3, 4, 6, 20–25, 27, 29, 31–32, 35, 39, 44–45, 53–56, 60, 62, 68–71, 130, 137–39, 142, 149, 155, 160, 162, 164, 167–68, 170, 172, 174–75, 256, 258–61, 268, 270, 275–77
John, Son of Zebedee 7–9, 29, 35, 182–83, 185–202, 209, 212, 216, 218–21, 226, 234–36, 239–40, 245–46, 249–50, 280–83, 287, 303–5
Johnson, Luke Timothy 226
Johnson, Mark 41, 43
Joseph 4–5, 13, 56, 70, 78, 80, 84, 96, 98, 104, 111–13, 119, 123, 125, 140, 159–60, 172–74, 260–62, 266, 268, 270–72, 276, 287
Joshua 36
Judas 34, 256

Judith 91, 113
Junod, Eric 184–85, 188–89, 195, 199, 235–36, 240
Justus 34
Kaestli, Jean-Daniel 184–85, 189, 195, 199, 235–36, 240, 289
Kennedy, George A. 130
Klauck, Hans-Josef 279
Knox, W. L. 131
Koester, Helmut 289
Lakoff, George 41, 43
Lalleman, Pieter J. 184, 190, 200–201, 235, 289
Lapham, Fred 190
Lazarus 301
Leah 85
Lee, Simon S. 181, 190, 202, 209, 219, 303
Levine, Amy-Jill 249
Libanius 265
Lieu, Judith 295
Limberis, Vasiliki 105
Lipsius, R. A. 184
Loisy, Alfred 230
Louw, Johannes P. 82
Luckmann, Thomas 43
MacDonald, Dennis R. 255
Malina, Bruce J. 43, 226
Mary 3–7, 10, 25–26, 34, 44, 55–57, 59–60, 62, 67–140, 142, 146, 148–49, 151–70, 173–74, 229–30, 245, 256, 259–77, 288, 307
Matthias 34
Meeks, Wayne 226
Melchizedek 20
Metzger, Bruce 210
Miles, Jack 17
Moloney, Francis J. 224, 228–31
Moses 15–16, 20–22, 26, 28–29, 36–37, 45–46, 53–54, 80, 116, 121, 125, 210, 219, 220–21, 276, 282
Nathan 121–22, 124
Nathaniel 287
Nebuchadnezzar 91, 116, 270
Nickelsburg, George W. E. 255
Nida, Eugene A. 82
Nikephorus 235
Noah 22
Nolland, John 209
Nutzman, Megan 114
Oakley, Todd V. 17, 44
O'Neil, Edward N. 265
O'Neill, J. C. 299
Origen 115
Parmenides 239
Patillon, Michel 130
Paul 37–38, 92, 101, 242
Peirce, Charles Sanders 41
Pelikan, Jaroslav 249
Pellegrini, Silvia 129, 147–49
Penner, Todd C. 21, 38
Perry, John 298
Pervo, Richard I. 22, 301, 303, 305
Peter 13, 29, 35–37, 186–87, 192, 194, 197–98, 201, 205, 209, 212, 216, 219–21, 226
Phillip 39, 287
Philo 223, 249, 285
Plato 240, 249
Pleše, Zlatko 67–68, 81, 89, 101, 103, 112, 147–48, 236, 260–61, 265, 268
Plotinus 238–39
Pontius Pilate 40, 228, 307–8
Potter, Jonathan 8–9, 253, 279–85, 287–88, 293, 300–306
Quarles, Charles L. 149
Reubel 264
Reuben 72
Robbins, Vernon K. 1–4, 7, 9, 14–17, 26, 43–44, 67, 69–72, 74, 81, 87, 103, 108, 110, 126, 130–31, 136, 142, 144, 146, 149–50, 172, 186, 195, 199–200, 206, 209, 212–13, 217, 221, 223–24, 227, 253–61, 272, 280, 291–94, 296, 302
Rohrbaugh, Richard 226
Rolf, Hurschmann 191
Ross, W. D. 249
Rusam, Dietrich 137, 141–42, 145, 156–57, 173

Ruthrof, Horst 41–44
Salome 126, 269, 271, 287
Samson 107
Samuel 5, 20, 22–23, 26–27, 74, 107–10, 125, 269
Sarah 53, 70, 88, 134, 138–39, 146, 263, 268
Saul 22–23
Schäferdiek, Knut 184
Schneider, Carl 297
Schneider, Paul G. 235
Shore, Bradd 43
Simeon 4, 27, 60–62, 68–70, 86–87, 94–95, 101, 143–44, 170, 172–73, 175, 256, 258, 265, 271, 274, 276
Simon of Cyrene 228
Simon the high priest 49–50, 54, 56, 60–61, 259
Simons, Robert 132
Smid, Harm Reinder 89, 147
Smith, D. Moody 182, 220, 229, 231
Socrates 240
Solomon 5, 16, 20, 23, 116, 119, 123, 125–27
Stempvoort, Pieter A. van 67
Stephen 36, 37, 40
Strelan, Rick 13–14, 23, 44, 51, 130, 132, 143
Suh, Michael K. W. 6–7, 9, 253, 261, 272
Tamar 284
Tannehill, Robert C. 131–32, 135, 143
Thaden, Robert H. von, Jr. 2–3
Thomas 200, 219, 283, 287, 303
Tilborg, Sjef van 229
Tuñí, Josep Oriol 297
Uzzah 53, 126, 271
Vico, Giambattista 42–43, 257
Vorster, Johannes N. 43
Vorster, Willem S. 67
Vuong, Lily C. 6–7, 72–73, 89, 95, 260
Watson, Duane F. 14, 18
Westermann, Claus 132
Wilson, Bryan R. 299
Wittgenstein, Ludwig 41
Wood, Laurence W. 239
Zaccheus 28
Zechariah 3–4, 6–7, 13–14, 20–21, 23–25, 34, 44–48, 50–59, 61–62, 68, 70–71, 77, 84–86, 130, 132, 134, 137–40, 149, 160–70, 172–73, 174–76, 209, 255–56, 258–61, 263, 268, 271, 273–77
Zwiep, Arie W. 34

CPSIA information can be obtained at www.ICGtesting.com
Printed in the USA
BVOW01s0703200315

392495BV00002B/5/P

9 781628 370638